THE READING RESOURCE HANDBOOK
FOR SCHOOL LEADERS

U17I

THE READING RESOURCE HANDBOOK
FOR SCHOOL LEADERS

Del Patty
Southern Illinois University
at Edwardsville

Janet D. Maschoff
Hazelwood School District
St. Louis, Missouri

Peggy E. Ransom
Ball State University
Muncie, Indiana

Christopher-Gordon Publishers, Inc.
Norwood, MA

Credits

Process definitions and questions from Jerry Johns used with permission.

Every effort has been made to contact copyright holders for permission to reproduce borrowed material where necessary. We apologize for any oversights and would be happy to rectify them in future printings.

Christopher-Gordon Publishers, Inc.
480 Washington Street
Norwood, MA 02062

Printed in the United States of America

10 9 8 7 6 5 4 3 2 1   00 99 98 97 96

ISBN: 0-926842-50-1

SHORT TABLE OF CONTENTS

LONG TABLE OF CONTENTS

LIST OF FORMS

ABOUT THIS BOOK

The purpose of *The Reading Resource Handbook* for school leaders is to help school principals, central office administrators, consultants, and supervisors improve school reading programs. The emphasis is on program improvement, whether the instructional approach is literature-based, basal reader, whole language, or cognitively based. An administrator using the book will gain a rapid overview of issues associated with school reading programs and begin to formulate a *snapshot* of needs. The *Resource Handbook* may be used to support a systematic, comprehensive, total-program improvement process, or to address specific management problems one at a time.

The *Resource Handbook* identifies specific problems in major areas of reading program administration and provides practical techniques, processes, and tools to deal effectively with those problems. Its worksheets are designed so that administrators who are not reading experts can confidently conduct staff development workshops and structure informal settings in which faculties may build consensus, talk about program options, and actually evaluate reading program components.

Each problem in reading program administration is presented in a clear, consistent format, including:

- a description of the problem.
- a rationale for dealing with the problem based on fundamental concepts and findings from professional practice.
- practical information and activities to address the problem, including procedures, flow charts, worksheets, and study activities.
- structures to identify program priorities to deal with reading problem areas.
- a plan-of-action form that helps the administrator to be an instructional leader in problem areas of the reading program.
- suggestions for further reading, a glossary of terms that may be unfamiliar to administrators, and a limited bibliography.

All chapters and activities are designed to *stand alone*, which accounts for the deliberate structural redundancy that occurs throughout the *Resource Handbook*.

The various problem-solving materials provided have been designed so that they can be photocopied directly from the book or adapted to meet local needs. No special permission is required for such copying by the *Resource Handbook* purchaser unless otherwise indicated, and the purchaser is free to make alterations. Each form may be revised to serve far more functions than those suggested.

Administrators will find the *Resource Handbook* useful in a number of ways—for example, in handling specific problems; in determining their own influence or desired influence on the reading program; and in carrying out step-by-step improvements in the entire program. To deal with a specific problem, the user consults the section of the *Resource Handbook* directly. To gain an overview of what constitutes an effective reading program, users may consider Chapter 1. Administrators may wish to review various leadership components periodically to self-assess growth. Principals may opt to self-study their leadership skills by using Chapter 2, while concurrently working with a Reading Advisory Board to pursue program review. To upgrade the program following a comprehensive, systematic program improvement process, Chapter 3 launches the change process, but is used in conjunction with the total *Resource Handbook*. Program study might be accomplished within a school year, yet could require more than one year, depending on the extent of program revision warranted. A marvelous benefit of a faculty's conducting a structured reading program change process is the way in which the faculty's knowledge is strengthened and rapport is enriched as the program is improved.

The focus of the *Resource Handbook* is the management of reading programs. There is no attempt to deal with classroom teachers' daily instructional concerns, and no effort is made to describe concepts about the teaching of reading from college textbooks. For that reason, minimal use of documentation may be found. Instead, the focus is on the essence of program leadership, helping to create a more effective reading program. Should an administrator or curriculum coordinator feel the need to tap experts in the field, several avenues are open. District-employed reading specialists or Title I (formerly Chapter I) teachers may provide immediate information or suggest sources. The administrator also may wish to consult a local university's faculty or education library to identify sources of support for reading programs. Another good source is the local reading council of the International Reading Association, whose membership may provide helpful information.

The authors acknowledge the cyclical nature of beliefs and practices about reading programs. Some present trends are recognized by many as revisitations of patterns of thirty and sixty years ago. At the same time, the authors are aware of enduring program components, found in the majority of school districts over time, regardless of trends. Reading consultants encounter a range of program options: contemporary literature-based textbook series; twelve-year-old, as well as recent, basal reading programs; whole language classrooms; combinations of these various approaches; and other less well known programs. The authors' intent is to address problems found in the administration of all of the program options.

Little of the content of the *Resource Handbook* may be documented in the professional literature. Instead, the *Resource Handbook*'s validity resulted, initially, from the authors' work with the national Right-to-Read effort, which involved programs to strengthen leadership skills of school administrators. Many of the worksheets were developed then, and have been revised over time for consultation work for state boards of education, school district staff development, and graduate reading leadership courses. The authors' presentations on reading leadership at preconvention institutes of the International Reading Association annual conferences lend credibility to the *Resource Handbook*. An important, little-recognized source of information about school reading leadership practice are the sales representatives of major textbook publishing companies. While the authors recognize the prospective bias and profit motives, we also have learned that those representatives have a great deal of accurate knowledge about programs in the various school districts they service. Still another source of credible information has been each authors' activities with advisory boards of International Reading Association local affiliates. Most of the members of those boards—particularly in our large, suburban affiliates—are the directors of reading or language arts programs in their respective school districts. Most have participated in one or more reading program studies and textbook selection processes. Those people, too, represent a wealth of information that has been shared generously, and many of their ideas have been adapted for use in the *Resource Handbook*.

However it is used, our hope is that the *Resource Handbook* will help administrators to improve the effectiveness of the reading programs in their schools. If that goal is met, young people will be the ones who will benefit most.

Del Patty
Janet D. Maschoff
Peggy E. Ransom

ACKNOWLEDGMENTS

The authors wish to thank those people who have assisted in one way or another with the preparation of the manuscript. Of those, Susan Bargiel, Collinsville District 10; Michele Bensa, Southern Illinois University at Edwardsville; Dr. John Borsa, Parkway School District; Kala Eydmann, Mehlville School District; Ann Goldsmith, Collinsville District 10; Al Granowsky, World Book Encyclopedia; Dr. Patricia Hughes, Ball State University; Mary Johnson, Belleville District 118; Dr. Joan Kirchoff, Belleville District 118; Dr. Dick Koblitz, Clayton School District; Gary Mosimann, Cahokia District 187; Dr. Barbara Negley, Noblesville Community Schools; Diana Rinker, Delaware Community Schools; Dr. C. Michael Thornburg, Pittsfield, Massachusetts; and Dr. James Thrasher, Dean, School of Education, University of Montana, are valued and thanked. The suggestions they have provided and the support they have given along the way are sincerely appreciated.

The authors are grateful to reviewers of the *Resource Handbook*. Dr. Ella Jones, Webster University and Hazelwood School District, St. Louis, Missouri; Jean Osborn, University of Illinois; Dr. Richard Vacca, Kent State University, Ohio; and our editor, Sue Canavan, offered valuable suggestions on manuscript organization and content.

Because of his quest for scholarship and his abiding motivation to excel, we would like to dedicate the *Resource Handbook* to Dr. William R. Powell, who, directly or indirectly, has been the authors' great teacher.

CHAPTER 1

CHARACTERISTICS OF OUTSTANDING READING PROGRAMS

Schools with outstanding reading programs commonly create learners who are able to read and like to read, building a foundation for students' lifetime literacy. Excellent programs may be founded on a vision developed by the faculty and supported by the building administrator's skilled instructional leadership (see Form 1.1). The administrator, in turn, conveys the school's vision of reading and writing to parents and community members. This foundation may support high student reading affect and achievement.

Outcomes of excellent reading programs are visible to the faculty, staff, parents, community, and anybody walking into the school. Pupils are seen participating in both direct instruction and child-centered activities. Students take joy in learning to read and write, and celebrate their literacy by sharing in small group, whole class, or individual activities. Displays of the books that children are reading might be prominently placed for all to see. Sampling the classroom book collection and the library or media center collection are favorite pupil endeavors. Visitors may look around and see written and artistic responses to children's reading.

Children bring home books they, or their class, have written, along with favorite trade books to read at home. Parents are active partners in the reading program, supporting and helping out whenever they can. Parents bask in feelings that they are welcome at school and that they make important contributions. Parents may frequently see the value of literacy volunteerism, and encourage others to also help at school. Family members often are seen reading to a group of students, helping with pupils' writing projects, listening to students read, or asking teachers to send home projects that pupils may be pleased to share.

OUTSTANDING READING PROGRAMS

Every school administrator may have a definite view of what constitutes an outstanding reading program. Even if two administrators have similar outlooks, each will envision parts of a program somewhat differently. In contrast, highly dissimilar judgments about excellent reading programs may also occur. An administrator with literature-based reading textbooks and a generously supplied library may manage an outstanding reading program. Another administrator may believe the school's reading program is excellent when it is based on a whole language model. A different principal may demonstrate that a program with a cognitive foundation is excellent. In other words, there are numerous models of effective reading programs.

The administrator or Reading Advisory Board (see Chapter 3, Form 3.5) may consider several excellent reading programs in deciding where the local school *is*, or *wants to be*, compared to various program descriptions. Below, readers will find abbreviated descriptions of three outstanding reading programs (see Forms 1.2 to 1.4). Following those descriptions, a matrix allows comparison of the programs against standards of excellence (see Form 1.5). Consideration may help a self-study group to identify characteristics to incorporate into a local reading program.

SYSTEMATIC SELF-STUDY OF READING PROGRAMS

The purpose of self-study is to identify and prioritize needs, then develop a program plan for improvement (see Chapter 3, Forms 3.19 to 3.21), building the foundation for an outstanding local reading program. That work ordinarily is undertaken by a representative committee, perhaps called a reading study committee, curriculum committee, or reading advisory board. Each member takes responsibility for gathering technical data to bring to the group for study and consideration.

Form 1.1
CHARACTERISTICS OF OUTSTANDING READING PROGRAMS

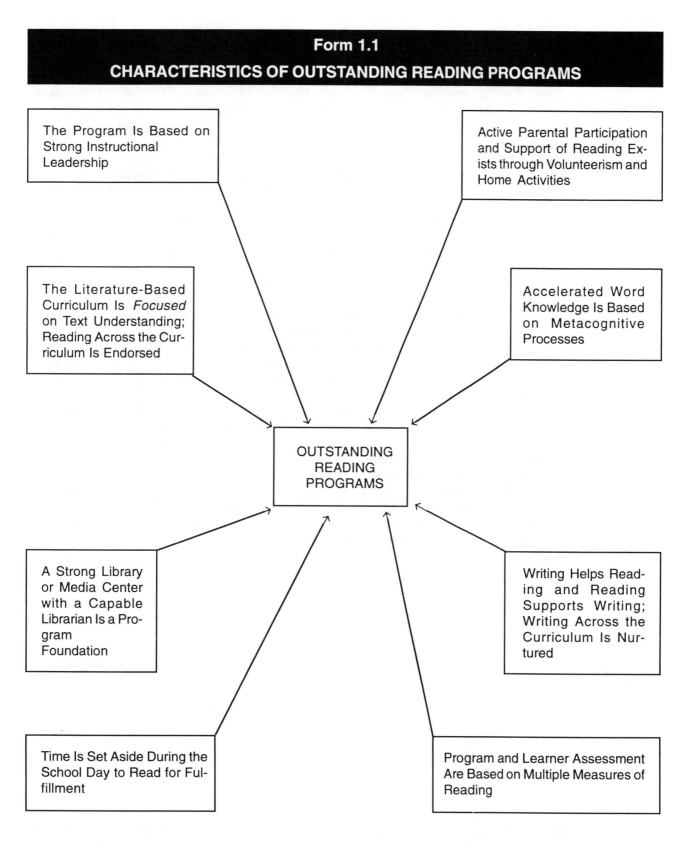

The Program Is Based on Strong Instructional Leadership

Active Parental Participation and Support of Reading Exists through Volunteerism and Home Activities

The Literature-Based Curriculum Is *Focused* on Text Understanding; Reading Across the Curriculum Is Endorsed

Accelerated Word Knowledge Is Based on Metacognitive Processes

OUTSTANDING READING PROGRAMS

A Strong Library or Media Center with a Capable Librarian Is a Program Foundation

Writing Helps Reading and Reading Supports Writing; Writing Across the Curriculum Is Nurtured

Time Is Set Aside During the School Day to Read for Fulfillment

Program and Learner Assessment Are Based on Multiple Measures of Reading

Form 1.2

MILES D. DAVIS ELEMENTARY SCHOOL

Miles D. Davis Elementary School. The school's suburban neighborhood is about 40 percent Hispanic-, 28 percent African-, 13 percent Asian-, and 19 percent Euro-American. Most students in this West Coast K–6 school are from households with lower middle class, minimum wage earning, or unemployed parents. Neighborhood children fear violence, drug trade, and abuse. Public housing creates a high student population turnover. The school enjoys high attendance, active parent involvement, and community pride.

A long-standing resistance to replacing basal readers with a literature-based textbook series was successfully overcome two years ago. The language experience approach and schoolwide recreational reading (DEAR˙) already enriched reading. Three popular classroom teachers coordinate study groups and willingly bring topics to the faculty for study. Peers appreciate those efforts and the principal offers all of the faculty strong support for professional growth. Classroom teachers requested inservice sessions on strategic comprehension, process writing, and spelling analogies this year. Student achievement is second highest in a large school district. Evaluation is based on standardized reading tests, state-mandated tests, running records,˙ text-based cloze tests, and portfolio assessment. The school pioneered an *accelerated schools˙* project, a *school power˙* effort, and an early reading intervention program, along with both pull-out and class-within-class Title 1.

The media center is located to the left of the school entrance. Wide double doors invite parents to adult- and child-sized chairs to wait and read from the collection. Intermediate level students have a primary grade *buddy* to read with for twenty minutes each week. The school nurtures university volunteers, senior citizens, and parents to read with, and to, children. A local businessmen's club asks each member to read with students two times a year, and most actually participate even more. Parents supervise students who publish a school newspaper and help pupils to get their articles ready for the paper. A grocery chain headquartered in the community sponsors in-class, monthly pizza parties for the six classes that read the most books.

˙Terms described in the glossary are signified with an asterik.

Form 1.3

FLETCHER ELEMENTARY SCHOOL

Fletcher Elementary School. The K–6 school's setting is an urban East Coast community with middle- to lower-class homes. While most students are Caucasian, about seven percent are minority children. Affect is positive toward reading and writing activities; attendance, too, is positive.

The principal takes full responsibility for the reading program and any related professional development. Building on the enthusiasm of a cadre of energetic teachers, the principal developed a whole language curriculum. Before initiating the program, the faculty participated in staff development and professional conferences to strengthen knowledge. In-school workshops presented by local university and central office consultants dealt with emerging literacy, strategic reading, process writing, cooperative grouping, and performance assessment. The faculty felt a need to enrich the total curriculum, and requested sessions dealing with reading-across-the-curriculum and writing-across-the-curriculum. Portfolio assessment, state-mandated tests, reading miscue analysis, and standardized reading tests are used. The faculty felt able to initiate each segment after workshop participation. Title 1 support is founded on whole language concepts and is augmented with Reading Recovery. Reading achievement was high before program revision, and continues to be one of the highest among schools in the district.

With the help of two manufacturing firms, a shopping center, and a regional fast-food franchise, a school board member paved the way to form an endowed foundation to support school literacy. Income funds have been used by a parent, community, and teacher advisory board to strengthen literacy efforts. The foundation matches funds earned by the PTA for its projects. The media center is generously stocked and is staffed to offer evening and summer circulation of books. Volunteers are on hand to read to student groups during daytime and evening hours. Each teacher takes pride in having three events a year in classrooms in which children invite their parents to participate. Attendance at those events runs about 70 percent and PTA participation, too, is high.

Form 1.4

MARK RICHARDS ELEMENTARY SCHOOL

Mark Richards Elementary School. The school is located in a mid-sized city in a large midwestern, metropolitan area. Attendance at this K–6 school is made up of equal numbers of the most impoverished and most prosperous children in the city, with fewer middle class pupils. Pride in the school and attendance are strong. Parents offer the highest rate of volunteer support of any school in the district.

Two highly regarded Title 1 teachers take responsibility for the school's staff development with the full support of the principal. After one year of whole language workshops, the principal announced that all basal texts would be collected and students would use trade books as the foundation for the reading and writing program. During the initial year, staff development was provided two afternoons each month for somewhat reluctant teachers. In two years, overall reading achievement suffered and *vocabulary* scores on standardized tests dropped seriously, causing upheaval among teachers and parents. The faculty insisted on access to literature-based textbooks and manuals. Teachers prevailed upon the principal to ask the Title 1 teachers to provide workshops on phonemic awareness, phonemic segmentation, and spelling analogies. The school uses standardized achievement tests, and the teachers requested that they be allowed to continue to use portfolio assessment. Title 1 teachers have worked alongside their case load pupils in regular classroom settings, strengthening pupils' regular assignments, but with mixed results. Richards school has quickly regained high reading achievement test scores in one year, and now considers reinstituting some components of whole language.

A local manufacturing firm supports *lunch with the principal* as an incentive for reading outside of school. Because of its popularity with students, groups, not individuals, dine with the principal, usually choosing a local fast-food restaurant. The school participates in Book-It, Six Flags, book fairs twice a year, and schoolwide recognitions of children who read the most books, with most students being recognized. The school has enjoyed total participation in SSR' for at least ten years. The school support staff takes pride and enjoys reading in classrooms with children during SSR and students are happy to share the time with staff.

Form 1.5

CRITERIA MET BY OUTSTANDING READING PROGRAMS

Directions: Criteria to identify outstanding reading programs may be found below. On the right, the names of the three schools described in Forms 1.2–1.4 are entered. Whenever a criterion is well met in the school description, a plus mark is entered at that point in the matrix.

Outstanding Reading Program Criteria:

	Miles D. Davis Elementary	Fletcher Elementary	Mark Richards Elementary
1. The reading program is founded upon strong instructional leadership and a shared reading program vision	+	+	+
2. Active parental participation at home and at school supports the reading program	+	+	+
3. A strong sense of volunteerism attracts community people into the school to help	+	+	+
4. The literature-based program is focused on text understanding; i.e., comprehension	+	+	+
5. Reading-across-the-curriculum is an important part of the program		+	+
6. Accelerated word knowledge is based on metacognitive learning processes	+		+
7. In this program, writing supports reading comprehension, and reading helps writing	+	+	
8. Writing-across-the-curriculum is a significant component of this literacy program	+	+	
9. A strong library or media center with a capable librarian is a foundation of the program	+	+	+
10. Time is set aside during each school day for recreational or enrichment reading	+	+	+
11. Remedial, intervention, and accelerated programs support basic reading	+	+	+
12. Both program and learner assessments are based on multiple measures	+	+	+
13. An effective, self-renewing staff development effort is an important program foundation	+	+	

The Principal's Role

As an equal participant in self-study, the principal learns alongside other members of the Reading Advisory Board. The principal's role is not as reading program expert, but as self-study cheerleader. The principal does not dominate the process, which might cause other members to become guarded, but functions as an active, fully participating member of the study.

Roles of Parents and Community Members

The primary purposes of community members' involvement in school affairs are to ensure local awareness and to support public participation in school policy. Parents or community members who participate in self-study or Reading Advisory Board processes (see Chapter 3, Forms 3.2 and 3.5) bring community concerns to program study, and take self-study deliberations back to the community to seek feedback. A strong case has been made for active parent participation, which clearly increases students' school achievement and enhances interactions between school and community (36).** Applications for federal grants to schools commonly require provisions for parent participation. Seasoned administrators tell us that people tend to stand behind those programs about which they were able to express their opinion during the decision-making process.

Roles of Faculty and Staff Members

Classroom teachers have the professional and practical experiences to study program needs and to plan for change. After careful study of objective data and program options, teachers may use their awareness of the community and its school needs to establish a new direction. Teachers have a strong sense of programs that will work, or will not work, in the setting. Teachers have a vested interest because they are on the *front line* when it comes to delivering prospective changes. Librarians, special reading teachers, and other support staff also lend their distinctive expertise to the self-study process. As evidence increases about the importance of authentic literature in children's lives, whether textbook-based or whole language, the librarian's knowledge is increasingly important to program study. The reading specialist may be particularly valuable because of contacts, networking with people who are knowledgeable about the professional literature and who have access to technical expertise.

Faculty Size

The size of a faculty may influence the functions of a Reading Advisory Board. Large schools would have no trouble finding enough faculty and staff to form self-study groups. Small schools, though, might not have enough faculty members to pursue a reading program self-study alone. Two or three small schools might have to work together and Reading Advisory Board members might have more than one job. Those smaller schools might have to adjust the time frame to complete all of the self-study tasks.

USES OF THE RESOURCE HANDBOOK

A school in pursuit of an outstanding reading program may find numerous uses for forms found in the *Resource Handbook*. Administrators may use various forms to structure teacher-administrator conferences, supervise instruction, prepare for staff development workshops, work with parents or community members, or as self-briefing sources. Reading Advisory Boards may use forms to structure program self-study and

---

**Bibliographic citations are indicated with item numbers in parentheses

goal-setting processes. Central office personnel may find forms helpful as they map goals with administrators from building to building. Teachers may find certain forms useful to self-assess their knowledge or effectiveness or to brief themselves prior to committee participation. Teachers also may wish to use forms to provide content for peer coaching, group or self-study.

TECHNICAL ASSISTANCE FOR READING PROGRAMS

Once Reading Advisory Boards have identified their programs' strengths and needs, a planning phase follows to address those needs. A school in pursuit of an outstanding reading program may wish to gain technical feedback as it organizes its program data. Planning processes involve various members of the Reading Advisory Board gathering information that may be used to select options suited to local needs. None of the members, individually, will feel that they have all of the information needed to address the local problem, but as the self-study group thinks together, data intrepretation usually falls into place. The Reading Advisory Board may sometimes seek information from outside sources, but may first need to identify those sources (see Form 1.6). Sometimes, a Reading Advisory Board benefits from developing flow charts of steps taken, and checks off each step as it is completed.

SUMMARY

Effective reading programs seem to affect how well children learn to read and like to read. Common characteristics are found in most outstanding reading programs. Excellent reading programs are founded on a strong vision and goals. The principal keeps goals at the forefront, supports the faculty to teach literacy well, monitors the program's qualities, and interprets for the community. Students tend to be engaged readers and writers, read to gain meaning, and read extensively from trade books. Parent and community participation and support augments the school's successes.

To pursue reading program improvement, self-study provides extensive data as a basis to change the program. Self-study ordinarily is undertaken by a committee, often referred to as a Reading Advisory Board. Reading Advisory Boards sometimes seek technical assistance as they pursue self-study.

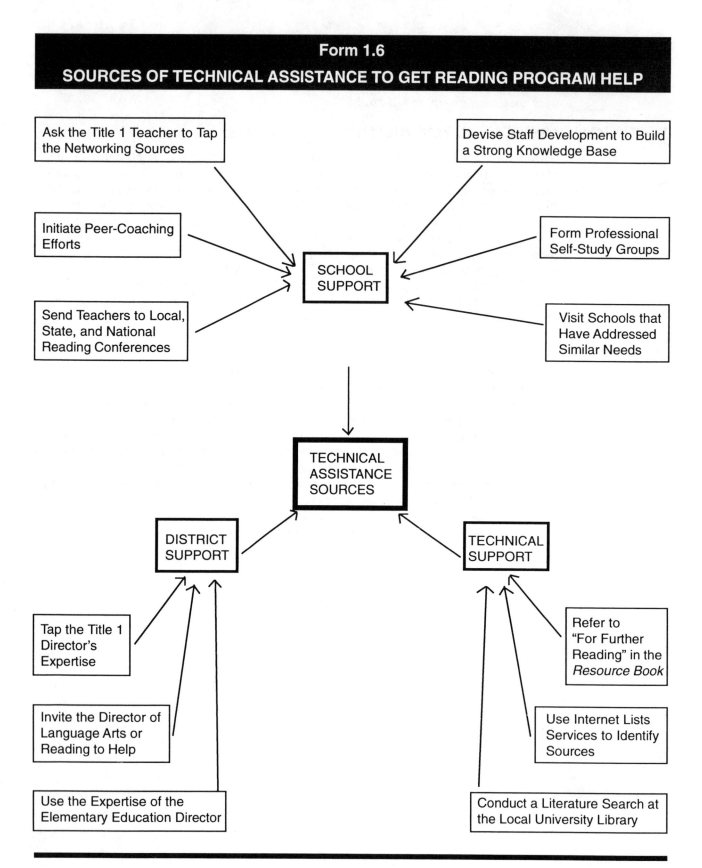

Form 1.6
SOURCES OF TECHNICAL ASSISTANCE TO GET READING PROGRAM HELP

Ask the Title 1 Teacher to Tap the Networking Sources

Devise Staff Development to Build a Strong Knowledge Base

Initiate Peer-Coaching Efforts

Form Professional Self-Study Groups

SCHOOL SUPPORT

Send Teachers to Local, State, and National Reading Conferences

Visit Schools that Have Addressed Similar Needs

TECHNICAL ASSISTANCE SOURCES

DISTRICT SUPPORT

TECHNICAL SUPPORT

Tap the Title 1 Director's Expertise

Refer to "For Further Reading" in the *Resource Book*

Invite the Director of Language Arts or Reading to Help

Use Internet Lists Services to Identify Sources

Use the Expertise of the Elementary Education Director

Conduct a Literature Search at the Local University Library

CHAPTER 2

INSTRUCTIONAL LEADERSHIP AND THE READING PROGRAM

At the building level, the principal is the key person to provide the leadership that results in reading program progress and success. In the context of the *Resource Handbook,* the reading program is comprised of personnel, curriculum, reading approach, instructional materials, organization, staff development, learning assessment, and program evaluation. Central office personnel possess neither the direct, continuous contact within schools, nor the direct authority to reinforce program growth in such a way as to effect long-term change. Individual classroom teachers and collaborative teams of teachers may develop model programs for their unit. Yet those individuals and groups are not able to effect a thorough, comprehensive reading curriculum that will permeate the entire building without the principal acting as the leader who pulls together its components. The principal, then, is uniquely able to articulate and advance program goals.

Basic strategies that aid program improvement include sharing information about effective schools research, management of change processes, and support of a positive school climate. Administrative skills, then, such as thoughtful decision-making, delegation of tasks, and effective time management, may enable principals to better use time and efforts, providing the clock hours to actually work on program improvement. Those factors of trust that free faculties to improve reading programs involve change processes, school climate, and strong communication. Principals with related knowledge are able to operate purposefully, and Reading Advisory Boards—the study groups made up of faculty, administrators, parents, and community members who assess programs—are empowered to take charge of planning for program improvements.

THE ADMINISTRATOR AS THE INSTRUCTIONAL LEADER   (see Form 2.1)

Effective instructional leaders hold strong views of reading programs, placing program goals at the forefront, and communicating them frequently to faculty, staff, students, and parents. Teachers have knowledge about reading approaches and components, enabling them to make good learning choices for students. The capable administrator is a team player who supports instructional decisions and assessment of pupil progress.

The Problem: Principals may not always know what makes a good reading program, so they rely on classroom teachers. In contrast, though, strong instructional leaders, themselves, know the program, how to teach children to read, and how to support teachers' best efforts.

Rationale: Principals able to model instructional leadership display a sense of excellence which, in turn, teachers expect of themselves and their students. Keen educational leadership may result in enhanced learning for each student, but particularly those pupils most at-risk of learning to read.

Procedures: The principal may choose to evaluate self-perceptions after completing Form 2.1. It is important for the administrator to be as honest and accurate as possible when checking responses, in order to gain accurate summary feedback. As an option, and only if extensive feedback is sought, it may be useful to ask the Reading Advisory Board (see Chapter 3, Form 3.5), faculty, staff, and the curriculum coordinator to complete Form 2.1 as they view the performance of the principal. A comparison would provide multiple perceptions, a foundation for the principal's professional growth.

For Further Reading

Parker, S. A. (1993). "So Now You're a School Leader: What Should You Do?" *Phi Delta Kappan,* 75, 3, 29–30.

> Parker reviews concepts from research at the National Center for School Leadership at the University of Illinois. The NCSL describes understanding the roles of school cultures and contexts as foundations for effective instructional leadership.

Wepner, S. B., et al. (1995) *The Administration and Supervision of Reading Programs.* New York: Teachers College Press. (P. O. Box 20, Williston, VT, 05449-0020. 1-800-488-2665.)

> The authors maintain that the management of reading programs is crucial to their effectiveness. Part I offers an overview of reading supervision, Part II guidelines for program development, Part III implementation and evaluation, and Part IV connections to reading comprehension development.

Form 2.1
THE READING ADMINISTRATOR AS AN INSTRUCTIONAL LEADER

Directions: Research from the effective schools literature is interpreted to suggest that one of the most important characteristics is the principal as an instructional leader. Form 2.1 may be used for principals' self-assessment, or if multiple perceptions are desired, others may complete the form at the principal's request. Participants may respond to each statement below by placing a checkmark on the right, along the continuum, which best describes the perceived effectiveness.

An Effective Reading Instructional Leader:	Highly Effective	Moderately Effective	Marginally Effective	Not Effective
	4	3	2	1

1. Demonstrates leadership that leads to program improvement

a. Considers instructional leadership the greatest priority .... ☐ ☐ ☐ ☐

b. Develops an organizational climate that encourages change and improvement .... ☐ ☐ ☐ ☐

c. Possesses and shares an understanding of effective schools based on current research .... ☐ ☐ ☐ ☐

d. Uses and elicits good communication skills .... ☐ ☐ ☐ ☐

e. Employs appropriate, open decision-making .... ☐ ☐ ☐ ☐

f. Manages time effectively in order to have the time available to be an instructional leader .... ☐ ☐ ☐ ☐

2. Possesses vision of the program goals

a. Actually plans for an effective program .... ☐ ☐ ☐ ☐

b. Knows the steps to be taken to get the program to its goals .... ☐ ☐ ☐ ☐

c. Articulates those goals frequently to keep them at the forefront .... ☐ ☐ ☐ ☐

d. Uses goals as the first checkpoint for making program decisions .... ☐ ☐ ☐ ☐

e. Leads the faculty to set high expectations of themselves and their students .... ☐ ☐ ☐ ☐

f. Guides faculty to expect authentic achievement results vs their only *feeling good* about how students are doing .... ☐ ☐ ☐ ☐

3. Involves faculty and staff in designing programs that meet the needs of students and the total community

a. Has a Reading Advisory Board or council at the building level .... ☐ ☐ ☐ ☐

b. Ascertains that faculty and staff articulate the reading program goals and support them .... ☐ ☐ ☐ ☐

c. Seeks consensus on steps to be taken to reach program goals .... ☐ ☐ ☐ ☐

d. Helps all factions of the school pull together to reach program goals .... ☐ ☐ ☐ ☐

–continues–

The Reading Administrator as an Instructional Leader –continued–	4	3	2	1

4. Supports selection of an instructional approach to meet program goals

   a. Guides the Advisory Board to consider a range of approaches; i.e., literature-based, language-experience, basal reader, whole language, or computer-based .... □ □ □ □

   b. Purchases instructional materials consistent with the program's goals .. □ □ □ □

5. Provides curricular and instructional support for teachers

   a. Assists teachers in selecting and designing activities to achieve instructional goals .... □ □ □ □

   b. Observes that teachers share instructional objectives with students ..... □ □ □ □

   c. Makes certain that teachers have the materials required for instruction □ □ □ □

   d. Works with teachers to plan for effective use of instructional time .... □ □ □ □

   e. Helps teachers to conduct preassessment in order to determine learning needs .... □ □ □ □

   f. Supports teachers to build an appropriate balance between curriculum-centered and child-centered needs .... □ □ □ □

   g. Stresses the importance of direct instruction .... □ □ □ □

   h. Stresses reading for understanding, or reading comprehension, as the major purpose .... □ □ □ □

   i. Asks teachers to nurture writing about what is read as a vehicle to improve comprehension .... □ □ □ □

   j. Supports accelerated vocabulary development as a metacognitive, functional process .... □ □ □ □

   k. Helps teachers offer sufficient guided practice to ensure successful independent learning .... □ □ □ □

   l. Aids teachers in establishing regular times for recreational reading in the program .... □ □ □ □

   m. Assists teachers with classroom organization and grouping .... □ □ □ □

   n. Provides the necessary support personnel for students who do not learn easily .... □ □ □ □

   o. Helps teachers to facilitate order, warmth, and self-confidence among students .... □ □ □ □

–continues–

The Reading Administrator as an Instructional Leader –continued–	4	3	2	1

6. **With faculty and staff, sets a good example; i.e., models the importance of reading and writing**

   a. Feels personal responsibility for modeling reading and writing .... ☐ ☐ ☐ ☐

   b. Supports Sustained Silent Reading (SSR) as a planned part of the reading curriculum .... ☐ ☐ ☐ ☐

   c. Reinforces faculty and staff modeling of good reading and writing .... ☐ ☐ ☐ ☐

   d. Utilizes the written word as an avenue of communication with students ☐ ☐ ☐ ☐

7. **Supervises each teacher's program organization and grouping processes**

   a. Monitors whether grouping is consistent with program goals .... ☐ ☐ ☐ ☐

   b. Oversees whether grouping is conducted to meet needs of all students ☐ ☐ ☐ ☐

   c. Sees a variety of flexibly formed, small groups functioning over the week to meet numerous goals .... ☐ ☐ ☐ ☐

   d. Checks whether grouping contains enough flexibility to avoid stigma .... ☐ ☐ ☐ ☐

   e. Notes whether each teacher has an optimal number of groups, neither too many nor too few .... ☐ ☐ ☐ ☐

   f. Monitors whether seat work or independent work is suited to each pupil; especially if whole class direct instruction is used .... ☐ ☐ ☐ ☐

   g. Helps improve the quality of seatwork time, with increased recreational reading and writing about completed reading .... ☐ ☐ ☐ ☐

   h. Supports teachers who use collaborative grouping to share developmental reading, recreational reading, and writing as vehicles for affective and cognitive development .... ☐ ☐ ☐ ☐

8. **Monitors use of the reading assessment system**

   a. Checks pupil and class programs at designated times throughout the year .... ☐ ☐ ☐ ☐

   b. Monitors objective test performances to assure that students make continuous progress .... ☐ ☐ ☐ ☐

   c. Oversees use of student portfolios as vehicles to judge students' reading and writing progress .... ☐ ☐ ☐ ☐

   d. Checks end-of-year progress of individual students and each class ...... ☐ ☐ ☐ ☐

   e. Checks that records are ready for next year's teacher......................... ☐ ☐ ☐ ☐

–continues–

The Reading Administrator as an Instructional Leader   –continued–

	4	3	2	1

9. Monitors continuously the progress of the total reading program

a. Supervises the use of portfolio and other independent assessments conducted by each teacher .... ☐ ☐ ☐ ☐

b. Helps teachers to check congruence among portfolio, standardized, and state-mandated tests for each member of their classes .... ☐ ☐ ☐ ☐

c. Checks periodically details of unit and level performance on important test items .... ☐ ☐ ☐ ☐

d. Oversees individual progress on standardized tests .... ☐ ☐ ☐ ☐

e. Checks class progress on standardized tests .... ☐ ☐ ☐ ☐

f. Assesses, monitors school progress on standardized achievement tests year-to-year .... ☐ ☐ ☐ ☐

g. Assesses library use by individuals, classes, and teachers .... ☐ ☐ ☐ ☐

10. Plans staff development programs to improve instruction and learning

a. Oversees staff development that is identified cooperatively by principal, faculty, and central office personnel .... ☐ ☐ ☐ ☐

b. Manages development that is continuous, long-range, and addressed to improvement of reading instruction and student learning .... ☐ ☐ ☐ ☐

c. Supports inservice that blends needs of the program with needs of the faculty .... ☐ ☐ ☐ ☐

11. Nurtures a climate that honors the concept of diversity

a. Develops a school that, through literature, studies and values various cultures from around the world .... ☐ ☐ ☐ ☐

b. Expects and accepts diversity in the pupil population of the local school ☐ ☐ ☐ ☐

c. Engenders a school climate that accepts the linguistic and dialectic diversity of the local school, using differences to teach about all languages .... ☐ ☐ ☐ ☐

d. Develops a climate that prevents diverse learners from being treated in such a way that they feel substandard .... ☐ ☐ ☐ ☐

12. Supervises pupil intake into Title 1-Chapter 1 special reading programs

a. Consults with classroom teachers so that appropriate students are referred .... ☐ ☐ ☐ ☐

b. Ascertains that diagnosis confirms the most suitable students for remedial programs .... ☐ ☐ ☐ ☐

c. Coordinates the organization of special reading teachers with other programs .... ☐ ☐ ☐ ☐

d. Arranges for reading specialists to diagnose new students, gifted students, and others needing specialized testing .... ☐ ☐ ☐ ☐

–continues–

The Reading Administrator as an Instructional Leader –continued–	4	3	2	1

13. **Coordinates a program that ties together Title 1 and classroom reading**

    a. Expects special teachers to communicate with classroom teachers as working teams .... ☐ ☐ ☐ ☐

    b. Encourages special reading teachers to teach within classrooms alongside regular teachers vs teaching pull-out programs .... ☐ ☐ ☐ ☐

    c. Monitors case loads of special reading teachers and guards for appropriate pupils .... ☐ ☐ ☐ ☐

    d. Expects special reading teachers to be resource consultants for classroom teachers .... ☐ ☐ ☐ ☐

Cover the page here and below before photocopying if users are not to see the interpretation until later.

Interpretation: Persons completing Form 2.1 are invited to look over the questionnaire to identify areas of strength and weakness. Once the total form has been studied, it might be helpful to look at sections that the administrator wishes to strengthen, and develop the section(s) with a plan of growth. Principals probably should be admonished to develop a plan that focuses on only a small number of sections at a time. The Administrator might choose to complete the worksheet, develop a plan, concentrate on growth, complete relevant parts of the worksheet again, then analyze changes.

    If the administrator chooses to compare self-assessment with the judgments of others, those parties involved may identify parts of the form, or choose the total instrument, for purposes of shared judgment. External judgments might help the administrator develop a plan of growth more accurately than self-assessment alone, increasing the depth of judgments.

READING PROGRAMS AND SCHOOL EFFECTIVENESS RESEARCH

(see Form 2.2)

A sizeable body of research has been amassed regarding the qualities of effective schools (56). Effective schools are goal-directed units. Program goals become the blueprint for all decisions. Reading programs are directed toward those affirmed goals with a singleness of purpose. Effective schools have high expectations for children, active parent participation, and high student achievement. Direct instruction of skills, inquiry processes, and searching for meaning are considered undergirding concepts.

The Problem: Principals may not have familiarized themselves or their faculties with the research on effective schools. As well, they may not have kept its concepts at the forefront of program decisions and inservice.

Rationale: Principals in possession of reading program expertise hold an advantage over those with less knowledge. Administrators who expect teachers to consider school effectiveness concepts in generating instructional blueprints and daily planning of learning activities may reap benefits.

Procedures: The principal may wish to complete Form 2.2 to judge self-understanding of key concepts. Administrators may ask Advisory Board members to complete the worksheet as a basis to compare judgments. Another application is to ask the faculty to complete Form 2.2 prior to initiation of discussions on effective schools research.

For Further Reading

Chubb, J. E. & Moe, T. M. (1990). *Politics, Markets, and America's Schools.* Washington, DC: The Brookings Institution. (1775 Massachusetts Avenue, N.W., Washington, DC, 20036-2188. 202-797-6000.)

> The authors' quest began when the public was asking what influence the money spent on education has on the learning of children. The text addresses effective schools in the context of public concern.

Edmonds, R. (1985). "Characteristics of Effective Schools: Research and Implementation." Edited by J. Osborn, et al. *Reading Education: Foundations for a Literate America.* Lexington, MA: Lexington Books, D. C. Heath and Company. (Out of print, but often available in major university libraries.)

> Edmonds reviewed studies of effective schools to conclude that administrators who balanced management and instructional skills, exercised strong leadership skills, maintained an orderly environment, developed and implemented a reading plan, held high expectations for all students, emphasized acquisition of reading skills, frequently monitored pupil progress, provided support services, and found teachers' job satisfaction, resulted in effective schools.

Form 2.2
READING PROGRAMS AND SCHOOL EFFECTIVENESS RESEARCH

Directions: Below, statements are presented to summarize research on effective schools. In some instances, criteria address reading curriculum and organization directly. In other cases, criteria function in a broader context, yet affect reading programs. The form may be completed by faculty, principals, or Reading Advisory Boards. In each instance, respondents may judge the school's status by placing checkmarks on the right.

School Effectiveness criteria:

	Highly Effective	Moderately Effective	Marginally Effective	Not Effective
	4	3	2	1
1. Develop an effective, coherent, school reading program with articulated goals that mesh	☐	☐	☐	☐
2. Encourage teachers to express confidence in their own abilities to instruct, and to be realistic	☐	☐	☐	☐
3. With a constant press for excellence, develop high achievement expectations in the basic skills of reading, writing, and mathematics as fundamental goals for *all* learners	☐	☐	☐	☐
4. Nurture and sustain positive learning climates that emphasize high expectations	☐	☐	☐	☐
5. Monitor collaboratively to establish and expect high success rates, recognizing that success breeds success	☐	☐	☐	☐
6. Understand that children will learn much of what they are taught; yet not nearly so much of what they *are not* taught	☐	☐	☐	☐
7. Operate with a balance of direct instruction; i.e., teacher teaches vs texts, trade books, workbooks, media, games, or social contexts doing the teaching	☐	☐	☐	☐
8. Take responsibility individually for pupil learning, providing adequate levels of difficulty for the learning of school tasks	☐	☐	☐	☐
9. Model those comprehension processes they want pupils to be able to perform before, during, and after reading	☐	☐	☐	☐
10. Sustain a philosophy within the building that the purpose of vocabulary and decoding is to improve reading comprehension, not to learn rules or "sound out" words	☐	☐	☐	☐
11. Develop adequate amounts of guided practice of children's comprehension before they pursue independent applications	☐	☐	☐	☐
12. Nurture cooperative activity and group interaction within groups to develop concepts, facilitate reading, provide practice, and enhance affect toward reading	☐	☐	☐	☐

–continues–

Reading Programs and School Effectiveness Research   –continued–

	4	3	2	1

13. Deliver direct instruction when needed, use reading groups, individualizing between and within groups to address distinctive needs and to enhance flexibility which avoids stigma .... ☐ ☐ ☐ ☐

14. Have operational objectives for each lesson, know what those objectives are, and communicate them purposefully to pupils .... ☐ ☐ ☐ ☐

15. Use appropriate and varied materials to help ensure a high rate of success and promote achievement .... ☐ ☐ ☐ ☐

16. Operate with continuous diagnosis, evaluation, and feedback vehicles to monitor and support student learning and motivation .... ☐ ☐ ☐ ☐

17. Allocate enough time for reading instruction, recognizing that students who read more become better readers, those who write more (compose) about what they read and share collaboratively become better readers and writers ☐ ☐ ☐ ☐

18. Minimize meaningless independent activity or seat work that does not increase learning, yet increases boredom .... ☐ ☐ ☐ ☐

19. Keep non-engaged and transitional times to a minimum; i.e., keep students on task with appropriate reading-related activities .... ☐ ☐ ☐ ☐

20. Provide public recognition and visible rewards for students' academic excellence and growth .... ☐ ☐ ☐ ☐

21. Involve parents meaningfully in their children's learning, sharing with them the research-based role of homework and shared reading .... ☐ ☐ ☐ ☐

22. Implement sound principles of classroom management .... ☐ ☐ ☐ ☐

23. Recognize that students learn better in secure, nurturing, friendly class-rooms and school environments .... ☐ ☐ ☐ ☐

24. Convey the idea that pupils are nurtured with order and direction that enhances learning and avoids disruptions and distraction .... ☐ ☐ ☐ ☐

25. Develop a public relations package that provides regular recognition of individual student success .... ☐ ☐ ☐ ☐

26. Generate public recognition for teacher effectiveness and successes .... ☐ ☐ ☐ ☐

Cover the page here and below before photocopying if users are not to see the interpretation until later.

Interpretation: The principal who understands concepts and research related to effective schools is best able to articulate those ideas to the faculty and to support the Reading Advisory Board as it pursues program planning. To assess self-knowledge about effective schools, columns of Form 2.2 may be totaled, giving four points to *highly effective* implementation, three to *moderately effective*, two to *marginally effective* and one to *not effective*. Totals between 79 and 104 should be judged as *highly effective*, those between 53 and 78 as *moderately effective*, between 27 and 52 *marginally effective*, and those between 1 and 26 *not effective*.

CHANGE PROCESSES AND IMPROVED READING PROGRAMS   (see Form 2.3)

Schools may not improve unless personnel are willing to change the way they operate. One philosophy maintains that *If you keep doin' what you did, you're gonna get what ya got.* A systematic needs-assessment and program-planning process (see Chapter 3) conducted by a Reading Advisory Board is a comprehensive way to support program improvement.

The Problem: Professionals may be reluctant to change the program, the way they teach, or their roles. Some school people seem to try harder vs trying new ways. Giving up old ways increases stress and reduces confidence.

Rationale: Change may best lead to program improvement if the process examines present strengths and identifies effective ways to deal with program needs. A representative Reading Advisory Board that maintains close contact with the faculty as planning and implementation occur creates an informed faculty less likely to resist changes.

Procedures: Form 2.3 may be completed by the principal to review concepts of change processes, to self-assess present knowledge, and to prepare for the initiation of change in the school. The Reading Advisory Board might complete Form 2.3 to determine their present understanding, then compare results with the principal. The Advisory Board might ask the total faculty to complete Form 2.3, using findings as the basis to conduct a needs-assessment.

For Further Reading

Educational Planning: Concepts, Strategies, Practices (1991). Edited by R. V. Carlson, & G. Awkerman. New York: Longman. (10 Bank Street, White Plains, New York 10606-1951. 914-993-5000.)

Twenty-five administrators analyze the theory and practice of educational planning. Social and political foundations are explicated. Policy is viewed from a process-to-product continuum.

Principals' Reading Leadership Program (1979). Developed by I. Aaron, D. Bingham, D. Brown, J. Hunt, C. Knight, T. McCalla, B. Moore, P. E. Ransom, & J. Thrasher Washington, DC: U. S. Office of Education.

A leadership training process was developed to help administrators generate *grass roots* support for instructional leadership in reading. Leadership training was followed by technical assistance.

Form 2.3

CHANGE PROCESSES AND IMPROVED READING PROGRAMS

Directions: Reading Programs may improve only if change is involved; in other words, programs do not get better by staying the same. Instructional leaders who are able to manage change processes enjoy an advantage as programs evolve. Principals should complete Form 2.3. Advisory Boards that foster change, too, may complete Form 2.3 to gain self-judgments. Below are found criteria related to change processes. On the right, please indicate present understanding of criteria.

Change Process criteria:	Thorough Understanding	Moderate Understanding	Marginal Understanding	No Understanding
	4	3	2	1
1. The most effective unit of change is the local school, vs the district or regional unit (1, 15, 45)	☐	☐	☐	☐
2. A change plan should concentrate on the educational leader's responsibility to sanction, support, and lead any change that occurs	☐	☐	☐	☐
3. Leadership factors in change are support, involvement, communication, climate, and good decision-making	☐	☐	☐	☐
4. Change occurs ultimately as a result of personnel's seeing a real need to change	☐	☐	☐	☐
5. Change that evolves from a systematic plan is superior to a shotgun approach of dealing with day-to-day crises or "putting out brush fires"	☐	☐	☐	☐
6. A firm time commitment is involved since at least two years are warranted to conduct needs-assessments, establish priorities, alter staff beliefs and attitudes, and improve instruction	☐	☐	☐	☐
7. Use of a team as change facilitators is better than use of one person	☐	☐	☐	☐
8. Persons involved with the change may take ownership of the plan best if involved in its formulation	☐	☐	☐	☐
9. The school must make substantial time commitments for the team to meet, plan, learn, and support implementation	☐	☐	☐	☐
10. Needs-identification or needs-assessment, with findings prioritized to address local needs, starts the plan (see Chapter 3)	☐	☐	☐	☐
11. Faculty ownership of program changes is necessary for changes to endure	☐	☐	☐	☐
12. Changes must be manageable and feasible for the average teacher	☐	☐	☐	☐
13. The change is best understood by the faculty if it is presented as it finally will appear or function	☐	☐	☐	☐
14. A series of sequential staff development strategies, offering specific knowledge and skills, is part of the change plan	☐	☐	☐	☐

–continues–

Change Processes and Improved Reading Programs —continued—	4	3	2	1
15. When change plans concentrate on improvements at the classroom level, the result is building organization, management, and values that fall into place	☐	☐	☐	☐
16. Breakthroughs occur when personnel are able to understand why the new way works better than the previous way	☐	☐	☐	☐
17. Faculty competence and commitment are developed during implementation of the process	☐	☐	☐	☐
18. Facing the unknown consequences of change can be stressful to faculty ...	☐	☐	☐	☐
19. Positive interactions with peers, support personnel, and administrators reduce stress	☐	☐	☐	☐
20. Principals are particularly vulnerable when expected to reconcile pressures from above with the resentment toward change which the faculty may feel .	☐	☐	☐	☐
21. Changing prior ways of behavior and treatment of the reading program requires careful monitoring	☐	☐	☐	☐
22. New skills are developed through practice and conscientious feedback	☐	☐	☐	☐
23. After initial training is completed, technical assistance, encouragement, peer support, and practice help to maintain the change	☐	☐	☐	☐
24. Assisting the faculty to examine its growth, share responses, and celebrate successes is a very important part of the process				
25. Corrective action is pursued as the implementation plan strays off course ..	☐	☐	☐	☐
26. Locking in new ways of behavior and treatment of the reading program requires careful monitoring	☐	☐	☐	☐
27. Successful program changes often require six years or more, total, to become fully institutionalized	☐	☐	☐	☐
28. The change plan must be monitored throughout, revised, and evaluated continuously	☐	☐	☐	☐
29. Change is viewed as a process, not an event, and change or improvement functions best when seen as a continuing, expected, and planned process.	☐	☐	☐	☐

Cover the page here and below before photocopying if users are not to see the interpretation until later.

Interpretation: To assist in self-checking knowledge of change processes, principals or Advisory Boards may wish to total responses to each criterion in each column above. Giving four points to *thorough under-standing,* three to *moderate understanding,* two to *marginal understanding,* and one point to *no understanding,* provides totals. Scores running between 88 and 116 suggest that the principal's knowledge of change processes represents *thorough understanding,* between 59 and 87 *moderate understanding,* between 30 and 58 *marginal understanding,* and between 1 and 29 is *no understanding.*

SCHOOL CLIMATE IN READING PROGRAM IMPROVEMENT   (see Form 2.4)

A wholesome school climate is important to improvement of reading programs, extending the trust to change. The environmental benefit of trust enables teachers to teach purposefully, confidently, and professionally. Children, likewise, benefit from learning in warm, accepting environments.

The Problem: Schools may operate in unhealthy climates in which neither the faculty nor principal recognizes the status, nor understands the impact of feelings on teaching and learning. Principals may be helpless to improve the school's climate without outside information, and teachers may feel frustrated with the administration, resisting change.

Rationale: A school seeking to improve its operations and change its ways of functioning may proceed in a setting in which people experience support from colleagues who are trying to change alongside each other. The trust and support which results from the principal's and peers' encouragement helps people to be willing to support program change.

Procedures: The principal may choose to complete Form 2.4 to assess personal knowledge, and to assess the status of the school. The administrator seeking judgments from the faculty or Advisory Board would be able to gain a collective status report. Schools conducting needs-assessment and program-planning change processes may benefit from assessment of the school climate.

For Further Reading

Halpin, A. (1966). *Theory and Research in Administration.* Toronto: Collier-Macmillan Canada, Ltd., 148–150. (Out of print, but found in many university education libraries.)

> A classic on organizational development. Part 1 develops theoretical and conceptual foundations. Part II summarizes empirical research on the *real world* of administration. The *Organizational Climate Description Questionnaire, Form IV* continues to be used extensively, and to be adapted by other authors.

Schmuck, R. A. & Runkel, P. J. (1985, 1988). *The Handbook of Organizational Development in Schools, Third Edition.* Prospect Heights, IL: Waveland Press. (P. O. Box 400, Prospect Heights, IL 60070. 1-708-634-0081.)

> The text is designed for administrators who plan to undergo organizational changes in their school. The purpose is to support improved student morale and raise achievement by developing more humane, consistent, and effective teaching. Topics include climate, and effective schools. The handbook strengthens adminstrators as helpful facilitators.

Form 2.4

SCHOOL CLIMATE IN READING PROGRAM CHANGE

Directions: A healthy school climate is essential to program change and improvement. Below are statements about climate which may be judged by teachers, Reading Advisory Board members, or principals. On the right, respondents may check the column which best represents their view of climate conditions in the local school.

School Climate criteria:	Highly Effective	Moderately Effective	Marginally Effective	Not Effective
	4	3	2	1
1. Teachers have close friends who also are faculty members at the school ...	☐	☐	☐	☐
2. There is no minority group of teachers who usually oppose the majority	☐	☐	☐	☐
3. Teachers do not exert group pressure on non-conforming faculty or staff	☐	☐	☐	☐
4. In faculty meetings, there is the feeling of "let's get things done"	☐	☐	☐	☐
5. Personnel at the school are helped to feel successful and worthy	☐	☐	☐	☐
6. Teachers talk about their personal lives to other faculty members and staff	☐	☐	☐	☐
7. Most teachers accept their colleagues' faults	☐	☐	☐	☐
8. There is considerable laughter when faculty gather informally	☐	☐	☐	☐
9. Teachers and staff at this school are treated with respect	☐	☐	☐	☐
10. Building personnel feel that they hold a great amount of credibility with the central office	☐	☐	☐	☐
11. Teachers show a great amount of school spirit	☐	☐	☐	☐
12. The principal goes out of his/her way to help teachers and staff	☐	☐	☐	☐
13. The principal sets the tone for the school by working hard, personally	☐	☐	☐	☐
14. The principal does personal favors for all teachers and staff	☐	☐	☐	☐
15. Teachers feel free to express themselves at faculty meetings, knowing that they will not be "put down" for their beliefs	☐	☐	☐	☐
16. Teachers ordinarily do not eat lunch by themselves in their classrooms	☐	☐	☐	☐
17. Teachers do not feel that some people are treated with favoritism	☐	☐	☐	☐
18. School personnel encourage and take seriously feedback from the community	☐	☐	☐	☐
19. Morale of teachers and staff is high	☐	☐	☐	☐
20. The principal uses constructive criticism	☐	☐	☐	☐
21. The principal stays after school to help teachers finish projects	☐	☐	☐	☐

–continues–

School Climate in Reading Program Change	—continued—	4	3	2	1
22. Teachers have positive contact with the principal each day		☐	☐	☐	☐
23. People at the school weigh carefully the feedback they get from students ...		☐	☐	☐	☐
24. The principal is well prepared when s/he speaks at school functions		☐	☐	☐	☐
25. The principal criticizes a specific act rather than a staff or faculty member ..		☐	☐	☐	☐
26. Teachers and staff feel free to question rules set by the principal		☐	☐	☐	☐
27. The principal looks out for the personal welfare of school personnel...........		☐	☐	☐	☐
28. The principal runs faculty meetings in an organized way with an established agenda		☐	☐	☐	☐
29. Teachers look forward to working with colleagues on projects.....................		☐	☐	☐	☐
30. Feedback from the community, parents, and students is shared with the faculty		☐	☐	☐	☐
31. The principal tells teachers of new ideas s/he has run across		☐	☐	☐	☐
32. Teachers do not talk about leaving the school or the school system		☐	☐	☐	☐
33. Teachers are informed of results of supervisors' visits		☐	☐	☐	☐
34. The principal supports teachers to work to their full capabilities		☐	☐	☐	☐
35. Teachers often spend more than the required amount of time at the school		☐	☐	☐	☐

Cover the page here and below before photocopying if users are not to see the interpretation until later.

Interpretation: The principal may want to complete Form 2.4 to gain a view of the climate in his/her school. The administrator might choose to ask faculty, staff, and parents active in the school to complete the worksheet, as well. The Reading Advisory Board would be able to use these aggregate data to analyze thoroughly the school's climate. Efforts then may be made to maintain strengths and improve areas warranting attention. As a result of completing Form 2.4, the principal might develop ways to improve the identified low or mediocre areas over which he has control.

Responses to columns of the School Climate worksheet may be totaled, giving four points to *highly effective,* three to *moderately effective,* two to *marginally effective,* and one to *not effective* responses. Totals between 106–140 may be considered *highly effective,* between 71–105 *moderately effective,* between 36–70 *marginally effective,* and between 1–35 *not effective.*

DECISION-MAKING SUPPORTS PROGRAM IMPROVEMENT   (see Form 2.5)

A school seeking to change its reading program and improve its ways of operation must be supported by a principal with strong decision-making skills. The principal who leads program-planning processes first prioritizes the program's needs and goals. Subsequently, decisions are directed toward goal fulfillment. Effective decisions may help to institutionalize program changes after they are initiated. Clearly communicating those decisions helps faculty and staff *pull together* to reach program goals.

The Problem: Principals are not always capable decision-makers; they may perform better in some settings and situations than in others. Advisory Board members, too, may be unskilled at making the strong decisions that support program-planning changes in reading.

Rationale: Capable decision-makers are able to use their time better, get more done, operate more effectively, and engender trust. Good decisions can support program change and improvements, providing a vehicle to have each action move toward program goals. As well, improved decision-making skills may be expected to increase overall administrative effectiveness.

Procedures: The principal may have had little opportunity to check her/his knowledge about decision-making, and may not have evaluated her/his decisions on the status of the school. An opportunity to do these things can be provided by using Form 2.5. The Reading Advisory Board and principal conducting a reading improvement process might use Form 2.5 as the benchmark piece of data to set the focus for program direction.

For Further Reading

Hughes, L. W. & Ubben, G. C. (1994). *The Elementary Principal's Handbook: A Guide to Effective Action, Fourth Edition.* Des Moines, IA: Longwood Division, Allyn & Bacon. (10 Bank Street, White Plains, NY 10606-1951. 914-993-5000.)

> The authors base the text on concepts and research applied directly to school settings. Effective school restructuring is a theme of the handbook. Hughes and Ubben offer examples, charts, forms, guidelines, and reports.

Keith, S. & Girling, R. H. (1991). *Education, Management, and Participation: New Directions in Educational Administration.* Boston: Allyn & Bacon. (Dept. 894, 160 Gould Street, Needham Heights, MA 02194-2310. 1-800-852-8024.)

> Keith and Girling offer a comprehensive school management text containing 12 chapters. The authors apply research findings to case studies of actual schools and districts. The section on solving problems and making decisions may be particularly helpful to practitioners.

Form 2.5
DECISION-MAKING SUPPORTS PROGRAM GOALS

Directions: Effective administrators make decisions consistent with program goals. Below, respondents will find criteria often employed when administrators are faced with school-related decisions. On the right, principals or Advisory Board members may check the extent to which their beliefs and knowledge are consistent with effective decision-making skills.

Decision-making criteria:	Thorough Knowledge	Moderate Knowledge	Marginal Knowledge	Little Knowledge
	4	3	2	1
1. Identify the problem				
a. Clear understanding of the issue	☐	☐	☐	☐
b. Issue is open, and known to others	☐	☐	☐	☐
c. Not a part of a larger problem	☐	☐	☐	☐
2. Dissect the problem				
a. Decide what is, or is not, important to deal with, going beyond symptoms	☐	☐	☐	☐
b. Recognize as a single, nonrecurring problem	☐	☐	☐	☐
c. Consider precedents that will aid in solving the problem	☐	☐	☐	☐
d. Determine whether individual or group decision-making is warranted	☐	☐	☐	☐
e. Define the goals the school has in addressing the problem	☐	☐	☐	☐
f. Conclude what the school wants to achieve, maintain, or avoid in the ultimate decision	☐	☐	☐	☐
3. Consider alternative solutions				
a. Identify criteria to meet in reaching the decision	☐	☐	☐	☐
b. Reflect upon remaining flexible	☐	☐	☐	☐
c. Brainstorm and consider all of the possible solutions and consequences that can be identified	☐	☐	☐	☐
d. Attempt to prevent experiences, prejudices, or personalities from limiting the alternatives explored	☐	☐	☐	☐
e. Examine alternatives without undue pressure because of time constraints	☐	☐	☐	☐
f. Reflect on the alternatives, but not for too long	☐	☐	☐	☐
g. Avoid dominant, or critical, persons' dominating the selection of alternatives	☐	☐	☐	☐
4. Evaluate alternatives and their consequences				
a. Consequences of possible solutions are considered	☐	☐	☐	☐
b. Guidelines for evaluating alternatives are applied	☐	☐	☐	☐
c. Advantages and disadvantages are weighed for significance	☐	☐	☐	☐

–continues–

Decision-making Supports Program Goals –continued–	4	3	2	1

5. Select an alternative and develop a plan of action

a. Alternative is selected that best fits the needs of the problem, using criteria chosen .... ☐ ☐ ☐ ☐

b. Time is taken to decide how to implement the decision .... ☐ ☐ ☐ ☐

c. A time line monitors flow of the decision .... ☐ ☐ ☐ ☐

d. Trouble-shooting the decision is conducted to consider what could go wrong .... ☐ ☐ ☐ ☐

6. Recognize that new ways of doing things interfere with old ways of operating

a. Lines of communication are kept open:

   communicate decisions to colleagues and receive feedback .... ☐ ☐ ☐ ☐

   gain feedback that aids understanding of the decision .... ☐ ☐ ☐ ☐

b. Evaluate whether the decision generally is suited to the problem .... ☐ ☐ ☐ ☐

c. Consider what new problems are created subsequently .... ☐ ☐ ☐ ☐

d. Recognize that this decision is part of a continuous cycle of decisions .. ☐ ☐ ☐ ☐

7. Opt for group decision-making

a. Shared decision-making is a factor in developing and sustaining teacher morale, empowerment, and program ownership .... ☐ ☐ ☐ ☐

b. Shared decision-making is positively related to teachers' satisfaction in teaching, and the school's climate .... ☐ ☐ ☐ ☐

c. Teachers prefer principals who involve them in decision-making .... ☐ ☐ ☐ ☐

d. Subordinates should be involved in shared decisions when they have a vested interest and possess expertise that they can contribute .... ☐ ☐ ☐ ☐

e. When a problem is structured, groups make more accurate decisions, but make them more slowly than does an individual .... ☐ ☐ ☐ ☐

Cover the page here and below before photocopying if users are not to see the interpretation until later.

Interpretation: Good decisions support daily and long-term operations of a school, and beyond that, lend help to the school as it attempts to improve its quality of reading program. Change warrants decisions consistent with the school's goals, and administrators can learn to improve those decision-making skills.

The Advisory Board or principal seeking to reflect upon their knowledge of decision-making, or ability to make quality choices, may total the columns of Form 2.5, giving four points to *thorough knowledge,* three to *moderate knowledge,* two to *marginal knowledge,* and one to *little knowledge* responses. Totals between 103–136 should be considered *thorough knowledge,* between 69–102 *moderate knowledge,* between 35–68 *marginal knowledge,* and between 1–34 *little knowledge.* A reminder is provided that self-analysis is valuable only if the administrator has checked, as accurately and realistically as possible, responses made on Form 2.5.

EFFECTIVE COMMUNICATION AND   (see Form 2.6)
READING PROGRAM IMPROVEMENT

When a school is undergoing a change process, clear communication* among all faculty, the principal, and staff about the reading program's goals and direction does matter. The administrator who is a successful communicator elicits trust from faculty and staff. As a result, personnel are able to understand the principal and the goals of the reading program.

The Problem: Principals may not recognize that their pronouncements do not always make sense to the faculty. Worse yet, the principal's manner of communication may offend faculty and negate the goals. Advisory Boards, too, risk being misunderstood.

Rationale: Reading program change and improvement warrants non-threatening, accurate communication. To operate effectively, both the principal and Reading Advisory Board strengthen change when they communicate clearly and non-offensively.

Procedures: Many administrators would like to be outstanding communicators, but gain little feedback about their effectiveness. Completion of Form 2.6 may provide such data. Upon analysis of a completed form, the principal could ask the district curriculum coordinator to fill out the form as s/he views the principal, using both forms as a basis for comparison.

Principals and Reading Advisory Board members pursuing change might complete Form 2.6 to identify strengths and weaknesses. They can then strengthen their own communication skills prior to initiating faculty participation in the program improvement process.

For Further Reading

Griffin, M. A. (1993). "Say It Like You Mean It," *School Business Affairs*, 59, 9, 15–19.

Griffin describes ways to communicate effectively. She deals with non-verbal, speaking, listening, and written communication skills.

Pfeiffer, J. W. & Jones, J. E. (1972–1995+). *A Handbook of Structured Experiences for Human Relations Training, Annual Volumes.* San Diego, CA: University Associates. (University Associates, Inc., 2780 Circleport Drive, Erlanger, KY 41018. 1-800-274-4434.)

Annual handbooks for group facilitators, trainers, and consultants published from 1972+. Topics deal with human relations leadership. Each edition contains sections on effective, facilitative communication practices.

Form 2.6
EFFECTIVE COMMUNICATION SUPPORTS PROGRAM CHANGE

Directions: Effective communication is a foundation of managing school program change. Criteria listed below may be related to principals' or Reading Advisory Board members' beliefs, skills, or knowledge about successful communication. On the right, participants may make checkmarks to represent the extent of present effectiveness.

Communication criteria:	Highly Effective 4	Moderately Effective 3	Marginally Effective 2	Not Effective 1
1. The purposes of communication within a school are for people to understand each other, to trust the environment where learning takes place, and to fulfill the mission of the school in a positive way	☐	☐	☐	☐
2. Communication is a process of interaction between individuals who send, receive, act on, and provide feedback about messages, any link of which may fail	☐	☐	☐	☐
3. Communication takes place in a social setting in which the receiver of the message may hold meanings different from those of the sender	☐	☐	☐	☐
4. The successful communicator knows his/her audience and anticipates reactions to messages	☐	☐	☐	☐
5. Initial meanings of the message reside with the sender	☐	☐	☐	☐
6. The effective communicator is a good listener who is interested in other people	☐	☐	☐	☐
7. The good communicator is open to receiving messages from others	☐	☐	☐	☐
8. Skilled communicators avoid jumping to conclusions about messages or their senders	☐	☐	☐	☐
9. The messages sent should be clear enough that the receiver will gain similar meanings	☐	☐	☐	☐
10. The choice of words is appropriate, neither too simple nor too complex	☐	☐	☐	☐
11. The sender is aware of how s/he is perceived by the receiver of the message	☐	☐	☐	☐
12. Good communicators operate in ways that the receiver will be satisfied with the message	☐	☐	☐	☐
13. Effective communicators function in such a way that the receiver will continue to be receptive to future messages	☐	☐	☐	☐
14. Opportunities for feedback that enhances accuracy of messages is greatest with one-on-one communication	☐	☐	☐	☐

–continues–

Effective Communication Supports Program Change   -continued-

	4	3	2	1
15. Possibilities for distortion of messages are increased in groups because several persons and points of view are present	☐	☐	☐	☐
16. With large groups and one-way communication, it is difficult to gain feedback	☐	☐	☐	☐
17. Persons should realize that messages may become distorted when they pass through several layers or levels of an organization	☐	☐	☐	☐
18. People should know that gaps in communication seem to be filled in with details that suit senders *and* receivers of messages	☐	☐	☐	☐
19. Senders recognize that receivers tend to hear what they expect, or at times, wish to hear..	☐	☐	☐	☐
20. Good communicators seek feedback and give feedback in order to gain common understanding and increase communication accuracy..................	☐	☐	☐	☐
21. Effective communicators keep channels open to include each appropriate member of the school	☐	☐	☐	☐
22. Administrators work to enhance communication skills of all with whom they affiliate through the use of effective activities to learn about communication processes	☐	☐	☐	☐

Cover the page here and below prior to photocopying if users are not to see the interpretation until later.

Interpretation: The principal may review the self-assessment of Form 2.6 to identify areas that are satisfactory or unsatisfactory. A personal growth plan, addressing unsatisfactory patterns, may lead to a "patch-it-up" stance toward communication skills. Another use of Form 2.6 is for the principal to anticipate first one, then another faculty member's responses to criteria and note discrepancies with self-assessment. The process may help to clarify areas warranting attention as the principal reflects upon communication skills as influences on decisions.

Results from the worksheet may be analyzed by totaling each column, giving four points to *highly effective*, three points to *moderately effective*, two to *marginally effective*, and one to *not effective*. Totals between 67–88 may be interpreted to mean that participants possess *highly effective* communication skills, between 45–66 *moderately effective,* between 23–44 *marginally effective*, and between 1–22 *not effective* communication skills.

DELEGATION OF TASKS AND RESPONSIBILITIES   (see Form 2.7)

The principal or Reading Advisory Board in pursuit of reading program-planning and the stresses of change may delegate shared leadership with others, creating a sense of program ownership and shared time demands. School administrators tend to be very busy people. Even prioritizing the day's challenges may identify uncompleted tasks and may signal tasks that can be appropriately delegated.

The Problem: The principal who leads and monitors program changes may become bogged down, and important tasks may not get done. Administrators may not trust faculty and staff to share tasks and responsibilities, a feeling often recognized more by the faculty than by the principal. This distrust and unshared ownership can interfere with program changes.

Rationale: Time required to lead program change is valuable for the principal and Reading Advisory Board. Trust, shared program ownership, and effective use of time may be actualized if suitable tasks are delegated.

Procedures: Principals may complete Form 2.7 to judge knowledge about task delegation, or to assess personal delegation skills. Knowing strengths and weaknesses can lead to a personal improvement process. Delegation gets more done, allowing the Reading Advisory Board to pursue more tasks concurrently. A program improvement process may result in the principal's or Advisory Board's asking numerous faculty and staff to gather data to assist in making decisions about program change.

For Further Reading

Luce, W. M. (1994). "Principles for Principals," *Executive Educator*, 16, 8, 23–25.

> A curriculum supervisor, previously a principal, presents principles for other principals. He describes the balance between principals' accountability to the central office and accountability to the school. Among management skills described, the author asserts the importance of appropriate delegation of tasks.

Vroom, V. H. & Jago, A. G. (1988). *The New Leadership: Managing Participation in Organizations.* Englewood Cliffs, NJ: Prentice-Hall. (113 Sylvan Avenue, Englewood Cliffs, NJ 07632. 1-800-526-0485.)

> Resource for upper-level business management and industrial organization psychology courses. The section on task delegation helps administrators think through steps taken.

Form 2.7

DELEGATION OF TASKS AND RESPONSIBILITIES

Directions: Administrators who are able to delegate may then address higher priorities such as instructional leadership of the reading program. Below, principals or Reading Advisory Board members will find step-by-step procedures related to the delegation of reading program-related tasks. On the right, participants may check the extent of their knowledge about those processes.

Task Delegation Procedures	Great Knowledge	Moderate Knowledge	Marginal Knowledge	Little Knowledge
	4	3	2	1
1. Recognize the need to use professional time more effectively	☐	☐	☐	☐
2. Be willing to give up some tasks, particularly favorite ones	☐	☐	☐	☐
3. List the tasks completed daily, weekly, monthly, or less frequently	☐	☐	☐	☐
4. List the key steps in each task above, and select a task to be delegated that has the clearest procedures	☐	☐	☐	☐
5. Write up a step-by-step explanation of how to do this task	☐	☐	☐	☐
6. Define any risks in performing this task, including mistakes an inexperienced person might make	☐	☐	☐	☐
7. Determine critical benchmarks of the project as checkpoints for a subordinate to meet with the delegator before going further	☐	☐	☐	☐
8. Estimate the time needed for training and handling the task	☐	☐	☐	☐
9. Communicate the notion that the delegator is looking for somebody to take over the task	☐	☐	☐	☐
10. Talk with prospective staff or faculty who might be interested and able to handle the task	☐	☐	☐	☐
11. Ask subordinates with the most potential for carrying out the task how they would handle the different steps	☐	☐	☐	☐
12. After gaining feedback from interested and capable persons, and weighing the options, make the assignment	☐	☐	☐	☐
13. Ask the subordinates what resources or support they will need	☐	☐	☐	☐
14. Authorize the delegatee publicly, so that others will know the appointment has the principal's support	☐	☐	☐	☐
15. Let go of the project by giving it up	☐	☐	☐	☐
16. If the subordinate runs into trouble with the task, help her/him to do it appropriately, rather than take the task back	☐	☐	☐	☐

–continues–

Delegation of Tasks and Responsibilities	-continued-	4	3	2	1

17. Recognize that the more the administrator is convinced of the importance of delegating, the more quickly the conviction will spread to subordinates and others .... ☐   ☐   ☐   ☐

18. Help others to become aware of the steps involved in delegating effectively .... ☐   ☐   ☐   ☐

Cover the page here and below prior to photocopying if users are not to see the interpretation until later.

Interpretation: Form 2.7, Task Delegation, may be useful if the principal shares management responsibilities, thereby freeing time to address the higher priority of the reading program's instructional leadership. Subordinates are able to feel ownership for the program, as well as empowerment.

    To interpret Form 2.7, the principal may total each column, giving four points to *great knowledge,* three to *moderate knowledge,* two to *marginal knowledge,* and one to *little knowledge* checkmarks. Totals between 55–72 may represent *great knowledge,* between 37–54 *moderate knowledge,* between 19–36 *marginal knowledge,* and between 1–18 *little knowledge.*

TIME MANAGEMENT ENHANCES READING LEADERSHIP   (see Form 2.8)

Principals who believe that instructional leadership is their most important responsibility, or those taking their faculty through reading program improvement processes, may find each day totally filled with tasks. Busy principals have difficulty getting all of the jobs done. Even those who are particularly effective may find the demands stressful and unable to be met during the number of hours in most days.

The Problem: Principals may become so involved with less important tasks that there is not adequate time to manage program change and improvements. Advisory Boards without time management training and knowledge of the effective use of the clock may delay program changes or actually not get around to initiating their goals.

Rationale: That administrators and Reading Advisory Board members can learn to manage time more effectively is a concept taken from executive training programs. Program change becomes more focused when leadership learns to use time better, and as they share that knowledge with colleagues.

Procedures: If the school is participating in a needs-assessment and program-planning study, all participants may benefit from enhanced time management skills, as time demands are great. The principal may benefit from completing Form 2.8 in order to assess present skills of time management. The principal might also conduct inservice workshops to help faculty and staff increase their skills at time management—both personal and professional competencies.

For Further Reading

Donahoe, T. (1993). "Finding the Way: Structure, Time, and Culture," *Phi Delta Kappan,* 75, 4, 298–305.

> Develops the importance of eliminating leadership dependency. Explicates the role of effective principals and external change agents in restructuring through time usage.

Raywid, M. A. (1993). "Finding Time for Collaboration," *Educational Leadership,* 51, 1, 30–34.

> Suggests 15 ways for schools to arrange time to facilitate professional collaboration.

Form 2.8
TIME MANAGEMENT ENHANCES READING LEADERSHIP

Directions: Principals who manage time well are better able to pursue the higher priority, instructional leadership of the reading program. Administrators may recognize that time management skills are cyclical, and that skill is not gained with just one effort. To pursue self-assessment, after reading each statement below, principals or Reading Advisory Board members may check on the right whether skills are presently effective or if improvement is warranted.

Time Management criteria:	Highly Effective	Moderately Effective	Marginally Effective	Not Effective
	4	3	2	1

1. Face the fact that managing time is a skill that must be developed

a. Make a commitment to learn the techniques of time management	☐	☐	☐	☐
b. Read, study, and think about managing time	☐	☐	☐	☐
c. Think about what can and cannot be done in the amount of time designated	☐	☐	☐	☐
d. Assess what the manager wants to do, what s/he has to do, and how much time is available to do it	☐	☐	☐	☐
e. Figure out what is taking the most time and decide if that time use fulfills what should be accomplished	☐	☐	☐	☐
f. Develop a plan for time management	☐	☐	☐	☐

2. Develop a more accurate sense of time by keeping a log

a. Keep a log recording activities in 15-minute increments on a daily basis	☐	☐	☐	☐
b. Review the log after six weeks to see if the ways the principal thinks time is spent are actually the ways the time is spent	☐	☐	☐	☐
c. Study whether the time spent on tasks is proportionate to task importance	☐	☐	☐	☐

3. Determine whether time spent is meeting goals, and if not, re-examine goals

a. List what is important to do today, tomorrow, next week, in a month, and in five years	☐	☐	☐	☐
b. State goals in concrete terms to aid attainment and evaluation	☐	☐	☐	☐
c. Re-establish goals in a frugal manner	☐	☐	☐	☐
d. Periodically, review, expand, delete, and set intermediate goals	☐	☐	☐	☐

–continues–

Time Management Enhances Reading Leadership	-continued-	4	3	2	1

4. Learn to say "no"

a. Assess the congruence of any new tasks with current goals .... ☐ ☐ ☐ ☐

b. Determine whether the new task is worthy of the time spent .... ☐ ☐ ☐ ☐

c. Recognize that a new task often includes a series of time-consuming activities .... ☐ ☐ ☐ ☐

5. Develop a "to do" list

a. Mark special days and deadline dates on a calendar .... ☐ ☐ ☐ ☐

b. Enter anything and everything that might be done into a notebook for that purpose .... ☐ ☐ ☐ ☐

c. Pick out items from the notebook, calendar, goal-referenced lists, and leftovers from previous days to make the "to do" list .... ☐ ☐ ☐ ☐

d. Discard items that have been transferred to new lists a number of times ☐ ☐ ☐ ☐

6. Do two things at the same time

a. Whenever possible, convert waiting time or traveling time into productive time .... ☐ ☐ ☐ ☐

b. Dictate letters or listen to tapes while traveling .... ☐ ☐ ☐ ☐

c. Carry materials to read while waiting for appointments at the central office, at airports, or doctor's office .... ☐ ☐ ☐ ☐

7. Set up arbitrary deadlines and limits

a. Stop being a perfectionist .... ☐ ☐ ☐ ☐

b. Set up arbitrary deadlines, based on importance and urgency of the project .... ☐ ☐ ☐ ☐

c. Create an extremely tight deadline and sprint for a short duration .... ☐ ☐ ☐ ☐

8. Avoid interruptions

a. When a long, complex task must be completed, hide out someplace .... ☐ ☐ ☐ ☐

b. Come to work before others or stay later .... ☐ ☐ ☐ ☐

c. Set aside a quiet hour at the office when no interruptions are permitted ☐ ☐ ☐ ☐

d. Schedule times for unanticipated tasks .... ☐ ☐ ☐ ☐

e. Let the secretary screen visitors and incoming calls .... ☐ ☐ ☐ ☐

f. Schedule a time to return telephone calls and stick to the schedule ...... ☐ ☐ ☐ ☐

g. Discourage drop-in visitors; talk with them standing up .... ☐ ☐ ☐ ☐

h. Become totally immersed in the task at a given moment .... ☐ ☐ ☐ ☐

–continues–

Time Management Enhances Reading Leadership -continued-	4	3	2	1

9. Invest time for a later payoff

   a. Learn new skills that save time. Learn to use a computer, word processor, or a dictating machine .... ☐ ☐ ☐ ☐

   b. Teach the staff those skills they should possess and procedures which they should follow .... ☐ ☐ ☐ ☐

   c. Spend time analyzing and improving the work flow and routine procedures .... ☐ ☐ ☐ ☐

   d. Prepare checklists and other job aids for the staff .... ☐ ☐ ☐ ☐

10. Learn to use formulas, forms, and frames

   a. Keep a collection of different types of letters, reports, proposals, articles, contracts, budgets, charts, tables, and other items used at work repeatedly .... ☐ ☐ ☐ ☐

   b. Rather than create something new from scratch, adapt and modify from previous formats to suit the present occasion .... ☐ ☐ ☐ ☐

11. Work as a team

   a. Cultivate a comfortable working style with colleagues and collaborators .... ☐ ☐ ☐ ☐

   b. Take time to build a team so that trust need not be reestablished with each new project .... ☐ ☐ ☐ ☐

   c. In working with a group, maintain a balance between people needs and task needs .... ☐ ☐ ☐ ☐

   d. Maintain a flexible leadership style that suits different situations, different groups, and different tasks .... ☐ ☐ ☐ ☐

   e. Do not be afraid to give up the control of a group, if needed .... ☐ ☐ ☐ ☐

   f. Be a follower if it will get the task done and save time .... ☐ ☐ ☐ ☐

12. Get organized

   a. Develop a filing and paper-sorting system and become adept at deciding which papers are worth keeping .... ☐ ☐ ☐ ☐

   b. Handle paper work only once .... ☐ ☐ ☐ ☐

   c. Sort papers into those requiring immediate action or warranting pending action. Make notations on pending items before filing .... ☐ ☐ ☐ ☐

   d. Sort papers deciding whether to read and file, read and distribute, or read and toss .... ☐ ☐ ☐ ☐

   e. Keep a file of reading material for "dead time" .... ☐ ☐ ☐ ☐

   f. Be generous with use of the trash can .... ☐ ☐ ☐ ☐

–continues–

Time Management Enhances Reading Leadership -continued-	4	3	2	1

13. Master the use of the telephone

   a. Tell the caller if this is not a convenient time to talk .... ☐ ☐ ☐ ☐

   b. Politely determine the purpose of calls and decide whether the information already is available, or if a return call should be made .... ☐ ☐ ☐ ☐

   c. Do not put off returning an unpleasant calld .... ☐ ☐ ☐ ☐

   d. Minimize socializing; answer each question with specific information .... ☐ ☐ ☐ ☐

   e. Walk a fine line between being brusque and being efficient .... ☐ ☐ ☐ ☐

   f. Buy and use a telephone answering service, voice mail, or e-mail that records messages .... ☐ ☐ ☐ ☐

   g. Collect messages, returning most calls at once, or select a time of day when people are likely to be available, such as early morning or late afternoon .... ☐ ☐ ☐ ☐

   h. Indicate time limitations, such as "I only have a minute," or "I just have a quick question" .... ☐ ☐ ☐ ☐

14. Delegate whenever appropriate

   a. Ask somebody else to take a task if the person can do it better or with more enjoyment .... ☐ ☐ ☐ ☐

   b. Outgrow "nobody-can-do-it-like-me," and realize it is bad for both mental health and time management to do it all .... ☐ ☐ ☐ ☐

   c. Ask a friend or assistant to do a job, or in their place, to have somebody do it .... ☐ ☐ ☐ ☐

   d. Delegate the task of delegating, if it is not possible to do the delegating .... ☐ ☐ ☐ ☐

15. Study the school calendar, plan the schedule

   a. Mark vacation beginnings and endings on the calendar .... ☐ ☐ ☐ ☐

   b. Mark special days and weeks to be observed on the calendar .... ☐ ☐ ☐ ☐

   c. Identify professional meetings to attend .... ☐ ☐ ☐ ☐

   d. Block out administrative team meetings regularly scheduled at the central office .... ☐ ☐ ☐ ☐

   e. Enter on the calendar routine staff meetings and begin to accumulate agenda content .... ☐ ☐ ☐ ☐

   f. Show meeting times for PTO and other parent groups that meet regularly .... ☐ ☐ ☐ ☐

   g. Indicate times for scheduling supervisory visits .... ☐ ☐ ☐ ☐

   h. Block out times for faculty evaluation conferences............................... ☐ ☐ ☐ ☐

      ☐ ☐ ☐ ☐

–continues–

Time Management Enhances Reading Leadership	-continued-	4	3	2	1

16. Relax, recognize when to stop and do nothing

    a.   Build relax time into the schedule to increase both efficiency and energy   ☐ ☐ ☐ ☐

    b.   Learn quick exercises to relieve tension during the day ....   ☐ ☐ ☐ ☐

If appropriate, do not photocopy the interpretation until after completion of the worksheet.

Interpretation: The principal with a strong commitment to both instructional leadership and program improvement must, of necessity, operate in both an efficient and an effective manner. Great amounts of time are required to acheive either goal. Administrators seeking to hone their time management skills might look at particular items or sections of Form 2.8 to identify areas warranting attention. Upon identifying the areas of desired growth, principals might develop skills and practice aggressively, then again complete Form 2.8 to study self-assessment of gains.

SYNTHESIS OF READING PROGRAM LEADERSHIP　(see Form 2.9)

The knowledge of instructional leadership and program effectiveness may support principals who lead their faculties toward program improvement. Understanding effective schools research, change processes, school climate, and strong communication skills, should enhance program-planning. Administrative effectiveness during program change processes can improve with advanced skills in decision-making, task delegation, and time management.

The Problem: Often, it is possible to get *side-tracked,* focusing and using up valuable time on lower priorities that prevent concentrated efforts toward instructional improvement. The administrator may have no sense of what the priorities should be as he or she tries to become a more effective instructional leader, and may not know how to retrieve helpful resources.

Rationale: Self-renewing leadership talent aids the principal in running an effective school, and lends support to teachers' abilities to function well, which, in turn, benefits students in the school. The principal who organizes himself/herself, and sets goals for the faculty, will stand a greater chance of having time available to influence reading program changes and improvement in the school.

Procedures: Administrators may complete Form 2.9 to gain self-assessment of reading leadership strengths and weaknesses. Reflection then should convert data to priorities (Form 2.10) for development of a professional growth plan (Form 2.11). Recognizing that growth requires concentrated effort and feedback, the principal is admonished not to take on too much at any one time but, instead, to set short-term, intermediate, and long-term goals, along with corresponding time lines, in pursuit of goals.

Form 2.9
SYNTHESIS OF READING PROGRAM LEADERSHIP

Directions: Administrators may benefit from knowing their reading leadership strengths and weaknesses. Categories are enumerated below. To assist in self-assessment or to establish priorities, administrators may check on the right whether the present status is highly, moderately, marginally, or not effective.

Leadership criteria:	Highly Effective	Moderately Effective	Marginally Effective	Not Effective
	4	3	2	1
1. Content of instructional leadership in the reading program (Form 2.1)	☐	☐	☐	☐
2. School effectiveness literature and reading leadership (Form 2.2)	☐	☐	☐	☐
3. Change processes and program improvement (Form 2.3)	☐	☐	☐	☐
4. School climate and leadership roles (Form 2.4)	☐	☐	☐	☐
5. Decision-making and leadership effectiveness (Form 2.5)	☐	☐	☐	☐
6. Effective communication and leadership (Form 2.6)	☐	☐	☐	☐
7. Delegation of tasks and leadership roles (Form 2.7)	☐	☐	☐	☐
8. Time management and instructional effectiveness (Form 2.8)	☐	☐	☐	☐
9. Development of a leadership growth plan (Form 2.11)	☐	☐	☐	☐

Interpretation: The principal seeking to improve leadership skills may benefit from identifying present strengths and weaknesses. To gain insight about present status, the administrator might total the columns of Form 2.9, giving four points to *highly effective*, three points to *reasonably effective*, two to *marginally effective*, and one to *not effective*. Totals between 28–36 may be judged *highly effective*, between 19–27 *reasonably effective*, between 10–18 *marginally effective*, and between 1–9 *not effective*, assuming accuracy of prior self-perceptions.

Form 2.10

PRIORITIZATION OF READING LEADERSHIP NEEDS

The principal may benefit from prioritization of data taken from Form 2.9, ranking criteria 1–9 based on perceived importance of improving skills. Each criterion may be converted to a personal goal statement that operationalizes what the principal seeks to accomplish. Taking on a manageable number of goals is important in order to reduce the chances of dissipated effort. To avoid this problem, the administrator might convert priorities to short-term, intermediate, and eventual goals:

Short-term goals for immediate attention: _____

_____

_____

_____

_____

_____

_____

Intermediate goals for early planning: _____

_____

_____

_____

_____

_____

_____

Eventual goals for later planning:_____

_____

_____

_____

_____

_____

_____

PERSONAL ADMINISTRATIVE GROWTH PLAN   (see Form 2.11)

Self-analysis of the administrator's developmental status may lead to a professional growth plan that supports the attainment of improved leadership skills, and as a result, stronger school programs. Carefully derived data from the summary (Form 2.9) should evolve into useful priorities (Form 2.10) based on analysis of the principal's identified strengths and weaknesses.

The Problem: As instructional leaders, principals may not always be as effective as the job warrants, or as their goals dictate. Results may be diminished support of principals and less than desired learning by children.

Rationale: Good administrators are good instructional leaders. Principals can learn to do better the job of supporting improved instruction, which creates wholesome learning environments.

Procedures: While some administrators work best independently, many benefit from a network that develops a feedback system. Participation with people who have a vested interest in shared success is useful, with colleagues who are able to be mutually supportive, yet are knowledgeable about reading programs. The principal who develops and follows a growth plan may benefit from peer coaching by another administrator, a small collaborative study group that meets regularly, or perhaps shared feedback with the Reading Advisory Board. The agenda might well deal with the content of all eleven forms, but particularly the content of Forms 2.9, 2.10, and 2.11, summary of leadership skills, priorities, and the growth plan. Monthly visits to local university libraries, using literature searches on key topics to study and share with a support group may stimulate professional development.

Comments and Cautions:

To avoid being overwhelmed by burnout and professional ineffectiveness, the principal may pace the professional growth plan by prioritizing Form 2.10, based on defined needs or program urgency, working on as many goals and activities at any one time as are manageable.

Form 2.11
PERSONAL ADMINISTRATIVE GROWTH PLAN

Directions: Principals who desire to develop a focus for professional growth in instructional leadership may benefit from being as specific as possible about what they seek to accomplish, how they will go about attaining growth, and how they will know when they have reached their goals. A review of Form 2.9 and Form 2.10 should lead the administrator to identify goals to pursue in this plan-of-action. Statements entered should be as simple as warranted and as useful as possible.

1. Goal Statement: _____

2. Objectives:

    a) _____

    b) _____

    c) _____

3. Activities: Dates; time checkpoints:

    a) _____   * _____

    b) _____   * _____

    c) _____   * _____

    d) _____   * _____

    e) _____   * _____

4. Resources: (professional reading, consultation, visitations)

    a) _____   * _____

    b) _____   * _____

    c) _____   * _____

5. How I will know when my goal is accomplished:

    _____

    _____

    _____

    _____

CHAPTER 3

READING PROGRAM STRENGTHS AND WEAKNESSES

The knowledge, experience, and research base exist to improve reading programs with a sense of direction and confidence. Principals are key change agents who support those structured change processes at local school levels (17, 46, 158). Strengths and weaknesses of reading programs (see Form 3.1) may be identified by a Reading Advisory Board's (see Form 3.5) conducting a comprehensive needs-assessment and program-planning process (59, 109). Before faculty are able to incorporate the desired change into their teaching, prerequisites are knowledge and ownership of the program as envisioned.

The principal who has the confidence of knowing strengths and weaknesses of the reading program is in a favorable position to lead a Reading Advisory Board through change processes and program improvements. Both may wish to look again at Chapter 2, particularly the section on *change processes*, to reflect upon issues and procedures worthy of careful pursuit.

Information for needs-assessment studies may be taken from student achievement data, curriculum analyses, and school resources inventories. Efforts are then made to prioritize data in order to plot program improvement. The subsequent program-planning process deals with studying ideal reading programs in order to make local decisions, generate supporting professional development, formulate assessments, and create or purchase new instructional materials. The plan-of-action at the end of Chapter 3 may function as the source of a structured change process for the total *Resource Book*.

For Further Reading

English, F. W. (1992). *Deciding What to Teach and Test: Developing, Aligning, and Auditing the Curriculum*. Newbury Park, CA: Corwin Press, Inc. (A Sage Publications Company, P. O. Box 2526, Newbury Park, CA 91319-8526. 805-499-9774).

> English places leadership in a context of dealing with teaching as political and educational activity. The author elaborates curriculum development with positive formats of site-based management. Sections deal with curriculum functions, alignment, and auditing.

Oliva, P. F. (1992). "Needs Assessment," *Developing the Curriculum, Third Edition*. New York: HarperCollins Publishers Inc., 218–254. (10 East 53rd Street, New York, NY 10022. 1-800-742-7831.)

> The textbook integrates curriculum with instruction. This edition analyzes processes of curriculum development with generously supplied examples and activities. The chapter on needs assessment explicates key components.

Form 3.1
NEEDS-ASSESSMENT AND READING PROGRAM-PLANNING

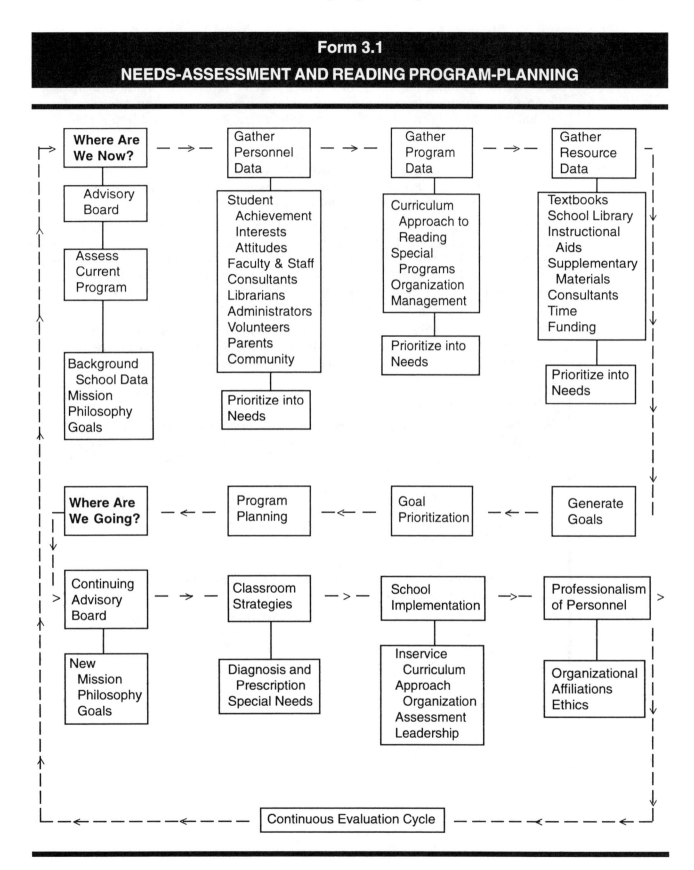

OVERVIEW OF NEEDS-ASSESSMENT AND PROGRAM-PLANNING (see Form 3.2)

The purpose of Form 3.2 is to help the faculty, staff, and parents to understand what is involved in a reading program review and to plan for a *straw vote*. While principals are seen as *key change agents* in structured change processes, Reading Advisory Boards ordinarily gather, organize, and interpret data that are translated into a plan-of-action.

The Problem: Principals and Advisory Boards may hold both expressed and undefined resistance to changing the program. There may be feelings that the program is fine, or there may be fear of and avoidance of change. Some may have been involved in establishing the present program, and feel a need to defend it.

Rationale: Program studies enable everybody to understand all of the components of the reading program and how elements go together. This perspective shows where the program *is*, and provides data to determine where the program *will go*. Planned change involves a principal's support and follow-through of innovations, resisting attempts to jump from program to program without giving the change an opportunity to be institutionalized, warranting a minimum of one to two years to launch.

Procedures: Using Form 3.2 to sample the staff and collate information, the Reading Advisory Board may gain a sense of whether there is a need to review the program. The process creates comparisons of the present program with some standard and, ordinarily, local reading data are used.

For Further Reading

Kaufman, R. A. (1983). "Needs Assessment," *Fundamental Curriculum Decisions*. Edited by F. W. English. Alexandria, VA: Yearbook of Association for Supervision and Curriculum Development, 53–67. (1250 North Pitt Street, Alexandria, VA 22314-1403. 1-703-549-9110.)

> The yearbook develops curriculum construction processes and skills as foundations for positive program change. Kaufman reviews major needs-assessment models, describes trends, and offers recommendations for curriculum development.

Radencich, M. C. (1995). *Administration and Supervision of the Reading / Writing Program*. Boston: Allyn and Bacon. (Dept. 894, 160 Gould Street, Needham Heights, MA 02194-2310. 1-800-852-8024.)

> As a supervisor and administrator, herself, Radencich addresses issues for district and school-based administrators, management of comprehensive district reading and writing programs, and management of schoolwide reading and writing programs.

Form 3.2
OVERVIEW OF NEEDS-ASSESSMENT AND READING PROGRAM-PLANNING

Directions: Prior to deciding whether to conduct a reading program needs-assessment, the principal and Reading Advisory Board may seek to identify participants' agreement with processes involved. Teachers and parents are asked to indicate whether they believe a Reading Advisory Board should review each criterion.

Criteria for conducting a needs assessment:	Strong Agreement 4	Moderate Agreement 3	Marginal Agreement 2	Little Agreement 1
1. Is an integral part of the total program-planning process; i.e., to develop a blueprint for the reading program	☐	☐	☐	☐
2. Attempts to find discrepancies between what does exist and what should be changed in the reading program and in content area reading	☐	☐	☐	☐
3. Is conducted by a committee consisting of carefully selected professional and community members	☐	☐	☐	☐
4. Keeps building faculty and appropriate central office personnel continuously aware of progress made	☐	☐	☐	☐
5. Determines how well students achieve in reading and in the content area texts	☐	☐	☐	☐
6. Appraises reading process and skill strengths and weaknesses of pupils as a result of instruction in the present program	☐	☐	☐	☐
7. Considers whether students enjoy reading and actually do a great amount of recreational reading at school and home	☐	☐	☐	☐
8. Appraises how well classroom and content area teachers are teaching reading	☐	☐	☐	☐
9. Examines whether the present curriculum is doing the job that is intended	☐	☐	☐	☐
10. Evaluates whether the building and classroom organization and grouping are effective.	☐	☐	☐	☐
11. Examines the need for staff development; i.e., whether teachers are appropriately knowledgeable about teaching students to read	☐	☐	☐	☐
12. Incorporates judgments of faculty, the principal, a central office representative, paraprofessionals, reading specialists, parent and community representatives, and a librarian in the needs assessment process	☐	☐	☐	☐

–continues–

Overview of Needs-Assessment and Reading Program Planning -continued-	4	3	2	1
13. Invites parents and community members to contribute opinions about the status of the reading program; to assess whether they judge the program as does school personnel	☐	☐	☐	☐
14. Reviews all reading-related resources of the school to identify what is available, how well it is used, and what is needed	☐	☐	☐	☐
15. Prioritizes needs identification throughout the process and converts those priorities into a plan for program improvement................................	☐	☐	☐	☐
16. Examines what money is available for changes in the program and for content area reading improvement	☐	☐	☐	☐
17. Recognizes that the fundamental reason to conduct a reading program needs-assessment is to determine whether changes are warranted	☐	☐	☐	☐

Cover the page here and below prior to photocopying if users are not to see the interpretation until later.

Interpretation: The Reading Advisory Board may choose to delete the comments that follow if this form is used with the faculty. Anybody who prefers to avoid the process may not respond objectively, if identified. The Board may total checkmarks, giving four points to each checkmark in the left column, *strong agreement,* three points to marks in the middle column, *moderate agreement,* two points to checkmarks in the next column, *minimal agreement,* and one point to checkmarks in the right column, *little agreement.* Totals between 52–68 may represent *strong agreement,* those between 35–51 may represent *moderate agreement,* those between 18–34 may be viewed as *minimal agreement,* and those between 1–17 may be judged *little agreement.* Totals of columns one and two may be combined to "get a vote" on conducting needs-assessment and program-planning.

BELIEFS AND DEFINITIONS RELATED
TO THE READING PROGRAM

(see Form 3.3)

A systematic needs-assessment and program-planning process is dependent upon some anchor, some commonly held assumptions and beliefs. Congruence between beliefs and practice is a foundation. For example, a faculty unwavering in its devotion to textbook-based reading instruction would have difficulty delivering an effective whole language curriculum.

The Problem: Schools only rarely develop commonly accepted mission statements, descriptions of the reading process, or philosophies and beliefs about teaching students to read. While many view those statements merely as academic exercises, others recognize that they are very basic to program change, and improvement depends on faculties' beliefs.

Rationale: The most difficult task of program review is for a Reading Advisory Board to ascertain what are the school reading beliefs, and what are the program's strengths and needs. Faculties may make extensive changes in reading programs if they recognize the need, take ownership, and believe they can handle program changes, beginning with analysis and agreement about beliefs and philosophy.

Procedures: The Reading Advisory Board may ask members of the faculty and selected community members to finish Form 3.3. It may be important to ask participants to complete all parts. The Board collects forms and collates questionnaire data. Three clear, culminating statements are desirable for the balance of the change study. Each will be tested against worksheets throughout the *Resource Book.*

For Further Reading

Fox, C. A. F. (1992). "The Critical Ingredients of Making Change Happen," *NASSP Bulletin*, 76, 541, 71–77.

Fox addresses the roles of change structures and leadership style in program advancement. The author explains the role of using outside facilitators. Fox presents criteria to review and structure planning methods. Processes to integrate innovations into present programs are developed.

Jones, R. R. (1992). "Setting the Stage for Program Change," *Executive Educator*, 14, 3, 38–39.

Central offices are able to empower local schools without giving up control completely. A key person should be selected to guide restructuring. Key sources of change in the building should be identified. Time should be provided to support change. Networking contacts in other districts should be located.

Form 3.3
BELIEFS AND DEFINITIONS RELATED TO READING PROGRAMS

Directions: Participants' responses to the following questions will help the principal to decide if we should undertake a study of the reading program. We will appreciate responses to mission, process, and philosophy statements. Please write generously in response to each section.

The Reading Program Mission Statement _____

_____

_____

_____

_____

The Reading Process What is reading? _____

_____

_____

_____

What do you do when you read? _____

_____

_____

_____

If a person did not know how to read, what would you tell that person he/she would need to learn?

_____

_____

_____

*Questions from a workshop conducted at the Lewis & Clark Reading Council annual meeting by Jerry L. Johns, Northern Illinois University.

–continues–

Beliefs and Definitions Related to Reading Programs   -continued-

The Reading Philosophy

How do you account for the various ways pupils learn to read? Include their intellectual, emotional, physical, and social development.

_____

_____

_____

_____

Please develop statements summarizing current research on reading instruction.

_____

_____

_____

_____

Please summarize current research on ways reading and writing are tied together.

_____

_____

_____

_____

Cover the page here and below prior to photocopying if users are not to see the interpretation until later.

Interpretation: The Reading Advisory Board may wish to compose three statements based on its aggregated summary of: (1) mission statement, (2) definition of the reading process, and (3) philosophy of reading, incorporating collective, prevailing comments from the questionnaire. Those statements may be widely circulated for response and approval. The importance of widespread acceptance is that these beliefs will become the foundation for reading program change and improvement.

STEPS TAKEN DURING A READING NEEDS-ASSESSMENT   (see Form 3.4)

A Reading Advisory Board charged to conduct a program study may benefit from a structure for time and tasks (see Form 3.4). Comprehensive reading curriculum study involves central office approval and faculty affirmation that the process should occur. After a scope is determined, data gathering may be pursued. Extensive study, data tabulation and prioritization, culminating in a plan of action for program improvement, follows.

The Problem: A serious problem may be that neither faculty, Reading Advisory Board, nor the principal has any idea of the time commitment or depth of tasks required to conduct a comprehensive curriculum study. As well, there may be little sense of the thoroughness of processes warranted to gather information. Being unwilling to change often is another challenge.

Rationale: Once a decision is reached to conduct a systematic needs assessment and program-planning process to identify reading strengths and weaknesses, a school may chart its time goals, identify people involved, and select procedures. The steps are logical and sequential, and, when they are completed, program priorities may fall into place, resulting in an operational plan.

Procedures: Using the calendar to commit participants to tasks and deadlines may organize people and affirm the scope of the study. In order to keep the balance of the faculty informed, the Reading Advisory Board may wish to display steps taken and time deadlines on chart paper located on a bulletin board in the faculty lounge. The faculty would already have had a chance to gain an overview of needs-assessment and program-planning (see Form 3.1).

For Further Reading

Coleman, P., et al. (1993). "Seeking the Levers of Change: Participant Attitudes and School Improvement," *School Effectiveness and School Improvement*, 4, 1, 59–83.

> A foundation of school change is to improve relationships among children, families, and faculty. Teacher practice is shown to affect student and parent feelings toward their school. The ways that those groups rate schools have long-term implications for learning and community support.

McNeil, J. D. (1990). *Curriculum: A Comprehensive Introduction, Fourth Edition*. New York: HarperCollins Publishers, 110–114. (10 East 53rd Street, New York, NY 10022. 1-800-742-7831.)

> McNeil's text is an inclusive introduction to curriculum theory and practice. Sections on curriculum design, implementation, and evaluation undergird the text. Contemporary issues are addressed, such as change processes, teacher empowerment, and trends in content fields.

		Form 3.4			

STEPS TAKEN DURING A READING NEEDS-ASSESSMENT

	Date of Initiation	Targeted Date of Completion	Actual Date of Completion

Directions: Steps followed during the needs-assessment are logical and may occur in a way that can be monitored on a calendar. The Reading Advisory Board, principal, or faculty may wish to pencil in, on the right, when steps are initiated, a target date for completion, and the date when steps actually are completed.

Steps Taken:	3	2	1
1. Confirm with the central office the importance of conducting a needs-assessment	—	—	—
2. Confirm with building personnel	—	—	—
3. Identify an Advisory Board or Council membership	—	—	—
4. Determine the scope of the needs-assessment	—	—	—
5. Assess the present program (***Where we are***)	—	—	—
6. Construct or select questionnaires that address:			
a. achievement (see Form 5.2).	—	—	—
b. attitudes (see Form 12.7)	—	—	—
c. interests (see Form 12.8)	—	—	—
d. curriculum (see Form 4.19)	—	—	—
e. organization (see Form 8.10)	—	—	—
f. personnel and staff development (see Forms 9.12–9.13)	—	—	—
g. selection of instructional materials (see Forms 7.24–7.25)	—	—	—
h. parent and community alliances (Forms 12.5–12.8)	—	—	—
7. Administer questionnaires	—	—	—
8. Analyze questionnaire data	—	—	—
9. Gather information	—	—	—

–continues–

Steps Taken During a Reading Needs-Assessment -continued-	3	2	1

10. Generate goals (***Where we want to be***) .... ___ ___ ___

11. Prioritize goals .... ___ ___ ___

12. Study, visit, and design the future program.. ___ ___ ___

13. Evaluate the results upon initiation and over time.. ___ ___ ___

14. Initiate a new needs-assessment and program planning process periodically
     to assure that a school's program remains current and relevant over time .. ___ ___ ___

Cover the page here and below prior to photocopying if users are not to see the interpretation until later.

Interpretation: The primary use of Form 3.4 is to enable participants to plot a sequenced structure of activities and time involved to conduct a program review. Assuming that no decision has yet been made to undergo the process, use of Form 3.4 may, in addition, help a principal, faculty, or Reading Advisory Board reflect upon the amount of time and the scope of tasks involved in conducting a needs-assessment and program-planning process. The overview may be of value in deciding which persons should pursue the process.

MEMBERSHIP OF THE READING ADVISORY BOARD   (see Form 3.5)

The structured program change process of needs-assessment and program-planning *maps* the program's future direction. Reading Advisory Boards—study groups made up of community, faculty, and administrative members who represent their constituencies—gather data and chart a new direction for the reading program. Members may be appointed or elected.

The Problem: In many cases, comprehensive reading program planning may not occur, and the only change may be in the selection of new textbooks, which improves programs only slightly, if at all. Principals may be active members of Advisory Boards, but need to exercise caution to avoid domination. Provision ordinarily is made to provide released time for Board work.

Rationale: The Reading Advisory Board's ultimate goal is improvement of the school's reading program. Support must be given to enable time and resources for staff meetings, assessment of needs, planning, implementation, and evaluation of educational change.

Procedures: The Reading Advisory Board, consisting of 7 to 15 members, functions with a majority made up of school personnel, particularly classroom teachers. The committee deliberates in ways that can be interpreted to school personnel and community members. Findings, placed on chart paper, may be placed on a bulletin board in the faculty lounge to keep people informed as the Reading Advisory Board plots its progress. Asking Reading Advisory Boards to keep minutes and perhaps publish a monthly bulletin outlining progress and giving details would keep people informed.

For Further Reading

Carrow-Moffett, P. A. (1993). "Change Agent Skills: Creating Leadership for School Renewal," *NASSP Bulletin*, 77, 552, 57–62.

> Steps in change processes are: affirm and interpret the vision frequently, empower those developing change, understand the values operating, identify facitliation and barriers to change, and resist attempts to return to earlier practice.

Steinburg, C., et al., (1992). "Making Choices about Change," *Training and Development Journal*, 46, 3, 33–42.

> Four articles are included in this report of an American Society for Training and Development's symposium. Content deals with approaches and views of change.

Form 3.5

MEMBERSHIP OF THE READING ADVISORY BOARD

Directions: The Reading Advisory Board may be appointed or elected. Election may assure faculty popularity in representation, perhaps ultimate faculty ownership of changes. Appointment may enhance balance in decisions and quality of membership. Suitable roles are those that follow:

Teachers:

Name _____ Position

Name _____ Position

Name _____ Position

Name _____ Position

Name _____ Position

Reading Specialist:

Name _____ Position

Librarian:

Name _____ Position

Building Administrator:

Name _____ Position

Central Office person:

Name _____ Position

School Board member:

Name _____ Position

Parents:

Name _____ Position

Name _____ Position

Community Representative:

Name _____ Position

Interpretation: A school may wish to achieve balance of representation in its Reading Advisory Board membership. The largest number of members should be classroom teachers, who together with the principal, librarian, or reading specialist constitute a majority. A central office person and school board member secure official approval for interpretations and decisions. The librarian's role supports program goals of literacy by developing a strong book collection. Teachers, parents, and community members should be people held in high regard, and who openly provide information to their constituencies. If the group selects the chair from its membership, the Reading Advisory Board is more likely to function effectively.

SCHOOL DEMOGRAPHICS DATA FOR PROGRAM STUDY (see Form 3.6)

Reading Advisory Boards who are planning program revisions are supported by accurate school information about their student population. Demographic information may be just as important as school achievement information in creating needs-appropriate, non-standard programs.

The Problem: Background school information often may be assumed, without anybody actually tabulating data to confirm the status. Programs and curricula may exist in a standard way, even though local clientele and needs are so distinctive as to warrant specialized programs.

Rationale: A careful description of background information provides the foundation for the school to develop a relevant, needs-specific reading program. Programs for rural, mountain children may be completely different from those of suburban children, or reading-related needs of second language students may differ greatly from those of dialect-divergent pupils. Urban students in Philadelphia may require programs different from those in Houston. The impact of poverty may affect the needs of reading programs.

Procedures: Exact enrollment numbers and demographic data are taken from school records. This information can be collected by a school secretary or clerk. Interpretation of those data by the Reading Advisory Board may set the stage for outlining the distinctive needs that emerge from the needs-assessment and program-planning process. To develop an accurate foundation, Boards may wish to identify total enrollments, type of community, racial and ethnic composition, and students receiving free or reduced lunches.

For Further Reading

Melvin III, C. A. (1991). "Translating Deming's 14 Points for Education," *School Administrator*, 48, 9, 20–23.

> The author describes four school districts' efforts to change educational operations. They opted for fitting purposes, infusing quality into educational *products*, and working toward zero *defects* using Deming's precepts.

Moore, L. E. (1993). "Restructured Schools: How, Why Do They Work?" *NASSP Bulletin*, 77, 553, 64–69.

> Visionary leadership provides a program structure, and clear goals the vehicle for change. Beliefs and behaviors in restructured schools are, by definition, altered. The purpose is to build students' trust in the school, forming bonds that help them to feel valued. Nurturing environments help teachers and students to feel that they are *the best*. Home, school, and community pride and interactions strengthen restructuring.

Form 3.6

SCHOOL DEMOGRAPHIC DATA FOR PROGRAM STUDY

Name of School _____

Name of School District _____

	K	1	2	3	4	5	6
Enrollment by Grade Level:							

Type of Community Represented:

____ % Inner City   ____ % Suburban

____ % Large City   ____ % Rural

____ % Small City

Ethnic/Racial Distribution:

____ % Asian-American   ____ % Native-American

____ % African-American   ____ % Mexican-American

____ % Causasian   ____ % Other Hispanic

____ % Other (please describe): _____

Percent of Distinct Needs Students

____ % Homeless Shelters   ____ % Transferred from Other Schools

____ % Agencies for Schools Neglected or Abused Children   ____ % Other

Percent of Free and Reduced Lunches

____ % Free Lunch   ____ % Reduced Lunch

USING ACHIEVEMENT DATA TO ESTABLISH NEEDS   (see Form 3.7)

The purpose of Form 3.7 is to provide a worksheet for use in local program review. The worksheet may be used as it exists, or may be modified. If adapted, criteria and sources of data may reflect locally available information. For practice purposes, a needs-assessment and program planning simulation (see Form 3.8) is available for use by the Reading Advisory Board.

The Problem: One problem is that many faculties and principals may not know how to go about collecting data for a local needs assessment. Once data are collected, it may be that Reading Advisory Board members have no structured way to analyze and interpret those data. Finally, the importance of a responsive plan-of-action may be unfamiliar to members.

Rationale: A Reading Advisory Board seeking to conduct a needs assessment and program-planning effort may collect, analyze, and interpret existing reading achievement data to determine its status and program scope. Accurate information supports the Board as it undertakes its tasks.

Procedures: Reading curriculum study committees may use Form 3.7 or a local modification to initiate a program review. To move ahead, a Reading Advisory Board may use the Hitchcock School simulation to practice and understand the processes that may be used locally. Wherever possible, it is desirable to use objective data. A committee may use the tabulated data from the chart in Form 3.8 as they complete a photocopied Form 3.7. Interpretation may come from the study of Form 3.9 and Form 3.10.

For Further Reading

Carr, J. F. & Harris, D. E. (1993). *Getting it Together: A Process Workbook for K-12 Curriculum Development, Implementation, and Assessment.* Needham Heights, MA: Allyn & Bacon, Inc. (Dept. 894, 160 Gould Street, Needham Heights, MA 02194-2310. 1-800-852-8024).

> The resource book supports teachers to improve children's functioning in classrooms. The text generously provides examples of assessments, activities and guidelines for curriculum planners. Charts and processes can be applied directly to practice.

Kaufman, R. et al. (1993). *Needs Assessment: A User's Guide.* Englewood Cliffs, NJ: Educational Technology Publications. (700 Palisade Avenue, Englewood Cliffs, NJ 07632. 201-871-4007.)

> Users may refer to the complete book, or specific topics, to conduct needs assessments. The text provides the structures to help a group determine if it is headed in the right direction. The authors develop the basics, the steps taken, and applications to organizations.

Directions: Form 3.7 assesses the reading curriculum, taught directly in basal texts, but addressed informally in whole language classrooms. In appropriate cells below, Reading Advisory Board judgments are structured by developing discrepancy data; i.e., a difference between expected and actual pupil performance, expressed positively or negatively. Grade levels evaluated are shown at the tops of columns. Discrepancy data should be taken from objective data, whenever possible, and calculated as in Form 3.9. Data finally are prioritized in Form 3.10 to establish program needs.

Criteria: Grade Level	K	1	2	3	4	5	6
Comprehension							
1. Factual, conceptual skills (basal-series tests)							
2. Organizing information (series tests)							
3. Interpretive, inference processes (series tests)							
4. Evaluative/critical skills (series tests)							
5. Standardized data (achievement tests)							
Vocabulary							
6. Context applications (basal-series tests)							
7. Sight word success (series tests)							
8. Phonic applications (series tests)							
9. Structural analysis (series tests)							
10. Standardized data (achievement tests)							

Grade one = percentiles; grades two–six = grade equivalents.

Assessment of Student Performance -continued-	**K**	**1**	**2**	**3**	**4**	**5**	**6**

Study Skills

11. Confirms searching, previewing, processes (interviews)

12. Verifies chapter-reading strategies (interviews)

13. Affirms paragraph reading processes (interviews)

14. Displays use of table of contents, index, text structures (interviews)

15. Verifies use of charts, illustrations, graphs, captions (interviews)

16. Standardized data (achievement tests)

Reading Affect

17. Displays evidence of extensive recreational reading (interviews)

18. Writes fluently about recreational reading undertaken (interviews)

19. Participates willingly in peer book-sharing and peer-sharing of writing (interviews)

20. Demonstrates evidence of various interests in reading (inventory)

21. Verifies a positive attitude toward reading and writing (inventory)

Form 3.8

NEEDS-ASSESSMENT AND PROGRAM-PLANNING SIMULATION

Hitchcock School is a k-6 elementary school in Brandtberg with approximately 675 students. The kindergarten enrollment is up to 150, 25 more than last year. Grades one and two have 125 students, grade three 100 students, grades four and five 60 students each, and grade six 55 students. The increase in students at the primary levels has been due to the construction of two new canning factories in Brandtberg which traditionally has been a farming community. About 70 percent of the population is Caucasian, 25 percent Mexican-American, and 5 percent Native American. Nineteen percent receive free and reduced lunches.

Reading Performance. Information to assess the status of the reading program at Hitchcock School has been gathered from several sources. To assess intellectual capabilities, the *Cognitive Abilities Test* is used. Reading data are taken from the *Metropolitan Achievement Test*, and end-of-unit, end-of-level tests of the reading series. Data reported below are based on early September status.

Grade Status			Comprehension					Vocabulary				
Grade	Norm in September	Expected Reading	Factual Recall	Organizing Skills	Interpretation of Conceptes	Evaluation of Ideas	Total Comprehension	Contextual Applications	Sight Words	Phonic Skills	Structual Analysis	Total Word Analysis
1	pc50	pc63	Listening Comp pc 59					Listening Vocab pc 58				
2	2.0	2.4	3.8	1.3	1.1	1.1	1.8	2.3	1.3	4.4	2.3	2.7
3	3.0	3.5	4.4	2.2	2.0	1.7	2.6	2.8	1.8	4.7	2.8	3.4
4	4.0	4.4	5.3	2.9	2.8	2.5	3.4	3.5	3.5	5.2	3.9	4.2
5	5.0	5.4	6.2	3.9	3.8	3.1	4.2	4.1	5.3	5.2	4.6	5.0
6	6.0	6.4	7.1	4.6	4.5	4.1	5.1	4.6	6.6	6.1	4.8	5.8

pc = percentile   Expected Reading = capacity or potential (Bond formula)*

Affect dimensions of the reading program are causing concern for some teachers, administrators, and many parents. Young children enjoy reading, but as they advance through the grades, they grow indifferent, or even negative. Neither teachers nor students like to be involved with low reading classes.

Personnel. Hitchcock School has hired seven new teachers in the last two years; currently, there are 26 teachers on the faculty. The seven new teachers have Master's degrees. Two of the older teachers are working on Master's degrees. The three most influential first grade teachers will retire at the end of the year. One third grade teacher and one fourth grade teacher, likewise, will retire.

With the increased numbers of students in the primary grades, the school has hired a part-time aide for each teacher of those grades. The philosophy of the teachers is that untrained personnel should not be used in the instructional program.

The school district is not large enough to have a reading consultant, although many teachers believe remedial reading is needed.

–continues–

Needs-Assessment and Program-Planning Simulation -continued-

Curriculum. The new reading series was purchased eleven years ago. That edition was adopted because the prior books were worn out, but the majority of teachers at that time did not want to change. The district purchased basal texts, manuals, workbooks, enrichment trade books, black-line ditto masters, and text-book-based end-of-level, end-of-book tests.

A new program, *Success in Reading and Writing*, was started by the three new kindergarten teachers but was discontinued because the first grade teachers felt that too much of the first grade work was already understood by kindergartners. One kindergarten teacher uses an unstructured, play-based program, and one uses *Alpha Time*, worksheets, and musical recordings.

First and second grade teachers are unwavering in their use of word skills from the reading textbook program; three at each grade level are determined, yet two are reluctant. Little is done with silent reading or meaning-making.

Of third grade teachers, three use basal texts, following manuals, with heavy workbook and worksheet use. Two have initiated whole language, learned in workshops, with no structured word skills, nor direct instruction of strategies to gain meaning. Those teachers get support from two second grade teachers. The whole language and basal-driven teachers each resent the other group.

The two fourth grade teachers follow the reading textbook series program, and attempt to focus on reading for meaning, noting that most of the students seem unskilled. They each attended recent workshops on teaching process writing.

The four teachers at fifth and sixth grade levels decided among themselves to use a literature study approach. None teach any word skills, study skills, nor direct instruction of comprehension. Those teachers are handicapped considerably by the absence of current library holdings to support contemporary literature study, so groups read basal text stories together and are asked to talk among themselves about the stories after they have finished reading.

Final approval of any new program rests with the school board. Most teachers in kindergarten, second, third, and fifth grades have all indicated that they are ready to change to a new, more contemporary program.

Organization: Teachers throughout the school place students into classroom groups based on available reading test scores and teacher suggestions. A reading record card is kept on each child which shows the book completed and the letter grade in reading.

About half of the teachers have two reading groups, and in many of those rooms, both groups use the same book. Most of the rest of the teachers have one reading group.

All classrooms at Hitchcock School are self-contained. Students are placed homogeneously by total classes, so some teachers have all top readers, while others have all low readers. Substantial stigma has emerged among teachers and pupils in low reading classes.

Three of the third grade teachers felt they were missing the needs of too many students and began to subgroup with differential tasks for multiple groups. Fourth grade teachers now complain that too many students do not "fit into their classes" and blame the third grade teachers.

Assessment: New students arrive at Hitchcock School in Brandtberg almost daily. They are generally placed for reading according to the point where their particular class happens to be reading in the book. One teacher in the third grade has all children read a series of stories from a test that she got in one of her university classes. She then assigns them to reading groups that read from library books instead of basal texts.

–continues–

Needs-Assessment and Program-Planning Simulation   -continued-

The district purchases end-of-unit and end-of-level tests from the textbook publisher and requires that those instruments be given. No teachers use them to reassign instruction, reteach, nor make diagnostic assessments.

Staff Development: When the reading textbook series was purchased eleven years ago, the company consultant spent five days in the district during the first year of use. The district has not provided other inservice programs for fourteen years because teachers then complained that the workshops were boring. At that time, a grievance was filed against the district's curriculum director, and she has been unwilling to support the Hitchcock School principal whenever reading program change is mentioned. The majority of teachers earned degrees years before, and have not updated their academic backgrounds.

Parents and Community: Teachers have complained that parents seem particularly apathetic about the school, the reading program, and other programs. Parents often have complained that they feel unwelcomed by the principal and teachers. A sizable uprising occurred when the kindergarten teachers were required to stop teaching the *Success* program.

Evaluation Cycle: Achievement data are published annually in the state-mandated School Report Card; copies are mailed home to each family, and must be published alongside results of other schools in a local newspaper. Central office administrators express uneasiness, and demand that principals push teachers to "get the scores up!" The district never has conducted cyclic needs-assessment and program-planning evaluations of the reading program. Thus, no goal prioritization and systematic program development has occurred.

Cover the page here and below before photocopying if users are not to see the interpretation until later.

Interpretation: (Caution—the interpretation probably should not be studied until after the Reading Advisory Board has studied Forms 9 and 10). Below, significant information regarding Hitchcock School is highlighted.

Reading Performance. Overall, the more years pupils attend this school, the lower performance becomes. The strength is in decoding, when balance or even an edge toward comprehension might be more healthy.

Personnel. For the most part, teachers have not remained current in reading instruction trends. Leadership is missing.

Curriculum. There is no reading *program*, as such. Coordination and articulation are non-existent. Students' active search for meaning is not at the heart of this program. Recreational reading is not developed.

Organization. Flexible grouping appears to be unimportant. No evidence exists of thematic instruction with integrated reading and writing, a current national emphasis. Ability grouping has extracted a cost.

Assessment. Those data collected do not appear to be used for improved instruction. Nothing appears to be done to analyze students' reading and writing progress. Text-based tests are administered, but not used.

Staff Development. No comprehensive inservice reading program appears to exist.

Parents and Community. Indifference and *underappreciated* characterize the feelings of local families.

Evaluation Cycle. A comprehensive, focused evaluation plan with feedback loops does not seem to be present.

IDENTIFICATION OF GOALS/NEEDS DISCREPANCIES (see Form 3.9)

The Reading Advisory Board may use discrepancy data to determine whether the program is functioning as it should. Similarly, those data may show the direction program improvements will take. Schools may wish to broaden understanding of needs-assessment processes by practicing with the use of the simulation.

Rationale: The Reading Advisory Board may judge the fit of local goals, pupil performance, and program effectiveness. Data showing discrepancies between the capabilities and achievement of students may point to the need for reading program revision. Next a Board may determine whether strengths and weaknesses are consistent with the program's beliefs and expectations.

Procedures: For practice, the Reading Advisory Board may wish to calculate the discrepancies between expected reading and actual reading from the Hitchcock School simulation using data taken from the chart in Form 3.8. Those differences may be entered into cells on the Form 3.7 practice sheet. For example, third grade *expected reading* (3.5) compared to *factual recall* (4.4) shows a positive discrepancy of +.9 months and that would be entered. Another example, fifth grade *expected reading* (5.4) compared to *contextual applications* (4.1) shows a negative discrepancy of –1.3 years. A Reading Advisory Board may check their practice calculations by referring to Form 3.9. The school's statement of philosophy of reading (Form 3.3), and definition of the reading process, represent the base line against which accurate and current achievement data ultimately are compared.

Comments and Cautions

Discrepancy scores measure congruence of program potential against program status.

Greatest need may be shown by locating the most negative discrepancies and may be addressed during program-planning. A school may also want to be sure to retain great strengths during program revision deliberations.

Form 3.9
IDENTIFICATION OF GOALS/NEEDS DISCREPANCIES

Directions: In appropriate cells below, Reading Advisory Board judgments are structured by developing discrepancy data; i.e., a difference between expected and actual pupil performance, expressed positively or negatively. Grade levels evaluated are entered at the tops of columns. Discrepancy data should be taken from objective data, whenever possible. Data finally are prioritized to establish program needs after completion of the worksheet.

Criteria:　　　　　　　　　　Grade Level	K	1	2	3	4	5	6
Comprehension							
1.　Factual, conceptual skills (basal-series tests)			+1.4	+.09	+0.9	+0.8	+0.7
2.　Organizing information (series tests)			-1.1	-1.3	-1.5	-1.5	-1.8
3.　Interpretive, inference processes (series tests)			-1.3	-1.5	-1.6	-1.6	-1.9
4.　Evaluative/critical skills (series tests)			-1.3	-1.8	-1.9	2.3	-2.3
5.　Standardized data (achievement tests)		-0.4	-0.6	-0.9	-1.0	-1.2	-1.3
Vocabulary							
6.　Context applications (basal-series tests)			-0.1	-0.7	-0.9	1.3	-1.8
7.　Sight word success (series tests)			-1.1	-1.7	-0.9	-0.1	+0.2
8.　Phonic applications (series tests)			+2.0	+1.2	+0.8	-0.2	-0.3
9.　Structural analysis (series tests)			-0.1	-0.7	-0.5	-0.8	-1.6
10.　Standardized data (achievement tests)		-0.5	+0.3	-0.1	-0.2	-0.4	-0.6

Grade one = percentiles; grades two–six = grade equivalents.

NEEDS-BASED ESTABLISHMENT OF PROGRAM PRIORITIES   (see Form 3.10)

Program-planning involves taking data from the needs-assessment, analyzing and prioritizing needs, and gaining consensus about the status of the program. Since the needs-assessment does test philosophy and mission (see Form 3.3) against program status (see Form 3.7), it is important that those two foundations are clearly established.

Rationale: A reading program with internal integrity has all of its components working together. Developmental, recreational, functional, and diagnostic reading all are delivered with a strong balance in the role of the parts.

Procedures: At this stage of the structured reading change process, the Board signifies items of strength and items of weakness from those discrepancies between program expectation and program status. Boards continuing a practice exercise may use Form 3.7, already labeled with discrepancies based on Form 3.9, to establish priorities. Items of strength are identified, and items of weakness, too, are located. With the example provided in the Hitchcock School simulation (Form 3.10), items of strength are marked with triangles, and areas warranting improvement are encircled. Those findings are then used to draw conclusions from Forms 3.11–3.13, synthesis of data, total program prioritization, and a comprehensive plan of action.

Comments and Cautions

Schools may go *galloping off in all directions* simultaneously without giving a program revision a chance to work. Implementation does require substantial time.

A basic concept is that teachers who are expected to make changes resulting from a needs-assessment, or their representatives, must be involved in the assessment process.

Form 3.10
NEEDS-BASED ESTABLISHMENT OF PROGRAM PRIORITIES

Directions: In appropriate cells below, Reading Advisory Board judgments are structured by developing discrepancy data; i.e., a difference between expected and actual pupil performance, expressed positively or negatively. Grade levels evaluated are entered at the tops of columns. Discrepancy data should be taken from objective data, whenever possible. Data finally are prioritized to establish program needs after completion of the worksheet. A way to signify important discrepancies may be to place triangles around positive numbers at least a half-year above significance, and encircle those a half-year below significance.

	K	1	2	3	4	5	6
Comprehension							
1. Factual, conceptual skills (basal-series tests)			+1.4	+.09	+0.9	+0.8	+0.7
2. Organizing information (series tests)			-1.1	-1.3	-1.5	-1.5	-1.8
3. Interpretive, inference processes (series tests)			-1.3	-1.5	-1.6	-1.6	-1.9
4. Evaluative/critical skills (series tests)			-1.3	-1.8	-1.9	-2.3	-2.3
5. Standardized data (achievement tests)		-0.4	-0.6	-0.9	-1.0	-1.2	-1.3
Vocabulary							
6. Context applications (basal-series tests)			-0.1	-0.7	-0.9	-1.3	-1.8
7. Sight word success (series tests)			-1.1	-1.7	-0.9	-0.1	+0.2
8. Phonic applications (series tests)			+2.0	+1.2	+0.8	-0.2	-0.3
9. Structural analysis (series tests)			-0.1	-0.7	-0.5	-0.8	-1.6
10. Standardized data (achievement tests)		-0.5	+0.3	-0.1	-0.2	-0.4	-0.6

Grade one = percentiles; grades two–six = grade equivalents.

SYNTHESIS OF NEEDS-ASSESSMENT AND PROGRAM-PLANNING (see Form 3.11)

The purpose of the simulation is to prepare a Reading Advisory Board to conduct a local needs-assessment and program-planning process. The process may culminate with a plan-of-action to improve the local reading program.

The Problem: The problem is that many reading review committees may have little idea of how to go about conducting a program study. Further, many principals will not trust the needs-assessment and program-planning process without a strong prior sense of how to proceed.

Rationale: A review process structured in such a way that a Board is enabled to study its reading program systematically aids chances of an accurate interpretation. A Reading Advisory Board with an understanding of structured change processes may feel confidence in the processes it pursues.

Procedures: Using data from Form 3.10 related to the simulation, a study group may synthesize information, formulate program priorities, and develop a plan-of-action (Forms 3.11–3.13). It may be noted that Form 3.11 employs specific worksheets from throughout the *Resource Book*. When completing Form 3.12, a Reading Advisory Board may refer to numerous worksheets from the volume to assure that the designated priorities are appropriate. Finally, the plan-of-action structures a school's program planning. Upon completion of the simulation to analyze the process, the Reading Advisory Board is then ready to pursue its program planning.

Comments and Cautions

Reading Advisory Board members who work with the needs-assessment and program-planning process should be willing participants in the effort.

The opportunity to pursue a simulation may be important to a Board's understanding the processes it will follow in the local curriculum study.

Board members must feel committed to the need for program improvement in its school, and actively seek to keep teachers and parents informed if impact is to occur.

Form 3.11
SYNTHESIS OF NEEDS-ASSESSMENT AND PROGRAM-PLANNING

Directions: Criteria related to needs-assessment and program-planning are listed below. On the right, principals or Reading Advisory Boards may respond to perceived needs for change regarding each criterion, ranging from great need to little need for program change. Participants may refer back to forms throughout the *Resource Book.*

Criteria:	Great Need for Change	Moderate Need for Change	Minimal Need for Change	Little Need for Change
	4	3	2	1
1. Beliefs, definitions of the reading process (see Form 3.3)	☐	☐	☐	☐
2. Instructional leadership in the reading program (see Forms 2.1, 2.9, 2.10) ..	☐	☐	☐	☐
3. Assessment of student performance (see Form 3.8)	☐	☐	☐	☐
4. The reading curriculum in the school (see Forms 4.19–4.20)	☐	☐	☐	☐
5. Assessment of reading performance (see Forms 5.15–5.16)	☐	☐	☐	☐
6. Approach to reading instruction (see Forms 6.7–6.8)	☐	☐	☐	☐
7. Selection of Instructional Materials (see Forms 7.24–7.25)	☐	☐	☐	☐
8. School and classroom reading organization (see Forms 8.10–8.11)	☐	☐	☐	☐
9. Professional reading development of teachers (see Forms 9.12–9.13)	☐	☐	☐	☐
10. Management of special reading programs (see Forms 10.9–10.10)	☐	☐	☐	☐
11. Paraprofessional Support of Reading (see Forms 11.12–11.13)	☐	☐	☐	☐
12. Public Relations and the Reading Program (see Forms 12.12–12.13)	☐	☐	☐	☐
13. Establish reading program priorities (see Form 3.12)	☐	☐	☐	☐

Form 3.12
READING PROGRAM STRENGTHS, WEAKNESSES, AND PRIORITIES

Directions: Below, in the left column, participants will find components of a representative reading program needs-assessment and program-planning process. On the right, space is provided to record program strengths, needs, and after careful deliberation, priorities. Checkmarks from Form 3.11, and the balance of the *Resource Book* may be used to cross-check judgments.

1. Beliefs, Definitions	*Strengths* 1. 2.	*Needs* 1. 2.	*Priorities* 1. 2.
2. Student Performance	*Strengths* 1. 2.	*Needs* 1. 2.	*Priorities* 1. 2.
3. Instructional Leadership	*Strengths* 1. 2.	*Needs* 1. 2.	*Priorities* 1. 2.
4. Reading Curriculum	*Strengths* 1. 2.	*Needs* 1. 2.	*Priorities* 1. 2.
5. Assessment of Reading	*Strengths* 1. 2.	*Needs* 1. 2.	*Priorities* 1. 2.

–continues–

Reading Program Strengths, Weaknesses, and Priorities -continued-

		Strengths	Needs	Priorities
6.	**Approach to Reading**	Strengths 1. 2.	Needs 1. 2.	Priorities 1. 2.
7.	**Instructional Materials**	Strengths 1. 2.	Needs 1. 2.	Priorities 1. 2.
8.	**Reading Organization**	Strengths 1. 2.	Needs 1. 2.	Priorities 1. 2.
9.	**Professional Development**	Strengths 1. 2.	Needs 1. 2.	Priorities 1. 2.
10.	**Special Programs**	Strengths 1. 2.	Needs 1. 2.	Priorities 1. 2.
11.	**Para-professional Support of Reading**	Strengths 1. 2.	Needs 1. 2.	Priorities 1. 2.
12.	**Public Relations the Reading Program**	Strengths 1. 2.	Needs 1. 2.	Priorities 1. 2.
13.	**Program Priorities**	Strengths 1. 2.	Needs 1. 2.	Priorities 1. 2.

Form 3.13
READING PROGRAM STRENGTHS AND WEAKNESSES: PLAN-OF-ACTION

Directions: Reading Advisory Boards or principals seeking to develop a comprehensive study of reading program strengths and weaknesses may wish to develop a functional plan-of-action. The committee may choose to complete Form 3.13 cooperatively, reaching consensus on the process to be undertaken. The benefit of being as specific as possible about goals is that a strong focus and sense of direction may emerge. A review of Form 3.11, followed by completion of Form 3.12, should aid the committee in completing Form 3.13. Statements should be as simple, direct, accurate, and useful as possible.

1. Goal Statement: _____

2. Objectives:

   a) _____

   b) _____

   c) _____

3. Activities: Dates; time checkpoints:

   a) _____   * _____

   b) _____   * _____

   c) _____   * _____

   d) _____   * _____

   e) _____   * _____

4. Resources: (professional reading, consultation, visitations)

   a) _____   * _____

   b) _____   * _____

   c) _____   * _____

5. How I will know when my goal is accomplished:

   _____

   _____

   _____

   _____

CHAPTER 4

THE READING CURRICULUM IN THE SCHOOL

Agreement among educators about a definition of what reading curriculum *is*, or *ought to be,* is not easily attained. The values, experiences, and preferences regarding reading curriculum frameworks differ widely among school leaders. Curriculum has been defined as "the *engagements* that pupils have under *the auspices* of . . ." school, mentioning: (a) what is taught, (b) how it is taught, (c) teachers' materials, (d) students' materials, and (e) school experiences as important factors (48, p. 6).

Whether faculties deliver contemporary whole language with trade books or conventional basal programs, most students must be taught to read, which constitutes much of the reading curriculum. Reading-related issues still being debated are readiness vs. emergent literacy, the role of phonics vs. words, and dealing with dialect-divergence and minority learners. The impact of schema and metacognition research is still in the developmental stages and yet to be implemented.

Reading Advisory Boards (see Form 3.5) and administrators may study the curriculum by using formats presented in Chapter 4. They may also review comprehensive needs-assessment and program-planning as developed in Chapter 3. While planning change, if the principal senses a need to sharpen instructional leadership, reference to Chapter 2 is appropriate.

For Further Reading

Doll, R. S. (1992). *Curriculum Improvement: Decision Making and Process, Eighth Edition*. Boston: Allyn & Bacon. (Dept. 894, 160 Gould Street, Needham Heights, MA 02194-2310. 1-800-852-8024.)

> Doll guides readers from curriculum assessment through methods of implementation and change processes. Sections explicate what curriculum should be, and processes for curriculum improvement. A focus is bottom-up processes for curriculum planning.

Oliva, P. F. (1992). *Developing the Curriculum, Third Edition*. New York: HarperCollins Publishers Inc. (10 East 53rd Street, New York, NY 10022. 1-800-742-7831.)

> The textbook develops relationships of curriculum and instruction. Examples and activities for practitioners are provided. Content deals with theory, roles, components and processes, and problems and products of curriculum development.

Form 4.1
ASSESSMENT OF CURRICULAR FRAMEWORKS

Directions: The reading curriculum is the driving force behind students' learning to read. With components listed below, each cell allows for decisions about how well the curriculum now meets criteria and how important each criterion will be to future planning. *On the left,* Reading Advisory Boards may judge whether the program now meets the criterion. *On the right,* they may judge the extent to which the criterion should be included in the future program. The beginning section of Form 4.1 deals with total program criteria, while the lower section addresses criteria by grade levels. Following Form 4.1, participants may encircle items of program strength and weakness.

Meets criterion now:

Y=Yes

N=No

Y/N / 1-5

Included in Prospective or Future Curriculum:

1. Extremely important
2. Fairly important
3. Maintain the present
4. Fairly unimportant
5. Unimportant

Criteria for School Decisions:

1. A comprehensive, planned, and articulated program is evident ....

2. A systematic scope and sequence is used ....

3. A suitable process-based focus monitors whole language or literature-based instruction ....

4. A curriculum guide provides the program focus ....

5. The content of curriculum has been converted into instructional objectives

6. Present content meets the needs of all students ....

7. Curriculum materials are adequate in quantity to meet the needs of all learners ....

8. Pupil placement for instruction is based on reading ability levels and specific needs ....

9. Provision is made for accurate placement of new students entering the program ....

10. As students advance to secondary school, records follow as part of an articulated plan ....

–continues–

Assessment of Curricular Frameworks -continued-	K	1	2	3	4	5	6
11. Teachers teach in such a way that they expect all students to learn to read							
12. Readiness, or emerging literacy, is the foundation for subsequent success							
13. Comprehension is the major thrust of the reading program							
14. The word analysis program (decoding) is developed to focus on clarity of meaning							
15. A comprehensive vocabulary program is part of the reading curriculum							
16. Learning to read content textbooks is a part of the reading curriculum							
17. Improved reading rate and efficiency are a part of the curriculum for students who have advanced beyond the basic skills							
18. Literacy appreciation is an important part of the curriculum							
19. The curriculum includes planned time for recreational reading							
20. The learning center-library is an integral part of planning for recreational reading							
21. Paraprofessionals are available to support teachers in meeting student needs							
22. Alternative formats are in place for classroom corrective reading							
23. Alternative formats are available for remedial students							
24. Alternative formats exist for second-language students							

Form 4.2
PRELIMINARY DECISIONS ABOUT THE READING CURRICULUM

Directions: The principal or Advisory Board may use Form 4.1 to gain overall faculty perceptions of reading curriculum components and how well its goals are being met. S/he or the Board may tally responses, averaging totals for each item, encircle on Form 4.2 the five highest program strengths and the lowest program weaknesses. After strengths and weaknesses are identified, priorities that meet program goals may be set; it is an important reminder that a priority may be either a present strength or a weakness. Items may be encircled below:

Curriculum Strength			Curriculum Weakness			Curriculum Priority		
1	2	3	1	2	3	1	2	3
4	5	6	4	5	6	4	5	6
7	8	9	7	8	9	7	8	9
10	11	12	10	11	12	10	11	12
13	14	15	13	14	15	13	14	15
16	17	18	16	17	18	16	17	18
19	20	21	19	20	21	19	20	21
22	23	24	22	23	24	22	23	24

Interpretation: Data tallied above may help the principal to gain an overview of the reading program, and with further consultation and input, decide whether the curriculum warrants in-depth study. This decision may lead the principal to appoint an Advisory Board or to pursue program study personally.

The Advisory Board or principal then may wish to review the local reading curriculum in-depth using Forms 4.3–4.18. Each component of the program is addressed across three pages in Chapter 4: (a) an overview, including a rationale, problems, or issues, (b) a flow chart identifying central concepts, and (c) a worksheet to support local review, signifying the degree of local implementation of each curriculum element. If review of Forms 4.3–4.18 is conducted, it is important to consider the present status and degree of goal fulfillment.

THE EMERGENCE OF LITERACY
(see Form 4.3)

The term *reading readiness* is slowly being reconceptualized as *emergent literacy* based on changes in understanding how children learn to read and write. In earlier times, any prerequisites to reading were considered part of pre-k/k/1 programs, as needed by individual pupils. Presently, pupils learn the conventions of reading and writing as they read and write.

The Problem: Many teachers operate as if young children already possess the prior knowledge and oral language required to be good readers. As well, they may not compensate for the laptime and bedtime reading absent from many homes. Finally, some teachers seem unaware of some pupils' low levels of knowledge about the reading process.

Rationale: Beginning readers benefit from a great amount of direct experience, oral language use, awareness of story structures, alphabet, phonemic awareness, and words. Whenever children enter school with underdeveloped literacy, it is the teacher's challenge to advance those pupils as quickly as possible. Print-rich classes with openness to pupils' risk-taking seem to benefit learners. Pupils should expect to read picture books and predictable books, as well as to write daily from the onset of kindergarten.

Procedures: Components of literacy emergence/readiness are presented in Forms 4.3 and 4.4. Form 4.3 represents a flow chart of literacy and Form 4.4 contains self-assessment criteria. Self-judgment may lead the principal, Advisory Board, or faculty to consider how well each element of Form 4.3 is taught, thus assessing needs to maintain or to change the program.

For Further Reading

Clay, M. M. (1991). *Becoming Literate: the Construction of Inner Control.* Auckland, NZ: Heinemann Education. (361 Hanover Street, Portsmouth, NH 03801-3912. 1-800-541-2086.)

> Children are shown how to exercise gradual, strategic control over their reading and writing. Teachers are shown how to help children develop different ways to gain inner control of their literacy growth. Topics include language development, concepts about print, interaction with books, etc.

Galda, L., et al. (1993). *Language, Literacy, and the Child.* Ft. Worth, TX: Harcourt Brace Jovanovich College Publishers. (301 Commerce Street, Suite 3700, Ft. Worth, TX 76102. 1-708-647-8822).

> The authors bridge language and literacy theories and realistic classroom applications into wholistic contexts for teaching literacy for new teachers. Galda, Cullinan, and Strickland generously provide teaching ideas. A focus on multicultural approaches stengthens the book.

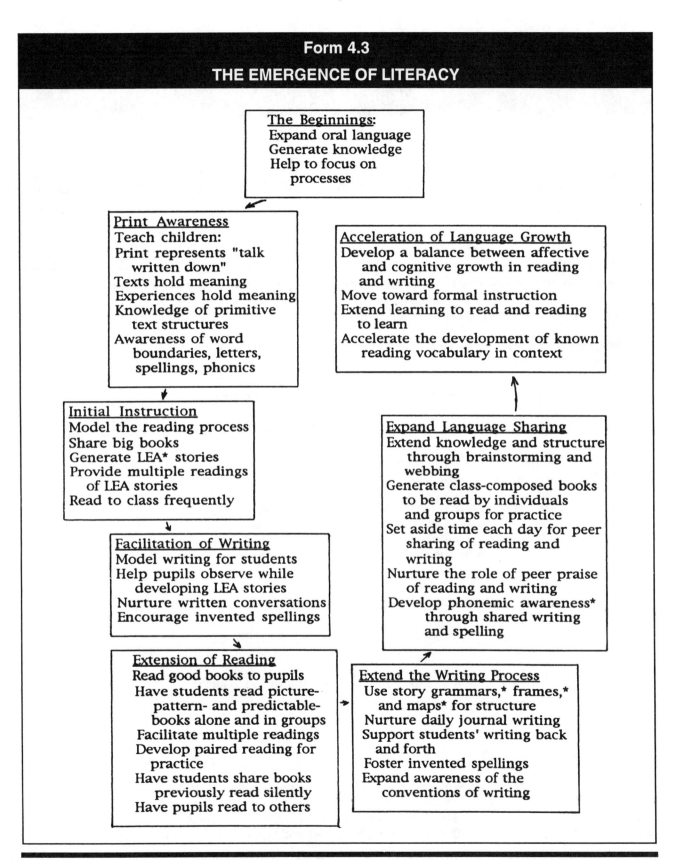

Form 4.3

THE EMERGENCE OF LITERACY

The Beginnings:
Expand oral language
Generate knowledge
Help to focus on
    processes

Print Awareness
Teach children:
Print represents "talk
    written down"
Texts hold meaning
Experiences hold meaning
Knowledge of primitive
    text structures
Awareness of word
    boundaries, letters,
    spellings, phonics

Acceleration of Language Growth
Develop a balance between affective
    and cognitive growth in reading
    and writing
Move toward formal instruction
Extend learning to read and reading
    to learn
Accelerate the development of known
    reading vocabulary in context

Initial Instruction
Model the reading process
Share big books
Generate LEA* stories
Provide multiple readings
    of LEA stories
Read to class frequently

Expand Language Sharing
Extend knowledge and structure
    through brainstorming and
    webbing
Generate class-composed books
    to be read by individuals
    and groups for practice
Set aside time each day for peer
    sharing of reading and
    writing
Nurture the role of peer praise
    of reading and writing
Develop phonemic awareness*
    through shared writing
    and spelling

Facilitation of Writing
Model writing for students
Help pupils observe while
    developing LEA stories
Nurture written conversations
Encourage invented spellings

Extension of Reading
Read good books to pupils
Have students read picture-
    pattern- and predictable-
    books alone and in groups
Facilitate multiple readings
Develop paired reading for
    practice
Have students share books
    previously read silently
Have pupils read to others

Extend the Writing Process
Use story grammars,* frames,*
    and maps* for structure
Nurture daily journal writing
Support students' writing back
    and forth
Foster invented spellings
Expand awareness of the
    conventions of writing

Form 4.4
CURRICULAR ASSESSMENT OF LITERACY EMERGENCE IN THE READING PROGRAM

Directions: A flow chart representing literacy emergence is found in Form 4.3. Below, in Form 4.4, principals, Reading Advisory Board members, and classroom teachers will find related criteria. On the right, participants may indicate the extent to which the school's curriculum fulfills each criterion. The glossary may define unfamiliar terms.

Criteria on literacy emergence:

	Strongly Implemented	Moderately Implemented	Marginally Implemented	Not Implemented
	4	3	2	1
1. Pupils are aware of print functions, that letters represent sounds, words represent speech, and texts represent meaning	☐	☐	☐	☐
2. Students attend schools in which print-rich environments support literacy development	☐	☐	☐	☐
3. Substantial amounts of authentic oral language and conversation occur	☐	☐	☐	☐
4. Teachers model reading for pupils by reading quality literature frequently	☐	☐	☐	☐
5. Youngsters benefit by early modeling with the language experience approach	☐	☐	☐	☐
6. Learners are actively engaged in early reading of picture books and predictable books	☐	☐	☐	☐
7. Pupils are encouraged to do early writing; and invented spellings are nurtured	☐	☐	☐	☐
8. Students read their compositions to peers and gain multiple approvals	☐	☐	☐	☐
9. Pupils are encouraged to use multiple readings of stories to various audiences across time	☐	☐	☐	☐
10. The social environment nurtures a lot of pupil reading and writing to each other	☐	☐	☐	☐

Interpretation: To judge literacy emergence, the principal may total columns in Form 4.4, giving four points to *strongly implemented*, three to *moderately implemented*, two to *marginally implemented*, and one point to *not implemented*. Totals between 31–40 may be viewed as *strongly implemented*, between 21–30 *moderately implemented*, between 11–20 *marginally implemented*, and between 1–10 *not implemented*.

THE COMPREHENSION OF NARRATIVE TEXT (see Form 4.5)

Effective reading comprehenders seem to have considerable topical knowledge about what they read. They tend to be fluent, automatic readers who focus less on words than meaning. They understand how texts are structured, or organized, and pursue texts as active searchers for meaning.

The Problem: Students whose early reading was oral, with a word focus rather than meaning, may have difficulty with comprehension. Those pupils may focus on intonation, accuracy, performance, letters, word parts, and words, instead of meaning. The reading may be slow, deliberate, and without purpose. The serious problem is that early habits and faulty definitions of the *process* are hard for students to *give up* over time.

Rationale: Strong reading programs help students to focus on meaning from the outset (52). Such programs deliver instruction leading to an understanding that reading is enjoyable and offering strategies for thinking about texts. The quality of materials read both expands knowledge of the language and promotes an abiding affect toward reading. Those pre-reading activities that augment topical knowledge may represent the most important part of instruction. Reading-as-thinking stresses high-level processes, such as inference, critical response, classification, and analysis.

Procedures: Form 4.5 may be used by an Advisory Board, administrator, or faculty to reflect upon reading comprehension in the curriculum. Form 4.6 then may be employed to identify strengths and weaknesses, in turn aiding a Board to set priorities for any program revisions.

For Further Reading

Cooper, J. D. (1993). *Literacy: Helping Children Construct Meaning, Second Edition.* Boston: Houghton Mifflin Company. (One Memorial Drive, Cambridge MA 02142. 1-800-225-1464.)

A preservice and inservice text in which teachers are shown how to help children construct meaning for themselves. The author's scope includes literacy contexts through thinking, reading, writing, speaking and listening. Cooper suggest that literacy should be taught through direct, real experiences.

Mason, J. M. & Au, K. H. (1990). *Reading Instruction for Today, Second Edition.* New York: HarperCollins College Publishers. (10 East 53rd Street, New York, NY 10022. 1-800-742-7831.)

Three strong chapters on reading comprehension and strategies undergird reading and study skills. Content supports reading-across-the-curriculum. Reading and writing processes are fully interrelated. Sections on emergent literacy and multicultural education are useful.

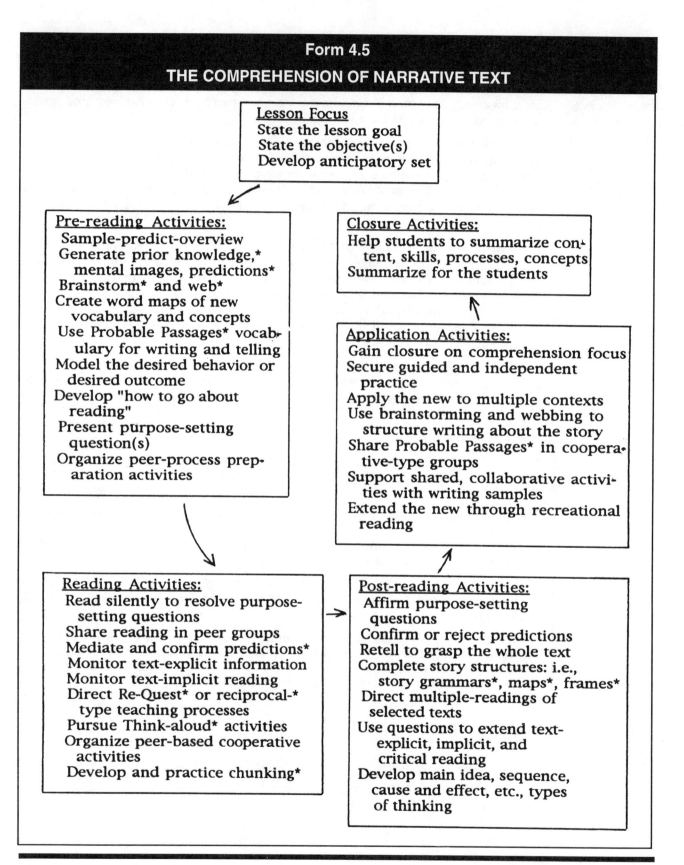

Form 4.5

THE COMPREHENSION OF NARRATIVE TEXT

Lesson Focus
State the lesson goal
State the objective(s)
Develop anticipatory set

Pre-reading Activities:
Sample-predict-overview
Generate prior knowledge,*
   mental images, predictions*
Brainstorm* and web*
Create word maps of new
   vocabulary and concepts
Use Probable Passages* vocab-
   ulary for writing and telling
Model the desired behavior or
   desired outcome
Develop "how to go about
   reading"
Present purpose-setting
   question(s)
Organize peer-process prep-
   aration activities

Closure Activities:
Help students to summarize con-
   tent, skills, processes, concepts
Summarize for the students

Application Activities:
Gain closure on comprehension focus
Secure guided and independent
   practice
Apply the new to multiple contexts
Use brainstorming and webbing to
   structure writing about the story
Share Probable Passages* in coopera-
   tive-type groups
Support shared, collaborative activi-
   ties with writing samples
Extend the new through recreational
   reading

Reading Activities:
Read silently to resolve purpose-
   setting questions
Share reading in peer groups
Mediate and confirm predictions*
Monitor text-explicit information
Monitor text-implicit reading
Direct Re-Quest* or reciprocal-*
   type teaching processes
Pursue Think-aloud* activities
Organize peer-based cooperative
   activities
Develop and practice chunking*

Post-reading Activities:
Affirm purpose-setting
   questions
Confirm or reject predictions
Retell to grasp the whole text
Complete story structures: i.e.,
   story grammars*, maps*, frames*
Direct multiple-readings of
   selected texts
Use questions to extend text-
   explicit, implicit, and
   critical reading
Develop main idea, sequence,
   cause and effect, etc., types
   of thinking

Form 4.6
CURRICULAR ASSESSMENT OF NARRATIVE TEXT COMPREHENSION

Directions: Advisory Boards or principals may review criteria on narrative comprehension from Form 4.5. Those criteria also are listed below in Form 4.6. On the right, respondents may signify the extent of local curriculum implementation. Respondents may refer to the glossary to identify highly unfamiliar terms.

Narrative comprehension criteria:	Strongly Implemented 4	Moderately Implemented 3	Marginally Implemented 2	Not Implemented 1
1. Silent reading is stressed for comprehension, meaning-making, or meaning-construction	☐	☐	☐	☐
2. Reading occurs best in a social or interactive context to aid motivation and interest	☐	☐	☐	☐
3. Brainstorming and webbing stories prior to reading enhances concepts and predictions	☐	☐	☐	☐
4. A problem-solving stance is developed with search, overview, predict, etc., processes	☐	☐	☐	☐
5. Probable passages, key word,* etc., activities tie together oral language, writing, reading	☐	☐	☐	☐
6. Silent reading comprehension is aided by think-aloud,* ReQuest*, etc., study	☐	☐	☐	☐
7. After reading, retellings are found to aid "recomprehension" or a whole text grasp	☐	☐	☐	☐
8. After reading, story grammars,* maps,* webs,*frames aid recomprehension, writing	☐	☐	☐	☐
9. Text-thinking, such as sequence, cause/effect, etc., are aided by visual or graphic structure	☐	☐	☐	☐
10. Shared rewriting of texts enhances writing, comprehension, and affect toward reading	☐	☐	☐	☐

Interpretation: To review narrative comprehension, the Advisory Board may total the columns in Form 4.6, giving four points to *strongly implemented*, three to *moderately implemented*, two to *marginally implemented*, and one point to *not implemented*. Totals between 31–40 may be viewed as *strongly implemented*, between 21–30 as *moderately implemented*, between 11–20 *marginally implemented*, and between 1–10 *not implemented.*

THE COMPREHENSION OF EXPOSITORY TEXT   (see Form 4.7)

Content textbooks, also described as expository texts, are designed to convey or expose information to students. Those texts are organized into chapters, units, sections, and paragraphs that function differently than do story texts. Pupils benefit from being taught specific strategies to deal with those new text structures. Graphic information, such as tables, maps, illustrations, and captions, likewise, requires new reading strategies.

Problem: One problem is that sometimes teachers do not teach students how to comprehend expository texts. Content texts increase substantially in size, volume, vocabulary, concept load, and sentence length after third grade, then take another jump at seventh grade. Texts report abstract, vicarious knowledge, not always of great interest to pupils. Content texts may be written at levels one to two years more advanced than are reading texts.

Rationale: Students may benefit from instruction in ways that content texts are written. Then, understanding the various strategies to address those text structures eases text reading. The social interaction of collaborative groups' talking and writing about texts, and sharing those interactions seems to make content more comprehensible and interesting for pupils.

Procedures: Form 4.7 may be used to reflect upon expository text content, while Form 4.8 may help an Advisory Board, principal, or faculty to judge the present status of this program component, supporting decisions to maintain the present role, or revise to meet future needs.

For Further Reading

Monahan, J., *et al.* (Eds.). 1988. *New Directions in Reading Instruction.* Newark, DE: International Reading Association. (800 Barksdale Road, P.O. Box 8139, Newark, DE, 19714-8139. 1-800-336-READ or 1-302-731-1600.)

> Content area teaching strategies are advanced with a flip-chart to support reading comprehension. Suggestions to organize cooperative learning, textbook use, and questioning strategies are offered. Content and graphics provide structures for staff development sessions.

Vacca, R. T. & Vacca, J. L. (1993). *Content Area Reading: Fourth Edition.* New York: HarperCollins College Publishers. (10 East 53rd Street, New York, NY 10022. 1-800-742-7831.)

> The text is supported by reading and writing strategies used across the curriculum. The authors develop sections on teaching with texts, thinking and learning with texts, and learning through literature.

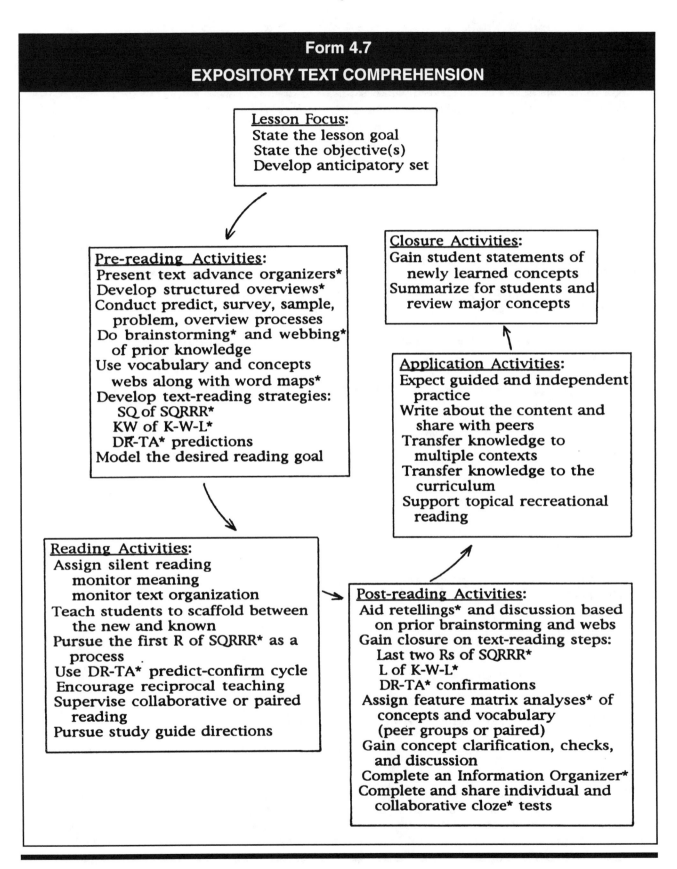

Form 4.7
EXPOSITORY TEXT COMPREHENSION

Lesson Focus:
State the lesson goal
State the objective(s)
Develop anticipatory set

Pre-reading Activities:
Present text advance organizers*
Develop structured overviews*
Conduct predict, survey, sample,
  problem, overview processes
Do brainstorming* and webbing*
  of prior knowledge
Use vocabulary and concepts
  webs along with word maps*
Develop text-reading strategies:
  SQ of SQRRR*
  KW of K-W-L*
  DR-TA* predictions
Model the desired reading goal

Closure Activities:
Gain student statements of
  newly learned concepts
Summarize for students and
  review major concepts

Application Activities:
Expect guided and independent
  practice
Write about the content and
  share with peers
Transfer knowledge to
  multiple contexts
Transfer knowledge to the
  curriculum
Support topical recreational
  reading

Reading Activities:
Assign silent reading
  monitor meaning
  monitor text organization
Teach students to scaffold between
  the new and known
Pursue the first R of SQRRR* as a
  process
Use DR-TA* predict-confirm cycle
Encourage reciprocal teaching
Supervise collaborative or paired
  reading
Pursue study guide directions

Post-reading Activities:
Aid retellings* and discussion based
  on prior brainstorming and webs
Gain closure on text-reading steps:
  Last two Rs of SQRRR*
  L of K-W-L*
  DR-TA* confirmations
Assign feature matrix analyses* of
  concepts and vocabulary
  (peer groups or paired)
Gain concept clarification, checks,
  and discussion
Complete an Information Organizer*
Complete and share individual and
  collaborative cloze* tests

Form 4.8

CURRICULAR ASSESSMENT OF EXPOSITORY TEXT COMPREHENSION

Directions: A flow chart of expository text comprehension may be found in Form 4.7, and those criteria are listed below in Form 4.8. On the right, principals, faculties, or Advisory Boards may indicate the extent of local criterion fulfillment. Highly unusual terms are defined in the glossary.

Expository Comprehension Criteria	Strongly Implemented — 4	Moderately Implemented — 3	Marginally Implemented — 2	Not Implemented — 1
1. The purpose of expository comprehension is to aid content or subject area text reading	☐	☐	☐	☐
2. Structured overviews* and advance organizers* are widely used to *visualize* content	☐	☐	☐	☐
3. Brainstorming* and webbing* occur often to help students "see" text to be read	☐	☐	☐	☐
4. Teachers display extensive use of pre-reading activities, such as predictions, searches, etc.	☐	☐	☐	☐
5. Students use K-W-L,* DR-TA,* SQRRR,* etc., to monitor meaning as they read content books	☐	☐	☐	☐
6. Students use reciprocal teaching* as valuable social interaction for interest and motivation	☐	☐	☐	☐
7. Teachers use vocabulary and context aids to tie together content socially after reading	☐	☐	☐	☐
8. Pupils gain post-reading closure on texts by completing DR-TA,* K-W-L,* etc., strategies	☐	☐	☐	☐
9. Collaborative peer groups complete forms as Information Organizers to tie up content	☐	☐	☐	☐
10. Cooperative groups gain closure by returning to organizers,* overviews,* webs,* etc.	☐	☐	☐	☐

Interpretation: To judge expository text use in the school, faculties may total columns in Form 4.8, giving four points to *strongly implemented* three to *moderately implemented*, two to *marginally implemented*, and one point to *not implemented*. Totals between 31–40 may be considered *strongly implemented*, between 21–30 *moderately implemented*, between 11–20 *marginally implemented*, and between 1–10 *not implemented*.

PROCESS WRITING SUPPORTS READING COMPREHENSION   (see Form 4.9)

Writing benefits students' writing skills and augments their reading comprehension. The National Writing Project has helped teachers to monitor class' brainstorming while teachers map or web collective knowledge, offering a visual structure for how students will compose. Pupils who create drafts that follow those webs add structure and confidence to writing. Carefully managed peer editing enhances skills and motivation.

The Problem: Prior generations have not been effective in teaching students to write with confidence or skill. The process previously was often based on the study of grammar and teachers' correcting pupil errors or misspellings, along with studying language arts textbooks. Resultant compositions have been brief and non-expressive for the most part.

Rationale: A widely-recognized idea across 40 years is that extensive writing benefits reading and considerable reading helps writing to develop. When students create their own texts, that embedded construction process aids future monitoring of their reading; pupils understand how texts function (226). As well, students who write about what they have read benefit from re-comprehension of the passage.

Procedures: To examine present program success, faculty, the principal, or Reading Advisory Board may review the content of Form 4.9. If participants seek to evaluate the present writing component alongside the reading curriculum, Form 4.10 may be used.

For Further Reading

Calkins, L. M. (1994). *The Art of Teaching Writing, New Edition.* Portsmouth, NH: Heinemann. (361 Hanover Street, Portsmouth, NH 03801-3912. 1-800-541-2086.)

Calkins approaches writing as the development of expression and the creation of a tool for understanding. She addresses poetry, fiction, and report writing. The author deals with the reading and writing connection. The book may be used in conjunction with available video.

Shanahan, T. (Ed.). (1990). *Reading and Writing Together: New Perspectives for the Classroom.* Norwood, MA: Christopher-Gordon Publishers, Inc. (480 Washington Street, Norwood, MA 02062. 1-800-934-8322.)

The authors bring together theory, research, and practice on interrelated reading and writing. The text is written for classroom teachers and reading leadership. Some of the best insights and perspectives on reading and writing to emerge in the last ten years are developed in this text.

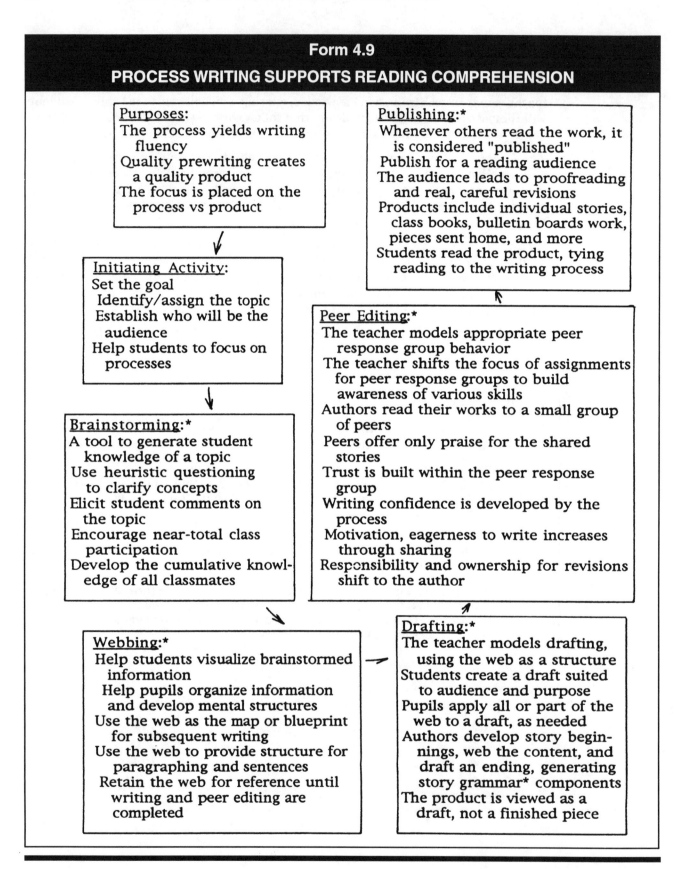

Form 4.9

PROCESS WRITING SUPPORTS READING COMPREHENSION

Purposes:
The process yields writing
  fluency
Quality prewriting creates
  a quality product
The focus is placed on the
  process vs product

Publishing:*
Whenever others read the work, it
  is considered "published"
Publish for a reading audience
The audience leads to proofreading
  and real, careful revisions
Products include individual stories,
  class books, bulletin boards work,
  pieces sent home, and more
Students read the product, tying
  reading to the writing process

Initiating Activity:
Set the goal
  Identify/assign the topic
Establish who will be the
  audience
Help students to focus on
  processes

Peer Editing:*
The teacher models appropriate peer
  response group behavior
The teacher shifts the focus of assignments
  for peer response groups to build
  awareness of various skills
Authors read their works to a small group
  of peers
Peers offer only praise for the shared
  stories
Trust is built within the peer response
  group
Writing confidence is developed by the
  process
Motivation, eagerness to write increases
  through sharing
Responsibility and ownership for revisions
  shift to the author

Brainstorming:*
A tool to generate student
  knowledge of a topic
Use heuristic questioning
  to clarify concepts
Elicit student comments on
  the topic
Encourage near-total class
  participation
Develop the cumulative knowledge of all classmates

Webbing:*
Help students visualize brainstormed
  information
Help pupils organize information
  and develop mental structures
Use the web as the map or blueprint
  for subsequent writing
Use the web to provide structure for
  paragraphing and sentences
Retain the web for reference until
  writing and peer editing are
  completed

Drafting:*
The teacher models drafting,
  using the web as a structure
Students create a draft suited
  to audience and purpose
Pupils apply all or part of the
  web to a draft, as needed
Authors develop story beginnings, web the content, and
  draft an ending, generating
  story grammar* components
The product is viewed as a
  draft, not a finished piece

Form 4.10

CURRICULAR ASSESSMENT OF WRITING WITH READING

Directions: Form 4.9 contains criteria related to the ways in which writing supports reading, as does the list of criteria below in Form 4.10. On the right, participants may signify the extent of local school application of those criteria. Highly unusual terms are defined in the glossary.

Criteria on Writing's Support of Reading:	Strongly Implemented	Moderately Implemented	Marginally Implemented	Not Implemented
	4	3	2	1
1. Writing is viewed by all school people as a vital, integral part of the language arts	☐	☐	☐	☐
2. Teachers and pupils recognize that writing helps reading and reading helps writing	☐	☐	☐	☐
3. Teachers ease the process and aid pupil confidence by creating visual structures	☐	☐	☐	☐
4. Students gain topical knowledge by participating in brainstorming* activities	☐	☐	☐	☐
5. Teachers web/map* the brainstorming to structure the writing assignment ..	☐	☐	☐	☐
6. Students create a draft of their assignment by using the web as their structure	☐	☐	☐	☐
7. Learners use the web to construct both the paragraphs and sentences	☐	☐	☐	☐
8. Pupils share their drafts collaboratively with peers who make positive responses	☐	☐	☐	☐
9. Writers participate in peer-editing by refering back to the web as their structure to review the use of writing and to support reading	☐	☐	☐	☐
10. Students sometimes publish their papers, i.e., prepare them for public sharing	☐	☐	☐	☐

Interpretation: To review writing's support of reading, the principal or faculty may total columns in Form 4.10, giving four points to *strongly implemented*, three to *moderately implemented*, two to *marginally implemented*, and one point to *not implemented*. Totals between 31–40 may be judged *strongly implemented*, between 21–30 *moderately implemented*, between 11–20 *marginally implemented*, and between 1–10 *not implemented*.

DEVELOPMENT OF MEANING VOCABULARY   (see Form 4.11)

The purpose of vocabulary instruction is to help students to understand new terminology they encounter when reading both narrative and expository texts. The teaching of meaning vocabulary and concepts is highly intertwined with reading comprehension.

The Problem: Many teachers either give perfunctory support to vocabulary development in teachers' manuals or may disregard the area altogether. Vocabulary instruction may consist of teachers' listing words and students' self-locating dictionary definitions. Teachers may be unaware of the importance of extensive recreational reading and classroom social interactions regarding the use of new terminology. Rarely do teachers employ social interaction to advance content text vocabularies. Likewise, use of visual and structural supports from cognitive science may be minimal.

Rationale: Vocabulary and concepts help reading comprehension and reading helps to increase meaning vocabulary, overall language development, and general knowledge. From cognitive psychology, structural aids such as word maps,* semantic maps,* and semantic feature matrixes* provide visual representations of terms and their super- and sub-structure relationships. Use of new terminology in classroom social interactions seems to augment new concepts in ways meaningful to students.

Procedures: The Advisory Board, faculty, or principal may use Form 4.11 to consider vocabulary content in the reading curriculum, and Form 4.12 to judge the extent of integration in the present reading program.

For Further Reading

Johnson, D. D. & Pearson, P. D. (1984). *Teaching Reading Vocabulary, Second Edition*. New York: Holt, Rinehart & Winston. (6277 Sea Harbor Drive, Orlando, FL 32887. 407-345-2000.)

> The authors explicate the importance of vocabulary development, instuctional components, developing meaning vocabulary, sight vocabulary, and word identification. Sections deal with vocabulary instruction in basal reading systems and content reading.

Vacca, R. T. & Vacca, J. L. (1993). *Content Area Reading: Fourth Edition*. New York: HarperCollins College Publishers. (10 East 53rd Street, New York, NY 10022. 1-800-742-7831.)

> The text is supported by reading and writing strategies used across the curriculum. The authors develop sections on teaching with texts, thinking and learning with texts, and learning through literature. A strong section on vocabulary development supports the text.

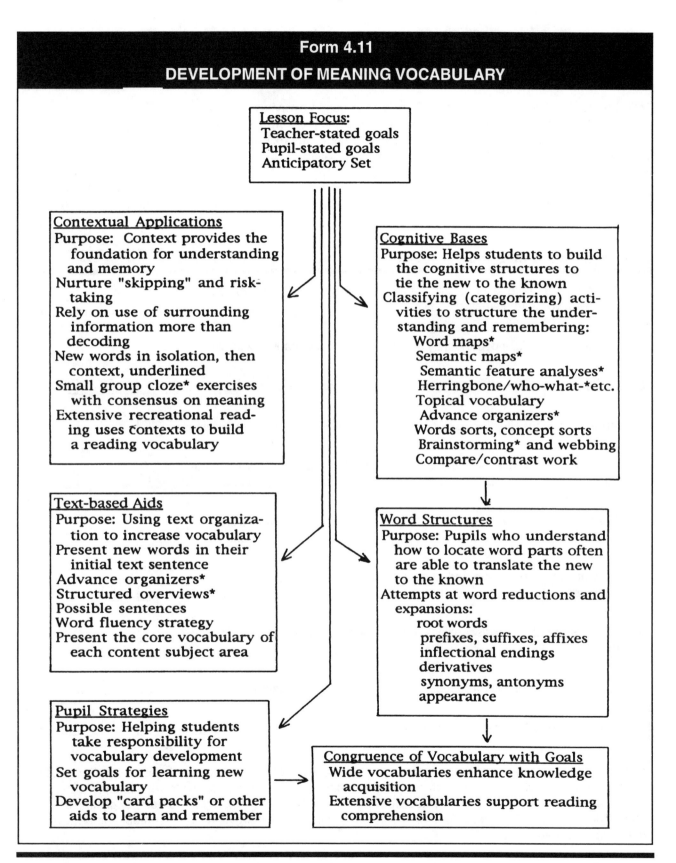

Form 4.11

DEVELOPMENT OF MEANING VOCABULARY

Lesson Focus:
Teacher-stated goals
Pupil-stated goals
Anticipatory Set

Contextual Applications
Purpose: Context provides the
    foundation for understanding
    and memory
Nurture "skipping" and risk-
    taking
Rely on use of surrounding
    information more than
    decoding
New words in isolation, then
    context, underlined
Small group cloze* exercises
    with consensus on meaning
Extensive recreational read-
    ing uses contexts to build
    a reading vocabulary

Cognitive Bases
Purpose: Helps students to build
    the cognitive structures to
    tie the new to the known
Classifying (categorizing) acti-
    vities to structure the under-
    standing and remembering:
        Word maps*
        Semantic maps*
        Semantic feature analyses*
        Herringbone/who-what-*etc.
        Topical vocabulary
        Advance organizers*
        Words sorts, concept sorts
        Brainstorming* and webbing
        Compare/contrast work

Text-based Aids
Purpose: Using text organiza-
    tion to increase vocabulary
Present new words in their
    initial text sentence
Advance organizers*
Structured overviews*
Possible sentences
Word fluency strategy
Present the core vocabulary of
    each content subject area

Word Structures
Purpose: Pupils who understand
    how to locate word parts often
    are able to translate the new
    to the known
Attempts at word reductions and
    expansions:
        root words
        prefixes, suffixes, affixes
        inflectional endings
        derivatives
        synonyms, antonyms
        appearance

Pupil Strategies
Purpose: Helping students
    take responsibility for
    vocabulary development
Set goals for learning new
    vocabulary
Develop "card packs" or other
    aids to learn and remember

Congruence of Vocabulary with Goals
Wide vocabularies enhance knowledge
    acquisition
Extensive vocabularies support reading
    comprehension

FORM 4.12

CURRICULAR ASSESSMENT OF MEANING VOCABULARY DEVELOPMENT

Directions: Participants may employ Form 4.11 to get an overview, or flow chart, of the place of meaning vocabulary in the reading program. Criteria are also listed below in Form 4.12. School people may check the extent of implementation. Highly unusual terms are defined in the glossary.

Criteria related to meaning vocabulary:	Strongly Implemented	Moderately Implemented	Marginally Implemented	Not Implemented
	4	3	2	1
1. Young readers take responsibility for their growing vocabularies; choose their own words for self-study	☐	☐	☐	☐
2. Children set goals, independently and with peers, for vocabulary growth	☐	☐	☐	☐
3. Pupils may prepare index cards with new words and meanings	☐	☐	☐	☐
4. Students display effective use of contexts in identifying new word meanings	☐	☐	☐	☐
5. Pupils are able to use the organization of texts to develop new word meanings	☐	☐	☐	☐
6. Readers use the structures of words, i.e., roots, affixes, to learn word functions	☐	☐	☐	☐
7. Students develop graphic and visual aids, word maps, etc., to develop meanings	☐	☐	☐	☐
8. Learners are active in discussions and brainstorming that aid word meanings	☐	☐	☐	☐
9. Pupils learn to cluster words together by categories or meaning groups	☐	☐	☐	☐
10. Students are able to explain the benefits of extensive meaning vocabularies	☐	☐	☐	☐

Interpretation: To assess meaning vocabulary's role, the Advisory Board may total columns in Form 4.12, giving four points to *strongly implemented*, three to *moderately implemented*, two to *marginally implemented*, and one point to *not implemented*. Totals between 31–40 may be regarded as *strongly implemented*, between 21–30 *moderately implemented*, between 11–20 *marginally implemented*, and between 1–10 *not implemented*.

LITERATURE-BASED READING AND WRITING   (see Form 4.13)

The purpose of literature-based programs is to help students become better readers and writers by studying authentic literature. Pupils pursue the various literary forms and authors of sets of books, and in the process, take on the conventions of writing and reading. Recent popularity of literature-based programs involves several forms. Some advocate use of trade books taken from library shelves, while others support textbook series of anthologies. Reading is grounded in cooperative learning, thematic instruction, and literature sets.

The Problem: Staff development may be warranted wherever teachers have no prior experience with literature-based teaching. While many students may learn to read by studying literature, others may warrant greater amounts of structure provided through the use of direct instruction, particularly at-risk learners.

Rationale: Students may benefit from process-based reading and writing founded on authentic literature. The richness of the quality of language used in high-level literature may result in enhanced oral language, advanced writing, augmented reading comprehension, vocabulary enhancement, and strongly positive feelings about reading and writing.

Procedures: Principals, faculties, or Advisory Boards may refer to Form 4.13 to gain an overview of literature-based instruction, then complete Form 4.14 to identify program implementation. Further information may be found in the *Whole Language* section of Chapter 6.

For Further Reading

McGee, L. M. (1992). "Focus on Research: Exploring the Literature-based Reading Revolution," *Language Arts*, 69, 7, 529–37.

> McGee describes the challenges involved in teaching literature based reading. She interprets research on innovative approaches, literacy experiences, and literary analysis. The author comments on teachers' reluctance and accomplishments.

Hiebert, E. H. & Colt, J. M. (1989). "Patterns of Literature-based Reading Instruction," *The Reading Teacher*, 43, 1, 14–20.

> The authors summarize three teachers' views, stressing a blend of those patterns in a total reading program. Descriptions are given of teacher-led and selected, and student-led and selected, formats. Hiebert and Colt also describe roles of independent reading.

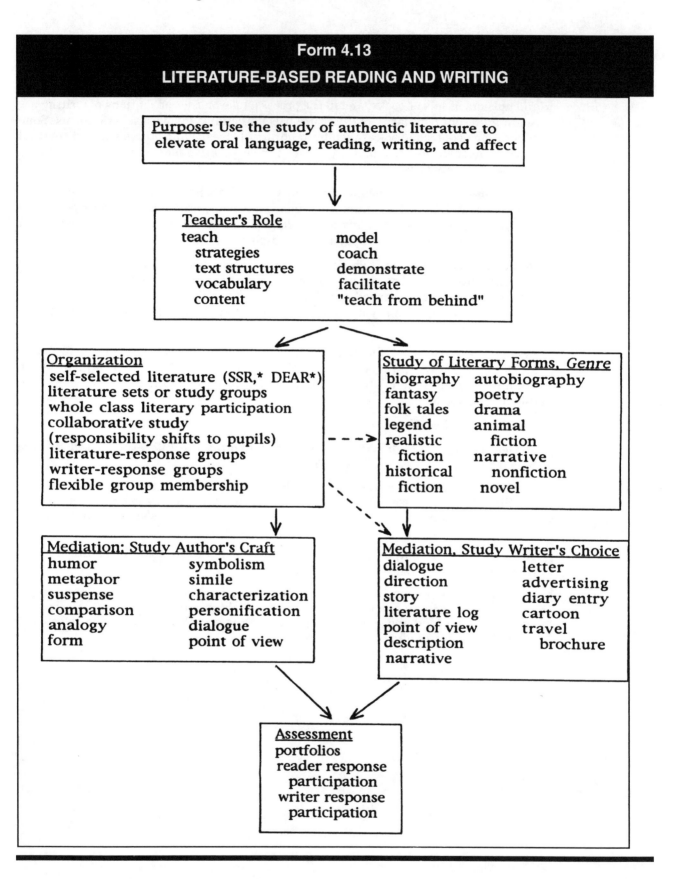

Form 4.13

LITERATURE-BASED READING AND WRITING

<u>Purpose</u>: Use the study of authentic literature to elevate oral language, reading, writing, and affect

<u>Teacher's Role</u>
teach	model
strategies	coach
text structures	demonstrate
vocabulary	facilitate
content	"teach from behind"

<u>Organization</u>
self-selected literature (SSR,* DEAR*)
literature sets or study groups
whole class literary participation
collaborative study
(responsibility shifts to pupils)
literature-response groups
writer-response groups
flexible group membership

<u>Study of Literary Forms, *Genre*</u>
biography	autobiography
fantasy	poetry
folk tales	drama
legend	animal
realistic	fiction
fiction	narrative
historical	nonfiction
fiction	novel

<u>Mediation: Study Author's Craft</u>
humor	symbolism
metaphor	simile
suspense	characterization
comparison	personification
analogy	dialogue
form	point of view

<u>Mediation, Study Writer's Choice</u>
dialogue	letter
direction	advertising
story	diary entry
literature log	cartoon
point of view	travel
description	brochure
narrative	

<u>Assessment</u>
portfolios
reader response
participation
writer response
participation

Form 4.14

CURRICULAR ASSESSMENT OF LITERATURE-BASED READING AND WRITING

Directions: Form 4.13 may be used as a flow chart or overview of literature-based instruction in reading curriculum. Related criteria are found below in Form 4.14. On the right, school personnel may check the extent of local implementation. Highly unusual terms are defined in the glossary.

Criteria for Literature-based programs:	Strongly Implemented	Moderately Implemented	Marginally Implemented	Not Implemented
	4	3	2	1
1. The classroom overflows as a print-rich environment, filled with children's work	☐	☐	☐	☐
2. Instruction is mediated through thematic, topical, unit study, and cooperative learning	☐	☐	☐	☐
3. Reading done by pupils involves literary forms, or genre, and author studies	☐	☐	☐	☐
4. The empowering teacher nurtures self-selection and self-pacing of literature	☐	☐	☐	☐
5. Direct instruction includes strategies, text structures, vocabulary, and content	☐	☐	☐	☐
6. Organization may involve literature sets, literature response groups, individuals, or the whole class	☐	☐	☐	☐
7. Students are empowered to make extensive entries into reading response journals	☐	☐	☐	☐
8. Writing samples in students' journals show developmental improvement over time	☐	☐	☐	☐
9. Pupils participate actively in literature response groups	☐	☐	☐	☐
10. Portfolios of student writing are organized to demonstrate periodic improvement	☐	☐	☐	☐

Interpretation: Faculty members may total columns in Form 4.14 to judge the local role of literature-based instruction, giving four points to *strongly implemented*, three to *moderately implemented*, two to *marginally implemented*, and one point to *not implemented*. Totals between 31–40 may be considered *strongly implemented*, between 21–30 *moderately implemented*, between 11–20 *marginally implemented*, and between 1–10 *not implemented*.

THE DECODING OR WORD ANALYSIS INSTRUCTION CYCLE   (see Form 4.15)

Unfamiliar words may be met by good readers as a logical, hypothesis-testing process of identification while they search for meaning. The language is alphabetic enough that, even during non-phonic eras, most people learned spelling patterns that were taught as components of a phonic curriculum. Phonics is rediscovered in thirty-year cycles, and the value diminishes between cycles; reasons must exist for both rediscoveries and reduced use.

The Problem: Many teachers have stressed phonic rules, sounding out words, and oral reading. Each has been emphasized more than reading for meaning, and students often are unable to do both concurrently. Many phonic patterns are stable and predictable, but some are not, yet teachers have not used this distinction with caution in order to reduce learner confusion.

Rationale: A reasoned approach may be to teach pupils to use context, configuration, phonics, and syllabication in a searching, problem-solving, metacognitive manner that retains meaning. Students should be taught to select any of the strategies above based on contextual need at any moment.

Procedures: Form 4.15 may be used to review those decoding elements ordinarily found in reading curriculum, and then Form 4.16 for the Advisory Board, principal, or faculty to review the present program as a basis for program maintenance or revision.

For Further Reading

Cunningham, P. M. (1995). *Phonics They Use: Words for Reading and Writing, Second Edition*. New York: HarperCollins College Publishers. (10 East 53rd Street, New York, NY 10022. 1-800-742-7831.)

> Cunningham deals with approaches to teaching little words, high-frequency words, and big words. She develops children's foundation of reading and writing with concepts about print, emerging literacy, and phonological awareness.

Stanovich, K. E. (1993–94). "Romance and Reality," *The Reading Teacher*, 47, 4, 180–191.

> The author reasons that direct instruction in spelling-sound relationships will enable whole language to endure. He acknowledges that some of his research will be popular with all scholars, other research will not be popular with some.

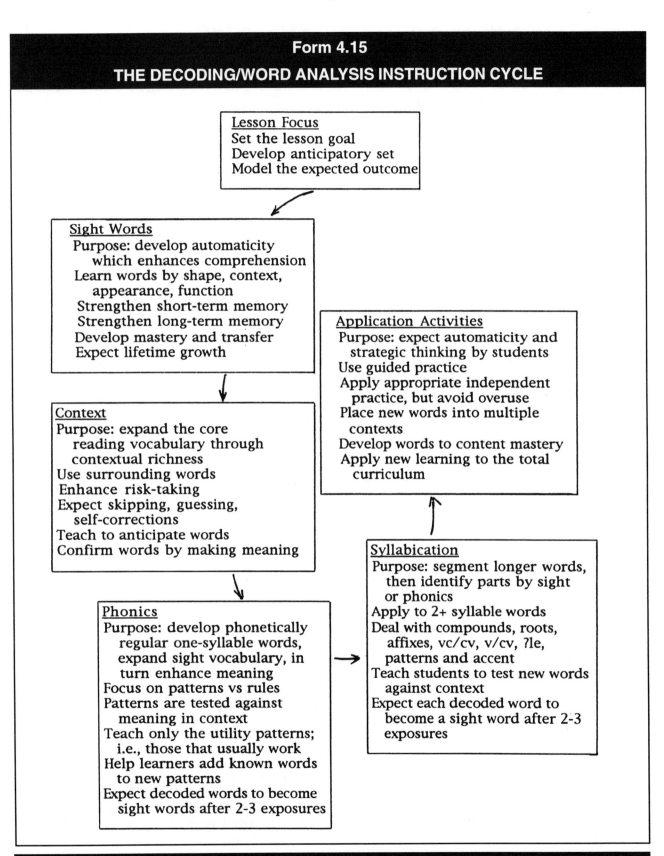

Form 4.15

THE DECODING/WORD ANALYSIS INSTRUCTION CYCLE

Lesson Focus
Set the lesson goal
Develop anticipatory set
Model the expected outcome

Sight Words
Purpose: develop automaticity
  which enhances comprehension
Learn words by shape, context,
  appearance, function
Strengthen short-term memory
Strengthen long-term memory
Develop mastery and transfer
Expect lifetime growth

Application Activities
Purpose: expect automaticity and
  strategic thinking by students
Use guided practice
Apply appropriate independent
  practice, but avoid overuse
Place new words into multiple
  contexts
Develop words to content mastery
Apply new learning to the total
  curriculum

Context
Purpose: expand the core
  reading vocabulary through
  contextual richness
Use surrounding words
Enhance risk-taking
Expect skipping, guessing,
  self-corrections
Teach to anticipate words
Confirm words by making meaning

Syllabication
Purpose: segment longer words,
  then identify parts by sight
  or phonics
Apply to 2+ syllable words
Deal with compounds, roots,
  affixes, vc/cv, v/cv, ?le,
  patterns and accent
Teach students to test new words
  against context
Expect each decoded word to
  become a sight word after 2-3
  exposures

Phonics
Purpose: develop phonetically
  regular one-syllable words,
  expand sight vocabulary, in
  turn enhance meaning
Focus on patterns vs rules
Patterns are tested against
  meaning in context
Teach only the utility patterns;
  i.e., those that usually work
Help learners add known words
  to new patterns
Expect decoded words to become
  sight words after 2-3 exposures

FORM 4.16
CURRICULAR ASSESSMENT OF DECODING/WORD ANALYSIS INSTRUCTION

Directions: Form 4.15 contains a flow chart of decoding, or word analysis, in the reading curriculum. Below, those criteria are also listed in Form 4.16, and on the right, participants may check the extent of implementation in the local school. Highly unusual terms are defined in the glossary.

Criteria for Decoding/Word Analysis:	Strongly Implemented 4	Moderately Implemented 3	Marginally Implemented 2	Not Implemented 1
1. The focus on word analysis or decoding is to provide tools to increase comprehension	☐	☐	☐	☐
2. Students are taught to select the decoding strategy warranted in any particular context	☐	☐	☐	☐
3. Learners are seen skipping words, taking risks that a word may not be correct	☐	☐	☐	☐
4. Pupils are aware of a growing number of their known sight words requiring no analysis	☐	☐	☐	☐
5. Readers are active in using both immediate and surrounding contexts for new words	☐	☐	☐	☐
6. Students utilize phonics as a strategic behavior vs a rule-bearing, sound-it-out response	☐	☐	☐	☐
7. Pupils are taught to rely more on consonants plus context than on vowels	☐	☐	☐	☐
8. Readers identify words phonically, then return them to context to confirm meaning	☐	☐	☐	☐
9. Learners segment longer words into their parts, then apply phonics or sight to parts	☐	☐	☐	☐
10. Readers grow toward fluency and automaticity which increases comprehension	☐	☐	☐	☐

Interpretation: To judge the role of decoding in the curriculum, principals, faculties, or Advisory Boards may total columns in Form 4.16, giving four points to *strongly implemented*, three to *moderately implemented*, two to *marginally implemented*, and one to *not implemented*. Totals between 31–40 may be considered *strongly implemented*, between 21–30 *moderately implemented*, between 11–20 *marginally implemented*, and between 1–10 *not implemented*.

THE RECREATIONAL READING COMPONENT   (see Form 4.17)

Conventional thinking has viewed recreational reading as a supplement to text-based reading classes. Recent curriculum thinking places authentic literature and recreational/personal reading at the heart of the reading program. The concept is so important that the federal government has set aside partial funding to support pupil ownership of books.

The Problem: The most serious problem may be those teachers who neither accept nor believe that vast amounts of reading are important to pupils' literacy advancement. SSR* and DEAR* activities, curriculum time set aside only for recreational reading, are not always planned, integral parts of school curricula. Faculties without school or classroom libraries have been hard-pressed to offer adequate recreational reading as part of a program.

Rationale: Great amounts of recreational reading enrich students' lives, expand language, increase vocabulary, augment overall knowledge, and improve reading achievement. Social interaction through shared reading and writing in cooperative groups, literature sets, and thematic study, improves affect for reading. Several ways of providing inexpensive books, such as book clubs, fairs, drives, and shopping for children's books at flea markets or garage sales, warrant effort in some communities without library resources.

Procedures: Form 4.17 may be employed to review recreational reading components, while Form 4.18 may be used to judge present status in the local school. Faculties, Advisory Boards, or principals may use findings from Form 4.18 to reconsider the present program.

For Further Reading

Gunning, T. G. (1992). *Creating Reading Instruction for all Children*. Boston: Allyn & Bacon. (Dept. 894, 160 Gould Street, Needham Heights, MA 02194-2310. 1-800-852-8024.)

> A comprehensive preservice and inservice text with basic information and strategies for effective teaching of reading and writing. Strong sections are developed on emergent literacy, reading comprehension, and vocabulary development. The section on literature is particularly well developed.

Vacca, J. L., et al. (1995). *Reading and Learning to Read, Third Edition*. New York: HarperCollins Publishers, Inc. (10 East 53rd Street, New York, NY 10022. 1-800-742-7831.)

> The text is supported by reading and writing strategies used across the curriculum. The authors develop sections on teaching with texts, thinking and learning with texts, and learning through literature. The section on teaching literature is helpful.

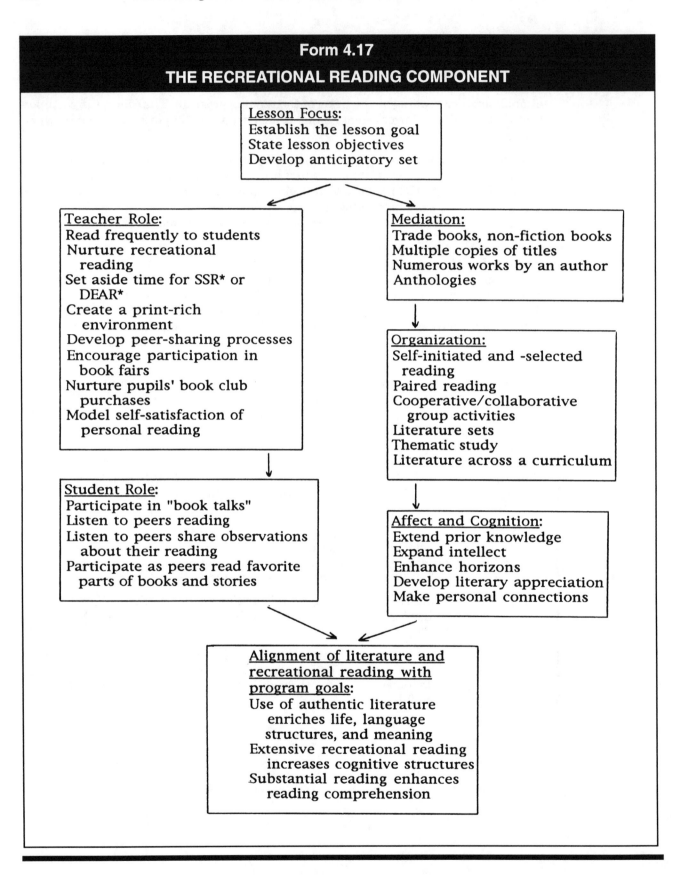

Form 4.17

THE RECREATIONAL READING COMPONENT

<u>Lesson Focus:</u>
Establish the lesson goal
State lesson objectives
Develop anticipatory set

<u>Teacher Role:</u>
Read frequently to students
Nurture recreational
   reading
Set aside time for SSR* or
   DEAR*
Create a print-rich
   environment
Develop peer-sharing processes
Encourage participation in
   book fairs
Nurture pupils' book club
   purchases
Model self-satisfaction of
   personal reading

<u>Mediation:</u>
Trade books, non-fiction books
Multiple copies of titles
Numerous works by an author
Anthologies

<u>Organization:</u>
Self-initiated and -selected
   reading
Paired reading
Cooperative/collaborative
   group activities
Literature sets
Thematic study
Literature across a curriculum

<u>Student Role:</u>
Participate in "book talks"
Listen to peers reading
Listen to peers share observations
   about their reading
Participate as peers read favorite
   parts of books and stories

<u>Affect and Cognition:</u>
Extend prior knowledge
Expand intellect
Enhance horizons
Develop literary appreciation
Make personal connections

<u>Alignment of literature and
recreational reading with
program goals:</u>
Use of authentic literature
   enriches life, language
   structures, and meaning
Extensive recreational reading
   increases cognitive structures
Substantial reading enhances
   reading comprehension

Form 4.18
CURRICULAR ASSESSMENT OF RECREATIONAL READING

Directions: Form 4.17 and criteria below in Form are 4.18 are related to recreational reading in the curriculum. On the right, participants may judge the extent to which criteria are implemented locally. Highly unusual terms are defined in the glossary.

Criteria regarding recreational reading:	Strongly Implemented 4	Moderately Implemented 3	Marginally Implemented 2	Not Implemented 1
1. The principal promotes reading through modeling, listening to pupils' reading, etc.	☐	☐	☐	☐
2. The principal and supervisors remind teachers continuously of reading's role	☐	☐	☐	☐
3. Teachers set aside time daily for students' self-selected reading, such as DEAR or SSR	☐	☐	☐	☐
4. Teachers provide time frequently for sharing favorite books or parts with peers	☐	☐	☐	☐
5. Teachers model for students their own enjoyment and satisfaction of reading	☐	☐	☐	☐
6. Teachers nurture peer interaction through students' reading in pairs, literature sets, etc.	☐	☐	☐	☐
7. Faculties nurture trade book collections with book fairs, clubs, RIF* participation, etc.	☐	☐	☐	☐
8. Schools nurture participation in contests such as Pizza Hut's *Book It*, Six Flags' program, etc.	☐	☐	☐	☐
9. Teachers make efforts to creating an extensive classroom library collection	☐	☐	☐	☐
10. A goal of the school board and school people is to continuously increase library holdings	☐	☐	☐	☐

Interpretation: To review the role of recreational reading in the reading curriculum, Advisory Boards, faculties, or principals may total the columns in Form 4.18, giving four points to *strongly implemented*, three to *moderately implemented*, two to *marginally implemented*, and one to *not implemented*. Totals between 31–40 may be viewed as *strongly implemented*, between 21–30 *moderately implemented*, between 11–20 *marginally implemented*, and between 1–10 points *not implemented*.

SYNTHESIS OF READING CURRICULUM COMPONENTS   (see Form 4.19)

The reading curriculum is comprised of learning activities, content that is read, methodologies, and text mediation. A widely accepted reading curriculum concept is that all of the language arts—that is, thinking, listening, speaking, reading, and writing—if unified, ease the learning of each element.

The Problems: Reading programs do not always meet desired goals. A curriculum may not be balanced and comprehensive if important parts have been inadvertently left out. Programs may not always be meaning-focused.

Rationale: Schools usually operate with an officially adopted or an implied reading program. Some develop curriculum guides; others use textbook series to define the curriculum. Schools may function with curriculum- or child-centered reading programs. In one way or another, though, schools address beginning or early reading. Comprehension of narrative and expository text reading, supported by expanding meaning vocabulary, is the heart of the curriculum. Comprehension is vastly enhanced by writing, accelerating word recognition ability, and recreational reading.

Procedures: The faculty, principal, or Reading Advisory Board may revisit Form 4.1 and complete Form 4.19 to synthesize, then affirm program strengths, needs and, ultimately, priorities. The program goals and mission statement, along with needs-assessment and program-planning formats from Chapter 3 may be considered at this time, as well. A great deal of discussion, including thorough faculty feedback, is warranted to ensure accuracy of interpretation. Finally, with the widest amount of open deliberation, personnel may reconsider Form 4.19 to synthesize, Form 4.20 to identify uppermost strengths and weaknesses, then set priorities for the program that best meets curriculum goals. A plan-of-action, Form 4.21, may be used to move a school toward desired curriculum goals.

Form 4.19
CURRICULUM COMPONENTS OF THE READING PROGRAM

Directions: Central components of reading programs are found throughout Chapter 4 and below. On the right, participants may check their views of the component's status in the local school. Respondents may feel free to refer back to individual worksheets in Chapter 4, as needed.

Criteria:	Strongly Implemented 4	Moderately Implemented 3	Marginally Implemented 2	Not Implemented 1
1. A reasonable balance exists in content of the reading curriculum (Forms 4.1 and 4.2)	☐	☐	☐	☐
2. Quality literacy emergence supports reading affect and achievement (Forms 4.3 and 4.4)	☐	☐	☐	☐
3. The comprehension of narrative texts (story) is the core of the reading curriculum (summary of Forms 4.5 and 4.6)	☐	☐	☐	☐
4. Comprehension of expository texts (content reading, study skills) is the basis for reading subject area textbooks (Forms 4.7 and 4.8)	☐	☐	☐	☐
5. Process writing extends awareness of text construction, reading comprehension, and writing skills (summary of Forms 4.9 and 4.10)	☐	☐	☐	☐
6. The development of meaning vocabulary supports reading comprehension, thinking and oral language (Forms 4.11 and 4.12)	☐	☐	☐	☐
7. Literature-based reading and writing add authenticity to language learning (see Forms 4.13 and 4.14)	☐	☐	☐	☐
8. Decoding taught strategically strengthens fluency and automaticity and, thus, reading comprehension (Forms 4.15 and 4.16)	☐	☐	☐	☐
9. Recreational reading's role is emphasized, both for student fulfillment and for the "practice effect" on reading achievement (summary of Forms 4.17 and 4.18)	☐	☐	☐	☐
10. The fundamental approach to reading instruction (see Form 6.7) is consistent with reading curriculum goals	☐	☐	☐	☐

Form 4.20
THE READING CURRICULUM'S STRENGTHS, WEAKNESSES, AND PRIORITIES

Directions: Below are components of the reading curriculum. On the right of each entry, space is provided to record strengths, weaknesses, and priorities of each component. Checkmarks on each respective worksheet in Chapter 4, particularly Form 4.19, may help in completing Forms 4.20 and 4.21.

1. Emerging Literacy (readiness)	*Strengths* 1. 2.	*Needs* 1. 2.	*Priorities* 1. 2.
2. Narrative Comprehension	*Strengths* 1. 2.	*Needs* 1. 2.	*Priorities* 1. 2.
3. Expository Comprehension	*Strengths* 1. 2.	*Needs* 1. 2.	*Priorities* 1. 2.
4. Process Writing	*Strengths* 1. 2.	*Needs* 1. 2.	*Priorities* 1. 2.
5. Meaning Vocabulary Growth	*Strengths* 1. 2.	*Needs* 1. 2.	*Priorities* 1. 2.
6. Literature-based Approach	*Strengths* 1. 2.	*Needs* 1. 2.	*Priorities* 1. 2.
7. Decoding Processes	*Strengths* 1. 2.	*Needs* 1. 2.	*Priorities* 1. 2.
8. Recreational Reading	*Strengths* 1. 2.	*Needs* 1. 2.	*Priorities* 1. 2.

Form 4.21
READING CURRICULUM: PLAN-OF-ACTION

Directions: Principals who wish to develop a focus on professional growth in curriculum leadership may benefit from being as specific as possible about what they seek to accomplish, how they will go about attaining growth, and how they will know when they have reached their goals. Reference to Form 4.19 and Form 4.20 may help the principal or Advisory Board to summarize, then set strengths, weaknesses, and priorities of the reading curriculum. A review of Form 4.20 may lead the administrator to identify goals to pursue in the plan-of-action. Statements entered should be as simple as warranted and as useful as possible.

1. Goal Statement: _____

2. Objectives:

   a) _____

   b) _____

   c) _____

3. Activities: Dates; time checkpoints:

   a) _____   * _____

   b) _____   * _____

   c) _____   * _____

   d) _____   * _____

   e) _____   * _____

4. Resources: (professional reading, consultation, visitations)

   a) _____   * _____

   b) _____   * _____

   c) _____   * _____

5. How I will know when my goal is accomplished:

   _____

   _____

   _____

   _____

CHAPTER 5

ASSESSMENT OF READING PERFORMANCE

An effective assessment plan could be expected to monitor how well each student is progressing through the curriculum, and how well the curriculum is functioning. Schools usually operate as though each pupil is expected to learn all of the content and processes of curriculum, and to hold positive feelings. The assumption is that monitoring individual pupil progress will support teachers as they alter instruction, materials, organization, pupil practice, and evaluation to enhance continued student growth.

The principal or Reading Advisory Board reflecting on the reading assessment plan considers issues such as whether there is a need to review:

1. what it wishes to know about curriculum effectiveness, student learning, and evaluation.
2. how well the curriculum is functioning at the program level.
3. how well individual students are progressing through the curriculum.
4. which content of the curriculum it wishes to assess.
5. how it will measure the content to be assessed.
6. whether to purchase or to use locally-developed instruments.
7. how to distinguish the role of standardized, state-mandated, portfolio, locally-developed, and text-based assessments to fulfill the popular concept of *multiple measures* of assessment.

The principal's or Advisory Board's study of reading assessment may be direct and focused only on this one goal. That goal would warrant the use of Chapter 5, alone. However, the Board may wish to review reading assessment in the greater context of overall reading program review. If that is the goal, the Board may want to study reading assessment as it is inter-related with needs-assessment and program-planning, Chapter 3, then the reading curriculum, Chapter 4. To begin, Boards might gain preliminary feedback from use of Forms 5.1 and 5.2, then, perhaps, the balance of Chapter 5.

READING PROGRAM ASSESSMENT OPTIONS   (see Forms 5.1 and 5.2)

Student assessment is governed by district desires to know how well its curriculum is functioning, which components warrant program revisions, how well each teacher is functioning, ways of making instruction more effective, and how well each pupil is advancing. While standardized tests and text-based tests are widely used, performance assessment holds the most promise for authentic judgments about pupils' reading.

Problem: Schools may not always have a comprehensive assessment plan, use existing data purposefully, create congruence between curriculum and testing, nor understand the accuracy of tests used. Districts often use standardized achievement tests and textbook-based instruments exclusively.

Rationale: A good school reading assessment plan should first be functional. School personnel and community members hold expectations that teachers will be able to tell just how well each student is doing. Additionally, people involved are expected to know how well the program, itself, is doing. A consensus exists that multiple measures of pupils' reading abilities provide a balanced view of status and progress; that is, a mix of options often is used.

Procedures: Principals, faculties, and Reading Advisory Boards may use Form 5.1 to gain an overview of assessment options. Form 5.2 may be used to judge the extent to which the local district has integrated options into its reading assessment program.

For Further Reading

Costa, A. (1989). "Re-assessing Assessment," *Educational Leadership*, 46, 7, 2—3.

> Costa presents the guest editorial in a themed edition of *EL*. He calls for process-oriented assessments to measure process-oriented learning. He endorses systematized process assessments with school-based accountability. The author recommends re-educating legislatures, parents, school boards, and communities to point out inadequacies of standardized tests.

Hiebert, E. H. & Calfee, R. (1992). "Assessing Literacy: From Standardized Tests to Portfolios and Performances." Edited by S. J. Samuels & A. E. Farstrup. *What Research Has to Say about Reading Instruction, Second Edition*. Newark, DE: International Reading Association. (800 Barksdale Road, P. O. Box 8139, Newark, DE 19714-8139. 1-800-336-READ or 302-731-1600.)

> Samuels and Farstrup describe the way current theory and research are reflected in practices and changes in reading instruction. Hiebert and Calfee interpret how thinking about assessment is being brought in line with reading and writing as constructive processes. They assert that multiple measures strengthen indicators of students' progress.

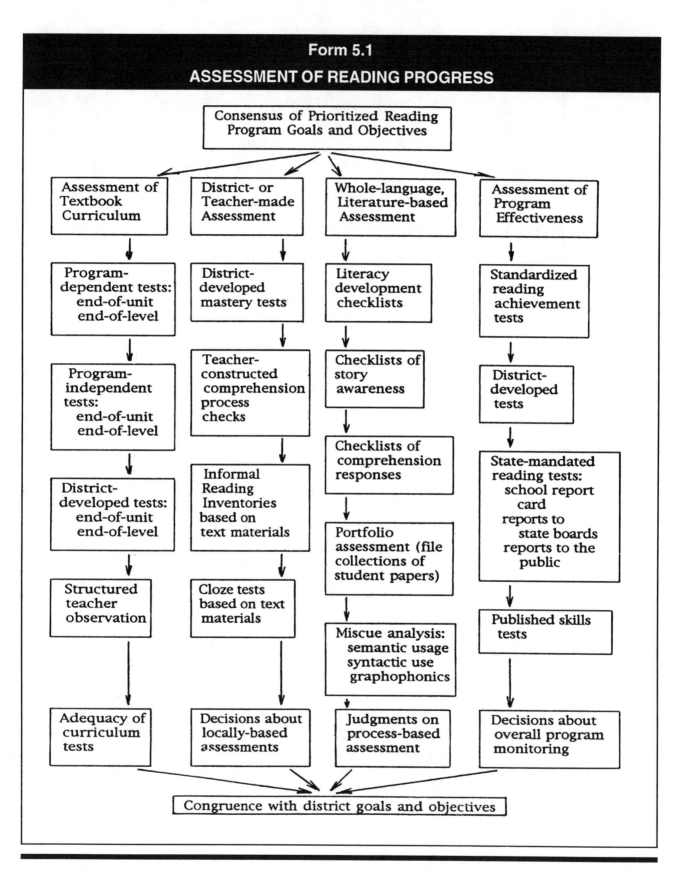

Form 5.1

ASSESSMENT OF READING PROGRESS

Consensus of Prioritized Reading Program Goals and Objectives

Assessment of Textbook Curriculum	District- or Teacher-made Assessment	Whole-language, Literature-based Assessment	Assessment of Program Effectiveness
Program-dependent tests: end-of-unit end-of-level	District-developed mastery tests	Literacy development checklists	Standardized reading achievement tests
Program-independent tests: end-of-unit end-of-level	Teacher-constructed comprehension process checks	Checklists of story awareness	District-developed tests
District-developed tests: end-of-unit end-of-level	Informal Reading Inventories based on text materials	Checklists of comprehension responses	State-mandated reading tests: school report card reports to state boards reports to the public
Structured teacher observation	Cloze tests based on text materials	Portfolio assessment (file collections of student papers)	Published skills tests
		Miscue analysis: semantic usage syntactic use graphophonics	
Adequacy of curriculum tests	Decisions about locally-based assessments	Judgments on process-based assessment	Decisions about overall program monitoring

Congruence with district goals and objectives

Form 5.2

ASSESSMENT OPTIONS FOR LOCAL CONSIDERATION

Directions: Below, the faculty, Reading Advisory Board, or principal will find a range of assessment options for consideration in the local school. On the right, participants may wish to decide if any option is now thoroughly, partially, minimally, or not implemented.

Reading Program Assessment Options:	Thouroughly Implemented	Partially Implemented	Minimally Implemented	Not Implemented
	4	3	2	1
1. Standardized reading achievement tests	☐	☐	☐	☐
2. Test results reviewed annually and compared with data from previous years	☐	☐	☐	☐
3. Out of those annual reviews come current program and class goal-setting	☐	☐	☐	☐
4. Instructional planning based on useable data from goal-setting	☐	☐	☐	☐
5. Current program goals compared to those of past years to mark progress	☐	☐	☐	☐
6. End-of-unit and end-of-level tests correlated with basal or literature-based textbooks	☐	☐	☐	☐
7. State-mandated tests given to all or certain grade levels of students to monitor at the state level and locally to monitor *school report cards* in newspapers	☐	☐	☐	☐
8. Generic, purchased program-independent testing packages	☐	☐	☐	☐
9. District-developed instruments that monitor the local curriculum	☐	☐	☐	☐
10. Item analyses of any of the above options	☐	☐	☐	☐
11. Running records* that offer on-the-job simple structures to analyze the *processing* students use as they read	☐	☐	☐	☐
12. Informal instruments, such as Informal Reading Inventories* or Cloze* tests	☐	☐	☐	☐
13. Miscue analysis* to monitor children's print-processing and thinking as they read	☐	☐	☐	☐
14. Checksheets for periodic judgments about student progress in any dimensions of the curriculum (see Forms 5.6–5.13)	☐	☐	☐	☐

–continues–

Assessment Options for Local Consideration -continued-	4	3	2	1
15. Formative processes including worksheets for the structuring of individual teacher observations	☐ ☐	☐ ☐	☐ ☐	☐ ☐
16. Portfolio assessment, incorporating student writing, samples of reading responses, audio tapes, video tapes, photos, etc.	☐	☐	☐	☐
17. Teacher-developed and student prepared anecdotes related to reading development	☐	☐	☐	☐
18. Reading response journals and literature response journals	☐	☐	☐	☐
19. Questionnaires for monitoring affective dimensions of reading; i.e., interest inventories, attitude inventories, etc.	☐	☐	☐	☐
20. Data from students' cumulative records to find learning patterns and discrepancies	☐	☐	☐	☐
21. Pupil information from standardized, text-based, and state-mandated tests is used alongside portfolio assessment to mark students' strengths and needs	☐	☐	☐	☐
22. Data kept on individuals and classes at least as long as students attend the school	☐	☐	☐	☐

Cover the page here and below prior to photocopying if users are not to see the interpretation until later.

Interpretation: Principals or Advisory Boards may make judgments about local assessment by tallying columns of Form 5.2, giving four points to checkmarks in *thoroughly implemented*, three points to *partially implemented*, two to *minimally implemented*, and one to *not implemented.* Totals between 51–68 may be considered *thoroughly implemented*, those between 35–51 *partially implemented*, between 18–34 *minimally implemented,* and between 1–17 *not implemented.* As well, participants may consider criteria one at a time to judge applicability and to set priorities.

STANDARDIZED TESTS IN READING PROGRAM ASSESSMENT   (see Form 5.3)

School administrators often seek to know how well local performance compares with larger populations of students. Frequently, too, principals wish to know how the present students' reading achievement compares to the previous year's classes. Teachers may wish to monitor achievement in classes, year by year, to see if their own teaching is steady, or is advancing over time.

The Problem: Frequently, neither the principal nor the faculty understands the amount of confidence that may be placed in individual test scores. Reference to the *standard error of measurement* will disclose the accuracy of individual test scores. Additionally, school personnel do not always understand the extent to which standardized reading achievement test scores are higher than actual reading levels in textbooks.

Rationale: Schools almost always have some level of curriculum, whether formal with published curriculum guides, or the occasionally found contemporary curriculum that emerges spontaneously from the children. Regardless of which they have, assessment components are likely to provide comprehensive data about the program and about individual students, each of which provides data to support program goal attainment.

Procedures: Form 5.3 may be used by Reading Advisory Boards, principals, and faculties to judge how effectively the local school is using its standardized achievement testing services. Either present use or future implementation of test use may be reviewed.

For Further Reading

Farr, R. & Carey, R. (1986). *Reading: What Can be Measured? Second Edition.* Newark, DE: International Reading Association. (800 Barksdale Road, P. O. Box 1839, Newark, DE 19714-8139. 1-600-336-READ or 302-731-1600.)

The authors present the research on measurement and evaluation in reading, explicating implications and interpretation. Educators are admonished to reflect on testing programs and what they hope to learn from instruments.

Lyman, H. (1991). *Test Scores and What They Mean, Fifth Edition.* Englewood Cliffs, NJ: Prentice-Hall. (113 Sylvan Avenue, Englewood Cliffs, NJ 07632. 1-800-526-0485.)

A readable, resourceful text for educator or layman to learn about test score interpretation. A section in the revision addresses new ideas about testing, including computer, performance, and adaptive tests, and assessment of diverse populations.

Form 5.3
STANDARDIZED ACHIEVEMENT TESTS IN READING PROGRAM ASSESSMENT

Directions: Below, the principal or Reading Advisory Board will find criteria to review program assessment and to evaluate individual student status. In columns on the right, participants may wish to check whether present standardized testing is fully implemented, partially implemented, minimally implemented, or not implemented.

Criteria are:	Thoroughly Implemented	Partially Implemented	Minimally Implemented	Not Implemented
	4	3	2	1
1. Standardized reading achievement testing provides data to judge how well the program meets its goals	☐	☐	☐	☐
2. Standardized test selection is based on the congruence of tests with the district's reading curriculum	☐	☐	☐	☐
3. Test results seem valid (accurate) and reliable (dependable) for the school, for each class, and for individuals	☐	☐	☐	☐
4. Test batteries are selected to yield accurate, non-inflated results	☐	☐	☐	☐
5. Test batteries are selected to remain current across time to permit assessment of the program with a stable testing foundation	☐	☐	☐	☐
6. Timing of test administration supports continuity of assessment; i.e., tests given at the same grade levels and at the same time of the year	☐	☐	☐	☐
7. Teachers, counselors, and administrators acknowledge a high correspondence between test results and classroom performance	☐	☐	☐	☐
8. Test batteries are chosen to provide optimal information in minimal testing time	☐	☐	☐	☐
9. Testing systems are chosen for optimal personnel efficiency; administration, scoring, and interpretation	☐	☐	☐	☐
10. Staff development is offered by publishers upon purchase to help faculty and administrators to use and interpret test results	☐	☐	☐	☐
11. The faculty understands the concept of standard error of measurement and can identify the error of appropriate grade levels, subtests, and individuals	☐	☐	☐	☐
12. The faculty understands that approximately one-third of subtest scores on a class summary sheet are substantially inaccurate	☐	☐	☐	☐
13. The faculty is aware that standardized test data are more useful to make program and class decisions than for making individual judgments	☐	☐	☐	☐

–continues–

Standardized Achievement Tests in Reading Program Assessment -continued-	4	3	2	1

14. Attempts are made to consider program success in comparison with student intellectual and economic capabilities; i.e., high economic level, high achievement; low economic level, low in school .... ☐ ☐ ☐ ☐

15. Substantial discrepancies between capability and achievement, high ability, low achievement, are used to screen students for Chapter I and district-financed remedial reading program .... ☐ ☐ ☐ ☐

16. Administrators and faculty together plot school progress year-by-year to monitor program effectiveness... ☐ ☐ ☐ ☐

17. The principal sets aside a faculty meeting upon receipt of test scores to interpret school achievement data for the faculty .... ☐ ☐ ☐ ☐

18. The principal schedules a conference with each faculty member to interpret class and individual data... ☐ ☐ ☐ ☐

19. Item analyses are provided for the school and for each class to aid personnel in monitoring content taught well and content in need of more careful attention .... ☐ ☐ ☐ ☐

20. Item analyses aid teachers to monitor content learned by each student and content in need of further instruction .... ☐ ☐ ☐ ☐

21. The format is efficient for record keeping and entering data into pupil cumulative records... ☐ ☐ ☐ ☐

22. Guidelines are provided for teachers to interpret results at parent-teacher conferences .... ☐ ☐ ☐ ☐

23. A summary and interpretation is provided for the family of each student who was given achievement tests .... ☐ ☐ ☐ ☐

Cover the page at this point and below before photocopying if users are not to see the interpretation until later.

Interpretation: To make judgments about how well achievement test data are used to assess reading program and student progress, check marks on the questionnaire may be totaled. Four points may be given to *thoroughly implemented*, three points to *partially implemented*, two to *minimally implemented*, and one point to *not implemented*. Scores between 70–92 may be considered *thoroughly implemented*, between 47–69 *partially implemented*, between 24–46 *minimally implemented*, and between 1–23 *not implemented*.

The principal may wish to make personal use of the form for self-reflection, or may choose to ask building employees to complete the form, using collective scores to make judgments about achievement test use. If the latter is used, the two paragraphs on this page might be deleted from the photocopied form.

PERFORMANCE ASSESSMENT AND THE READING CURRICULUM (see Form 5.4)

Authentic assessment is direct, and removes those risks that come with inferred evaluation. Standardized or mastery testing that samples student performance, in contrast, sometimes results in inaccurate student outcomes, or even errors in interpretation. Present theory prefers "multiple measures" of assessment, of which performance assessment complements other sources.

The Problem: At the present time, many teachers may have little knowledge about performance assessment. The need for staff development, therefore, may be evident if school districts expect teacher implementation. In order to secure teacher ownership, many districts will need to address the time demands warranted.

Rationale: The complexity of learning to read and write is multi-dimensional and multi-faceted—an ongoing, continuous orchestrational process calling for realistic monitoring. Thus, performance assessment is founded on teacher- and self-judgments about the direct work of students. The concept nurtures teachers' assessment of each learner while teaching, along with saving work samples in portfolios for later evaluation (87, 215).

Procedures: Administrators, Advisory Board members, and particularly individual faculty members may determine strengths and weakness by totaling sections of worksheets, and by "eyeing" responses to specific items.

For Further Reading

Hill, B. C. & Ruptic, C. (1994). *Practical Aspects of Authentic Assessment: Putting the Pieces Together*. Norwood, MA: Christopher-Gordon Publishers, Inc. (480 Washington Street, Norwood, MA 02062. 617-762-5577.)

> The authors provide balanced background and thinking about authentic assessment. Forms support performance judgments on emergent literacy, writing, reading, spelling, and content reading. Organization of assessment processes is described.

Valencia, S. W., et al. (1994). *Authentic Reading Assessment: Practices and Possibilities*. Newark, DE: International Reading Association. (800 Barksdale Road, P.O. Box 8139, Newark, DE 19714-8139. 1-800-336-READ.)

> The text begins and ends with chapters describing the assessment reform movement. The authors present nine case studies to interpret authentic assessment. Those studies are written by educators *in the trenches*. Challenges facing this reform movement are interpreted.

Form 5.4
PERFORMANCE/PORTFOLIO ASSESSMENT

Directions: Below, administrators, Reading Advisory Boards, and faculty will find criteria related to performance, or authentic assessment. On the right, respondents may check the extent of implementation in the local school or classroom.

Criteria:	Thoroughly Implemented	Partially Implemented	Minimally Implemented	Not Implemented
	4	3	2	1

Purposes of authentic assessment

1. Improves instruction, augments pupil learning, and supports reporting to others .... ☐ ☐ ☐ ☐

2. Demands a focus on student construction of meaning (comprehension) from texts .... ☐ ☐ ☐ ☐

3. Complements the idea of multiple measures of assessment, alongside other accepted and conventional forms .... ☐ ☐ ☐ ☐

4. Links literacy assessment to classroom teaching and practice; i.e., merges instruction and assessment .... ☐ ☐ ☐ ☐

5. Provides instructional outcomes that reflect current theories and research on learning to read and write .... ☐ ☐ ☐ ☐

6. Collects authentic information for each student's literacy development .... ☐ ☐ ☐ ☐

7. Creates instruments of political change to reform reading and writing instruction .... ☐ ☐ ☐ ☐

8. Recognizes that teachers, schools, and/or districts may be "jarred into action" by external forces to change local instruction .... ☐ ☐ ☐ ☐

Interpretation: Districts considering performance assessment, seeking to weigh its purposes, may tally columns in Form 5.4, giving four points to *thoroughly implemented*, three points to *partially implemented*, two to *minimally implemented*, and one point to *not implemented*. Totals between 25–32 may be regarded as *fully implemented*, between 17–24 *partially implemented*, between 9–16 *minimally implemented*, and 1–8 *not implemented*.

–continues–

Performance/Portfolio Assessment	-continued-	4	3	2	1

Content of authentic assessment

Student Contributions to Portfolios

1. Responses to reading, including literature logs, response journals, story frames, story maps, etc. .... ☐ ☐ ☐ ☐

2. Written retellings using story frames .... ☐ ☐ ☐ ☐

3. Periodic writing samples .... ☐ ☐ ☐ ☐

4. Individual and group compositions .... ☐ ☐ ☐ ☐

5. Students' published books .... ☐ ☐ ☐ ☐

6. Think-aloud protocols .... ☐ ☐ ☐ ☐

7. Video or audio tapes and photo-documentation of cooperative and individual reading .... ☐ ☐ ☐ ☐

8. Pupil notes about their own reading and and writing development .... ☐ ☐ ☐ ☐

9. Lists or card packs of materials read, such as stories during direct instruction, enrichment reading, resource reading, recreational reading, poetry, plays, readers' theater, etc. .... ☐ ☐ ☐ ☐
    ☐ ☐ ☐ ☐

10. Lists or card packs of items read at home for recreation, information, homework, etc. .... ☐ ☐ ☐ ☐

11. Summary analyses of process and product of cooperative learning projects ☐ ☐ ☐ ☐

12. Reading attitude and interest inventories entered periodically across the year .... ☐ ☐ ☐ ☐

13. Checksheets to assess curriculum participation (Forms 5.6–5.13) .... ☐ ☐ ☐ ☐

Interpretation: Personnel considering the content of portfolios may tally columns, giving four points to *fully implemented*, three points to *partially implemented*, two to *minimally implemented*, and one point to *not implemented*. Totals between 40–52 may be considered *fully implemented*, between 27–39 *partially implemented*, between 14–26 *minimally implemented*, and between 1–13 *not implemented*.

–continues–

Performance/Portfolio Assessment -continued-	4	3	2	1

Teacher Contributions to Portfolios

	4	3	2	1
1. Observational checklists	☐	☐	☐	☐
2. Conference forms	☐	☐	☐	☐
3. Interview forms	☐	☐	☐	☐
4. Anecdotal summaries	☐	☐	☐	☐
5. Checklists to judge congruence of literacy development with school curriculum (Forms 5.6–5.13)	☐	☐	☐	☐
6. Running records of oral reading to assess *the process* of reading	☐	☐	☐	☐
7. Required school forms	☐	☐	☐	☐
8. District-developed formative assessments	☐	☐	☐	☐
9. District-developed summative assessments	☐	☐	☐	☐

Interpretation: To judge teacher contributions to pupil portfolios, columns may be tallied, giving four points to *fully implemented*, three to *partially implemented*, two to *minimally implemented*, and one point to *not implemented*. Totals between 28–36 may be considered *fully implemented*, those between 19—27 *partially implemented*, between 10–18 *minimally implemented*, and between 1–9 *not implemented*

–continues–

		4	3	2	1
Performance/Portfolio Assessment	-continued-				

Management of authentic assessment

Teachers Establish the Goals for Portfolio Assessment

1. Help students decide *why* they will generate portfolios .... ☐ ☐ ☐ ☐

2. Help students to select samples of work which show that they can read, comprehend, interpret, and evaluate written content .... ☐ ☐ ☐ ☐

3. Enable students to hold positive attitudes and feel motivated to read .... ☐ ☐ ☐ ☐

Teachers and Pupils, in Conjunction, Select the Content/Data for Portfolios

4. Choose content that demonstrates reading growth .... ☐ ☐ ☐ ☐

5. Identify samples that display writing development .... ☐ ☐ ☐ ☐

6. Enter informal measures of comprehending which display growth .... ☐ ☐ ☐ ☐

7. Create or select reading development checklists .... ☐ ☐ ☐ ☐

Teachers Develop Summary Sheets to Synthesize Information Contained in Portfolios

8. Use accepted criteria for adding new pieces to the portfolio and deleting the old .... ☐ ☐ ☐ ☐

9. Generate student responsibility and skills to maintain the portfolio .... ☐ ☐ ☐ ☐

10. Develop the importance of student and teacher collaboration on portfolio use .... ☐ ☐ ☐ ☐

Interpretation: To judge portfolio management, participants may total the columns above, giving four points to *fully implemented*, three to *partially implemented*, two to *minimally implemented*, and one to *not implemented*. Totals between 31–40 may be regarded as *fully implemented*, between 21–30 *partially implemented*, between 11–20 *minimally implemented*, and between 1–10 *not implemented*.

–continues–

Performance/Portfolio Assessment   -continued-

	4	3	2	1

Evaluation of authentic assessment

Student-related Criteria   ☐ ☐ ☐ ☐

1. Focus on what students actually *do* in classrooms ....   ☐ ☐ ☐ ☐

2. Has the construction of meaning as the undergirding theme of portfolios ...   ☐ ☐ ☐ ☐

3. Display a collection of student reading responses and writing samples to demonstrate developmental literacy growth ....   ☐ ☐ ☐ ☐

4. Show fluency and automaticity over time with advancing text difficulty ....   ☐ ☐ ☐ ☐

5. Collect higher-level literary responses representing higher-order thinking ....   ☐ ☐ ☐ ☐

6. Display outcomes of collaborative learning, discovery learning, inquiry processes, and problem-solving ....   ☐ ☐ ☐ ☐

7. Evaluate both processes *and* products of reading and writing ....   ☐ ☐ ☐ ☐

8. Nurture students' active involvement and empowerment ....   ☐ ☐ ☐ ☐

9. Give evidence that student transfer of learning to real-world contexts exists   ☐ ☐ ☐ ☐

10. Provide a strong feedback function for pupil self-evaluation and growth plans ....   ☐ ☐ ☐ ☐

11. Assure equity, fairness, and accuracy for each student being assessed .....   ☐ ☐ ☐ ☐

12. Generate assessment data that closely parallels reading and writing instruction ....   ☐ ☐ ☐ ☐

Interpretation: To judge student-related criteria for portfolio success, totals may be calculated for each column, giving four points to *thoroughly implemented*, three to *partially implemented*, two to *minimally implemented*, and one point to *not implemented*. Totals between 37–48 may be considered *thoroughly implemented*, between 25–36 *partially implemented*, between 13–24 *minimally implemented*, and between 1–12 as *not implemented*.

–continues–

Performance/Portfolio Assessment	-continued-	4	3	2	1

Program-related Criteria

1. Underscore specific forms and procedures that must be decided upon, developed, and revised in the local setting .... ☐ ☐ ☐ ☐

2. Recognize performance assessment as a growing, evolving process that does not begin in full-blown fashion .... ☐ ☐ ☐ ☐

3. Bridge the demands of being useful and manageable inside classrooms, yet meaningful and interpretable outside the classroom; representing both assessment *and* accountability .... ☐ ☐ ☐ ☐

4. Optimize student learning objectives from the school district curriculum ..... ☐ ☐ ☐ ☐

5. Warrants step-by-step implementation that can be handled by classroom teachers in typical settings... ☐ ☐ ☐ ☐

6. Acknowledge the role of staff development to understand the *why*s and *how*s of authentic assessment.. ☐ ☐ ☐ ☐

7. Review periodically the methods of collecting data and the value of the actual data collected .... ☐ ☐ ☐ ☐

8. Encourage an assessment process that underscores higher levels of literacy learning... ☐ ☐ ☐ ☐

Interpretation: Schools planning to judge effectiveness of their performance assessment status may tally columns, giving four points to *fully implemented*, three points to *partially implemented*, two to *minimally implemented*, and one point to *not implemented*. Totals between 32–25 may be judged *fully implemented*, between 17–24 *partially implemented*, 9–16 *minimally implemented*, and 1–8 *not implemented*.

BASAL READER/LITERATURE-BASED ASSESSMENTS   (see Form 5.5)

The popularity of recent text-based end-of-unit, end-of-level reading tests has been supported by concepts of mastery learning, criterion-referenced tests, and public demand for school accountability. Reading test publishers may offer mastery tests, unstructured portfolio and journal writing packages, or some combination. The degree of acceptance of literature-based reading instruction may affect district selection of text-based assessments.

The Problem: Traditionally, districts have delivered curriculum-centered reading and writing programs; presently there is growing "grass-roots" interest in child-centered reading and writing. Many districts may have to alter teachers' belief systems through staff development if child-centered assessment is to flourish. The second problem is that mastery-type tests deal better with assessment of basic reading skills than with higher-level comprehension and text-thinking, viewed as a national need.

Rationale: School people and taxpayers may wish to know how well students progress through the curriculum. Whenever textbook programs are purchased, districts often purchase accompanying end-of-unit, end-of-level tests. Districts seem to trust publishers to use "experts" to develop and field-test those instruments, resulting in assumed credibility and accountability.

Procedures: Participants may complete Form 5.5 to explore criteria to select textbook-based tests. In order to consider the content of textbook-based assessments, please refer to Forms 5.6–5.13, content basic to reading programs, no matter what reading approach is used locally.

For Further Reading

Harp, B. (Ed.). (1994). *Assessment and Evaluation for Student Centered Learning: Expanded Professional Version, Second Edition.* Norwood, MA: Christopher-Gordon Publishers, Inc. (480 Washington Street, Norwood, MA 02062. 617-762-5577.)

An overview of background, concepts, tools, and strategies to make authentic assessment and evaluation functional in classrooms. Holistic assessment is described for primary, intermediate, bilingual, multicultural, and special education classes.

Valencia, S. W. & Greer, E. A. (1992). "Basal Assessment Systems: It's Not the Shoes," *The Reading Teacher,* 45, 8, 650–651

The authors develop a case for the use of *multiple measures* of reading. Their survey reports suggest that teachers use widely tests accompanying basal readers. Valencia and Greer then go ahead to describe components of three basal publishers' current assessment programs.

Form 5.5
BASAL READER/LITERATURE-BASED ASSESSMENTS

Directions: Schools often select text-based tests corresponding with new purchases of basal or literature-based programs. Below, participants will find criteria related to choices of tests. On the right, Reading Advisory Board members, principals, or faculty may judge the extent to which a criterion was implemented in present assessments options.

Test selection criteria:	Thoroughly Implemented	Partially Implemented	Minimally Implemented	Not Implemented
	4	3	2	1
1. Textbook-based reading program assessment is considered only one of the multiple measures of evaluation used to monitor pupil progress	☐	☐	☐	☐
2. The content of tests actually assesses those reading program components that school people and the community wish to know about	☐	☐	☐	☐
3. The content of text-based tests measures pupil success when learning the district's curriculum	☐	☐	☐	☐
4. The publisher addresses the concept that criterion-tests measure specific items or basic skills effectively, yet are not able to assess higher-level comprehension or thinking about text	☐	☐	☐	☐
5. Congruence is high between test content and the reading program's scope and sequence	☐	☐	☐	☐
6. Content of tests is sequenced carefully to correspond with the order of instruction in reading classes	☐	☐	☐	☐
7. Items throughout the test battery are field-tested and offer evidence of content validity and reliability	☐	☐	☐	☐
8. Assessments help teachers to identify both the strengths *and* needs of pupils	☐	☐	☐	☐
9. Formats of tests are direct, easy for pupils to follow, and easy to score	☐	☐	☐	☐
10. Pupil performance is compared with the objectives of instruction vs the performance of classmates	☐	☐	☐	☐
11. Performance is set against some standard, or criterion; i.e., perhaps 75 or 80 percent success	☐	☐	☐	☐
12. Publishers describe the role of test instruments as pre- or post-tests, or both	☐	☐	☐	☐

–continues–

Basal Reader/Literature-Based Assessments -continued-	4	3	2	1
13. Adequate numbers of assessments of any one skill are provided so that a teacher may feel confident that a student can use that skill in any context ..	☐	☐	☐	☐
14. Teachers are given indications of when students may proceed to the next unit of instruction, or whether reteaching is warranted	☐	☐	☐	☐
15. Success of students corresponds well enough with actual pupil performance in class that classroom teachers in ordinary settings may have confidence in the instruments; i.e., redibility exists	☐	☐	☐	☐
16. Formats are provided that make it easy to counsel with students about strengths and needs, then to plan jointly how the student will proceed	☐	☐	☐	☐
17. Suggestions are given for the teacher to address needs of students who do not perform adequately on particular items and the total end-of-unit, end-of-level tests	☐	☐	☐	☐
18. A simple, useful structure is provided that corresponds with both the curriculum and test instruments for record keeping	☐	☐	☐	☐

Interpretation: Selection committees or Advisory Boards often seek objective criteria to use when choosing text-based tests for reading programs. To aid this process, columns may be totaled, with four points given to *thoroughly implemented*, three points to *partially implemented*, two to *minimally implemented*, and one point to *not implemented*. Totals between 55–72 may be judged *thoroughly implemented*, between 37–54 *partially implemented*, between 19–36 *minimally implemented*, and between 1–18 *not implemented*.

CURRICULUM-BASED ASSESSMENT
OF STUDENT PERFORMANCE

(Forms 5.6 to 5.13)

Some educators have attempted to politicize differences, yet the curriculum and assessment of text-based reading programs and child-centered reading programs are more similar than different. Either creates a focus on meaning, or comprehension, and both support an accelerating reading vocabulary. In child-centered programs, learning is more random, emerging from the social context. In text-based programs, the curriculum may be more pre-planned and comprehensive. Regardless, most districts do operate from either a defined or an implied reading curriculum.

The Problem: Many teachers appear unaware of individual student status and progress, instead teaching "to the group." Teachers often seem to stress some elements of curriculum, disregarding or minimizing other dimensions.

Rationale: District personnel ordinarily want to know if individuals, and the total pupil population, are advancing in narrative and expository text comprehension. A near-universal concern also is pupil success in vocabulary meaning and decoding, writing, and enjoyment of recreational reading. The way a school district assesses its reading curriculum often is the foundation of monitoring individual student growth. Encouraging teachers to be as accurate and objective as possible increases the value of Forms 5.6 to 5.13.

Procedures: Forms 5.6 to 5.13 may be used to monitor individual student progress in the reading program. Reading Advisory Boards, principals, and faculties may review those forms to consider local use, or as a basis to develop local formats. Such forms, completed by teachers, students, or peers, may be entered periodically into individual student portfolios. The next eight forms may be considered one at a time as curriculum elements, or examined collectively to look at individual students' orchestration of the reading process.

Form 5.6
PERIODIC ASSESSMENT: LITERACY EMERGENCE (READING READINESS)

Student _____ Teacher _____ Date _____

☐ teacher assessment   ☐ self-assessment   ☐ peer assessment

	Always	Usually	Sometimes	Never
Reading Process				
Has a sense of *what reading is*	☐	☐	☐	☐
Expects texts to make sense	☐	☐	☐	☐
Uses extensive oral language	☐	☐	☐	☐
Understands words and concepts	☐	☐	☐	☐
Has ability to retell stories	☐	☐	☐	☐
Text Structure Awareness				
Understands story parts (grammars)	☐	☐	☐	☐
Knows reading is for fun *and* information	☐	☐	☐	☐
Aware of left-to-right direction of print	☐	☐	☐	☐
Perceives word boundaries, paragraphs	☐	☐	☐	☐
Knows letter names, spellings, sounds	☐	☐	☐	☐
Developing a sense of phonemic awareness	☐	☐	☐	☐
Strategic Applications				
Participates in group and class reading	☐	☐	☐	☐
Conducts book previews independently	☐	☐	☐	☐
Reads picture books, predictable books	☐	☐	☐	☐
Shares independent reading with peers	☐	☐	☐	☐
Writes about reading and shares the writing	☐	☐	☐	☐
Employs invented spellings when writing	☐	☐	☐	☐
Moves toward spelling approximations	☐	☐	☐	☐

Please place comments on the back of the page.

Form 5.7
PERIODIC ASSESSMENT: NARRATIVE TEXT COMPREHENSION (STORY READING)

Student _____ Teacher _____ Date _____

☐ teacher assessment   ☐ self-assessment   ☐ peer assessment

	Always	Usually	Sometimes	Never
The Process				
Reads fluently, chunks* effectively	☐	☐	☐	☐
Extends reading vocabulary	☐	☐	☐	☐
Uses context clues appropriately	☐	☐	☐	☐
Searches, predicts for meaning	☐	☐	☐	☐
Text Structure				
Uses story structures* such as story	☐	☐	☐	☐
grammars,* frames,* maps*	☐	☐	☐	☐
Uses title, graphics to aid story previews	☐	☐	☐	☐
Strategic Applications				
Applies prior knowledge to the task	☐	☐	☐	☐
Monitors story meanings	☐	☐	☐	☐
Skips unknown words when appropriate	☐	☐	☐	☐
Employs a systematic process when understanding is not reached	☐	☐	☐	☐
Uses main idea and supporting details to understand text structure	☐	☐	☐	☐
Summarizes effectively	☐	☐	☐	☐
Infers beyond print information	☐	☐	☐	☐
Analyzes text information critically	☐	☐	☐	☐
Employs think-alouds* independently	☐	☐	☐	☐
Participates in retellings	☐	☐	☐	☐

Please place comments on the back of the page.

Form 5.8
PERIODIC ASSESSMENT: EXPOSITORY TEXT COMPREHENSION
(CONTENT READING)

Student _____   Teacher _____   Date _____

☐ teacher assessment   ☐ self-assessment   ☐ peer assessment

	Always	Usually	Sometimes	Never
The Process				
Previews, searches total text to be read	☐	☐	☐	☐
Participates in brainstorming,* webbing* to provide text structure	☐	☐	☐	☐
Predicts meaning, surveys text	☐	☐	☐	☐
Applies prior knowledge independently	☐	☐	☐	☐
Confirms or denies predictions	☐	☐	☐	☐
Text Structure				
Gains independence using SQRRR* or other text-reading structure	☐	☐	☐	☐
Able to apply QARs,* PreP*, etc.	☐	☐	☐	☐
Uses text features: graphics, headings, subheads, captions, etc.	☐	☐	☐	☐
Strategic Applications				
Uses DR-TA* and other thinking-about-text structures	☐	☐	☐	☐
Employs text organizers and text overviews	☐	☐	☐	☐
Actively uses ReQuest,* reciprocal teaching,* or other text-integration processes	☐	☐	☐	☐
Integrates K-W-L,* DR-TA* and other predict-confirm structures	☐	☐	☐	☐
Uses compare/contrast (classification)	☐	☐	☐	☐
Discerns cause and effect	☐	☐	☐	☐
Interacts with peers to expand learning	☐	☐	☐	☐

Please place comments on the back of the page

Form 5.9
PERIODIC ASSESSMENT: WRITING ABOUT READING

Student _____ Teacher _____ Date _____

☐ teacher assessment   ☐ self-assessment   ☐ peer assessment

	Always	Usually	Sometimes	Never
Brainstorming*				
Shares existing knowledge on topic or story just read	☐	☐	☐	☐
Uses peer comments to expand knowledge	☐	☐	☐	☐
Webbing*				
Contributes to brainstorming, webbing	☐	☐	☐	☐
Uses the web to organize for writing	☐	☐	☐	☐
Employs web to create paragraphs, sentences	☐	☐	☐	☐
Refers to the web when writing and participating in peer editing	☐	☐	☐	☐
Drafting*				
Creates a draft suited to the lesson goal	☐	☐	☐	☐
Applies all or part of the web to make a draft	☐	☐	☐	☐
Uses story grammars to self-assess	☐	☐	☐	☐
Views the product as a first draft, not a final product	☐	☐	☐	☐
Peer Editing*				
Participates in peer response groups	☐	☐	☐	☐
Accepts ownership for revisions	☐	☐	☐	☐
Outcomes				
Ties writing to text reading	☐	☐	☐	☐
Publishes at appropriate times	☐	☐	☐	☐

Please write comments on the back of the page

Form 5.10
PERIODIC ASSESSMENT: MEANING VOCABULARY

Student _____ Teacher _____ Date _____

☐ teacher assessment ☐ self-assessment ☐ peer assessment

	Always	Usually	Sometimes	Never
Student Goals				
Expresses goals for improved reading vocabulary	☐	☐	☐	☐
Maintains dictionaries, card packs, or journals with vocabulary study words	☐	☐	☐	☐
Contextual Applications				
Uses context to aid word meanings	☐	☐	☐	☐
Skips unknown words when warranted	☐	☐	☐	☐
Word Structures				
Uses root word functions	☐	☐	☐	☐
Analyzes prefixes, suffixes, inflections	☐	☐	☐	☐
Uses appearance plus context to infer word meaning	☐	☐	☐	☐
Text Structure				
Participates in new word introductions	☐	☐	☐	☐
Employs *possible sentence* strategy	☐	☐	☐	☐
Uses advance organizer* formats	☐	☐	☐	☐
Applies structured overview* preteaching	☐	☐	☐	☐
Cognitive Aids				
Uses word maps,* semantic maps	☐	☐	☐	☐
Gains structure from semantic feature forms	☐	☐	☐	☐
Maintains use of word sorts, concept sorts	☐	☐	☐	☐

Please write comments on the back of the page.

Form 5.11
PERIODIC ASSESSMENT LITERATURE-BASED READING AND WRITING

Student _____ Teacher _____ Date _____

☐ teacher assessment   ☐ self-assessment   ☐ peer assessment

	Always	Usually	Sometimes	Never
Organizational Activities				
Productive in collaborative groups	☐	☐	☐	☐
Shares in reader response groups	☐	☐	☐	☐
Contributes to writer response groups	☐	☐	☐	☐
Active in literature set activities	☐	☐	☐	☐
Participates actively in SSR,* DEAR, SSW	☐	☐	☐	☐
Studies Literary Forms/Genre (see Forms 4.13, 7.15)				
Ties modeled genre to written and oral response	☐	☐	☐	☐
Analyzes literary forms, integrates into writing	☐	☐	☐	☐
Pursues Author's Craft (see Forms 4.13, 7.16)				
Understands craft options	☐	☐	☐	☐
Employs options when generating writer's response to literature	☐	☐	☐	☐
Includes craft in journal entries	☐	☐	☐	☐
Uses Writer's Choice (see Forms 4.13, 7.15)				
Analyzes processes employed in literature study	☐	☐	☐	☐
Thinks through options for response group participation	☐	☐	☐	☐
Adapts new skills to classroom writing	☐	☐	☐	☐

Please write comments on the back of the page.

Form 5.12
PERIODIC ASSESSMENT: WORD ANALYSIS

Student_____ Teacher _____ Date _____

☐ teacher assessment   ☐ self-assessment   ☐ peer assessment

	Always	Usually	Sometimes	Never
Monitors Meaning				
Uses strategies vs rules for unknown words	☐	☐	☐	☐
Self-corrects appropriately	☐	☐	☐	☐
Chunks effectively, reads fluently	☐	☐	☐	☐
Expands Basic Vocabulary				
Uses context to identify words	☐	☐	☐	☐
Skips words whenever appropriate	☐	☐	☐	☐
Learns words through shape and function	☐	☐	☐	☐
Maintains word banks of new words	☐	☐	☐	☐
Uses new words in speaking and writing	☐	☐	☐	☐
Analyzes One-syllable Phonic Words				
Tests phonic hypotheses against meaning	☐	☐	☐	☐
Thinks strategically using phonemic awareness	☐	☐	☐	☐
Uses beginning and ending consonants, combinations	☐	☐	☐	☐
Employs stable vowels, disregards others	☐	☐	☐	☐
Avoids mispronunciations (non-words)	☐	☐	☐	☐
Analyzes Two-plus Syllable Words				
Understands compounds, roots, prefixes, suffixes, inflectional endings	☐	☐	☐	☐
Applies vc/cv, v/cv, ?le, patterns to decode two-syllable words	☐	☐	☐	☐

Please place comments on the back of the page.

Form 5.13
PERIODIC ASSESSMENT: RECREATIONAL READING

Student _____ Teacher _____ Date

☐ teacher assessment   ☐ self-assessment   ☐ peer assessment

	Always	Usually	Sometimes	Never
The Process				
Demonstrates ongoing interest in reading for pleasure and information	☐	☐	☐	☐
Expresses pride in reading completed...	☐	☐	☐	☐
Exhibits a wide range of recreational reading interests	☐	☐	☐	☐
Text Structure				
Uses text structures; i.e., titles, illustrations, etc., to aid meaning	☐	☐	☐	☐
Understands literary forms, such as poetic, narrative, etc.	☐	☐	☐	☐
Monitors story grammars, such as setting, plot, characters, problem resolution...	☐	☐	☐	☐
Reading Growth				
Participates actively in SSR* or DEAR*	☐	☐	☐	☐
Shares with peers during *book talks*...	☐	☐	☐	☐
Supports group tasks in *literature set* activities	☐	☐	☐	☐
Maintains a reflective reading response journal	☐	☐	☐	☐
Enjoys preferred genre and expands reading interests	☐	☐	☐	☐
Has developed favorite authors who are often chosen..	☐	☐	☐	☐
Makes deliberate efforts to expand knowledge, enjoy reading, and read better	☐	☐	☐	☐

Please place comments on the back of the page.

COACHING STUDENTS FOR TEST-TAKING   (see Form 5.14)

Despite the strong professional call for performance assessment, perhaps nothing strikes more fear into the hearts of school superintendents, school boards, and principals than do state-mandated or standardized achievement results displayed prominently on the front page of the local newspaper. Collectively, there is a goal of making schools *look good* and many educational leaders *want those scores up* almost more than anything.

The Problem: Staff development often has not dealt with the concept of helping teachers help students to take important tests successfully. Rather than teaching process-based strategies that would increase student reading and writing performance, teachers often feel pressured to spend weeks rehearsing test-taking practices with their classes.

Rationale: School personnel desire to gain an optimal performance from students as they complete important tests. Students who do not know how to participate in test-taking in a systematic, effective way may penalize their own status, as well as that of their school. At some point between teaching test-taking skills and reducing test-anxiety that diminishes results is an appropriate place to educate teachers on supporting students as they take tests.

Procedures: Faculties, principals, or Reading Advisory Boards may use Form 5.14 to examine the extent of coaching for test-taking within the school. Content of Form 5.14 might be studied and discussed at faculty meetings within districts prior to administration of standardized reading tests or state-mandated tests.

For Further Reading

Kilian, L. J. (1992). "A School District Perspective on Appropriate Test-Preparation Practices . . .," *Educational Measurement: Issues and Practices*, 11, 4, 13–15+.

> Kilian addresses concerns about appropriate test preparation. He suggests guidelines to prepare for and administer high-stakes tests in school settings.

Stewart, O. & Green, D. S. (1983). "Test-taking Skills for Standardized Tests of Reading," *The Reading Teacher*, 36, 7, 634–39.

> The authors assert that pupils' performance on tests can be improved with practice. Stewart and Green recommend that teachers assign tasks that are similar to test formats. Simulations are recommended well in advance of serious tests. An extensive set of recommendations is provided.

◊

Form 5.14
COACHING STUDENTS FOR TEST-TAKING

Directions: Many students benefit from instruction, or coaching, in test-taking skills. Those skills help with taking standardized achievement tests, state-mandated assessment, or curriculum-based tests. Below, participants will find statements related to such coaching. On the right, principals, faculty members, or Reading Advisory Board members will find places to check for local implementation.

Test-coaching criteria:	Thoroughly Implemented	Partially Implemented	Minimally Implemented	Not Implemented
	4	3	2	1

1. *Understanding purposes of the test(s):*

a. Understand how the results will be used to assess individual pupils ...... ☐ ☐ ☐ ☐

b. Evaluate how well the district program is doing .... ☐ ☐ ☐ ☐

c. Provide information about instruction across the state (if state-mandated) .... ☐ ☐ ☐ ☐

2. *Attitudes toward the test affect results:*

a. Coach the class during preparation for tests, as well as during tests, to influence students' development of positive attitudes .... ☐ ☐ ☐ ☐

b. Balance the benefit to pupils of knowing that the test is important, yet avoid anxiety levels that reduce performance .... ☐ ☐ ☐ ☐

c. Encourage students with low expectations toward test performance to increase their efforts .... ☐ ☐ ☐ ☐

Cover the page at this point and below if use is desired before referring to the interpretation.

Interpretation: Personnel wishing to assess respondents' understanding of test purposes and attitudes toward tests may tally columns in Part 1, giving 4 points to checkmarks in the left column, three to marks in the next column, two to marks in the third column, and one point to checkmarks in the right column. Totals between 10–12 may be considered *thoroughly implemented*, between 7–9 *partially implemented*, 4–6 *minimally implemented*, and 1–3 *not implemented*. The same process and calculations may be followed to gain separate assessments of responses to Part 2, attitudes toward tests.

–continues–

Coaching Students for Test-Taking   -continued-

	4	3	2	1

3. *Practicing test-taking skills:*

a. Practice occasionally throughout the school year on curriculum-based tests structured like the standardized or state-mandated tests that students must take to increase familiarity, confidence, and improved district-level results .... ☐ ☐ ☐ ☐

b. Recognize that test-taking instruction is a periodic part of classroom activities .... ☐ ☐ ☐ ☐

c. Coach students on procedures to use both before and during practice tests .... ☐ ☐ ☐ ☐

d. Review items after practice tests, asking students with correct answers to explain how they chose answers to pupils who missed those items . ☐ ☐ ☐ ☐

e. Administer practice tests at the grade level that will be tested, as well as to students in other grades who may not be tested for a year or two ☐ ☐ ☐ ☐

f. Administer a similar practice test within 1–2 days before official tests .. ☐ ☐ ☐ ☐

g. Develop curriculum-based practice tests in teams who teach the same grade level .... ☐ ☐ ☐ ☐

Cover the page at this point and below if use is desired before referring to the interpretation.

Interpretation: Reading Advisory Boards may summarize responses to Part 3 by tallying checkmarks in columns, giving four points to marks in the left column, three to the next column, two to the third column, and one point to checkmarks in the right column. Totals between 22–28 may be judged *thoroughly implemented*, between 15–21 *partially implemented*, between 8–14 *minimally implemented*, and between 1–7 *not implemented.*

Coaching Students for Test-Taking	-continued-	4	3	2	1

4. *Understanding multiple-choice formats:*

a. Read directions carefully as students follow along .... ☐ ☐ ☐ ☐

b. Ask students to tell them whenever they do not understand directions ☐ ☐ ☐ ☐

c. Ask a student to restate the directions in her/his own words .... ☐ ☐ ☐ ☐

d. Encourage pupils to look at *all* of the possible answers before making a choice .... ☐ ☐ ☐ ☐

e. Teach pupils that on some tests, more than one answer may be correct .... ☐ ☐ ☐ ☐

f. Show students how the best of several correct answers is chosen ...... ☐ ☐ ☐ ☐

g. Model how to disregard items that could not possibly be correct .... ☐ ☐ ☐ ☐

h. Teach that, in some formats, each of the correct answers should be marked .... ☐ ☐ ☐ ☐

i. Show pupils that some choices are deliberate distracters .... ☐ ☐ ☐ ☐

j. Encourage students to read questions more than one time to reach understanding .... ☐ ☐ ☐ ☐

k. Demonstrate for students how to base the answer on as much information as they can "figure out" .... ☐ ☐ ☐ ☐

Cover the page at this point and below if use is desired before referring to the interpretation.

Interpretation: Respondents seeking to assess understanding multiple-choice may tally columns, giving four points to checkmarks in the left column, three to the next column, two to the third column, and one point to checkmarks in the right column. Totals between 34–44 may be viewed as *thoroughly implemented*, between 23–33 *partially implemented*, 12–22 *minimally implemented*, and between 1–11 *not implemented*.

–continues–

Coaching Students for Test-Taking -continued-	4	3	2	1

5. *Marking test items:*

a. Provide students with practice on how to mark separate answer sheets .... ☐ ☐ ☐ ☐

b. Show young students how sometimes the test booklet will have to be folded flat to manage .... ☐ ☐ ☐ ☐

c. Supervise young students when multiple columns are used on answer sheets, showing that they may need to slide the answer sheet under the test booklet to align the correct column .... ☐ ☐ ☐ ☐

d. Monitor pupils to be sure they have marked the right choice on the answer sheet .... ☐ ☐ ☐ ☐

e. Remind pupils that, to stay at the right place on answer sheets, they may need to check the test and answer sheet numbers after each five items .... ☐ ☐ ☐ ☐

f. Model for students that if they skip an item on the test, planning to think further and return to the item, they should also skip that place on the answer sheet .... ☐ ☐ ☐ ☐

g. Instruct pupils that if there are skipped items, they should mark lightly at that place on the booklet and go back later to reconsider the item .... ☐ ☐ ☐ ☐

h. Ask students to make no extraneous marks on the answer sheet, but instead on scratch paper .... ☐ ☐ ☐ ☐

i. Assure students that, if answers are changed, erasures should be made carefully .... ☐ ☐ ☐ ☐

j. Ask students to not "give up," but to try to keep doing as much as possible .... ☐ ☐ ☐ ☐

k. Tell pupils, whenever time remains, the importance of double-checking any answers they felt uncertain about .... ☐ ☐ ☐ ☐

l. Encourage students to double-check their work whenever time is available .... ☐ ☐ ☐ ☐

m. Teach students a "searching" attitude when the test is becoming unduly difficult, skimming the balance to see if there are parts they can answer .... ☐ ☐ ☐ ☐

n. Coach pupils on making reasonable guesses if no penalties are given for guesses that are missed .... ☐ ☐ ☐ ☐

–continues–

Coaching Students for Test-Taking	-continued-	4	3	2	1

6. *Budgeting time to complete tests:*

   a. Show students that tests are easiest at the beginning, becoming more difficult as the end is approached .... ☐ ☐ ☐ ☐

   b. Administer practice tests with time limits, particularly to young students without prior test experience .... ☐ ☐ ☐ ☐

   c. Explain to pupils that they should sit and think for two minutes to "feel" how long that amount of time seems.. ☐ ☐ ☐ ☐

   d. Deliver a *two minute warning* to show the the amount of time remaining ☐ ☐ ☐ ☐

   e. Remind the class when ten, twenty, and twenty-five minutes have passed, to practice pacing.. ☐ ☐ ☐ ☐

   f. Teach pupils to work deliberately and not rush, yet keep moving along . ☐ ☐ ☐ ☐

Cover the page at this point and below if use is desired before referring to the interpretation.

Interpretation: Those seeking analysis of Part 5, marking test items, may tally columns, giving four points to marks in the left column, three to the next column, two to the third column, and one to the right column. Totals between 43–56 may be considered *thoroughly implemented*, between 29–42 *partially implemented*, 15–28 *minimally implemented*, and 1–14 *not implemented*. Part 6 is similarly tallied. In Part 6, budgeting time, totals between 19–24 are judged *thoroughly implemented*, between 13–18 *partially implemented*, 7–12 *minimally implemented*, and between 1–6 *not implemented*.

Coaching Students for Test-Taking   -continued-

| | 4 | 3 | 2 | 1 |

7. *Spreading out the testing "load":*

   a. Recognize that students with state-mandated, standardized, and curriculum-based tests may be involved with a lot of hours of testing .... ☐ ☐ ☐ ☐

   b. Note that it is important to avoid both teacher and student test "burn out" .... ☐ ☐ ☐ ☐

   c. Observe that primary grade students should be involved in no more than one hour of testing per day, spread over a.m. and p.m. .... ☐ ☐ ☐ ☐

   d. Realize that intermediate students should have no more than one hour of testing in the morning and another hour of testing in the afternoon of test days .... ☐ ☐ ☐ ☐

   e. Recognize that exceeding reasonable time limits reduces test accuracy, and results in lower achievement than the actual status .... ☐ ☐ ☐ ☐

   f. Agree that testing should be scheduled for Tuesdays, Wednesdays, and Thursdays, avoiding first and last days of school weeks .... ☐ ☐ ☐ ☐

Cover the page at this point and below if use is desired before referring to interpretation.

Interpretation: Personnel wishing to assess spreading out the testing load may give four points to each response in the first column, three points to checkmarks in the second column, two to choices in the third column, and one point to responses in the last column. Scores between 19 and 24 may signify that the criterion is *thoroughly implemented.* Those totals between 13 and 18 suggest that this criterion is *partially implemented.* Scores between 7 and 12 may show that *minimally implemented* is the status. Sums between 1 and 6 may suggest that *not implemented* is the condition.

SYNTHESIS OF READING PROGRAM ASSESSMENT   (see Form 5.15)

Reading assessment has received recent, widespread attention. The forces of authentic-portfolio-performance assessment have led educators to rethink reading evaluation, going beyond standardized and text-based tests. A strong call is being made for the use of multiple measures of reading.

The Problem: Teachers often have not monitored just how well students are reading and writing. Standardized reading tests provide little instructionally specific information. State-mandated tests tend to report only how well reading programs in districts and schools are functioning, but provide little individual pupil feedback. Text-based tests are widely used, measuring the elements, but not the process of reading.

Rationale: A fully functioning reading assessment plan may provide evidence of reading status and advancement of each pupil. As well, aggregated data may reflect on overall reading curriculum effectiveness. Finally, each teacher may use assessment information to reflect on the quality of instruction.

Procedures: The Reading Advisory Board, faculty, or principal may re-examine all of the forms in Chapter 5, but especially Form 5.15, to summarize reading assessment internally. After reviewing forms in Chapter 3 on needs-assessment and program-planning processes, deliberations about Form 5.16 in Chapter 5 may be reconsidered in the context of curriculum and program goals. Substantial discussion and input from faculty, staff, parents, and community members is warranted to determine strengths, needs, but particularly, priorities. A plan-of-action to fulfill goals and needs regarding reading assessment may be found in Form 5.17. The Advisory Board may use the form as a path to undergo program improvement processes.

Form 5.15
SYNTHESIS OF READING PROGRAM ASSESSMENT

Directions: Basic elements of reading assessment programs are found throughout Chapter 5 and below. On the right, principals, Reading Advisory Board members, or faculty may check their view of the element's status in the local school. Respondents may feel free to refer back to forms presented throughout Chapter 5.

Criteria:

	Thoroughly Implemented	Partially Implemented	Minimally Implemented	Not Implemented
	4	3	2	1
1. Various options for assessment of the reading program have been considered (see Form 5.2)	☐	☐	☐	☐
2. The place of standardized reading achievement testing has been reviewed (see Form 5.3)	☐	☐	☐	☐
3. Performance assessment, portfolios, have been judged for congruence with the reading program (see Form 5.4)	☐	☐	☐	☐
4. Those assessments accompanying both basal reading texts and literature-based text series have been considered (see Form 5.5)	☐	☐	☐	☐
5. Assessment of individual student performance to address curriculum demands has been reviewed (see Forms 5.6–5.13)	☐	☐	☐	☐
6. The role of coaching for test-taking has been given appropriate deliberation (see Form 5.14)	☐	☐	☐	☐

Interpretation: Advisory Boards, faculties, or principals who seek to gain closure on local program assessment components may give four points to each checkmark in the first column, three in the second column, two for the third column, and one point for the fourth column. Totals between 22–28 may be judged *thoroughly implemented*, between 15–21 *partially implemented*, between 8–14 *minimally implemented*, and between 1–7, *no implementation.*

Form 5.16

READING ASSESSMENT: STRENGTHS, NEEDS, AND PRIORITIES

Directions: Below, respondents will find on the left elements of many reading program assessment packages. On the right, space is provided to enter present program strengths, needs, and priorities based on the interpretation of Form 5.15.

1. Reading Assessment Options	*Strengths* 1. 2.	*Needs* 1. 2.	*Priorities* 1. 2.
2. Standardized Reading Tests	*Strengths* 1. 2.	*Needs* 1. 2.	*Priorities* 1. 2.
3. Performance Assessment	*Strengths* 1. 2.	*Needs* 1. 2.	*Priorities* 1. 2.
4. Basal and Literature-based Assessment	*Strengths* 1. 2.	*Needs* 1. 2.	*Priorities* 1. 2.
5. Curriculum-based Student Performance	*Strengths* 1. 2.	*Needs* 1. 2.	*Priorities* 1. 2.
6. Coaching for Test-taking	*Strengths* 1. 2.	*Needs* 1. 2.	*Priorities* 1. 2.

Form 5.17
READING ASSESSMENT: PLAN-OF-ACTION

Directions: Principals, Reading Advisory Boards, or faculty who wish to develop a focus on professional growth in reading assessment leadership may benefit from being as specific as possible about what they seek to accomplish, how they will go about attaining growth, and how they will know when they have reached their goals. Reference to Form 5.15 and Form 5.16 may help to summarize, then set strengths, weaknesses, and priorities of reading assessment. A review of Form 5.16 may lead the Board or principal to identify goals to pursue in the plan-of-action. Statements entered should be as simple as warranted and as useful as possible.

1. Goal Statement: _____

2. Objectives:

    a) _____

    b) _____

    c) _____

3. Activities: Dates; time checkpoints:

    a) _____   * _____

    b) _____   * _____

    c) _____   * _____

    d) _____   * _____

    e) _____   * _____

4. Resources: (professional reading, consultation, visitations)

    a) _____   * _____

    b) _____   * _____

    c) _____   * _____

5. How I will know when my goal is accomplished:

_____

_____

_____

_____

CHAPTER 6

APPROACHES TO READING INSTRUCTION

Curriculum scholars caution that alternative approaches seem to represent frustrations with basal readers and attempts to provide increased curricular options. Each approach holds numerous strengths and advantages along with learning and curriculum flaws. Short-term innovations, likewise, do contain faults. The enduring approaches seem to ease teaching efforts and make the most economical use of teachers' time. The challenge apparently is to get faculties to search all of the options and to select programs and components that best address local needs.

Fundamental beliefs, goals, materials, methodologies, and assessment processes vary from one reading approach to another. The most popular approaches may be basal reader systems, literature-based textbooks, whole language, and the language experience approach (see Form 6.1). The current, prevailing iteration of basal readers is the literature-based textbook series. Recent influences of whole language and cognitive science are changing the way many teachers operate and the ways reading textbooks are used.

A strong case has been developed that liberal vs conservative swings occur in American institutions in about 30-year cycles (171). This stance may be interpreted to support the revolving-cycles concept related to American reading instruction (181, 191). Seasoned observers affirm this pattern, noting that current innovations have their roots in programs that appeared about thirty and sixty years ago. Child-centered reading programs were represented by progressive education, individualized reading, language-experience, and open education. Present related concepts are founded on cognitive science, linguistic studies, and whole language. Even so, the majority of teachers continue to develop curricula using reading textbooks.

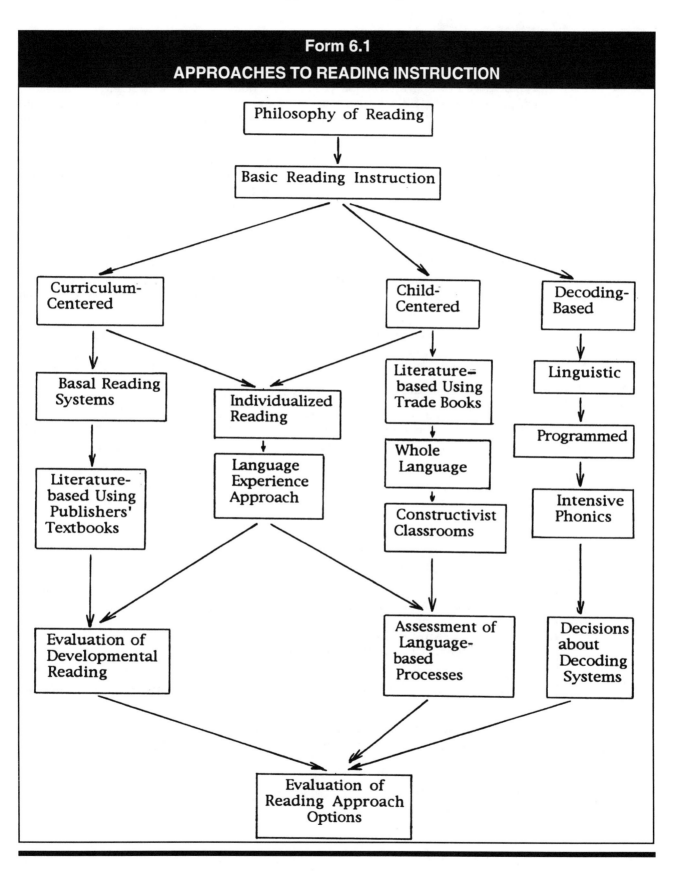

Form 6.1

APPROACHES TO READING INSTRUCTION

OVERVIEW OF APPROACHES TO READING
(see Form 6.2)

The statement in *Becoming a Nation of Readers* that "the observation that basal programs 'drive' reading instruction is not to be taken lightly" characterizes American reading instruction. Influences of cognitive science and whole language may have contributed to the shift now occurring in literature-based teachers' manuals and the content of children's texts.

The Problem: Many teachers who have taught the same program for several years, or their principal, motivated by a desire for higher achievement test results, seek alternatives. The quest for the perfect program may lead schools to *throw out the baby with the bath water* periodically, voiding effective and unsuccessful components alike, then starting over, and in a few years, starting over again, jumping on endless *bandwagons*, yet finding little improvement.

Rationale: Schools benefit from using research bases and reasoned searches to select reading programs and components that best meet the needs of local students. Local schools may review all of the curriculum options, finally selecting a needs-grounded program (see Chapter 3).

Procedures: Participants may complete Form 6.2 to gain overall status views, then complete Forms 6.3 to 6.5 to consider suitability of the most popular reading curriculum options, and finally Form 6.6 to judge congruence of curriculum and approaches.

For Further Reading

Anderson, R. *et al.* (Eds.). 1985. *Becoming a Nation of Readers*. Washington, D.C.: The National Institute of Education. (International Reading Association, 800 Barksdale Road, P.O. Box 8139, Newark, DE 19714-8139. 1-800-336-READ or 302-731-1600.)

A state-of-the-art publication supported by the National Institute of Education. The authors developed the concept that grasping meaning and efficient word recognition were companion processes. The authors studied environmental influences, teaching strategies and tools, and assessment.

Lehr, F. & Osborn, J. (Eds.). (1994). *Reading, Language, and Literacy: Instruction for the Twenty-First Century*. Hillsdale, NJ: Lawrence Erlbaum Associates, Inc. (365 Broadway, Hillsdale, NJ 07642. 201-666-4110.)

The text emerged from a combined meeting of the School Division of the Association of American Publishers, International Reading Association, and Center for the Study of Reading. Contributors attempted to bring together the best available research evidence about the teaching of reading and how children learn to read, bridging the various instructional approaches.

Smith, N. B. (1963). *Reading Instruction for Today's Children*. Englewood Cliffs, NJ: Prentice-Hall, Inc., pp. 78–107. (Out of print, but found in many university education libraries.)

Smith chose to acquaint preservice and inservice teachers with theory and research, applying those elements to actual teaching. An inclusive classic that contains a section on reading approaches, some current with the book's publication date, some again popular.

Form 6.2

OVERVIEW OF READING APPROACHES

Directions: Each cell below allows for decisions about whether the present approach to reading is effective, and how important that approach will be in the future reading program. On the upper left of each cell below, respondents may judge whether or not the approach is now suitable. On the lower right, judgments may be made about how important the approach will be in the future program. Following the worksheet, decisions may be made about which approaches are most and least suited, then priorities established.

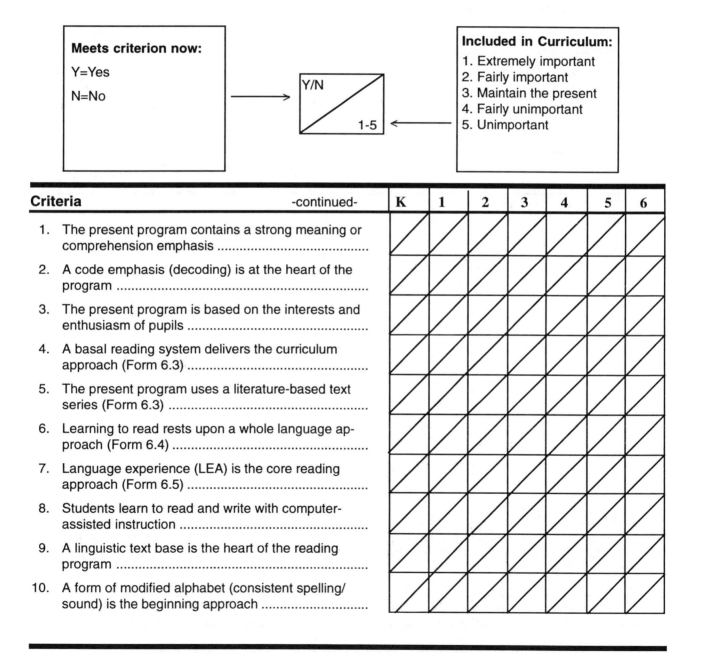

Meets criterion now:

Y=Yes

N=No

Y/N

1-5

Included in Curriculum:

1. Extremely important
2. Fairly important
3. Maintain the present
4. Fairly unimportant
5. Unimportant

Criteria -continued-	K	1	2	3	4	5	6
1. The present program contains a strong meaning or comprehension emphasis							
2. A code emphasis (decoding) is at the heart of the program							
3. The present program is based on the interests and enthusiasm of pupils							
4. A basal reading system delivers the curriculum approach (Form 6.3)							
5. The present program uses a literature-based text series (Form 6.3)							
6. Learning to read rests upon a whole language approach (Form 6.4)							
7. Language experience (LEA) is the core reading approach (Form 6.5)							
8. Students learn to read and write with computer-assisted instruction							
9. A linguistic text base is the heart of the reading program							
10. A form of modified alphabet (consistent spelling/sound) is the beginning approach							

–continues–

Overview of Reading Approaches -continued-	K	1	2	3	4	5	6

11. A self-instructional, programmed format is the basis for learning to read ....

12. Computer-mediated instruction is used supplementally ....

13. An individualized reading approach is the fundamental approach ....

14. Intensive phonics is the fundamental instructional means ....

15. An eclectic approach is employed, combining two or more of the above: ....

16. _____

17. _____

18. _____

Interpretation: The Reading Advisory Board, principal, or faculty which completes Form 6.2 may have a sense of its present reading status, but even more, a strong sense of where it wants its reading program to be in the future. To refine curriculum goals, a Reading Advisory Board may choose to select components from more than one approach.

A solid approach would be to refer back to needs-assessment and program-planning in Chapter 6, data to strengthen present decisions about a basic reading approach, along with program sub-components. Subsequently, referral to Forms 6.2 to 6.6 may expand applications of the reading approach.

BASAL READING/LITERATURE-BASED TEXTBOOKS   (see Form 6.3)

The dominant force in American reading instruction beginning with the McGuffey's Eclectic Primer more than a century ago has been the basal reader. The current iteration, literature-based textbook series, is produced by six to ten major textbook publishers. Estimates across thirty years are that 91 to 96 percent of elementary teachers have taught from reading textbooks.

The Problem: Many American educators believe the time is right to use child-centered vs curriculum-centered mediation to teach children to read and write. Basal readers represent a wholly curriculum-centered approach. A second problem is that many teachers have disregarded the intent of basal texts, asking pupils to read *round robin*, with little direct instruction.

Rationale: Literature-based/basal texts are used by a great majority of elementary-level teachers. Given the widespread popularity of the texts, knowing the current status and trends supports teachers who examine effectiveness, misuses, and shortcomings when updating language arts curricula.

Procedures: A principal, Reading Advisory Board (RAB), teacher, or faculty may wish to gain feedback about strengths and weaknesses of reading texts in the local setting. A RAB may ask participants to complete Form 6.3, perhaps adding criteria 16–30 from Form 6.4, since those criteria now apply to text series. RABs may collate judgments, display findings, set priorities and new goals, and pursue staff development. Whether judging present status or prospective revisions, aggregate data, publicly displayed, should support faculty acceptance.

For Further Reading

Cooper, J. D. (1993). *Literacy: Helping Children Construct Meaning, Second Edition.* Boston: Houghton Mifflin Company. (Wayside Road, Burlington, MA 01803. 1-800-733-1717.)

> A preservice and inservice text in which teachers are shown how to help children construct meaning for themselves. The author's scope includes literacy contexts through thinking, reading, writing, speaking, and listening. Cooper addresses various approaches to teaching literacy skills to children.

Mason, J. M. & Au, K. H. (1990). *Reading Instruction for Today: Second Edition.* New York: HarperCollins College Publications. (10 East 53rd Street, New York, NY 10022. 1-800-742-7831.)

> The authors' treatment emphasizes reading for meaning, or comprehension. Reading and study skills are developed. Writing processes are interrelated with reading. Multicultural issues are developed. A section on approaches to reading is offered.

Form 6.3

BASAL READING/LITERATURE-BASED TEXTBOOKS IN THE SCHOOL READING CURRICULUM

Directions: Literature-based or basal reading programs consist of reading texts, charts, teachers' manuals, journals, practice books, reproducible masters, etc., to show students *how to* read. Below, participants will find statements related to reading/literature texts. On the right, judgments may be made about the extent of local implementation of criteria.

Criteria:

	Thoroughly Implemented	Moderately Implemented	Minimally Implemented	Not Implemented
	4	3	2	1

1. There is some sort of glue that holds the program together, a master plan, blueprint, curriculum guide, or scope and sequence that paces the program, the learners, the teachers, and provides a common core of curriculum .... □ □ □ □

2. The master plan is embedded in teachers' manuals that support teachers with extensive suggestions about how to present the curriculum .... □ □ □ □

3. Content of students' books is expected to provide the contextual applications to support the program's underlying philosophy, master plan, blueprint, or scope and sequence.. □ □ □ □

4. Instructional materials are edited to represent the core of instruction, assuming that additional recreational, enrichment, writing, and study skills will be included for teachers in appropriate learning contexts .... □ □ □ □

5. The difficulty level of texts goes from very easy, with text predictability in kindergarten, to progressively more difficult over the elementary years; vocabulary in primary texts is carefully developed and presented .... □ □ □ □

6. Differentiated instruction assists the pacing of learning, with enrichment provided for accelerated students and suggestions for intensified learning to meet the needs of students who do not learn easily .... □ □ □ □

7. Students are taught comprehension of narrative text, expository text, writing about reading, decoding, vocabulary, and literary foundations, using stories, and including appropriate direct instruction.. □ □ □ □

8. Suggestions of classroom organization and grouping may be offered in manuals, including whole class, cooperative, skill-specific, ability, and social groups .... □ □ □ □

9. Provision is adequate to extend and practice the strategies, abilities, and skills that are developed in the textbook program... □ □ □ □

10. An underlying assumption is that a textbook series represents economy of teachers' time; i.e., teachers need not gather all of the stories, enrichment, practice and teaching ideas for every lesson they teach .... □ □ □ □

–continues–

Basal Reading/Literature-Bases Textbooks in the School Reading Curriculum -continued-	4	3	2	1
11. Another editorial assumption is that teachers will choose selectively from among the range of suggestions given in teachers' manuals, and will make no attempt to teach the whole manual	☐	☐	☐	☐
12. The forms, or genre, of literature, such as biography, fiction, and legend, support meaning and feelings about reading, while strengthening students' abilities to write as they learn to analyze genre	☐	☐	☐	☐
13. Crafts used by authors—for example, humorous writing, comparison, or point-of-view—are studied during reading and practiced during pupils' writing activities	☐	☐	☐	☐
14. Formats for writing—i.e., letters, diaries, literature logs, stories—are studied while reading texts, and applications are made to the writing of students, increasing both writing skills and reading comprehension	☐	☐	☐	☐
15. In contemporary textbook series, reading comprehension, or meaning, is more important than accuracy of word pronunciation or identification	☐	☐	☐	☐
16. Teachers' manuals have embedded into their content the thinking-about-text which supports reading comprehension	☐	☐	☐	☐
17. Classification of knowledge, the building-block of thinking and comprehension, is aided in manuals with webbing, mapping, etc.; i.e., structuring activities	☐	☐	☐	☐
18. Exaggerated, excessive predictions precede the reading of any stories to enhance understanding of the reading *process,* to strengthen comprehension and to increase chances of recognizing new words while reading	☐	☐	☐	☐
19. Comprehension of content books is strengthened in manuals through structural activities such as advance organizers, structured overviews, K-W-L,* DR-TA,* etc.	☐	☐	☐	☐
20. Comprehension content includes reading to understand factual information, make inferences, and develop critical thinking	☐	☐	☐	☐
21. Literacy emergence materials are designed to enhance oral language, social interactions, reading of picture books and predictable books, letter names, letter sounds, a small number of sight words, with writing (composition), invented spellings, and copying	☐	☐	☐	☐
22. Balanced decoding applies context clues, sight word vocabulary, phonics, syllabication, and picture clues to a vocabulary-accelerating system in order to increase fluency and automaticity	☐	☐	☐	☐
23. The ultimate purpose of decoding is to increase reading comprehension—not to sound out words or learn phonic rules	☐	☐	☐	☐
24. Contemporary research on learning of vocabulary in contexts, phonemic awareness, accuracy, fluency, automaticity, and vocabulary acceleration, is evident	☐	☐	☐	☐

–continues–

Basal Reading/Literature-Bases Textbooks in the School Reading Curriculum -continued-	4	3	2	1
25. End-of-unit, end-of-level tests corresponding with each level of textbook are designed to assess student learning..	☐	☐	☐	☐
26. Performance assessment is an ongoing, integral part of the textbook's total program	☐	☐	☐	☐
27. A management assumption is that textbook packages represent the greatest cost savings, with competition between publishers holding down costs	☐	☐	☐	☐
28. If desired, planning is available and thoroughly developed in each teachers' manual, and the challenge is managing materials, flexibly grouping students, and teaching effectively	☐	☐	☐	☐
29. Teachers' manuals may represent *the only* staff development within many districts	☐	☐	☐	☐

Cover the page here and below before photocopying if users are not to see the interpretation until later.

Interpretation: Participants may total each of the columns, giving four points to each response in the left column, three to the next column, two to the next column, and one to the column on the right. Totals between 88 and 116 may be viewed as having *thoroughly implemented* basal/literature-based criteria, between 59 and 87, *moderately implemented,* between 30 and 58 *minimally implemented,* and between 1 and 29 *not implemented* in the local setting.

The goal is to identify the quality of the present basal or literature-based program. Those judgments, then, are tested against needs for future program expectations. If warranted, a summary interpretation of Form 6.3 may be entered onto Form 6.7, enabling a comparison of approaches.

N.B.: Shifts in contemporary literature-based text series cause them to be somewhat indistinguishable from whole language concepts. Principals or Reading Advisory Boards may opt to revise Form 6.3 to include items 16–30 of Form 6.4. *Thoroughly implemented* would then range from 178–236, *moderately* from 199–177, *minimally* from 60–118, and *not implemented* from 1–59.

WHOLE LANGUAGE IN THE SCHOOL READING CURRICULUM   (see Form 6.4)

The whole language movement emerged from concepts of linguistic and cognitive sciences. Scholars such as Clay (33), Goodman (75), and Smith (189) used those academic foundations to study the learning of good readers. The major influence of whole language may be to create shifts in regular instruction. Some educators now replace the term whole language with the terms constructivist or transactional classrooms.

Problem: Whole language is a child-centered approach vs the more widely accepted curriculum-centered models. Although child-based concepts dominate the professional literature, classroom teachers have been slow to adopt whole language approaches. Considerable staff development is warranted when districts initiate a whole language philosophy.

Rationale: Whole language is a child-centered belief system about how students learn. All of the language arts are integrated into a meaning-focused, holistic classroom with an authentic literature base. Its prospects are to create effective, empowered readers, fully engaged, with positive affect toward reading and literature.

Procedures: In order to judge congruence with their personal belief systems, teachers, faculties, administrators, or Reading Advisory Boards who seek an alternative to basal-text instruction may wish to complete Worksheet 6.4 to judge present status, suitability of whole language, and the range of staff development that would be warranted.

For Further Reading

Clay, M. M. (1991). *Becoming Literate: The Construction of Inner Control*. Auckland, New Zealand: Heinemann Education. (361 Hanover Street, Portsmouth, NH 03801-3912. 1-800-541-2086.)

Children are shown how to exercise gradual, strategic control over their reading and writing. Teachers are shown how to help children to develop different ways to gain control of their literacy growth. Topics include language development, concepts about print, interaction with books, etc.

Goodman, K. (1986). *What's Whole About Whole Language*. Portsmouth, NH: Heinemann Educational Publishers. (361 Hanover Street, Portsmouth, NH, 02801-3912. 1-800-541-2086.)

Goodman suggests ways to enhance whole language programs and ways to evolve present programs into whole language formats. The author describes whole language foundations of reading and writing and provides criteria for teachers to self-assess.

Form 6.4

WHOLE LANGUAGE IN THE SCHOOL READING CURRICULUM

Directions: Whole language holds a contemporary set of beliefs which endorses learning all of the language arts concurrently, reading whole texts, reading for meaning, learning skills only as needed, and reading only authentic literature. Below are criteria related to whole language. On the right, judgments about the degree of local implementation may be made.

Criteria:

	Thoroughly Implemented	Moderately Implemented	Minimally Implemented	Not Implemented
	4	3	2	1
1. The fundamental belief is that language is learned naturally through experimentation, risk taking, and use, and that instruction should complement that learning	☐	☐	☐	☐
2. Teacher empowerment, or teachers taking charge of curriculum, materials, and learning, rather than depending on manuals, texts, and workbooks, is basic to whole language	☐	☐	☐	☐
3. Whole language teachers, redefining teaching and learning, spend a greater portion of their time both planning for teaching and reflecting on student learning than do typical teachers	☐	☐	☐	☐
4. Whole language functions best in a classroom that keeps language whole; i.e., reading, writing, listening, speaking, and thinking are unified throughout the day	☐	☐	☐	☐
5. An environment of trust and security is important to encourage children to take the risks and make the mistakes that undergird language learning	☐	☐	☐	☐
6. The medium, or content, of whole language is more likely to consist of trade books, children's magazines, newspapers, and peer-published books than basal texts	☐	☐	☐	☐
7. Students are empowered as decision-makers, choosing books they will read, topics they will write about, and interests to pursue	☐	☐	☐	☐
8. The language learned is natural language, or the way children speak, as well as the language of good literature, and students become better language users through reading and writing authentic literature	☐	☐	☐	☐
9. The teacher reads to pupils every day as a vehicle for modeling the process of reading	☐	☐	☐	☐
10. The medium for instruction is authentic literature, including multiple copies to support literature sets, and immersion in print-rich environments	☐	☐	☐	☐
11. Pattern books selected and for students to read, and for teachers to read to classes, are text-redundant, using predictable, repetitive language	☐	☐	☐	☐

–continues–

Whole Language in the School Reading Curriculum -continued-

	4	3	2	1

12. The intuitive sense of knowing what comes next in the story enables students to develop predicting strategies, and to expand their reading vocabularies .... □ □ □ □

13. Thinking underlies language processes; and reading involves a series of thinking options to get to meaning .... □ □ □ □

14. Teachers view reading and writing as developmental processes, and children become better at both by reading and writing .... □ □ □ □

15. Good readers use three cueing systems, semantic (meaning), syntactic (grammar), and graphophonic (print), interdependently to get meaning .... □ □ □ □

16. Students are taught to develop self-monitoring processes, such as "does this make sense?" "what will happen next?" "does this sound like language?" so that they will know when they understand .... □ □ □ □

17. Pupils are encouraged to make predictions and take guesses (risk-taking) as they encounter difficult words, skipping when appropriate .... □ □ □ □

18. Letters, sound patterns, or words are not learned in isolation, but in the context of language that is real and whole .... □ □ □ □

19. Language unity is demonstrated as pupils listen and speak when they are prewriting a piece, conferencing, and sharing .... □ □ □ □

20. Journal writing as a daily activity increases writing abilities, which in turn improves reading capabilities .... □ □ □ □

21. Concentration is placed on children's thinking as they write, and invented spellings are encouraged as needed to aid written expression .... □ □ □ □

22. Writing activities often are conducted at writing and publishing centers, and it is the publishing stage at which correct spellings and grammatical forms are important .... □ □ □ □

23. Whole language advocates encourage thematic approaches in content classes to integrate the language arts into the total curriculum .... □ □ □ □

24. The role of collaboration (i.e., sharing a story with a friend, or group) increases interests, aids motivation, and increases long-term affect .... □ □ □ □

25. Time spent in recreational reading, sustained silent reading (SSR), or drop everything and read (DEAR), is viewed as a daily part of the curriculum ..... □ □ □ □

26. Constructing meaning is seen as providing its own intrinsic motivation and its own rewards, thus enhancing affect toward reading .... □ □ □ □

27. Child-teacher conferences are planned routinely to include reading, writing, book talks, and follow-up activities .... □ □ □ □

28. Evaluation is conducted, in the main, through "kidwatching" or observing student development in reading and writing, and by keeping performance and anecdotal records .... □ □ □ □

—continues—

Whole Language in the School Reading Curriculum -continued-	4	3	2	1
29. Portfolio assessment is holistic and ongoing; it monitors meaning making, miscues, and attempts to get at student thinking...	☐	☐	☐	☐
30. Parents are encouraged to be partners in children's language learning, supporting and reinforcing at home any activities undertaken at school	☐	☐	☐	☐

Cover the page here and below before photocopying if users are not to see the interpretation until later.

Interpretation: Persons seeking to summarize scores on the inventory may give four points to checkmarks in the *thoroughly implemented* column, three to *moderately implemented*, two to *minimally implemented*, and one point to *not implemented*. Scores with totals between 91 and 120 may be interpreted as *thoroughly implemented*, those between 61 and 90 as *moderately implemented*, between 31 and 60 as *minimally implemented*, and those between 1 and 30 would mean *not implemented*. Participants are invited to enter summary scores from Form 6.4 into the appropriate place on the matrix of Form 6.7, assuming a desire to compare suitability of whole language with that of other approaches.

THE LANGUAGE EXPERIENCE APPROACH   (see Form 6.5)

Language experience is a fundamental component of whole language, is used as an integral, transitional medium in the pre-reading and formal text reading of basal and literature-based instruction, and gains widespread use in remedial reading programs. The language experience approach (LEA) may only rarely be used as a comprehensive reading curriculum, yet its influence over time, and its integration into other curricula, is substantial.

The Problem: Teachers may not be aware of the way LEA helps pupils to grasp the reading *process*, to grasp the construction of meaning through the observation of writing, and to read those compositions. Teachers may not realize how well LEA complements literature-based and basal texts, whole language, or remedial programs.

Rationale: Teachers who are able to employ LEA possess the means to support learners as meaning makers. Students who do not know *what reading is* (and many educationally at-risk students do not) observe the *process* as it unfolds. They note the constructions of text founded on *talk*, and gain the foundation for meaning and comprehension vs becoming word-bound, a risk encountered by pupils who misconstrue the *process*.

Procedures: Teachers who wish to explore LEA may use Form 6.5 to judge personal beliefs, skills, and needs. Principals may use data from the form to plot staff development for teachers, regardless of the reading approach used in the curriculum.

For Further Reading

Allen, R. V. & Allen, C. (1982). *Language Experience Activities, Second Edition.* Boston: Houghton Mifflin Company. (Wayside Road, Burlington, MA 01803. 1-800-733-1717.)

> A classic written by the developers of the approach. Allen attributes the concepts as *rooted in antiquity*. Among numerous additional concepts, the text describes a curriculum rationale, the role of shared experiences, discussion, listening, telling stories, dictating stories, making and reading stories, and writing independently.

Harp, B. & Brewer, J. (1991). *Reading and Writing: Teaching for the Connections.* Ft. Worth, TX: Harcourt Brace Jovanovich, Publishers. (301 Commerce Street, Suite 3700, Ft. Worth TX 76102. 1-708-647-8822.)

> The authors weave the language, reading, and writing connections into a process in which each area supports the other areas. Content addresses language development and integration, teachers' decisions, basic approaches, literacy skills, and applying literacy skills to other curricular areas.

Form 6.5
THE LANGUAGE EXPERIENCE APPROACH IN THE READING CURRICULUM

Directions: LEA combines learning all of the language arts while planning and reflecting upon direct experiences. Below, participants will find statements related to teaching LEA. On the right, faculty, Reading Advisory Board members, and the principal may make judgments about the degree of local implementation.

Criteria:	Thoroughly Implemented 4	Moderately Implemented 3	Minimally Implemented 2	Not Implemented 1
1. Books are read to students from the beginning of kindergarten as a means of modeling reading and providing good literature experiences	☐	☐	☐	☐
2. Children construct their own knowledge by participating in common experiences and talking about those experiences	☐	☐	☐	☐
3. Pupils learn through direct activities that integrate the language components of thinking, listening, speaking, writing, and reading	☐	☐	☐	☐
4. The settings or locations of common events are chosen carefully to support oral language and curriculum needs	☐	☐	☐	☐
5. Choices are extensive for activities, and may include classroom, building, school grounds, walking trips, or field trips	☐	☐	☐	☐
6. The experience story is recorded by the teacher based on conversations before and after direct activities shared by pupils and the teacher	☐	☐	☐	☐
7. Students express themselves and the teacher records on chart paper or a chalkboard those stories dictated by the group	☐	☐	☐	☐
8. Students are asked to think, talk about their ideas, brainstorm, express themselves collaboratively, and share with peers as teachers record their comments	☐	☐	☐	☐
9. As the teacher writes, children observe, learning that print and meaning emerge from oral language	☐	☐	☐	☐
10. The teacher reads the dictated story back to the individual, group, or class, pointing to story parts as she reads	☐	☐	☐	☐
11. Children read both their own individual stories dictated to the teacher, and group stories	☐	☐	☐	☐
12. Multiple readings are desirable, and first one, then another student may read a sentence until the story has been completed	☐	☐	☐	☐
13. Each child is encouraged to read the story to others—a peer, small group, the class, another class, parents, grandparents, neighbors, etc.	☐	☐	☐	☐

–continues–

The Language Experience Approach in the Reading Curriculum -continued-

	4	3	2	1
14. Individual students may be called to the chalkboard or story chart to identify certain words, letters, spellings, grammatical forms, or phonic patterns	☐	☐	☐	☐
15. As teachers record, they may call attention to letter formations, sound-symbol patterns, spellings, and grammatical conventions	☐	☐	☐	☐
16. Teachers are able to point out the onset and rime (rhyme) of spelling patterns which, when understood cognitively, support those spelling *analogies* to accelerate vocabulary, and subsequently, comprehension	☐	☐	☐	☐
17. After group composition, teachers may type or prepare a hand-printed copy to duplicate for each student	☐	☐	☐	☐
18. Stories may be collected and bound into books, either a single copy for the classroom library or copies for each class member	☐	☐	☐	☐
19. LEA charts may be kept and displayed for periods of time to aid pupils in locating words, spellings, or ideas	☐	☐	☐	☐
20. Students may copy parts of their individual or group stories as a means of reading and writing familiar text	☐	☐	☐	☐
21. Early writing is nurtured by invented spellings that help pupils focus on the process and avoid distractions that come from early emphasis on correct spellings	☐	☐	☐	☐
22. Pupils develop basic reading vocabularies through writing, and may place each new word into a personal word bank	☐	☐	☐	☐
23. The specific subject matter of the experience story may follow a shared activity, or be a part of a thematic unit of study	☐	☐	☐	☐
24. Opportunities to conduct research are provided in the language curriculum, and appropriate trade books and library books are used in the process	☐	☐	☐	☐

Cover the page here and below prior to photocopying if users are not to see the interpretation until later.

Interpretation: Individuals or faculty groups seeking to identify the congruence between their beliefs and implementation of LEA may complete Form 6.5, giving four points to each checkmark in the column on the left, three points to checkmarks in the next column, two points to marks in the third column, and one point to the column on the right. Totaling those points, the participant would consider scores between 72 and 96 as *thoroughly implemented*, those between 49 and 72 as *moderately implemented*, between 25 and 48 as *minimally implemented*, and those between 1 and 24 as *not implemented*. A summary of Form 6.5 may be entered onto Form 6.7 to aid comparison of local approaches and expectations

CONGRUENCE BETWEEN READING APPROACH AND CURRICULUM

(see Form 6.6)

Congruence between the reading approach and language arts curriculum is important whenever Reading Advisory Boards seek to revise, retain, or improve the reading program. A mismatch between locally-derived needs and any fundamental reading approach would frustrate the principal, faculty, and parents, alike, and program goals would not be fulfilled.

The Problem: The faculty or principal may prefer or be comfortable with the present reading program, and that may cause open exploration to be a serious problem. Some purchased programs may have content segments unrelated to, or in conflict with, local curriculum goals.

Rationale: Introducing the notion that there are no perfect programs may help faculties to explore options (see Form 6.1). The present approach to reading instruction is valid if achievement is high, pupil performance is strong, and affect toward reading and the language arts is highly positive. The present curriculum may be judged effective if students are neither harmed nor alienated by its delivery. The approach may be executed best when teachers use it with confidence and enthusiasm.

Procedures: Initially, respondents might complete Form 6.6 individually. After reflection, collated information may be used by an Advisory Board or principal to judge status beliefs of the faculty. Shared, aggregate summaries may lead to ownership and support from faculty toward program change, or affirm that the present approach is suitable to the faculty.

For Further Reading

Adams, M. J. (1990). *Beginning to Read: Thinking and Learning About Print*. Cambridge, MA: The MIT Press. (The MIT Press, Massachusetts Institute of Technology, Cambridge, MA 02142. 1-617-253-5646.)

A text for people studying cognitive and reading theories. Adams uses constructivist theory to build the case that capable readers employ automatic print perception along with the thought-getting of reading comprehension. Meaning and print are shown to be both independent and interdependent.

Veatch, J. (1966). *Reading in the Elementary School*. New York: The Ronald Press. (Out of print, but found in many university education libraries.)

A text for preservice and inservice teachers seeking a more comprehensive approach to teaching reading and writing. The person most associated with individualized reading describes the roles of key vocabulary, language experience, good literature, and classroom management. The author hoped to repersonalize the teaching of reading and writing.

Form 6.6

MATRIX TO JUDGE CONGRUENCE OF READING APPROACH WITH CURRICULUM CONTENT

Directions: Below, you will find listed curriculum content. On the right, Reading Advisory Board members, faculty, or principals will find reference to three reading curriculum models. In each cell, please signify the degree of congruence between curriculum criteria and the reading approach by entering (+) when there is high congruence, or agreement, (o) in cases of some congruence, and (-) whenever no congruence occurs.

Criteria:	Literature-based or Basal Texts	Whole Language	Language Experience (LEA)
	3	2	1

Mission/purpose

1. Emphasizes reading for meaning			
2. Integrates the language arts			
3. Develops active readers (non-passive)			

Affect

4. Incorporates recreational reading			
5. Uses authentic literature			
6. Promotes success			

Narrative Text Comprehension

7. Teaches *wholeness* of text			
8. Prediction processes			
9. Chunking*			
10. Mental images			
11. Schema matches			
12. Meaning vocabularies			
13. Word maps,* semantic maps*			
14. Interactive reading, think-alouds*			
15. Confirmation processes			
16. Text explicit reading			
17. Text implicit reading			
18. Self monitoring			
19. Narrative text structures			

–continues–

Matrix to Judge Congruence of Reading Approach with Curriculum Content

-continued-

	3	2	1

Expository Text Comprehension

	3	2	1
20. Elements of narrative comprehension (7-19)			
21. Study of expository text structures			
22. Understanding of chapter, paragraph structures			
23. Uses of advanced organizers*			
24. Adaptations of structured overviews*			
25. Generation of study guides			
26. Study of technical vocabularies			

Literary elements

	3	2	1
27. Author studies			
28. Understanding of the crafts of authors			
29. Study of the genre of literature			
30. Investigations of forms of authors			

Writing

	3	2	1
31. Brainstorming*			
32. Webbing*			
33. Drafting*			
34. Peer editing*			
35. Revising*			
36. Publishing*			

Decoding

	3	2	1
37. Skipping/risk taking			
38. Context			
39. Sight words			
40. Phonemic awareness*			
41. Phonics			
42. Syllabication			
43. Clustering			
44. Chunking*			

–continues–

**Matrix to Judge Congruence of Reading
Approach with Curriculum Content**   -continued-

	3	2	1

Teaching Resources

	3	2	1
45. Stories, the reading materials, packaged			
46. Accompanying teachers' manuals			
47. End-of-unit and end-of-level assessment			
48. Portfolio assessment			
49. Student journals			
50. Student workbooks			

Cover the page here and below prior to photocopying if users are not to see the interpretation until later.

Interpretation: Scanning each column and all lines may help an administrator, Reading Advisory Board, or faculty to identify strengths and weaknesses of approaches applied locally, along with judgments of suitability of those curricula to the local setting. Collated, or tallied results from the form might be left on a bulletin board in the faculty work room for several days prior to any action or discussion. A summary interpretation of Form 6.6 may be moved forward to Form 6.7 to tie approach and curriculum congruence to an overall chapter summary.

SYNTHESIS OF IMPLEMENTATION OF APPROACHES   (see Form 6.7)

Participants may feel, after reviewing Forms 6.3 to 6.5, that more is the same, than different, about various reading approaches. The challenge is to use the planning process to address local goals, needs, and priorities.

The Problem: The problem may be that the participants may not want the approach to be reviewed openly, fearing change, confusion, or dissension. Consensus on meanings of Forms 6.2-6.6 may be difficult to reach. Inaccurate interpretations may lead a school toward a reading approach that would not be effective in the local setting.

Rationale: A way to examine reading approaches is to study congruence with program strengths and needs. Based on findings, a curriculum may be reexamined. Once a needs-based curriculum has been developed, a fitting fundamental reading approach would be identified. Subsequently, decisions about instructional materials, organization, learning assessment, and staff development may emerge.

Procedures: Participants may review Forms 6.2-6.6, indicating the extent of local use on Form 6.7. Using those forms, people may undertake Form 6.8 to identify approach strengths and needs, tied to local priorities. A subsequent, clear set of priorities may support a strong plan-of-action.

Comments and Cautions

The approach to reading may support a faculty to attain its curriculum goals. Many schools employ components of the three approaches in Chapter 3.

A love of language should drive the reading approach, with positive, shared feelings about reading and writing.

The approach should develop a solid, meaning-based comprehension component.

Pupils' rapidly expanding reading vocabularies can only strengthen good reading comprehension.

The approach should be expected to enable students to learn to read content textbooks successfully.

Form 6.7
SYNTHESIS OF IMPLEMENTATION OF APPROACHES

Directions: Below, the principal, Reading Advisor Board, or faculty will find criteria related to fundamental approaches to teaching students to read. On the right, participants may choose to signify the extent to which the local school has implemented components of those approaches.

Criteria:	Thoroughly Implemented	Moderately Implemented	Minimally Implemented	Not Implemented
	4	3	2	1
1. Literature-based or basal reading texts (Form 6.3)	☐	☐	☐	☐
2. Whole language in the curriculum (Form 6.4)	☐	☐	☐	☐
3. The language experience approach (Form 6.5)	☐	☐	☐	☐
4. Congruence between approach and curriculum (Form 6.6)	☐	☐	☐	☐

Interpretation: Giving four points to checkmarks in the left column, *thoroughly implemented,* three points to checkmarks in the second column, *moderately implemented,* two points to checkmarks in the next column, *minimally implemented,* and one point to marks in the left column, *not implemented,* will help Reading Advisory Board participants to total the four columns. Totals between 13–16 may be judged *thoroughly implemented* in the reading curriculum, between 9–12 considered *moderately implemented*, totals between 5–8 may be viewed as *minimally implemented*, and those between 1–4 may be considered *not implemented*.

Form 6.8
READING APPROACH: STRENGTHS, NEEDS, AND PRIORITIES

Directions: Below, you will find components of various approaches to reading instruction. On the right of each entry, space is provided to record strengths, weaknesses, and ultimately, priorities of each component. Checkmarks on each respective worksheet in Chapter 4, particularly Forms 4.2, 4.7, and 4.8, may help in completing Form 6.9.

1. **Approaches to Reading Instruction**	*Strengths* 1. 2.	*Needs* 1. 2.	*Priorities* 1. 2.
2. **Literature-based and Basal Textbooks**	*Strengths* 1. 2.	*Needs* 1. 2.	*Priorities* 1. 2.
3. **Whole Language in the Reading Program**	*Strengths* 1. 2.	*Needs* 1. 2.	*Priorities* 1. 2.
4. **Language Experience Approach**	*Strengths* 1. 2.	*Needs* 1. 2.	*Priorities* 1. 2.
5. **Congruence between Approach and Curriculum**	*Strengths* 1. 2.	*Needs* 1. 2.	*Priorities* 1. 2.

Form 6.9

PLAN-OF-ACTION FOR READING APPROACHES

Directions: Administrators seeking to develop a focus for professional growth may benefit from being as specific as possible about what they seek to accomplish, how they will go about attaining growth, and how they will know when they have reached their goals. A review of Forms 6.7 and 6.8 should lead the principal or Board to identify goals to pursue in the growth plan. Statements entered should be as simple, direct, and useful as possible.

1. Goal Statement: _____

2. Objectives:

   a) _____

   b) _____

   c) _____

3. Activities: Dates; time checkpoints:

   a) _____   * _____

   b) _____   * _____

   c) _____   * _____

   d) _____   * _____

   e) _____   * _____

4. Resources: (professional reading, consultation, visitations)

   a) _____   * _____

   b) _____   * _____

   c) _____   * _____

5. How I will know when my goal is accomplished:

   _____

   _____

   _____

   _____

CHAPTER 7

SELECTION OF INSTRUCTIONAL READING MATERIALS

A comprehensive reading program is balanced—that is, instruction, activities, and experiences are provided for developmental, functional, recreational, and diagnostic reading. Textbook selection includes careful examination of that balance. Recent insights into the reading process and related roles of both comprehension and decoding call for reflection as materials are purchased. Balance is offered between reading and writing, recognizing that reading helps writing, and that writing helps reading comprehension. Decoding needs to be considered, knowing that word knowledge helps reading, and that comprehension expands word knowledge.

Fundamental reading materials usually consist of a series of reading textbooks, a collection of library books, and computer software. Some educators believe that only the purchased textbook program is needed; others believe that only trade books are needed. Each component, individually, is judged important in schools, and all are seen as complements to each other. The fit of each program's scope should be matched with local goals to see how component parts relate to each other.

The extensive range of support, or pupil enrichment, materials made available by publishing houses deserves a committee's analysis. Care may be taken to judge whether those materials help a school to meet its reading goals. Materials for Title 1 (previously Chapter 1) programs warrant consideration by the administrator who is accountable for the specialist's decisions. School administrators may contemplate the importance of professional books for teachers who recognize that, with a new program, staff development may be as important as decisions about literature-based textbook series purchases.

SELECTION OF READING MATERIALS   (see Form 7.1)

Most schools ordinarily purchase basal reader textbook series when they opt to update the reading program (see Forms 7.2 to 7.13). Others, however, base reading programs on trade books and choose titles independently or use comprehensive criteria (see Forms 7.14 to 7.19) to match curriculum goals. Software purchases may enrich the curriculum (see Form 7.21). The most universally used teacher inservice education comes from teachers' manuals.

The Problem: Schools may start the purchase of new reading textbooks when it might be more appropriate to begin with a needs-assessment and program-planning process (see Forms 3.11 and 3.12). Some schools plan to purchase new textbooks without reviewing the curriculum objectives. Purchasers may consider a new series without looking at library holdings.

Rationale: A balanced reading program instructs, models, and provides opportunities for students to learn *how to read*. Judgments about the program's instructional materials will influence the quality of students' learning and their affect about reading. A purposeful way to coordinate the selection of materials may be for the Reading Advisory Board (see Form 3.5) to conduct a comprehensive study (see Forms 3.12, 4.20, and 6.8).

Procedures: The Reading Advisory Board, Textbook Selection Committee, or administrator may use Form 3.3 to review beliefs and then Forms 7.1 to 7.22 as structures to select new reading materials. Particular care might be given to Forms 7.24 to 7.26, which support a summary and analysis of the process.

For Further Reading

Frager, A. M. & Vanterpool, M. (1993). "Point-Counterpoint: Value of School Textbooks," *Reading Horizons*, 33, 4, 300–312.

> The authors view textbooks as efficient compilations of source materials, comprehensive, cost effective, and written by knowledgeable and experienced people. For each strength, there is a negative counterpoint.

Pagels, C. F. & Adams, J. B. (1981). "Here's a Well-Oiled Textbook Adoption Process," *Executive Educator*, 3, 12, 25–26.

> Pagels and Adams describe a textbook selection process used most frequently *then and now*. Committees often assess needs, review choices in materials, prioritize three choices, invite publishers' presentations, and make a selection.

Form 7.1

SELECTION OF READING MATERIALS

Directions: Below, Textbook Selection Committees or principals will find criteria for selection of reading materials. On the right, respondents may identify whether their decisions will deliver thorough, moderate, minimal, or no congruence with defined program goals.

Criteria for Reading Materials Selection:	Thorough Congruence	Moderate Congruence	Minimal Congruence	No Congruence
	4	3	2	1
1. Decisions are based on pupils' acceleration of reading abilities and reading for fulfillment	☐	☐	☐	☐
2. Needs are defined for purchase of new basal- or literature-based materials	☐	☐	☐	☐
3. Reasons are identified for the purchase of new trade books	☐	☐	☐	☐
4. Criteria are established for the selection of new computer-based reading software	☐	☐	☐	☐
5. Judgments exist about designation of new special reading program purchases	☐	☐	☐	☐
6. Purchases of professional books to support faculty development fit program decisions	☐	☐	☐	☐
7. Congruence is found in the program's needs (see Form 3.12) and materials selected	☐	☐	☐	☐
8. Alignment occurs with curriculum content (see Form 4.20) and reading materials named	☐	☐	☐	☐
9. Agreement exists between reading approach (see Form 6.8) and materials purchased	☐	☐	☐	☐
10. The organization (see Form 8.11) is consistent with purchases of reading materials	☐	☐	☐	☐
11. Assessment (see Form 5.16) decisions are congruent with reading materials selected	☐	☐	☐	☐

Interpretation: Participants may total columns, giving four points to the left column, three points to the second, two to the third column, and one point to the right column. Totals between 34–44 represent *thorough congruence*, between 23–33 *moderate congruence*, between 12–22 *minimal congruence*, and between 1–11 *no congruence*.

BASAL OR LITERATURE-BASED READING TEXT SELECTION   (See Form 7.2)

Reading textbook programs represent the standard vehicle for teaching children to read in American schools. Across decades, those text materials have been described as *basal readers*. Presently, textbook publishers often refer to those materials as *literature-based* readers. Shifts in content of teachers' manuals and stories have followed changes in textbook programs.

The Problem: The process may begin without the establishment of solid criteria for selecting reading materials. Many educators have little awareness of how to select materials for a reading program. At times, the preferences of a few faculty dominate the choices. Rigid insistence on one reading approach may restrict open deliberation to consider alternatives.

Rationale: The total reading program usually is thought of as all that is packaged and taught from textbooks, trade books, or software. This program ordinarily is displayed through some blueprint of all that is taught and learned. The content of teachers' manuals conveys the program. Children's stories are developed to share content and to improve reading abilities.

Procedures: About five to seven major publishing houses sell most of the instructional programs. The Reading Advisory Board (long-term) or Textbook Selection Committee (short-term) may prioritize those programs it wishes to review, using one set of Forms 7.2 to 7.12 to judge criteria and Form 7.13 to synthesize judgments for each publisher's series. Forms 7.2 to 7.13 may be stapled together, one set of forms for each series to be reviewed. Participants concerned about the difficulty of basal texts or trade books may refer to the *Fry Graph for Estimating Readability* (see Appendix A).

For Further Reading

Dole, J. A., et al. (1990). *Guide to Selecting Basal Reading Programs*. Urbana, IL: Center for the Study of Reading. (Dissemination Director, Room 173 CRC, 51 Gerty Drive, Champaign, IL 61820. 1-217-244-4083 or 217-333-2552.)

A comprehensive process to select reading textbook programs is advanced. Nine self-study bulletins support committees with research syntheses, understanding issues, selection guidelines, and procedures to evaluate various series.

Lamb, P. (1993). "Literature-Based Language Arts Programs: Promises and Problems," *Reading and Writing Quarterly: Overcoming Learning Difficulties*, 9, 2, 135–50.

Lamb provides the structures to evaluate the success of several types of literature-based programs. She offers descriptions of the options and outlines the issues involved in implementation.

Publisher _____

	Form 7.2					

Form 7.2
BASAL OR LITERATURE-BASED SERIES SELECTION

Directions: Administrators or Textbook Selection Committees may use Forms 7.2–7.12 to evaluate reading textbook series. Those forms should be photocopied, with one set for each series being reviewed. Criteria from each form should be reviewed, and extent of publishers' implementation of criteria checked on Form 6.12.

Criteria for Reading Program Selection:

	Thoroughly Implemented 4	Moderately Implemented 3	Minimally Implemented 2	Not Implemented 1

Purpose

1. The stated purpose of the series is consistent with the school's reading mission, definition of reading, and philosophy (see Form 3.4) .... ☐ ☐ ☐ ☐

2. The content of the reading program matches the district reading approach (see Forms 6.6–6.7) .... ☐ ☐ ☐ ☐

3. The content of teachers' manuals, i.e., the program, is both current and timeless .... ☐ ☐ ☐ ☐

4. The Textbook Selection Committee reviews publishers with purposes and research bases matching the school's curriculum goals (see Forms 4.19–4.20) .... ☐ ☐ ☐ ☐

Content

5. The description of a wholesome reading process is evident to teachers and pupils .... ☐ ☐ ☐ ☐

6. The focus of the program is on teaching students *how* to read, balancing the components that go into the process .... ☐ ☐ ☐ ☐

7. The content of the program represents a balance among developmental, functional, and recreational reading .... ☐ ☐ ☐ ☐

8. Strategies, processes, and skills can be taught using the content of manuals .... ☐ ☐ ☐ ☐

9. The materials support teaching to respect diversity in gender, race, culture, and ethnicity—pupil texts address diversity .... ☐ ☐ ☐ ☐

Program Foundations

10. Teachers' economy of time is evident and all suggestions are at teachers' fingertips .... ☐ ☐ ☐ ☐

Publisher_____

Basal- or Literature-Based Series Selection -continued-	4	3	2	1
11. Thorough suggestions are provided to model, demonstrate, or teach new strategies	☐	☐	☐	☐
12. Thematic units are congruent with the needs and interests of students	☐	☐	☐	☐
13. Thematic units develop reading alongside the other language arts	☐	☐	☐	☐
14. A balanced range of literary genre is used as the vehicle to accelerate learning to read	☐	☐	☐	☐
15. The story selections represent high-quality, authentic literature	☐	☐	☐	☐
16. Illustrations are carefully chosen to convey the story line and serve as an aid to reading comprehension	☐	☐	☐	☐
17. New strategies are taught prior to reading, which permits contextual application and aids memory for new learning	☐	☐	☐	☐
18. Ongoing assessment of individual and class learning is a part of the teaching format, with specific evaluative activities..............................	☐	☐	☐	☐

Readability

	4	3	2	1
19. Vocabulary and concept load of materials are suitably difficult, with defined readability	☐	☐	☐	☐
20. Students enjoy a ratio of new-to-known words that aids contextual use to learn new words	☐	☐	☐	☐
21. Sentence length, number of sentences, story and paragraph length, and complexity of concepts are aligned with students' development..................	☐	☐	☐	☐
22. Writing style is consistent with linguistic development; i.e., predictable words, redundancy, strong match between illustrations and story	☐	☐	☐	☐

Teachers' Manuals

	4	3	2	1
23. Content of teachers' manuals matches the school's curriculum goals	☐	☐	☐	☐
24. The objectives of the program are clearly identified in teachers' manuals	☐	☐	☐	☐
25. The lesson format in the manual is easy to follow	☐	☐	☐	☐
26. Pre-reading, reading, and post-reading activities are fully explicated	☐	☐	☐	☐
27. Teachers are able to locate strategies and skills with an index or scope and sequence chart	☐	☐	☐	☐
28. Teachers' manuals contain embedded, high-quality staff development support	☐	☐	☐	☐

–continues–

Publisher_____

Basal- or Literature-Based Series Selection	-continued-	4	3	2	1

Services offered

29. Consultant services are available with purchase, and across years of use, at no cost .... ☐ ☐ ☐ ☐

30. Bulletins and monographs related to reading instruction are available periodically at no additional cost to purchasers .... ☐ ☐ ☐ ☐

31. Publishers will package school districts with the specific items needed for each building on its own pallet, and delivered directly to the school .... ☐ ☐ ☐ ☐

Cover the page here and below prior to photocopying if users are not to see the interpretation until later.

Interpretation: Columns may be tallied, giving four points to marks in the left column, three to the next column, two to the third column, and one point to the right column. Totals between 94–124 may be judged *thoroughly implemented,* 63–93 *moderately implemented,* 32–62 *minimally implemented,* and 1–31 *not implemented* in this program.

Publisher _____

Form 7.3			
TEXT SELECTION FOR EMERGENT LITERACY			

Directions: The Textbook Selection Committee and administrator are invited to review Forms 4.3, 4.4, and 5.6 to consider criteria for curriculum and assessment of emergent literacy. Criteria are listed below and places are provided on the right to check the extent to which programs under review are congruent with those criteria.

	Thoroughly Implemented	Moderately Implemented	Minimally Implemented	Not Implemented
Criteria on Emergent Literacy	4	3	2	1

Teachers' Manuals Address:

1. The editors advocate children's learning to read and write by reading and writing .... ☐ ☐ ☐ ☐

2. Reading is founded on modeling for students what reading *is*, and how good readers do read .... ☐ ☐ ☐ ☐

3. Publishers support extensive use of the language experience approach (see Form 6.5) to introduce the reading process .... ☐ ☐ ☐ ☐

4. Teachers are encouraged to model reading with big books to engage students .... ☐ ☐ ☐ ☐

5. Early texts in this series hold an intensive congruence between content of illustrations and content of the story line .... ☐ ☐ ☐ ☐

6. Students read *lots* of pages using alphabet books, picture books, and predictable books from the series .... ☐ ☐ ☐ ☐

7. Pupils are encouraged to write as they learn to read, with invented spellings accepted .... ☐ ☐ ☐ ☐

8. Students are provided the story structures to strengthen writing fluency and confidence .... ☐ ☐ ☐ ☐

9. Teachers develop students' knowledge of letter names, phonemic awareness* (44, 72, 79), and how spellings work, from the beginning .... ☐ ☐ ☐ ☐

Interpretation: Columns may be tallied, giving four points to marks in the left column, three to the next column, two to the third column, and one point to the right column. Totals between 28–36 may be judged *thoroughly implemented*, 19–27 *moderately implemented*, 10–18 *minimally implemented*, and 1–9 *not implemented* in this series.

Publisher_____

	Form 7.4
	TEXT SELECTION FOR NARRATIVE READING COMPREHENSION

Directions: The Textbook Selection Committee or administrator may opt to reconsider Forms 4.5, 4.6, and 5.7 when considering criteria on text selection. Respondents may check on the right the extent of implementation of each series being reviewed.	Thoroughly Implemented	Moderately Implemented	Minimally Implemented	Not Implemented
Criteria on Narrative Comprehension Teachers' Manuals Address:	4	3	2	1
1. The underlying focus of the total reading program is to help students learn to read for meaning, or comprehension	☐	☐	☐	☐
2. Teachers are shown how to teach explicitly, and model each strategy for comprehension	☐	☐	☐	☐
3. Guided silent reading is an integral part of instruction, sharpening pupils' ability to focus on text and their processing of text	☐	☐	☐	☐
4. Teachers are supported to develop *pre-reading* strategies that nurture student predictions, or images of what the story will be	☐	☐	☐	☐
5. The program provides suggestions to teach *during-reading* strategies for active reading	☐	☐	☐	☐
6. Editors offer suggestions to teach *post-reading* strategies, supporting recomprehension	☐	☐	☐	☐
7. Students are shown how to use text-explicit (fact) information and text-implicit (inference, critical reading) strategies to understand	☐	☐	☐	☐
8. Pupils are taught story structures to use when monitoring comprehension ..	☐	☐	☐	☐
9. Students are shown how to gain meaning if they do not understand the text	☐	☐	☐	☐
10. The program provides structures to classify information, such as cause/effect, sequence, compare/contrast, etc.	☐	☐	☐	☐

Interpretation: Columns may be tallied as shown in Form 7.3. Totals between 31–40 may be judged *thoroughly implemented*, 21–30 *moderately implemented*, 11–20 *minimally implemented*, and 1–10 *not implemented.*

Publisher_____

Form 7.5			
TEXT SELECTION FOR EXPOSITORY TEXT COMPREHENSION			

Directions: The Textbook Selection Committee, or principal may wish to review Forms 4.7, 4.8, and 5.8 as criteria are considered related to text selection and expository comprehension. Criteria on expository text selection are shown below. Respondents may check how well the reviewed materials implement criteria on the right. **Criteria on Expository Comprehension Teachers' Manuals Address:**	Thoroughly Implemented	Moderately Implemented	Minimally Implemented	Not Implemented
	4	3	2	1
1. Prior to reading, students are helped to visualize text to be read with structured overviews or advance organizers	☐	☐	☐	☐
2. Students are taught the distinctive features of expository text structures with unit-, chapter-, and paragraph-reading strategies	☐	☐	☐	☐
3. Classes are taught to generate predictions, surveys, overviews, and form questions about content, which create images and aid comprehension	☐	☐	☐	☐
4. Pupils are shown how to read graphics i.e.—maps, photographs, charts, graphs, illustrations, and their captions	☐	☐	☐	☐
5. Learners are taught to map or web terms or concepts to aid classification, to enhance memory and understanding	☐	☐	☐	☐
6. Students are taught to participate in, and to create their own, classification strategies to organize information in their minds	☐	☐	☐	☐
7. Manuals are used to show pupils how to adapt study skills to the reading of subject area texts and non-fiction trade books	☐	☐	☐	☐
8. Teachers show students how to use study guides as structures to read content textbooks	☐	☐	☐	☐

Interpretation: Columns may be tallied as shown in Form 7.3. Totals between 25–32 may be judged *thoroughly implemented*, 17–24 *moderately implemented*, 9–16 *minimally implemented*, and 1–8 *not implemented*.

Publisher_____

Form 7.6

TEXT SELECTION FOR READING AND WRITING ALIGNMENT

Directions: The Textbook Selection Committee or administrator may examine Forms 4.9, 4.10, and 5.9 when considering the role of writing in support of reading better. Related criteria are presented below. Participants may indicate the extent to which reviewed materials meet the criteria on the right.

Criteria on Reading and Writing Teachers' Manuals Address:	Thoroughly Implemented	Moderately Implemented	Minimally Implemented	Not Implemented
	4	3	2	1
1. Manuals develop the concept that writing has a system or structure to help students with writing	☐	☐	☐	☐
2. The program conveys strategies and skills to help students become *process* writers who may improve over a lifetime	☐	☐	☐	☐
3. The program demonstrates that writing helps reading, reading helps writing	☐	☐	☐	☐
4. Teachers' editions support brainstorming, i. e., students' contributing information through discussion of topics provides considerable collective knowledge prior to writing	☐	☐	☐	☐
5. Manuals develop the concept that previewing the process with webs or maps helps students to *see* what they will be doing	☐	☐	☐	☐
6. Students are helped when creating a first draft by reference back to the brainstorming and the web, which organizes those meanings	☐	☐	☐	☐
7. Students are taught cooperative processes of peer editing to gain positive feedback on their writing, and ways to know how to revise	☐	☐	☐	☐
8. Teachers' editions promote children's publishing their works to display or share with peers	☐	☐	☐	☐

Interpretation: Columns may be tallied, giving four points to marks in the left column, three to the next column, two to the third column, and one point to the right column. Totals between 25–32 may be judged *thoroughly implemented*, 17–24 *moderately implemented*, 9–16 *minimally implemented*, and 1–8 *not implemented* in this reading program.

Publisher_____

Form 7.7

TEXT SELECTION FOR MEANING VOCABULARY DEVELOPMENT

Directions: The administrator or Textbook Selection Committee may choose to evaluate Forms 4.11, 4.12, and 5.10 when reviewing texts for purchase. Below, criteria on meaning vocabulary may be found. On the right, participants may judge the extent to which materials being reviewed meet the criteria.

Criteria on Meaning Vocabulary Teachers' Manuals Address:	Thoroughly Implemented	Moderately Implemented	Minimally Implemented	Not Implemented
	4	3	2	1
1. The program builds emphasis on expanding students' knowledge of word meanings	☐	☐	☐	☐
2. Students are encouraged to choose and record words they wish to know ...	☐	☐	☐	☐
3. Pupils are supported to set goals of the number of words they wish to learn each day or week..........................	☐	☐	☐	☐
4. Students are taught that the number of words they know increases over a lifetime	☐	☐	☐	☐
5. Teachers are directed to introduce new vocabulary in the first context in which the word will appear in the text	☐	☐	☐	☐
6. Learners are shown how to create word maps and semantic maps to increase structure which aids memory for new words	☐	☐	☐	☐
7. Word maps are developed in class, later independently to classify new terms into super- and sub-structure categories	☐	☐	☐	☐
8. Teachers develop new terms and concepts into semantic feature matrixes to nurture peer definitions in cooperative groups	☐	☐	☐	☐
9. The students' texts and teachers' manuals develop word foundations—i.e., roots, inflectional endings, prefixes, suffixes, etc.	☐	☐	☐	☐

Interpretation: Columns may be tallied, giving four points to marks in the left column, three to the next column, two to the third column, and one point to the right column. Totals between 28–36 may be judged *thoroughly implemented*, 19–27 *moderately implemented*, 10–18 *minimally implemented*, and 1–9 *not implemented* in this series.

Publisher_____

Form 7.8
TEXT SELECTION FOR LITERARY CONTENT

Directions: The Textbook Selection Committee or principal may wish to reconsider Forms 4.13, 4.14, and 5.11 when reviewing literary formats for text selection. Criteria to select for literary content are developed below. On the right, participants may check how well the reviewed materials meet criteria.

Criteria on the Literature Foundation Teachers' Manuals Address:	Thoroughly Implemented 4	Moderately Implemented 3	Minimally Implemented 2	Not Implemented 1
1. Literary content and instruction in the series aligns well with local reading program goals	☐	☐	☐	☐
2. The program's literary component is congruent with local decisions about the approach (see Forms 6.6–6.7) to reading that is to be used	☐	☐	☐	☐
3. Teachers' manuals support teachers to conduct direct instruction and to model the literary dimensions of stories	☐	☐	☐	☐
4. Students are taught the tools of writer's choice (see Form 7.15) and writer's craft (see Form 7.16), benefiting writing ability and reading comprehension	☐	☐	☐	☐
5. Students are taught that story structures (see Form 7.17) help them to monitor, strengthen retellings, and provide writing structures	☐	☐	☐	☐
6. Students are taught to understand the genre (see Form 7.18) of literature to enhance comprehension, enjoyment, and writing	☐	☐	☐	☐
7. Author studies, reading numerous books by the same author, are encouraged in the program	☐	☐	☐	☐
8. Literary studies are supported with use of cooperative groups or *literature sets*	☐	☐	☐	☐
9. Pupils are taught, during non-fiction reading, and practice those study skills that apply to subject area textbooks	☐	☐	☐	☐

Interpretation: Columns may be tallied as shown in Form 7.3. Totals between 28–36 may be judged *thoroughly implemented*, 19–27 *moderately implemented*, 10–18 *minimally implemented*, and 1–9 *not implemented*.

Publisher_____

Form 7.9

TEXT SELECTION FOR DECODING DEVELOPMENT

Directions: Textbook selection committees or the principal may elect to study Forms 4.15, 4.16, and 5.12 to review decoding criteria. Listed below are word identification criteria related to text selection. Respondents may check on the right the extent to which reviewed materials meet the criteria.

Criteria on Decoding Instruction Teachers' Manuals Address:	Thoroughly Implemented	Moderately Implemented	Minimally Implemented	Not Implemented
	4	3	2	1
1. Students are taught that learning to know new words is a lifetime, expansive process	☐	☐	☐	☐
2. The program develops the concept that word knowledge helps reading, reading comprehension helps word knowledge	☐	☐	☐	☐
3. The program displays a definite thrust toward accelerating students' word recognition	☐	☐	☐	☐
4. The program helps students to see that all four decoding vehicles (sight, context, phonics, and syllabication) each support the other	☐	☐	☐	☐
5. Young readers learn to understand the role of letters, spellings, phonemic awareness, and phonics as cues to gain meaning	☐	☐	☐	☐
6. Early trade books and series' stories offer a concentration of alphabet books, picture books, and predictable books to build a foundation for recognition of known words	☐	☐	☐	☐
7. Pupils are taught to use decoding as a strategic process, using context along with visual and auditory information, to determine words vs. learning rules that may or may not apply	☐	☐	☐	☐
8. Words that were difficult during reading are analyzed in isolation, then returned to context to confirm identification	☐	☐	☐	☐

Interpretation: Columns may be tallied, giving four points to marks in the left column, three to the next column, two to the third column, and one point to the right column. Totals between 25–32 may be judged *thoroughly implemented*, 17–24 *moderately implemented*, 9–16 *minimally implemented*, and 1–8 *not implemented* in the program.

Publisher_____

Form 7.10
SELECTION OF SUPPLEMENTARY INSTRUCTIONAL MATERIALS

Directions: Textbook Selection Committees or administrators will find below criteria related to the purchase of supplementary materials. On the right, respondents may check the extent that each criterion is met in the publication reviewed.

Criteria to Select Supplements:

	Thoroughly Implemented	Moderately Implemented	Minimally Implemented	Not Implemented
	4	3	2	1
1. Practice materials hold high story, strategy, and vocabulary congruence with content of children's texts and teachers' manuals	☐	☐	☐	☐
2. Supplementary materials are chosen to complement the basic reading materials, to extend new strategies and skills................................	☐	☐	☐	☐
3. Multimedia materials (filmstrips, photos, video tapes, software) are available, using content aligned with manuals and students' texts	☐	☐	☐	☐
4. Supplementary materials (word cards, kits, teaching charts) are attractive, durable, and clearly organized for student understanding	☐	☐	☐	☐
5. Supplementary materials are developed to nurture pupils' repeated reading	☐	☐	☐	☐
6. Practice materials have easy vocabulary that enables students to read independently...	☐	☐	☐	☐
7. Practice materials require student responses in complete sentences for higher-level task fulfillment..	☐	☐	☐	☐
8. Practice materials are suited for independent work and cooperative groups	☐	☐	☐	☐
9. Literature response journals include both unstructured pages and pages that aid pupils in writing, such as story frames	☐	☐	☐	☐

Interpretation: Columns may be tallied, giving four points to marks in the left column, three to the next column, two to the third column, and one point to the right column. Totals between 28–36 may be judged *thoroughly implemented*, 18–27 *moderately implemented*, 10–18 *minimally implemented*, and 1–9 *not implemented* in the reading program.

Publisher_____

Form 7.11					
ASSESSMENT COMPONENT OF READING TEXT SELECTION					

Directions: Textbook Selection Committees or principals may review the criteria listed below to judge the assessment component of each publishers' textbook package. On the right, the extent to which a publishing house addresses those criteria may be checked.

Criteria on Assessment Components:	Thoroughly Implemented 4	Moderately Implemented 3	Minimally Implemented 2	Not Implemented 1
1. Assessments appear to judge exactly what teachers have taught, along with pupil applications of those new learnings	☐	☐	☐	☐
2. Provisions are made in assessment options to support teachers when students have difficulty with reading	☐	☐	☐	☐
3. Structures are provided for the most important assessments, those structured observations teachers make as they teach (see Forms 5.6–5.13)	☐	☐	☐	☐
4. Assessments appear to have validity and reliability; i.e., they seem to be accurate	☐	☐	☐	☐
5. Assessment instruments are easy to administer, score, and interpret..........	☐	☐	☐	☐
6. Practice sessions are developed for teachers to help students use test formats prior to actual administration of those assessments	☐	☐	☐	☐
7. End-of-unit, end-of-level assessments are developed to analyze comprehension, study skills, vocabulary, decoding, word knowledge acceleration, known literary qualities, ability of students to monitor and adapt their reading	☐	☐	☐	☐
8. Unit and level tests are adequately diagnostic to identify strengths and weaknesses of students as they progress through the curriculum	☐	☐	☐	☐
9. Structures are provided to organize and assess student portfolios of reading and writing..	☐	☐	☐	☐
10. Student literature response journals are developed to relate to stories in pupils' texts	☐	☐	☐	☐
11. Pupil placement instruments are available to quickly identify text levels at which new students are able to function effectively	☐	☐	☐	☐

–continues–

Publisher_____

Assessment Component of Reading Text Selection -continued-	4	3	2	1

12. Teachers' monitoring of pupil fluency is structured and supported (fluency demonstrates student orchestration of the reading process, effective comprehension and word use) in the assessment process .... ☐ ☐ ☐ ☐

13. An Informal Reading Inventory* and Cloze Test* based on textbook content are provided by the publisher .... ☐ ☐ ☐ ☐

14. Record-keeping is simple and functional, requiring minimal teachers' time, including graphs to show pupil progress, individual pupil progress charts, and cumulative file forms .... ☐ ☐ ☐ ☐

Interpretation: Columns may be tallied, giving four points to marks in the left column, three to the next column, two to the third column, and one point to the right column. Totals between 43–56 may be judged *thoroughly implemented*, 29–42 *moderately implemented*, 15–28 *minimally implemented*, and 1–14 *not implemented* in the series.

SYNTHESIS OF BASAL OR
LITERATURE-BASED SELECTION

(see Forms 7.12 and 7.13)

The Reading Advisory Board and administrator may have a sense that each textbook series that has been examined has goals closely congruent with local curriculum goals. Committees may use each Form 7.12, one for each series reviewed, to compare one program with another, using Form 7.13.

The Problem: Purchasing new reading books is a serious challenge for textbook selection committees and administrators. Doing the job well is time-consuming and stressful, with sales representatives' pressures, colleagues' expectations, and administrators' preferences all having to be considered. Committee members often have no prior experience with complex, comprehensive curriculum studies.

Rationale: Well-chosen literature-based reading series provide the very foundation for children's learning to read and write. Moreover, teachers' manuals may provide the anchor for teachers' planning and teaching, and in many school districts, virtually the only inservice education. The quality of purchases, then, may facilitate or limit teaching and learning opportunities.

Procedures: The purpose of Form 7.12 is to synthesize data from earlier parts of the chapter, Forms 7.2 to 7.11, dealing with selection of reading textbook series. The accumulated information from all the copies of Form 7.12, and finally, the summary matrix, Form 7.13, may be used to interpret selection decisions for administrators, a district curriculum committee, and the school board. Summary and analyses may lead committees to see that some reading materials have clear advantages over alternative selections.

Comments and Cautions

Textbook purchases *do not* comprise the total reading program. Applications of the reading process to expository text and resource book reading must be taught outside of reading textbooks. The recreational reading component may have as much value as direct instruction from reading textbooks.

Form 7.12

EVALUATION OF A BASAL OR LITERATURE-BASED TEXT SERIES

Directions: Forms 7.1–7.11 pull together criteria related to textbook series selection. One set of those forms may be completed for each publisher's materials. On the right, Textbook Selection Committees, administrators, or Reading Advisory Boards may judge agreement with local goals.

Series Selection Synthesis:

	Thoroughly Implemented 4	Moderately Implemented 3	Minimally Implemented 2	Not Implemented 1
1. All of this publisher's materials align well with local reading curriculum goals	☐	☐	☐	☐
2. Content of the program, teachers' manuals, and children's text are integrated (see Form 7.2)	☐	☐	☐	☐
3. The series' emergent literacy component meets the needs of young readers (see Form 7.3)	☐	☐	☐	☐
4. Teachers' manuals and pupils' texts deal well with narrative text comprehension (see Form 7.4)	☐	☐	☐	☐
5. The program develops expository text reading comprehension very well (see Form 7.5)	☐	☐	☐	☐
6. Interrelatedness of reading and writing is important in the series (see Form 7.6)	☐	☐	☐	☐
7. Teaching meaning vocabulary to students is well addressed in the program (see Form 7.7)	☐	☐	☐	☐
8. The reading textbook program develops literary content authentically (see Form 7.8)	☐	☐	☐	☐
9. The reading program uses a current approach to teach students to decode (see Form 7.9)	☐	☐	☐	☐
10. Supplemental teacher and pupil materials aid instruction and learning (see Form 7.10)	☐	☐	☐	☐
11. The literature-based series' assessment monitors pupils' advancement (see Form 7.11)	☐	☐	☐	☐

Interpretation: Columns may be tallied as in Form 7.3. Totals between 34–44 may be viewed as *thoroughly implemented*, 23–33 *moderately implemented*, 12–22 *minimally implemented*, and 1–11 *not implemented* in this series. This evaluation of one publisher may be combined with Form 7.12 for each publisher being considered, and final selection decisions made on Form 7.13.

Form 7.13
SYNTHESIS OF ALL READING PROGRAMS REVIEWED

Directions: Separate evaluations (7.12) may have been completed by the textbook selection committee. On the right, participants may enter the names of each publisher whose materials were reviewed. Finally, checkmarks taken from the respective Form 7.12 for each series may be entered in the appropriate cell below on the right.

Reading Text Selection Criteria:

1. Publishers' materials are aligned with local reading curriculum goals ☐ ☐ ☐ ☐ ☐

2. Content in manuals and readers seems suitable .... ☐ ☐ ☐ ☐ ☐

3. Emerging literacy is well addressed .... ☐ ☐ ☐ ☐ ☐

4. Narrative comprehension is well developed .... ☐ ☐ ☐ ☐ ☐

5. Expository text comprehension is thoroughly presented .... ☐ ☐ ☐ ☐ ☐

6. Writing and reading are integrated .... ☐ ☐ ☐ ☐ ☐

7. Meaning vocabulary evolves well in the materials .... ☐ ☐ ☐ ☐ ☐

8. Literature is authentically displayed .... ☐ ☐ ☐ ☐ ☐

9. Decoding is adequately developed .... ☐ ☐ ☐ ☐ ☐

10. Supplementary materials provide adequate teacher and pupil benefits ☐ ☐ ☐ ☐ ☐

11. The assessment component is appropriate for curriculum and each student .... ☐ ☐ ☐ ☐ ☐

Interpretation: Each committee member may complete Form 7.13 independently before a group interpretation is pursued. Comparisons of checkmarks on each criterion may help the committee to identify component strengths and weaknesses. Totaling each column may provide evidence for the committee about which program gains the greatest number of points. Thereafter, the committee may deliberate to consider all factors involved in the selection process before formulating a recommendation.

SELECTION OF TRADE BOOKS
FOR READING INSTRUCTION

(see Forms 7.14 to 7.20)

Library books, or trade books, as they are described among librarians and curriculum specialists, are highly important to reading programs. Many educators use trade books supplementally. Other educators believe a quality library collection should be the foundation for reading instruction. In those cases, trade book selection should be aligned with language arts curriculum. Classroom libraries, too, hold great significance in children's lives.

The Problem: Principals are key personnel for literacy advancement in schools, but some principals have little vision of the importance of enrichment reading in the personal and literacy development of students. Many schools have neither classroom nor central libraries. Classroom teachers often have little knowledge of how to select titles for classroom collections.

Rationale: Schools rich in trade books, resource books, and other learning center collections possess an important literacy component. The foundation of whole language classrooms is a strong collection of trade books. Beyond literature for its own sake, study of literary structures aids comprehension through knowledge of writers' choice and craft, story structures or grammars, and the fullest range of genre.

Procedures: Educators who select trade books or literature-based texts may refer to Forms 7.14 to 7.20 as structures to apply criteria to purchases. One set of forms may be developed for each literature-based series reviewed or for selected criteria to use in selection of individual trade book titles.

For Further Reading

Canney, G. & Neuenfeldt, C. (1993). "Teachers' Preferences for Reading Materials," *Reading Improvement*, 30, 4, 238–45.

> The authors conducted surveys of 600+ elementary and middle school teachers and learned that most have a preference for a mix of basal readers and trade books in their instructional program. There was no difference based on grade level taught, years of experience, or number of reading courses completed.

Cullinan, B. E. & Galda, L. (1994). *Literature and the Child, Third Edition*. Ft. Worth, TX: Harcourt Brace College Publishers. (College Publishing, 301 Commerce Street, Suite 3700, Fort Worth, TX 76102. 1-708-647-8822.)

> The authors describe different models of literature programs. Checklists are provided to select children's literature. Consistent with current practice, structures to analyze children's responses are provided. Addresses the range of genre, including multicultural treatment.

Title, Set, Series _____

Form 7.14

CRITERIA TO SELECT TRADE BOOKS

	Yes	No
Directions: Trade books usually represent supplemental purchases for school districts. Sometimes, though, those purchases comprise the foundation for the language arts curriculum. Pupils may learn about writing and may expand reading comprehension by studying the craft and choice of authors, story structures, or genre. Related criteria used by librarians, classroom teachers, or administrators are presented below as guidelines for purchases. The criteria will not always be reasons for selection, but may help to avoid books that violate criteria. On the right, respondents may check whether the prospective book, set, or series meets those criteria.		
Criteria for Trade Books:	2	1

Overall Criteria

1. This book captures the interests of pupils; topics are attractive and appropriate ☐ ☐

2. The possible purchase is of high quality and is well written ☐ ☐

3. Students are able to identify with or relate to appropriate characters in the trade book ☐ ☐

4. The quality of language and expression is suited to children's conceptual and linguistic development ☐ ☐

5. The selection is of appropriate readability and conceptual match ☐ ☐

6. The prospective purchase supports the curriculum of the school in a desired way ☐ ☐

7. If a curriculum-enrichment source, it is agreed that the book will not be used by teachers in prior years ☐ ☐

8. This book or series is suitable as a source of pupils' use in literature sets, or literary study group ☐ ☐

9. The book's primary use would be as a whole class title ☐ ☐

10. The book would be most suitable as a title to be read aloud to students ☐ ☐

11. The choice is suitable for use in paired, or dyad reading ☐ ☐

12. The book's role on the master list of titles indicates that this book is appropriate for its proposed use ☐ ☐

13. The physical makeup of the book is suitable, with appropriate print, illustrations, and durability ☐ ☐

14. The book has gained professional recognition from the American Library Association or other groups ☐ ☐

15. The title or series would be acceptable to the community that the school serves ☐ ☐

Interpretation: Respondents may check each criterion, when relevant, to judge whether new selections meet general standards. It may be helpful for participants to look at patterns of checkmarks for various titles or sets of books to discern whether their goals are being met objectively, and according to criteria.

Title, Set, Series _____

Form 7.15

TITLES LEND THEMSELVES TO THE STUDY OF WRITER'S CHOICE

	Yes	No
Directions: Students learn to monitor their reading comprehension by studying how authors select forms or types of writing. As well, pupils may learn to follow those forms in their own writing. Reading Advisory Boards or principals may use the following criteria to judge whether the present collection or new purchases offer balance to the range of books supporting study of writer's choice. On the right, those judgments may signal whether prospective selections do meet those criteria. **Writer's Choice Criteria:**		
	2	1

1. Study of personal writing, such as *get well* cards, *thank you* notes, *letter* writing, giving and receiving *directions*, *diary* entries, *literature logs*, which may advance both reading comprehension and writing .... ☐ ☐

2. Persuasive writing, such as *advertising, cartoon, point of view, travel brochure,* teaches students to *convince* audiences, and to be sensitive to their own *critical* thinking skills as they monitor texts or as they write .... ☐ ☐

3. Descriptive writing, including *narration*, written *dialogues*, *descriptions*, and *stories* that aid comprehension monitoring structures .... ☐ ☐

4. Expository writing, such as *report* writing, giving *directions*, writing from *multiple sources*, and *summarizing* articles or topics .... ☐ ☐

Interpretation: The Reading Advisory Board or other curriculum planners may use checkmarks from Form 7.15 to identify books that would promote each criterion. Checkmarks may signal needs for age-appropriate materials for curriculum development to meet writer's choice criteria. Individual teachers may opt to develop their own copy of Form 7.15 to assess whether classroom titles support this balance. Teachers may make lists of books at the bottom of the page that would demonstrate balance.

Title, Set, Series _____

Form 7.16
TITLES LEND THEMSELVES TO THE STUDY OF WRITER'S CRAFT

Directions: Students may learn to self-monitor their reading comprehension by studying the processes involved in writer's craft. Pupils may study those processes, also, to follow when they construct their own writing. Curriculum committees or Reading Advisory Boards may study related criteria, listed below, as they review present school holdings, or consider the selection of new books or literature sets. On the right, respondents may mark whether titles do meet locally desired criteria.

Writer's Craft Criteria:

	Yes	No
	2	1
1. Authors evoke *feeling*, *tone*, *sense*, etc., with the various tools of the craft, any of which may be suited to the contents of reading or students' construction of texts	☐	☐
2. Writers employ sources of identification with humanity through *personification*, *point of view*, *characterization*, or *dialogue*	☐	☐
3. Writers develop impressions with use of *simile*, *symbolism*, *metaphor*, or *analogy*	☐	☐
4. Authors apply readers' structures to stories with crafts of *comparison*, *form*, *cause and effect*, *dialogue*, *sequence* or *classification*	☐	☐
5. Authors are able to use *suspense*, *curiosity*, *humor*, etc., to develop readers' sense of emotion as they monitor texts for meaning	☐	☐

Interpretation: The Reading Advisory Board or administrator may use checkmarks from Form 7.16 to study patterns of books that would promote each criterion. Checkmarks may indicate needs for age-appropriate materials for curricular development to address writer's craft. Individual teachers may prepare their individual Form 7.16 to judge whether classroom titles support a balance in writer's craft. Teachers may make lists of books at the bottom of the page that would demonstrate this balance.

Title, Set, Series _____

Form 7.17
PURCHASES LEND THEMSELVES TO THE STUDY OF STORY STRUCTURES

Directions: Pupils may improve their comprehension monitoring and writing skills by understanding story structures. The Reading Advisory Board or principal may complete Form 7.17 to judge balance in library titles to support pupils' study of story structures. Criteria are listed below, and checkmarks to signify presence or absence in purchase options may be made on the right.

Story Structure Criteria:	Yes 2	No 1
1. Lends itself to understanding of story structures, or story grammars, which help readers to monitor as they read, aiding comprehension	☐	☐
2. Enables study of setting to structure the understanding of time and place, aiding students to relate content to existing knowledge	☐	☐
3. Uses character development to help readers to see stories as lifelike, aiding identification or meaningful interaction with characters	☐	☐
4. Lends itself to the study of plot to offer students a structure to follow the story as its action unfolds	☐	☐
5. Develops an emergence of conflict, which provides the vehicle to help the character(s) to accomplish the goals	☐	☐
6. Develops a theme to create an underlying core to tie together the plot, characters, etc., to convey a deeper level of author's message	☐	☐
7. Conveys meaning of the author's or character's point of view	☐	☐
8. Supports readers' imagery through the author's style, which demonstrates ways to arrange words or sentences	☐	☐
9. Creates visual imagery with editors' choices of illustrations to support story sequence	☐	☐

Interpretation: Checkmarks may indicate balance in the collection to meet criteria in Form 7.17, or may signal the need for age-appropriate books to meet story structure curriculum criteria. Individual teachers also may create their own copy of Form 7.17 to evaluate balance in their classroom collection to meet the criteria.

Title, Set, Series _____

	Form 7.18		
	PURCHASES LEND THEMSELVES TO THE STUDY OF LITERARY GENRE		

Directions: Pupils study of genre may enhance comprehension through monitoring those formats and may improve writing as students construct pieces representing the genre. Reading Advisory Boards or principals may use the following criteria to evaluate whether the present collection or new purchases represent balance in titles to use for genre study. On the right checkmarks may indicate whether the criterion is, or is not, met.

Literary Genre Criteria:	Yes	No
	2	1

1. This genre may be used to teach its form, to use its form when monitoring text, or to employ the form when writing .... ☐ ☐

2. The picture book options help readers to understand a story by studying its illustrations, and to appreciate the quality of its art work .... ☐ ☐

3. The predictable book titles help young readers to develop meaning and vocabulary by studying illustrations and using text redundancy to know words they are reading .... ☐ ☐

4. The folk tales and folklore, without known authors, tell stories of particular cultures or times to help readers encounter other beliefs and mores .... ☐ ☐

5. Purchase choices representing age-appropriate fables, myths, and epics address human life, explain ancient worlds, or tell the struggles of heroes .... ☐ ☐

6. Titles representing multicultural literature offer stories of ethnic or racial groups, past or present, that help readers to understand those lives and values, both people of their own *and* other cultures .... ☐ ☐

7. Options of fantasy show the authors' use of imagination through narration to alter familiar realities to go outside of natural law or scientific fact .... ☐ ☐

8. The poetry choices gives readers the sounds and images to *play with words* to understand and to create artistic forms of literature .... ☐ ☐

9. Titles of modern fiction convey stories that could happen, and are consistent with the lives of real people, yet are fictitious .... ☐ ☐

10. Choices among historical fiction create a story consistent with a distinctive time and place, helping the past to come alive, employing authentic settings and conditions .... ☐ ☐

11. Titles representing science fiction, often focused on technology, develop stories that may be, or may become with further research, scientifically feasible .... ☐ ☐

–continues–

Title, Set, Series _____

Purchases Lend Themselves to the Study of Literary Genre -continued-	2	1
12. Titles representing biography describe the accomplishments and lives of real people in ways that children can see themselves in those lives, creating role models	☐	☐
13. Purchase options including informational books develop nonfiction concepts to gain knowledge about the world	☐	☐
14. Purchase options include a range of children's and adult's magazines to address interests and hobbies, and to support the school's curriculum	☐	☐
15. Selections include appropriate children's and adults' newspapers to meet individual pupil needs and to fulfill the curriculum	☐	☐
16. Options to purchase nonfiction do lend themselves to study skills applied to various reading contexts—i.e., use of tables of contents, index, glossary, chapter sections and subsections	☐	☐

Interpretation: The Reading Advisory Board, administrator, or other curriculum planners may study checkmarks in Form 7.18 to see if the present collection or prospective purchases would show balance in meeting the above criteria. Checkmarks may indicate that balance exists, or that new age-appropriate purchases should be completed. Individual teachers may opt to create their personal copy of Form 7.18 to judge whether the classroom collection has a desired balance.

Form 7.19
MATRIX TO EVALUATE TRADE BOOK OPTIONS

Directions: Categories of trade book options are listed below. The Reading Advisory Board, librarian, or administrator may tally titles by category, and by grade level, on the right to monitor balance in the collection. The core part of Form 7.19 may be enlarged on the photocopy machine to provide additional space to contain tally marks.

Trade Book Categories:	K	1	2	3	4	5	6
1. Picture books							
2. Predictable books							
3. Big books							
4. Folk tales, folklore							
5. Fables, myths, epics							
6. Multicultural books							
7. Fantasy titles							
8. Modern fiction							
9. Historical fiction							
10. Science fiction							
11. Biography							
12. Poetry							
13. Informational books							

Interpretation: The Reading Advisory Board or principal may ask the library staff to complete a copy of Form 7.19 to assess balance in the collection to meet categories of literary study. As well, the Board might ask each teacher to complete Form 7.19 as it represents classroom collections. Collating that information might lead to judgments about whether the collection is comprehensive, or warrants purchases by categories. The library staff might generate a computerized list of the school's collection by categories. Teachers at grade levels, or grouped by primary and intermediate levels, might work with the principal or Reading Advisory Board to make decisions about when books would be age- or grade-appropriate to support literary study goals.

Form 7.20

SYNTHESIS OF CRITERIA TO PURCHASE TRADE BOOKS

Directions: Trade books enrich both children's lives and the school curriculum. Categories related to tying together trade book purchases are listed below. On the right, the Reading Advisory Board, librarian, or administrator may check the extent to which categories have been implemented.

Synthesis for Trade Book Selection:

	Thoroughly Implemented	Moderately Implemented	Minimally Implemented	Not Implemented
	4	3	2	1
1. Decisions about purchases are consistent with the school's curriculum goals (see Form 4.20) and reading approach (see Form 6.8)	☐	☐	☐	☐
2. Choices of trade book purchases are congruent with school and classroom organization options (see Forms 7.2, 7.4, 7.11, 8.10)	☐	☐	☐	☐
3. Overall qualities of books reviewed are considered during selection (see Form 7.14)	☐	☐	☐	☐
4. Writer's choice is well represented among new titles selected to aid literary interpretation, support writing, and increase reading comprehension (see Form 7.15)	☐	☐	☐	☐
5. Writer's craft is well represented among new titles selected to aid literary interpretation, enhance writing, and aid comprehension (see Form 7.16)	☐	☐	☐	☐
6. Selections model story structures to faciliate analysis and to aid development of reading comprehension and writing development (see Form 7.17) .	☐	☐	☐	☐
7. The fullest range of genre options is addressed, to understand literary forms and to monitor reading comprehension (see Form 7.18)	☐	☐	☐	☐
8. Balance is evident in the school's range of trade book selections (see Form 7.19)	☐	☐	☐	☐

Interpretation: Reading Advisory Boards, librarians, teachers, or principals may study patterns of checkmarks in Form 7.20 to judge how comprehensively they have directed the selection of trade books and library holdings. Cumulative data may support decisions to revise selection, or may affirm the present choices.

SELECTION OF READING SOFTWARE MATERIALS   (see Form 7.21)

Rapid advancements in technology cause educators to experience frustration. Any current purchases are replaced by technological advancements within months. To remain current, and to make purchasing decisions with longevity, administrators need to network in active ways. The talents of the educational service center, university consultant, expert colleague, and computer sales and consultant personnel are invaluable.

The Problem: Identifying quality software that actually advances pupils' reading and writing, rather than simply being electronic workbooks, is a challenge. A great concern is how not to make costly investments that will be regretted almost at once. The selection of *user friendly* hardware sometimes seems less important than cost.

Rationale: Computers can motivate and advance students' reading abilities. To provide visionary leadership, the administrator may need support to enable teachers to select both suitable hardware and quality software. Administrators or knowledgeable colleagues usually provide the necessary staff development to support teacher use of computers.

Procedures: Reading Advisory Boards or textbook committees often are asked to make recommendations regarding selection of technology. Assuming that suitable hardware exists, the challenge is to identify software that advances pupils' reading in school curriculum. Form 7.21 offers those criteria.

For Further Reading

Kincade, K. M. & Stange, T. V. (1993). "Theory into Practice: Issues to Consider When Selecting Reading Software to Meet Different Readers' Needs," *Reading Horizons*, 34, 2, 151–69.

> The authors recommend that teachers scrutinize software manuals and programs to assure that content matches students' needs and the school's curriculum. Kincade and Stange appraise software programs to judge ease of use, format, and management ease.

Wepner, S. B. (1991). "Linking Technology to Genre-Based Reading," *The Reading Teacher*, 45, 1, 68–70.

> The author describes the limits of one-computer classrooms. She reviews software that supports various literary genre. Wepner advocates software that parallels trade book functions, but with the bonus of social communication and text interaction.

Form 7.21

SELECTION OF READING SOFTWARE MATERIALS

Directions: Reading Advisory Boards, Textbook Selection Committees, or principals may review software purchasing processes by studying the criteria below. To judge the extent to which criteria meet local needs, checkmarks may be made on the right.

Criteria to Select Reading Software:	Meets Criteria Thoroughly	Meets Criteria Moderately	Meets Criteria Minimally	Does Not Meet Criteria
	4	3	2	1
1. Program rationale and goals are stated so that purchasers *know* what they are buying	☐	☐	☐	☐
2. Content complements the school's reading curriculum goals and objectives	☐	☐	☐	☐
3. Content fits the needs and interests of the student population	☐	☐	☐	☐
4. Content is accurate, complete, and logically sequenced to aid learner use	☐	☐	☐	☐
5. Ample opportunities are provided to practice strategies stated in sales materials	☐	☐	☐	☐
6. Directions for pupils to support reading and writing are simple, direct, and easy to follow	☐	☐	☐	☐
7. Reading experiences are provided that advance pupils' abilities and may be tailored to individual needs	☐	☐	☐	☐
8. Materials warrant students' problem-solving interaction rather than skill, drill, or practice applications	☐	☐	☐	☐
9. Students are provided appropriate feedback to nurture reading gains and motivation	☐	☐	☐	☐
10. The editorial foundation of the program stresses reading to comprehend, or making sense of text—and appears transferable to text reading	☐	☐	☐	☐
11. Content uses writing, or the construction of text, as a vehicle to advance comprehension	☐	☐	☐	☐
12. Content accelerates word knowledge to help comprehension, comprehension to advance word knowledge	☐	☐	☐	☐
13. Program content lends itself to classroom instruction, i.e., teachers may enrich the curriculum options with this program	☐	☐	☐	☐

–continues–

Selection of Reading Software Materials -continued-	4	3	2	1
14. Software content supports the themes studied in the classroom	☐	☐	☐	☐
15. Reading difficulty of content is suited to those students who use the program	☐	☐	☐	☐
16. Program assessments or tests accurately measure pupil success	☐	☐	☐	☐
17. Program materials accurately record and track each pupil's progress	☐	☐	☐	☐
18. Teacher support materials, such as guides and resource materials, are included	☐	☐	☐	☐
19. The program has been adequately field-tested to insure practicality and increase purchaser confidence	☐	☐	☐	☐
20. Cost of the software is consistent with local use of the materials	☐	☐	☐	☐

Cover the page here and below prior to photocopying if users are not to see the interpretation until later.

Interpretation: Software evaluators may tally columns in Form 7.21, giving four points to checkmarks in the left column, three points to marks in the second column, two points to the next column, and one point to checkmarks on the right. Totals between 61–80 may be interpreted as *meets criteria thoroughly*, between 41–60 *meets criteria moderately*, between 21–40 *meets criteria minimally*, and between 1–20 *does not meet criteria*.

SELECTION OF MATERIALS FOR   (see Form 7.22)
SPECIAL READING PROGRAMS

Instructional and recreational reading materials for students in special education programs must be interesting, appropriately challenging, satisfying, and used in a way to accelerate learning. Students and educators probably would prefer to have special and regular students read from the same materials, and may seek strategies to adapt regular texts to special students.

The Problem: Text and trade book materials suitable for the mainstream of children in classrooms may not be equally suitable for special education students. Strategies to adapt mainstream materials for use with both slow and advanced special education students may not suffice to expand pupils' reading success.

Rationale: Students learn more easily if textbooks are of appropriate difficulty and do not draw unusual attention from peers. Materials for special education students may lend themselves to learning how to learn. Those materials should help special students, just as regular students, to understand and remember text information. Components for teachers may be used most effectively if teachers' strategies are task-specific. Enrichment trade books may be adapted particularly to special education needs.

Procedures: Reading Advisory Boards, Textbook Selection Committees, administrators, or teachers may use Form 7.22 to consider criteria for choosing instructional materials for special education programs. Those criteria may also be used to reconsider the suitability of currently used instructional materials.

For Further Reading

Kirk, S. A., et al. (1993). *Educating Exceptional Children, Seventh Edition.* Boston: Houghton Mifflin Company. (Wayside Road, Burlington, MA 01803. 1-800-733-1717.)

The text is addressed to special education and classroom teachers, counselors, and psychologists who function as teams to help pupils. The volume is written to assist in the preparation of those who will meet the needs of exceptional people in a contemporary society.

Smith, D. D. & Luckasson, R. (1995). *Special Education: Teaching in an Age of Challenge, Second Edition.* Boston: Allyn and Bacon. (Dept 894, 160 Gould Street, Needham Heights, MA 02194-2310. 1-800-852-8024.)

The text brings research to practical applications. Current teaching strategies are described, case studies are integrated into the text, and current issues are interpreted. This edition adds inclusion, cultural diversity, bilingual issues, and technology.

Form 7.22
SELECTION OF MATERIALS FOR SPECIAL READING PROGRAMS

Directions: Below, Reading Advisory Boards, administrators, or Textbook Selection Committees will find criteria for the selection of textbooks and trade books for special education programs. On the right, respondents may check the extent to which titles or textbook series implement those criteria. Unfamiliar terms are described in the glossary.

Criteria for Special Reading Materials:	Thoroughly Implemented	Moderately Implemented	Minimally Implemented	Not Implemented
	4	3	2	1
1. Support *learning strategies** or *cognitive strategies** to learn *how* to learn ...	☐	☐	☐	☐
2. Apply advance organizers* and mnemonics* to enhance understanding and memory	☐	☐	☐	☐
3. Lend themselves to task analysis* that breaks instruction into smaller parts	☐	☐	☐	☐
4. Adaptable to teachers' modeling for students concepts and processes to be learned	☐	☐	☐	☐
5. Effectively adaptable for direct instruction* and generalization*	☐	☐	☐	☐
6. Yields readability levels suitable for the clientele, including high-interest/low vocabulary texts and trade books, picture books, and predictable books	☐	☐	☐	☐
7. Accelerates phonological skill, word recognition, and decoding development	☐	☐	☐	☐
8. Lend themselves to support parent tutoring to enrich school activities	☐	☐	☐	☐
9. Uses computer-based instruction that supplements traditional teaching, drill, practice, supplementary work, and word processing	☐	☐	☐	☐

Interpretation: Columns may be totaled, giving four points to marks in the left column, three points to marks in the next column, two to the next column, and one point to checkmarks in the right column. Totals between 28–36 may be judged *thoroughly implemented*, between 19–27 *moderately implemented*, between 10–18 *minimally implemented*, and between 1–9 *not implemented*.

SELECTION OF PROFESSIONAL BOOKS FOR TEACHERS AND ADMINISTRATORS

(see Form 7.23)

An informed faculty is more likely to have effective reading teachers than is an uninformed faculty. While the youngest teachers may possess current knowlege about teaching children to read, some older teachers may not have studied for a number of years. The principal may be in a position to nurture professional reading. Having a current library is a key source.

The Problem: Some schools have no professional library, at all. Others have only a few professional books, often given by teachers who finished master's degrees a decade or so in the past. Given the turnover of ideas based on research in cognitive psychology and learning, outdated books on reading instruction hold little value. Some principals may not understand the importance of teachers' remaining current on literature about teaching children to read.

Rationale: A current, well-informed faculty that is able to use contemporary ideas about teaching children to read is likely to operate at a high professional level. Faculties that are encouraged to share *book reports* or reviews of professional articles at faculty meetings may set a tone for shared professional development.

Rationale: The Reading Advisory Board or principal may study Form 7.23 to gain feedback on how comprehensive the collection of professional books and journals is in order to identify titles that might be purchased. Participants may refer to *For Further Reading* sections of the *Resource Book* to identify professional books regarding Form 7.23 criteria and Appendix B to consider names of professional journals.

For Further Reading

Sanacore, J. (1993). "Using Study Groups to Create a Professional Community (Reading Leadership)," *Journal of Reading*, 37, 1, 62–66.

> Sanacore describes components of effective study groups and provides examples of how to apply components to local settings. He recommends study groups as complements to traditional staff development.

Slusarski, S. B. (1992). *Enhancing Professional Development through Reading Professional Literature* (ED 351 496).

> The author makes three time-management suggestions: scheduling, planning, and prioritizing to complete the needed reading of professional literature. She suggests reading book reviews, publishers' brochures, and abstracts to efficiently get background information.

Form 7.23
SELECTION OF PROFESSIONAL BOOKS FOR TEACHERS AND ADMINISTRATORS

Directions: Schools purchasing new reading materials often also select new professional books and journals for teachers. Criteria are listed below for use by the Reading Advisory Board or principals. On the right, participants may check desirability of materials under review.

Criteria for Professional Materials:	Highly Desirable	Moderately Desirable	Minimally Desirable	Not Desirable
	4	3	2	1
1. Books dealing with classroom reading instruction	☐	☐	☐	☐
2. Books addressing *current* concepts of reading comprehension	☐	☐	☐	☐
3. Books that develop *contemporary* thinking about accelerated decoding ability	☐	☐	☐	☐
4. Books to teach students how to read content or expository textbooks	☐	☐	☐	☐
5. Books that have to do with recreational or enrichment reading	☐	☐	☐	☐
6. Books that develop contemporary concepts of organization or grouping	☐	☐	☐	☐
7. Books that help teachers to think through present beliefs about reading assessment	☐	☐	☐	☐
8. Books dealing with whole language concepts	☐	☐	☐	☐
9. Books addressing concepts that involve literature-based reading and writing	☐	☐	☐	☐
10. Journals and monographs from the International Reading Association on topics above and numerous other topics on reading	☐	☐	☐	☐
11. Journals and monographs from the National Council of Teachers of English on topics listed above and additional topics on reading	☐	☐	☐	☐

Interpretation: Form 7.23 may be assessed by participants seeking congruence between new textbook or trade book purchases and staff development. Respondents may study checkmarks to determine topics warranting purchases of books, journals, or monographs.

SYNTHESIS TO SELECT INSTRUCTIONAL READING MATERIALS (see Form 7.24)

Instructional materials become the medium for children's learning and for effective teaching of reading and writing. Content of the reading textbook series may affirm attention to developmental, functional (content reading), recreational, and diagnostic reading. Choices of materials that help students to *think about text meanings* or active reading comprehension are a challenge to textbook committees, as is decoding treated as a strategic vs a skill process.

The Problem: In many districts, an administrator asks faculties to choose representatives for a textbook selection committee. Members may be principal's favorites, outspoken and dominant, but neither representative nor thoughtful. Ultimate committee decisions may sometimes be disregarded.

Rationale: The materials selected warrant careful reflection by the faculty and its representation. The quality of instructional materials may influence directly the quality of pupils' learning. The committee, fully representative of each grade level, or primary and intermediate teachers, is very important. Members should be knowledgeable and objective about reading, and about trade books. An outside, expert resource person may help the committee to remain objective.

Procedures: Reading Advisory Boards or principals who study alignment of program goals with textbook purchases may complete Form 7.24. Reflection on Form 7.24 should ease completion of Form 7.25 to develop statements of strengths, needs, and priorities for selection of materials and Form 7.26 to develop an action plan.

Comments and Cautions:

New reading program purchases may not cure old problems, at all. New texts may not change the way some teachers teach, or what some teachers believe is important, regardless of teachers' manual content.

A distinctive challenge to educators is to choose instructional materials that help students to think about text meaning as a process rather than as a skill.

Form 7.24

SYNTHESIS TO SELECT INSTRUCTIONAL READING MATERIALS

Directions: Reading Advisory Board members or administrators may study Forms 3.11–3.13, 4.19–4.21, 6.7–6.9 and 7.1–7.22 to synthesize data regarding selection of new reading materials. Criteria are listed below, and respondents may check the extent to which those criteria have been applied during the present investigation.

Criteria for Materials Selection:	Thoroughly Applied	Moderately Applied	Minimally Applied	Not Applied
	4	3	2	1
1. Reading textbook materials from numerous publishing houses have been evaluated prior to selection (see Forms 7.2–7.13)	☐	☐	☐	☐
2. Trade books are chosen to address congruence with program goals, either to enrich literature-based textbook use, or as the fundamental medium for instruction in non-textbook programs (see Forms 7.14–7.20)	☐	☐	☐	☐
3. Suitable software is selected to complement, to enrich, or to supplant the basic reading curriculum (see Forms 7.21)	☐	☐	☐	☐
4. Materials for special reading programs are selected by those specialists in conjunction with the Reading Advisory Board or principal (see Form 7.22) ..	☐	☐	☐	☐
5. A range of books, monographs, and journals on teaching children to read is selected for the professional library (see Form 7.23)	☐	☐	☐	☐
6. Suitable reading assessment materials to evaluate individual student progress, and to monitor overall reading program status, are selected (see Form 7.20)	☐	☐	☐	☐

Cover the page here and below prior to photocopying if users are not to see the interpretation until later.

Interpretation: Participants may tally respondents' checkmarks, giving four points to marks in the left column, three points to the next, two to the third column, and one point to each mark in the right column. Totals between 19–24 may be interpreted as *thoroughly applied*, between 13–18 as *moderately applied*, between 7–12 as *minimally applied*, and between 1–6 as *not applied*. This synthesis supports completion of Forms 7.25–7.26.

Form 7.25

SELECTION OF INSTRUCTIONAL READING MATERIALS: STRENGTHS, NEEDS, AND PRIORITIES

Directions: Below, principals, textbook selection committees, or Reading Advisory Boards will find categories related to the selection of reading instructional materials. On the right, space is provided for respondents to enter reading program-related strengths, needs, and priorities based on worksheets throughout the chapter, but particularly Form 7.24.

	Strengths	*Needs*	*Priorities*
1. Literature-based or Basal Reading Materials	1. 2.	1. 2.	1. 2.
2. Trade Books for Reading Program Selection	1. 2.	1. 2.	1. 2.
3. Reading-based Computer Software Selection	1. 2.	1. 2.	1. 2.
4. Materials for Special Reading Programs	1. 2.	1. 2.	1. 2.
5. Professional Books and Journals for Faculty	1. 2.	1. 2.	1. 2.
6. Assessment Component for Reading Materials Selection	1. 2.	1. 2.	1. 2.
7. Plan-of-Action for Selection of Reading Materials	1. 2.	1. 2.	1. 2.

Form 7.26

**SELECTION OF INSTRUCTIONAL READING MATERIALS:
ADMINISTRATIVE PLAN-OF-ACTION**

Directions: Principals, Reading Advisory Board members, or textbook selection committees may culminate study with a plan-of-action for selection of reading materials. Participants should be as specific as possible about what they seek to accomplish, how they will pursue selection, and how they will know when they have reached their goals. Application of conclusions from Forms 7.24 and 7.25 may support the writing of the plan-of-action. Statements should be as simple, direct, and as useful as possible.

1. Goal Statement: _____

2. Objectives:

   a) _____

   b) _____

   c) _____

3. Activities: Dates; time checkpoints:

   a) _____   * _____

   b) _____   * _____

   c) _____   * _____

   d) _____   * _____

   e) _____   * _____

4. Resources: (professional reading, consultation, visitations)

   a) _____   * _____

   b) _____   * _____

   c) _____   * _____

5. How I will know when my goal is accomplished:

   _____

   _____

   _____

   _____

CHAPTER 8

ORGANIZATION OF SCHOOL AND CLASSROOM READING

Organization of the reading program deals with the ways in which the principal or faculty members assign pupils to classroom units. Similarly, classroom organization addresses the ways in which teachers assign pupils to instructional groups. Various organizational models have emerged over time designed to enhance teacher effectiveness and to increase the quality of student learning. In order to address reading organization, various segments of the chapter may be used for general information, teacher-administrator conferences, staff development workshops, or goal-setting processes.

Curriculum influences now addressing reading program organization are thematic, unit-based, integrated instruction, and reading-across-the-curriculum, writing-across-the-curriculum. Present theories tying active involvement and social interaction with reading and writing address the hope and need to build positive feelings toward literacy. Many educators are troubled by the hostility toward both reading and writing as learners approach middle-school and junior high school ages. The evident way to address this alarming social concern may be to change what is taught, how teaching occurs, and to change the interaction of students as active problem-solvers vs listeners while they learn to read and write in social contexts.

Reading organizational change has emerged slowly across decades, often returning to whole class instruction. Innovations have run short life cycles, except for (a) self-contained classes and departmentalization at school levels, and (b)whole-class and ability group instruction within classrooms. Innovations of reading organization require years to become *institutionalized*, supported with frequent goal-setting reminders, praise, staff development, focused supervision, and peer nurturance.

READING PROGRAM ORGANIZATION   (see Form 8.1)

Reading program organization suggests assigning students to classes, assigning children to instructional groups in classes, and developing classroom environments. Decisions may be addressed at the central office, by the principal, by the faculty, or by individual teachers.

The Problem: Many schools may have no defined organizational plan. Students may be assigned to class without careful reflection. Teachers may group children without evidence of effectiveness or consideration of district philosophy. Faculty may not always feel empowered to attempt alternatives.

Rationale: A well-planned reading program organization may reflect on good practice, local needs, and research effectiveness. Issues to resolve are direct instruction vs incidental discovery, strategies vs skills, authentic literature vs literature-based text series, heterogeneous vs homogeneous groups, and implicit organizational structures accompanying those decisions. Old concepts that are returning, such as thematic instruction and cooperative grouping, may warrant non-traditional organization. Prior to changing reading organization, faculties may need to decide what their goals are. Staff development would be warranted if program change occurs.

Procedures: Form 8.1 may be used to gain an overview of the present status of reading program organization. Using worksheets from Chapter 8, the Reading Advisory Board or principal may choose to conduct a more thorough study, maintain the present program, or revise based on needs and evidence.

For Further Reading

Spencer, C. & Allen, M. G. (1989). *Grouping Students by Ability: A Review of the Literature* (ED 302 326).

> The authors' review of literature suggests that students learn best in classes where ability levels are average or higher. This concept is suggested as a starting point for changing attitudes and practices. Heterogeneous grouping is then endorsed.

Wilson, M. C. (1947). "The Teacher's Problems in a Differentiated Reading Program," *Elementary English*, 24, 2, 77–85+.

> Wilson's article addresses timely and timeless issues in regard to adjusting instruction for individuals and groups. Teachers, then and now, are concerned with limited instructional time, changes to gain high level thinking, and an adequate range of materials. Early concerns about ability groups are comparable to present efforts to group flexibly for social, interest, skills, or cooperative groups.

Form 8.1

READING PROGRAM ORGANIZATION

Directions: Each cell below allows for decisions about how well the reading program organization functions, and how the present organization should be revised or maintained as a result of needs assessment. *On the upper left* of each cell respondents may judge the extent to which the organization now meets the criteria below. *On the lower right,* judgments may be made on the extent to which the criterion needs to be met in the program's future organization.

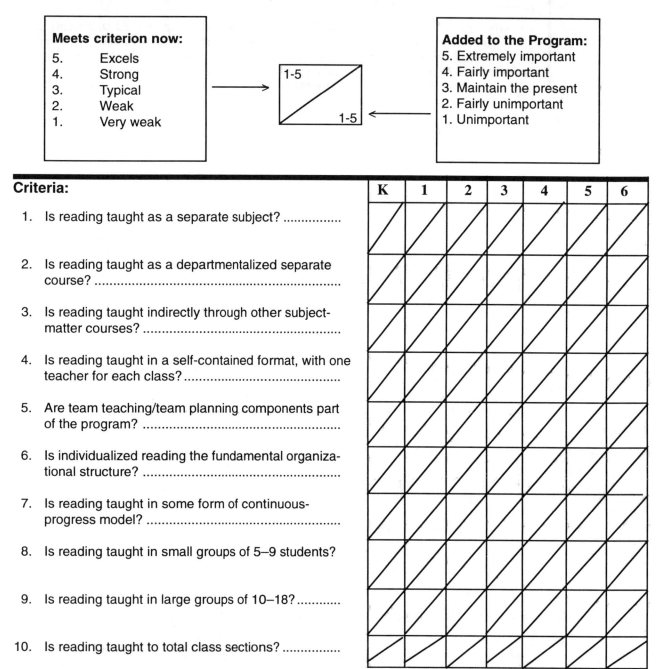

Meets criterion now:
5. Excels
4. Strong
3. Typical
2. Weak
1. Very weak

Added to the Program:
5. Extremely important
4. Fairly important
3. Maintain the present
2. Fairly unimportant
1. Unimportant

Criteria:

	K	1	2	3	4	5	6
1. Is reading taught as a separate subject?							
2. Is reading taught as a departmentalized separate course?							
3. Is reading taught indirectly through other subject-matter courses?							
4. Is reading taught in a self-contained format, with one teacher for each class?							
5. Are team teaching/team planning components part of the program?							
6. Is individualized reading the fundamental organizational structure?							
7. Is reading taught in some form of continuous-progress model?							
8. Is reading taught in small groups of 5–9 students?							
9. Is reading taught in large groups of 10–18?							
10. Is reading taught to total class sections?							

–continues–

Reading Program Organization   -continued-   K   1   2   3   4   5   6

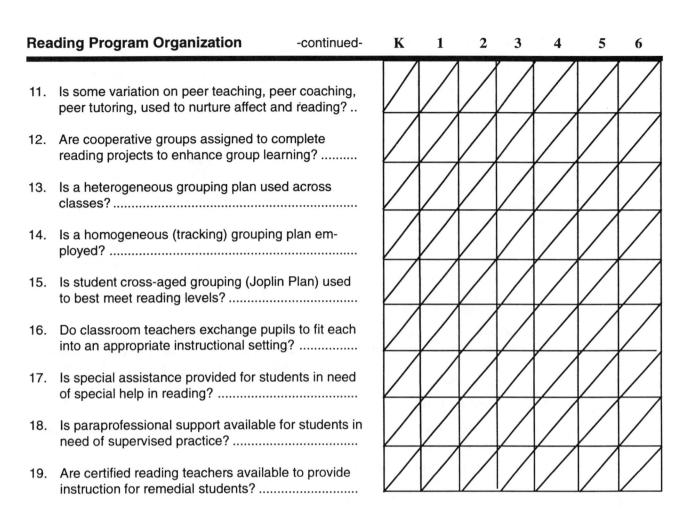

11. Is some variation on peer teaching, peer coaching, peer tutoring, used to nurture affect and reading? ..

12. Are cooperative groups assigned to complete reading projects to enhance group learning? ....

13. Is a heterogeneous grouping plan used across classes? ....

14. Is a homogeneous (tracking) grouping plan employed? ....

15. Is student cross-aged grouping (Joplin Plan) used to best meet reading levels? ....

16. Do classroom teachers exchange pupils to fit each into an appropriate instructional setting? ....

17. Is special assistance provided for students in need of special help in reading? ....

18. Is paraprofessional support available for students in need of supervised practice? ....

19. Are certified reading teachers available to provide instruction for remedial students? ....

Interpretation: The Reading Advisory Board or principal may use Form 8.1 in several ways. One use is to judge present effectiveness of organization. Another function is to judge how the program is to advance when revised. A caution is to study interaction between present use and prospective change, to assure that valuable components are not lost with program revisions. To judge revision priorities, the Reading Advisory Board may wish to gain consensus by encircling those three to four items which are deemed clearly most important.

SCHOOL-LEVEL READING ORGANIZATIONAL OPTIONS   (see Form 8.2)

Classroom settings that support good teaching and good learning are positive for teachers, pupils, principals, the central office, and parents. Personnel are concerned about how to assign students to teachers in order to best form classes.

The Problem: Sometimes a teaching philosophy may be more important than individual learners or teacher survival. Principals in some cases may be most concerned with treating each teacher fairly and equally. In other cases, the principal may be concerned only with optimizing learning for each child on level. Assignments often are conducted randomly, developed to fulfill a program philosophy, and may segregate students by ability. Administrators may overstress cooperative groups, disregarding strategy and skill learning in the total curriculum.

Rationale: The annual quest to find the best learning combinations is troublesome to school people at all levels. Teachers are expected to help each pupil make strong reading gains. As well, teachers wish to operate effectively and efficiently. An oft-overheard concern is that teachers simply do not have two or three additional hours in their day to best plan for instruction.

Procedures: Numerous classroom options to organize for reading are found in Form 8.2. Consideration may lead a principal, Advisory Board, or faculty to discuss suitability of choices. Form 8.3 may be used to reflect thoroughly on options that may be adopted in a school.

For Further Reading

Flood, J., et al. (1992). "Am I Allowed to Group? Using Flexible Patterns for Effective Instruction," *Reading Teacher*, 45, 8, 608–16.

> The authors show how flexible groups may be used to create successful reading and writing activities. The authors opine that research on flexible grouping's effectiveness should be conducted.

Smith, N. B. (1963). *Reading Instruction for Today's Children.* Englewood Cliffs, NJ: Prentice H Hall, Inc., 108–160. (Out of print, but found in many university education libraries.)

> Smith chose to acquaint preservice and inservice teachers with theory and research, applying those elements to actual teaching. An inclusive classic that contains a section on organizational options, some current at the time of the book's publication, some that are presently rediscovered and popular.

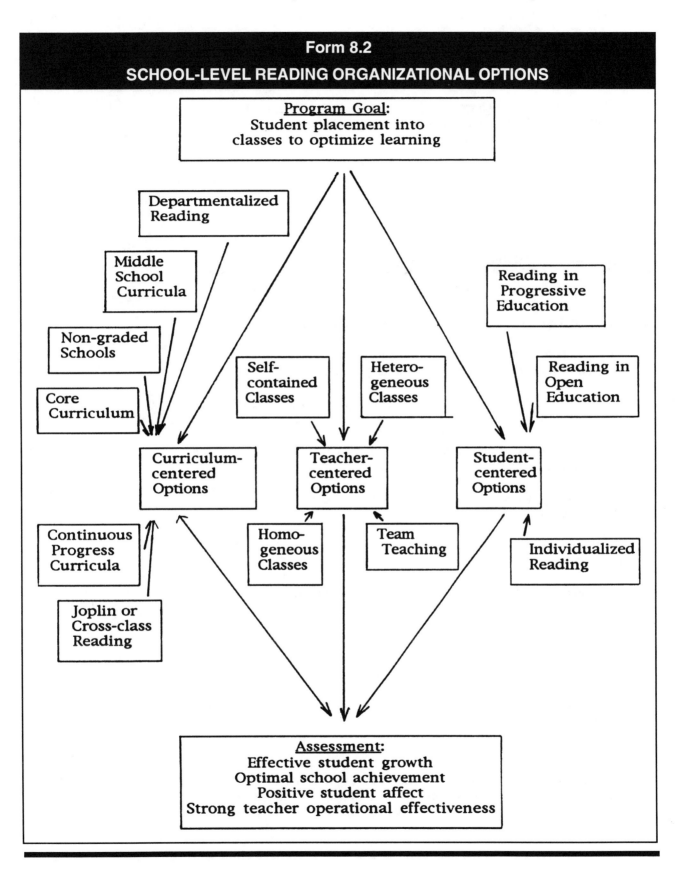

Form 8.2

SCHOOL-LEVEL READING ORGANIZATIONAL OPTIONS

<u>Program Goal</u>:
Student placement into
classes to optimize learning

Departmentalized
Reading

Middle
School
Curricula

Reading in
Progressive
Education

Non-graded
Schools

Self-
contained
Classes

Hetero-
geneous
Classes

Reading in
Open
Education

Core
Curriculum

Curriculum-
centered
Options

Teacher-
centered
Options

Student-
centered
Options

Continuous
Progress
Curricula

Homo-
geneous
Classes

Team
Teaching

Individualized
Reading

Joplin or
Cross-class
Reading

<u>Assessment</u>:
Effective student growth
Optimal school achievement
Positive student affect
Strong teacher operational effectiveness

Form 8.3

ASSESSMENT OF SCHOOL-LEVEL READING ORGANIZATION

Directions: School administrators assign pupils to classroom units using reasonable criteria, such as optimal pupil learning and effective teaching conditions. Below, criteria are given. On the right, respondents may check the extent to which the school applies those criteria.

School Reading Organization Criteria:	Presently Effective	Somewhat Effective	Not Effective
	3	2	1
1. Goals and needs of the reading program are addressed	☐	☐	☐
2. The typical teacher finds the school's organizational plan manageable	☐	☐	☐
3. All students are placed into instructional units that are designed to accelerate their advancement in reading and writing	☐	☐	☐
4. Faculty efforts to improve school reading organization are acknowledged and supported	☐	☐	☐
5. Decisions about reading program organization are based on pupil success in the reading curriculum...	☐	☐	☐
6. Organizational decisions are, to the extent possible, made to address child-centered learning	☐	☐	☐
7. The reading organization's highest priority is to support students' reading for meaning	☐	☐	☐
8. Attitudes and interests of students toward reading and writing are advanced by the school's reading organization	☐	☐	☐
9. Mediation of child-centered, teacher-centered, and curriculum-centered decisions about school-level reading organization is thoughtful and balanced	☐	☐	☐
10. Congruence is evident between reading organization and reading approach (see Chapter 6)	☐	☐	☐

Interpretation: The principal, Reading Advisory Board, or faculty may total columns, giving three points to checkmarks in the *presently effective* column, two to *somewhat effective*, and one to *not effective*. Totals between 21–30 may be considered *presently effective*, between 11–22 *somewhat effective*, and between 1–10 *not effective*.

CLASSROOM READING GROUP OPTIONS   (see Form 8.4)

The social setting of students as they grow in reading may affect both how well they make reading attempts, and how attitudes are formed. To address needs, teachers have mostly alternated between whole class groups and ability groups, each with advantages *and* serious flaws.

The Problem: Faculties often have not considered all grouping options when assigning children to groups to ease learning. Teachers who instruct children in what they are not capable of learning may cause great harm. Classrooms that stress easing the burdens of teachers may be least effective in optimizing learning for students. Across time little has been done to address social interaction in classrooms to benefit both learning and affect toward reading.

Rationale: Teacher use of the widest range of classroom organization possible may ease learning of and affect toward reading. Organization that concentrates on student interaction and shared decision-making may lead to empowered learning. All grouping options have positive strengths as well as have serious limitations that must be considered when addressing individual needs.

Procedures: School people may study Form 8.4 to consider a range of classroom grouping options. Open consideration may help teachers identify new combinations to try in various classroom contexts to meet a range of learning needs. Form 8.5 may be used to make school- or classroom-level decisions about grouping that result in the most benefit for learners *and* teachers.

For Further Reading

Gunning, T. G. (1992). *Creating Reading Instruction for all Children*. Boston: Allyn & Bacon, 490–517. (Dept. 894, 160 Gould Street, Needham Heights, MA 02194-2310. 1-800-852-8024.)

A comprehensive elementary methods textbook for preservice and inservice teachers. The basics of reading instruction are provided. The section on organization for reading instruction is helpful to practitioners.

Sanacore, J. (1992). "Intraclass Grouping with a Whole-Language Thrust," *Reading and Writing Quarterly: Overcoming Learning Difficulties*, 8, 3, 295–303.

To facilitate shared reading, literature circles, special needs, strategic reading, literature and writing response group activities, Sanacore describes five different patterns to support grouping flexibility.

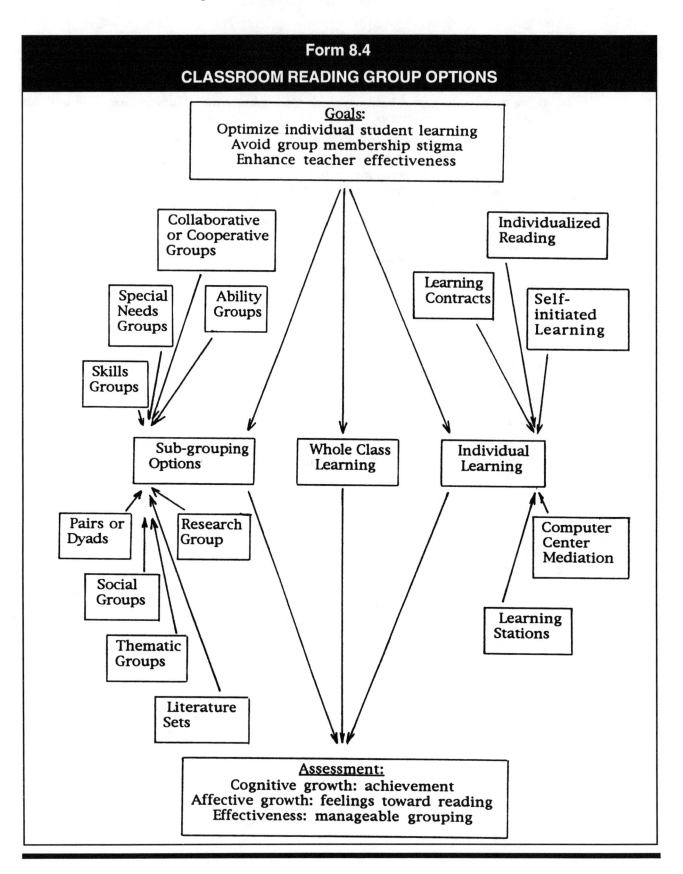

Form 8.4
CLASSROOM READING GROUP OPTIONS

Goals:
Optimize individual student learning
Avoid group membership stigma
Enhance teacher effectiveness

Collaborative or Cooperative Groups

Individualized Reading

Special Needs Groups

Ability Groups

Learning Contracts

Self-initiated Learning

Skills Groups

Sub-grouping Options

Whole Class Learning

Individual Learning

Pairs or Dyads

Research Group

Computer Center Mediation

Social Groups

Thematic Groups

Learning Stations

Literature Sets

Assessment:
Cognitive growth: achievement
Affective growth: feelings toward reading
Effectiveness: manageable grouping

Form 8.5
ASSESSMENT OF CLASSROOM READING GROUP OPTIONS

Directions: A wide range of options for grouping students to learn to read is available. Administrators or Reading Advisory Boards seeking to assess local implementations of those options may review criteria listed below. The extent of application may be checked on the right.

Classroom Grouping Options Criteria:	Presently Effective 3	Somewhat Effective 2	Not Effective 1
1. Grouping decisions within classes are consistent with program goals and learning needs	☐	☐	☐
2. The classroom organizational structure is developed so that the teacher can function effectively	☐	☐	☐
3. Every student is taught with peers, using instructional materials that ease learning, promote confidence, and assure academic success	☐	☐	☐
4. A variety of subgrouping options is used to fit the range of classroom academic and affective goals	☐	☐	☐
5. Each student feels the confidence of not belonging to only one group; no stigma, only positive feelings	☐	☐	☐
6. Teachers use subgroups to increase peer problem-solving and social interaction patterns	☐	☐	☐
7. Teachers use subgroups to support interaction and responses to strengthen reading comprehension	☐	☐	☐
8. Teachers develop subgroups to accelerate growth in reading vocabulary			
9. Teachers create subgroups to enhance values, attitudes, and motivation to read	☐	☐	☐
10. Appropriate options found in Form 8.4 are manageable and practical in classes	☐	☐	☐

Interpretation: The principal or Reading Advisory Board may total the columns in Form 8.5, giving three points to *presently effective*, two points to *somewhat effective*, and one point to *not effective*. Totals between 21–30 may be considered *presently effective*, those between 11–20 *somewhat effective*, and between 1–10 *not effective*.

SIMULATION TO FORM READING INSTRUCTIONAL GROUPS   (See Form 8.6)

Subgroups in classes may be formed to address pupils' cooperation, interests, abilities, research, or needs. Groups with changing memberships may increase students' learning from peers. Simulations may serve as staff development data for large group teachers' workshops, subgrouped to increase participation and ownership of conclusions, then shared.

Problem: All possible grouping options may not be considered. Students may be assigned to read with peers from texts that are too difficult, preventing growth, or too easy, diminishing growth. Pupils may be placed in low-ability groups in first grade and then never advance to higher groups.

Rationale: Students benefit from interaction with the widest range of peers while learning to read and write. Advanced peers provide strong role models and opportunities for peer identification. Subgroup assignments that frequently allow underdeveloped students to read with pupils of like needs and from like text levels may support skill and strategy development.

Procedures: Reading scores from a local class may be used to give the total faculty practice in assigning flexible subgroup memberships. The exercise provides opportunities to judge, value, and seek consensus on roles of subgroups. If there is reluctance to use an actual class, a choice from Form 8.6 may be used. While gaining consensus, participants are cautioned that placement decisions may not be nearly as important as reasons for placement.

For Further Reading

Sanacore, J. (1992). "Intra Class Grouping with a Whole Language Thrust," *Reading and Writing Quarterly: Overcoming Learning Difficulties*, 8, 3, 295–303.

> Sanacore stresses flexibility in grouping as he presents five options for whole language classrooms. The author posits ways to address shared reading, sharing meetings, literature circles, skill groups, and strategy groups.

Slavin, R. E. (1993). "Ability Grouping in the Middle Grades: Achievement Effects and Alternatives," *Elementary School Journal*, 93, 5, 535–52.

> Slavin explicates processes of between-class, ability grouping, cooperative grouping, and within-class grouping. He found little effect of grouping on achievement in 27 studies that addressed high, average, and/or low reading students.

Form 8.6

SIMULATION TO FORM READING INSTRUCTIONAL GROUPS

Directions: Below are found total reading grade scores for second grade, fourth grade, and sixth grade children at the beginning of the school year. Please feel free to use data below, or preferably, use achievement data from the local school district to simulate instructional groups, whether whole class, ability groups, or some form of interactive groups. Using what appears to be the best combinations found in Form 8.4 or data from the local school setting, please establish, in faculty groups of five to six teachers, the kinds and numbers of instructional groups and range of achievement within groups that would be needed to best help each student advance in reading ability. After each group has achieved consensus that they could "live with" the group's decision, reports should be made to the total study group about interpretations.

Grade Two			Grade Four			Grade Six		
3.4	1.9	1.5	7.9	4.7	3.8	8.8	5.6	4.8
3.0	1.8	1.5	7.8	4.7	3.7	8.3	5.5	4.7
2.9	1.7	1.5	6.4	4.7	3.7	7.8	5.5	4.4
2.7	1.7	1.4	6.0	4.6	3.6	7.7	5.3	4.2
2.4	1.7	1.4	6.0	4.5	3.6	7.3	5.2	3.7
2.1	1.7	1.4	5.9	4.5	3.3	6.9	5.0	3.0
2.1	1.7	1.3	5.6	4.3	2.9	6.4	5.0	2.9
2.1	1.6	1.3	5.5	4.3	2.9	5.8	5.0	2.7
2.0	1.6	1.3	5.3	4.1	2.8	5.7	5.0	2.3
	1.6		5.1	3.8	2.8	5.6	4.9	1.8
			4.8					

Interpretation: Concepts that are likely to be defined and shared are:

The range of achievement in grade level is extensive (usually greater than the grade in school; i.e., in fourth grade, the highest to lowest ranking reader is more than four years). The range is greater, of course, at the upper grade levels. The percent of pupils who actually read on grade level, i.e. 4.0–4.9 (in fourth grade), is small. The percent of students reading at or above grade level in September should be about 50% (i.e., in early September, about half of the class, if normal, would be at 4.0 or higher).

The number of students in instructional subgroups should be manageable for the teacher, yet functional for cooperative group activities if cooperative groups are the structure; i.e., often 5–7 students (enough for peer interaction, not so many that shy students are unwilling to participate).

Views of the approach to reading instruction (see Chapter 6) that will address these classes may affect decisions about group placement. For example, social grouping may fit some types of cooperative settings, while skills-based instruction might be suited to textbook-based classes—either example would influence grouping decisions based on the data above or in a local school.

MANAGEMENT OF COLLABORATIVE GROUPS   (see Form 8.7)

Collaborative groups may nurture students' literacy empowerment and motivation. To address this concern, educators are rediscovering cooperative pupil interaction in thematic curriculum units of study. Recent teacher- and text-dominated practice has often resulted in passive readers and undesirable pupil feelings toward reading and writing. Many teachers, though, fearing loss of class control and management problems, avoid subgroup use.

The Problem: Little opportunity exists in many classrooms for students to read and write, then talk with peers about their responses. The absence of sharing values, attitudes, and democratic participation during reading may result in pupil indifference. It is easier to *tell students* than to use collaborative group study. It is also easier to keep students in *straight rows* than to have them interacting with one another.

Rationale: Pupil learning may be enhanced as thematic study, cooperative grouping, reading participation, and writing processes are unified. Group study may augment both literacy acceleration and affect toward reading and writing. Problem-solving activities may create pupil empowerment that strengthens attitudes and interests. Whenever cooperative groups are initiated, teaching effective group participation is warranted.

Procedures: Form 8.7 may be used to self-assess cooperative grouping at all levels—district, school, Reading Advisory Board, teacher, and principal. The worksheet may aid judgment of present status, desired organizational use of cooperative groups, or planning for curricular improvement.

For Further Reading

Cummings, C. (1990). *Managing a Cooperative Classroom*. Edmonds, WA: Teaching, Inc. (Teaching, Inc., P.O. Box 788, Edmonds, WA 98020. 206-774-0755.)

> The author offers a practical monograph to introduce cooperative learning. Cummings describes cooperative classroom management, group development, required social skills, and maintenance of suitable classroom organization.

Johnson, D. W., et al. (1994). *The New Circles of Learning: Cooperation in the Classroom and School*. Alexandria, VA: Association for Supervision and Curriculum Development. (1250 North Pitt Street, Alexandria, VA 22314. 703-549-9110.)

> A revision of the pioneering monograph on cooperative learning. The authors address positive learning climates through cooperation. They describe lesson components, grade level adjustments, and conversions of lectures to cooperative activities. Added to the new edition is conflict resolution as a dimension of successful learning.

Form 8.7

MANAGEMENT OF COOPERATIVE GROUPS

	Thoroughly Implemented	Partially Implemented	Not Implemented
Directions: Cooperative groups and integral thematic units of study are challenging for teachers to manage. The teacher is developing pupils' reading gains, responses toward reading and writing, affect toward literacy, and social growth. Below, Reading Advisory Board members, classroom teachers, or principals will find criteria related to collaborative group management. On the right, participants may check the degree of implementation in in the local setting.			
Management of Cooperative Groups Criteria:	3	2	1

Goals of cooperative grouping

1. Increase students' successes in content of the reading curriculum	☐	☐	☐
2. Strengthen experiences and success with problem-solving strategies that improve reading inferences and critical responses to text	☐	☐	☐
3. Enhance social interaction that develops pupils' participative skills and democratic empowerment, which aids reading response and writing response	☐	☐	☐
4. Nurture positive affect toward learning to read	☐	☐	☐

Cooperative group assignments

5. Assignments are broad-based, applying curriculum themes, unifying most curriculum content	☐	☐	☐
6. Assignments are structured in open-ended, problem-solving formats with higher-level skill integration	☐	☐	☐
7. Assignments are designed for reading-across-the-curriculum and writing-across-the-curriculum	☐	☐	☐
8. Reading and writing strategies and skills are integrated into the problem-based themes	☐	☐	☐
9. Subgroup size merits monitoring; pupils may work best in groups of five to seven pupils	☐	☐	☐

Planning for productive learning procedures

10. The core of thematic/cooperative success is the process of learner planning and goal setting	☐	☐	☐

–continues–

Management of Cooperative Groups	-continued-	3	2	1

11. The process begins with only one subgroup while regular activities resume for the balance of pupils .... ☐ ☐ ☐

12. The first group's membership is chosen with a fair chance of achieving academic and behavioral success, in other words, no saboteurs .... ☐ ☐ ☐

13. Any students not able to participate productively in a group are not permitted to remain in the group and diminish its success .... ☐ ☐ ☐

14. That group's planning, goals, behaviors, knowledge gains, and assessments are developed for the total class, that all may learn from the planning that goes into one group .... ☐ ☐ ☐

15. Later, a second and concurrent group is assigned, with whole class planning and assessment of both groups' processes .... ☐ ☐ ☐

16. Additional subgroups are formed with each new assignment until all students are working in cooperative groups .... ☐ ☐ ☐

Group management

17. Collaborative groups have clear tasks "up front" .... ☐ ☐ ☐

18. Tasks and assignments ordinarily will be developed by the class and commitments will be established .... ☐ ☐ ☐

19. Group management warrants assignments that incorporate reading with shared responses, and writing with shared responses .... ☐ ☐ ☐

20. Group members have roles and responsibilities within the group, sometimes assigned, sometimes self-selected .... ☐ ☐ ☐

21. All members of the subgroup are responsible for all learning and all interaction processes .... ☐ ☐ ☐

Culminating cooperative group activities

22. Activities are pursued to tie together major concepts and integrate the learning involved .... ☐ ☐ ☐

23. Culminating activities include tying together knowledge, reconsideration of reading and writing processes in the assignment, assessment of group processes, participation of individuals and group .... ☐ ☐ ☐

24. Activities ordinarily would include the display of new knowledge for other subgroups to study .... ☐ ☐ ☐

–continues–

Management of Cooperative Groups   -continued-

	3	2	1
25. Summary activities ordinarily may include presenters' lists of books, with "book talks," that non-group classmates may enjoy as well	☐	☐	☐
26. Summary activities include written reports of both learning and interaction processes, using shared composition of reports	☐	☐	☐

Evaluation of cooperative grouping

	3	2	1
27. Evidence that content learning has occurred is objective and visible	☐	☐	☐
28. Evidence that social development, personal responsibility, and group effectiveness are displayed	☐	☐	☐
29. Total classes respond to reports from each of the subgroups, judging effectiveness of both content reported and process descriptions shared	☐	☐	☐

Cover the page here and below before photocopying if users are not to see the interpretation until later.

Interpretation: Principals, the Reading Advisory Board, or self-assessing teachers may total columns in Form 8.7, giving three points to *thoroughly implemented*, two to *partially implemented*, and one point to *not implemented*. There may be value in collating those data from each teacher to combine their perceptions. Totals from 59–87 may be considered *thoroughly implemented*, between 30–58 partially *implemented*, and between 1–29 *not implemented*.

USE OF CLASSROOM SPACE FOR READING   (See Form 8.8)

Strong decisions about space usage may benefit teachers' management of group processes, student ability to concentrate, and ease of learning. Separation of reading subgroups with space may reduce pupils' distraction and increase ability to interact as students read and write, then discuss their responses.

The Problem: Many teachers may not be aware of how the placement of subgroups supports their functions, classroom management, and pupils' participation. Administrators may be unaware of how much quality of classroom management influences pupils' reading achievement and attitudes. Teachers may avoid subgroups, cooperative- or ability-based, because of fear of losing control.

Rationale: Teachers who use classroom space wisely may benefit their learners. Students with reduced distraction during reading group activities may be better able to concentrate on text meanings. Cooperative groups separated from one another may participate more quietly because of reduced overall classroom noise, diminishing teacher management problems.

Procedures: Individual teachers may choose to use Form 8.8 for self-assessment purposes. The principal or Reading Advisory Board may complete Form 8.8 to judge school status, or may collect teachers' copies to gain collective perceptions. Subsequently, reading organization may be studied and staff development conducted.

For Further Reading

Jongsma, K. S. (1991). "Grouping Children for Instruction: Some Guidelines," *The Reading Teacher*, 44, 8, 610–11.

> The author develops five dimensions of planning involved for classroom groups. She posits the article as providing answers to the questions of beginning teachers.

Peck, G. (1989). "Facilitating Cooperative Grouping: A Forgotten Tool Gets it Started," *Academic Therapy*, 25, 2, 145–50.

> As cooperative grouping again becomes popular, issues involved in organization reappear. Peck advocates groups with mixed ability students and mutual choice pairs. His recommendation is that teachers use sociograms to formulate group membership.

Form 8.8
USE OF CLASSROOM SPACE FOR READING

Directions: Teachers who use instructional subgroups may find increased distractibility without careful management. Space is a good management tool. For each criterion below, respondents may check the category closest to the extent of implementation.

Classroom Space for Reading Criteria:	Thoroughly Implemented	Partially Implemented	Not Implemented
	3	2	1
1. Space use reflects the philosophy and goals of the school reading program	☐	☐	☐
2. The way space is used is based on instructional priorities	☐	☐	☐
3. The total amount of available space appears to be well used	☐	☐	☐
4. Certain sections of the room are clearly set aside for certain activities	☐	☐	☐
5. The use of space reflects the importance of direct instruction, independent practice, mastery of reading processes, and recreational reading	☐	☐	☐
6. Each pupil understands the role of various classroom functions and can operate effectively wherever assigned	☐	☐	☐
7. The amount of space available is suited to those activities undertaken	☐	☐	☐
8. Classroom areas are so organized that the teacher can observe each activity	☐	☐	☐
9. There are as many chairs and tables as pupils who work in any classroom area	☐	☐	☐
10. Students working within a group are very close together, with considerable space between groups	☐	☐	☐
11. Privacy and distraction are managed through furniture placement and distance	☐	☐	☐
12. Instructional materials are stored for easy access at pupils' eye levels, located near areas where used	☐	☐	☐
13. Furniture is of appropriate size to fit the needs of class members	☐	☐	☐
14. Recreational reading centers are comfortable, attractive, and cozy	☐	☐	☐
15. Locations are provided for cooperative-collaborative reading activities	☐	☐	☐

–continues–

Use of Classroom Space for Reading	-continued-	3	2	1

16. Learning centers are comfortable, functional, accessible, and conducive to their designated learning activities .... ☐ ☐ ☐

17. The classroom traffic patterns provide easy access to various parts of the room .... ☐ ☐ ☐

18. Traffic lanes do not pass close to quiet centers .... ☐ ☐ ☐

19. The overall atmosphere and organization appear to be conducive to learning to read .... ☐ ☐ ☐

Cover the page here and below before photocopying if users are not to see the interpretation until later.

Interpretation: Principals, Reading Advisory Boards, or school faculties may total columns, giving three points to *thoroughly implemented*, two points to *partially implemented*, and one point to *not implemented*. Totals between 39–57 may be judged *thoroughly implemented*, between 20–38 *partially implemented*, and between 1–19 *not implemented*.

ASSESSMENT OF CLASSROOM READING GROUPS   (see Form 8.9)

The management of both whole class reading and instructional subgroups represents challenges and problems to teachers. The challenge is to deliver successful instruction, attempting to address a functional level for each reader. This *politically incorrect*, yet empirically documented concept (39, 155) has been referred to traditionally as the instructional reading level.

The Problem: The compromise between meeting each student's needs and the teachers' being able to manage the total program often leaves teachers feeling frustrated. Teachers who only recently recovered from problems of managing three ability-based reading subgroups may be reluctant to take on management problems of subgroups founded on cooperative learning.

Rationale: Learning to read and write may be enhanced in classroom environments in which flexibly assigned subgroups are formed to meet pupils' instructional needs and interests, and reading achievement may be increased. Engaged time—that is, time spent actually reading—may be increased within subgroups. Shared student responses to reading and writing may enhance peer feedback, interest, and reading motivation.

Procedures: The worksheet may have several uses. Teachers may use the instrument individually for self-assessment. The teacher and principal might each complete the form and use shared interpretations for principal-teacher assessment conferences. The principal or Reading Advisory Board may use data from Form 8.9 to gain information for program assessment purposes.

For Further Reading

Cook, D. M., et al. (1986). *A Guide to Curriculum Planning in Reading*. Madison, WI: The Wisconsin Department of Public Instruction, 111–127. (125 South Webster Street, P.O. Box 7841, Madison, WI 53707-7841. 608-266-2188.)

A guidebook for use by reading program leaders, administrators, and supervisors. Its intent is to create interactive reading comprehension processes, integrate reading and writing, read a variety of texts for multiple tasks, and develop lifetime independent readers. Includes classroom assessment processes.

Smith, R. J., et al. (1978). *The School Reading Program: A Handbook for Teachers, Supervisors, and Specialists*. Boston: Houghton Mifflin Company, 126–149. (Wayside Road, Burlington, MA 01803. 1-800-733-1717.)

The text is written for reading specialists, classroom teachers and administrators concerned with reading curriculum development. The authors wrote for the three groups because of the belief that all roles are included in reading curriculum development. Group management is addressed in the handbook.

Form 8.9
ASSESSMENT OF CLASSROOM READING GROUPS

Directions: Subgrouped reading instruction is being rediscovered in new contexts. Teachers are forming cooperative study groups, literature response groups, skills groups, etc. For each classroom organization criterion below, Reading Advisory Board members, principals, or classroom teachers may check their present level of self-understanding.

Assessment of Reading Groups Criteria	Presently Effective	Somewhat Effective	Not Effective
	3	2	1
1. The major goal of reading groups in this class is to support effective learning and teaching	☐	☐	☐
2. Groupings are made from a variety of options, including interest, cooperative, ability, small, whole class, skills, social, to enhance reading and to avoid the stigma of inflexible grouping	☐	☐	☐
3. The classroom has the general appearance of a well-managed, productive classroom with wholesome interpersonal rapport	☐	☐	☐
4. Group memberships are based on objective diagnostic data about pupil reading levels, needs, processes, skills, and interests	☐	☐	☐
5. Students who do not fit classroom groups are sent for reading to a teacher where they can function, and equal numbers of pupils are received in exchange	☐	☐	☐
6. Instruction places primary students within a range of 3/4 of a year achievement and intermediate pupils within a 1 1/4 range of actual ability, avoiding functional withdrawal................................	☐	☐	☐
7. Primary students usually read from materials in which they make no more than 1/10 to 1/20 oral mistakes when reading; intermediate students 1/16 to 1/20................................	☐	☐	☐
8. Grouping and independent reading allow each student to maximize "time on task"................................	☐	☐	☐
9. Each group receives enough instructional time to meet the needs of each of its students	☐	☐	☐
10. The size of each group, ever flexible, is dependent upon the type of reading activity undertaken	☐	☐	☐
11. Each group is small enough that the teacher is able to observe the reading functions of every pupil	☐	☐	☐

–continues–

Assessment of Classroom Reading Groups   -continued-

	3	2	1

12. When total class reading is conducted, care is taken that each student is capable of completing the lesson objective .... ☐ ☐ ☐

13. Students almost never are required to sit through a lesson in which they could complete the tasks prior to instruction .... ☐ ☐ ☐

14. The classroom is organized in such a way that each student knows what is supposed to be happening .... ☐ ☐ ☐

15. During seat work sessions, independent practice is selected to help students learn to read better, rather than to occupy time .... ☐ ☐ ☐

16. Guided practice precedes any independent practice found in seat work, increasing chances of success .... ☐ ☐ ☐

17. Seat work time incorporates recreational reading as a planned curriculum objective .... ☐ ☐ ☐

18. Writing-about-reading assignments are a part of independent work, incorporating peer sharing and peer editing .... ☐ ☐ ☐

19. Evidence of shared responsibility for managing the class abounds; teachers and pupils have like goals .... ☐ ☐ ☐

20. The organizational structure tends to make pupils more responsible for their own reading growth .... ☐ ☐ ☐

21. There is no evidence of stigma or embarrassment found in any placement within any group .... ☐ ☐ ☐

22. Interests of students are considered when forming instructional groups ...... ☐ ☐ ☐

23. The affect and learning advantages of cooperative reading are extended with paired and small group assignments .... ☐ ☐ ☐

24. The class appears devoid of disruptive, aimless pupil behavior during reading classes, supporting students' ability to concentrate and to interact with peers .... ☐ ☐ ☐

Cover the page here and below if users are not to see the interpretation until later.

Interpretation: Teachers may self-assess classroom reading subgroups, or administrators and Reading Advisory Boards may use data from Form 8.9 to make program decisions. To summarize each form, totals may be made of each column, giving three points to *presently effective*, two points to *somewhat effective*, and one point to *not effective*. Totals between 49–72 may be considered *presently effective*, those between 25–48 *somewhat effective*, and between 1–24 *not effective*.

SYNTHESIS OF READING PROGRAM ORGANIZATION   (see Form 8.10)

A Reading Advisory Board, the principal, or faculty may improve pupil reading gains and feelings through social and academic mediation. Class assignments in the autumn influence literacy learning all year. Those reading together in subgroups affect individual performance. Subgroup management to avoid confusion and distraction affects literacy learning.

The Problem: The materials for instruction, textbooks, journals, trade books, etc., often gain more attention than does the classroom environment, or peers who read with students. When children must read with inappropriate classmates, their opportunities to learn may be diminished. Pupils who must read with a group that outperforms or underperforms them are handicapped.

Rationale: Choices of organization, or pupil grouping, may influence program success, individual pupil reading gains, and affect toward reading. Careful consideration of overall program goals may be reviewed to determine congruence with reading program organization.

Procedures: Forms 8.1 to 8.8 may be used to consider the extent of local implementation. Those judgments may be reported in Form 8.9 and Form 8.10. After careful group reflection, participants may consider each criterion in Form 8.11 to determine organizational strengths, needs, and priorities, and finally, use Form 8.12 to develop a plan-of-action for the study of reading organization. Those decisions may be cross-referenced to program and curriculum goals (Chapters 3 and 4), and reading approach (Chapter 6).

Comments and Cautions

All reading organization options have strengths and each choice has serious flaws.

Principals, Reading Advisory Boards, or faculties might reflect upon all options publicly to expand awareness.

Faculty selectiveness about options for various students, or combinations of students, may aid reading achievement and affective gains.

Form 8.10
SYNTHESIS OF READING PROGRAM ORGANIZATION

Directions: Below, participants will find a place to summarize various worksheets. On the right, places are provided to assess whether the program component is thoroughly, partially, or not implemented. The principal's or Reading Advisory Board's careful deliberation is required, if this information is to be used for program assessment.

Reading Organization Components:	Thoroughly Implemented	Partly Implemented	Not Implemented
	3	2	1
1. Overall reading program organization (see Form 8.1)	☐	☐	☐
2. School-level organizational options (see Form 8.2)	☐	☐	☐
3. Classroom grouping options (see Form 8.3)	☐	☐	☐
4. Classroom space usage (see Form 8.7)	☐	☐	☐
5. Management of cooperative learning (see Form 8.8)	☐	☐	☐
6. Assessment of classroom grouping (see Form 8.9)	☐	☐	☐
7. Reading organization is congruent with priorities identified as program strengths and weaknesses (see Form 3.12)	☐	☐	☐
8. Components of the reading curriculum (see Forms 4.19 and 4.20) are consistent with the reading organizational status	☐	☐	☐
9. The reading approach (see Forms 6.7 and 6.8) corresponds with reading program and class organization	☐	☐	☐

Interpretation: The Reading Advisory Board or principal may total the columns in Form 8.10, giving three points to *thoroughly implemented*, two to *partially implemented*, and one to *not implemented*. Totals between 19–27 may be judged *thoroughly implemented*, those between 10–18 *partially implemented*, and those from 1–9 *not implemented*.

Form 8.11
READING ORGANIZATION: STRENGTHS, NEEDS, AND PRIORITIES

Directions: Below, respondents will find components of reading program organizational options. On the right, space is provided to record program strengths, needs, and, after careful deliberation, priorities. Checkmarks from all of the worksheets in Chapter 8 have been synthesized to generate Form 8.10, which may be used to complete the present form.

1. **Overall Reading Program Organization**	*Strengths* 1. 2.	*Needs* 1. 2.	*Priorities* 1. 2.
2. **School-level Options**	*Strengths* 1. 2.	*Needs* 1. 2.	*Priorities* 1. 2.
3. **Classroom Grouping Options**	*Strengths* 1. 2.	*Needs* 1. 2.	*Priorities* 1. 2.
4. **Classroom Space Usage**	*Strengths* 1. 2.	*Needs* 1. 2.	*Priorities* 1. 2.
5. **Management of Cooperative Groups**	*Strengths* 1. 2.	*Needs* 1. 2.	*Priorities* 1. 2.
6. **Assessment of Classroom Grouping**	*Strengths* 1. 2.	*Needs* 1. 2.	*Priorities* 1. 2.

Form 8.12
READING ORGANIZATION: PLAN-OF-ACTION

Directions: Administrators seeking to develop a comprehensive plan to improve reading organization may benefit from being as specific as possible about what they seek to accomplish, how they will go about attaining growth, and how they will know when they have reached their goals. A review of Form 8.11 should lead the administrator to identify goals to pursue in the growth plan. Statements entered should be as simple, direct, and useful as possible.

1. Goal Statement: _____

2. Objectives:

    a) _____

    b) _____

    c) _____

3. Activities: Dates; time checkpoints:

    a) _____   * _____

    b) _____   * _____

    c) _____   * _____

    d) _____   * _____

    e) _____   * _____

4. Resources: (professional reading, consultation, visitations)

    a) _____   * _____

    b) _____   * _____

    c) _____   * _____

5. How I will know when my goal is accomplished:

    _____
    _____
    _____
    _____

CHAPTER 9

PROFESSIONAL DEVELOPMENT OF READING TEACHERS

Despite the best efforts of colleges and universities, teacher preparation is not complete when teaching degrees are conferred. Academic content courses, theory and methods courses, and practicum experiences are only the beginning of a lifelong learning process for teachers and their principals or supervisors. Frequently, courses present concepts and research in learning theory, teaching strategies and techniques, but fail to link the theory to real-life teaching situations.

Coupled with their inexperience in linking theory and practice, teachers carry within them preconceived notions of how classrooms should be managed and children taught based on their own prior experiences as students. For some, teaching *the way I was taught* is a more powerful influence than schooling in updated, research-based approaches.

In addition, teaching, like administration, is an isolated activity. Teachers tend to work independently, guarding planning time and break time as opportunities to prepare for immediate lesson objectives rather than engaging in long-term planning and sharing of techniques and content materials on a collegial basis. The result is that educators—teachers and principals alike—who do not talk with each other have no way of getting the feedback that lets them know just how capable they are.

It rests on the principal, then, as instructional leader, to provide the initial direction to work with teachers to set personal, professional goals. To accomplish this thrust, administrators supervise and coach teachers' growth toward goal attainment. Principals facilitate opportunities and follow-up for inservice training that is related to school-wide and individual goals that ultimately increase student achievement.

SELECTION OF CLASSROOM AND SPECIAL READING TEACHERS

(see Forms 9.1 and 9.2)

To enhance the quality of instruction and learning, principals seek to employ the best possible teaching candidates as classroom teachers and reading specialists. At the district level, purchased, structured interview programs may be used. Prospective candidates may be screened at one, two, or three levels before being interviewed by a principal or team at a local school. Whether or not the district uses a structured interview format, principals need to be prepared to ask questions that reflect the needs of an individual school unit.

The Problem: Unfortunately, many principals have no training in interview processes, nor have they developed a systematic procedure with routine questions to use in conducting interviews. Frequently, principals fail to see the value of inviting a cohort of staff members to participate in the interview process. Another problem for principals is that teachers may be assigned to their school, in some districts, without local agreement.

Rationale: Insightful interviewers will have at hand a list of questions that tap the potential of candidates for classroom or reading specialist positions. Principals may secure pertinent information in 30 to 45 minutes. Other administrators or staff members can clarify and verify the data collected by conferencing together briefly following each interview.

Procedures: Forms 9.1 and 9.2 contain sample interview questions that may be adapted for local school use. The principal, with the interview team, will want to order the questions and determine who will ask them to maintain consistency throughout the selection process.

For Further Reading

Vann, A. S. (1994). "The Pre-Employment Interview: Asking the Right Questions," *Principal*, 73, 3, 38–41.

> Vann has developed a set of key questions from which he draws objective observations and subjective reactions in appraising a candidate for employment.

Sanacore, J. (1995). "Guidelines for Hiring Qualified Reading Professionals," *Journal of Reading*, 38, 5, 396–99.

> Sanacore advocates selection of new personnel with assistance of a planning team, affirm mission in the context of a new reading educator, interview the best candidates, observe those candidates, and develop strategies to retain new appointees.

Candidate _____

Form 9.1
READING-RELATED CRITERIA TO INTERVIEW CLASSROOM TEACHERS

Directions: Below are sample interview questions; most are open-ended. Principals or interview committees may want to use a separate form for each candidate to note responses made. Space is provided for comments. After the interview, each member may make checkmarks on the right to indicate candidate's qualifications.

Classroom Reading Interview Criteria:

	Highly Qualified 4	Typically Qualified 3	Minimally Qualified 2	Not Qualified 1
1. Tell a little about yourself, personally and professionally (relax the candidate, embellish information from the resume)	☐	☐	☐	☐
2. How do you introduce yourself to students and parents? and get to know them? (content and process)	☐	☐	☐	☐
3. What communication techniques will you practice? (frequency, form, reason)	☐	☐	☐	☐
4. What do you think is the key to good classroom management and discipline? (behavior expectations, rewards, incentives, consequences)	☐	☐	☐	☐
5. Walk through a lesson or unit in reading for grade _____ (teaching style, lesson planning, alternative approaches)	☐	☐	☐	☐
6. If you got the _____ grade position, how many reading groups would you anticipate having? How much time per day for reading? (curriculum scope, priorities, personal philosophy on grouping/curriculum integration)	☐	☐	☐	☐
7. What are your thoughts about phonics, whole language, literature-based instruction? (flexibility, understanding, child-centered)	☐	☐	☐	☐
8. How would you vary instruction to meet needs of gifted as well as low ability or disabled students? (differentiated instruction, peer tutoring, grouping)	☐	☐	☐	☐
9. What are your thoughts on cooperative learning—advantages and disadvantages? (understanding, risk-taker)	☐	☐	☐	☐
10. What relationship do you see between reading and writing? (how each supports the other)	☐	☐	☐	☐
11. Are you computer-literate? What software programs have you used in reading? (knowledge or eagerness to learn)	☐	☐	☐	☐

–continues–

Candidate_____

Reading-Related Criteria to Interview Classroom Teachers -continued-	4	3	2	1
12. Tell about one or two important influences in your life (how influenced, stage in life)	☐	☐	☐	☐
13. What would you do if a student did not turn in homework for a whole week? Do you believe in daily homework? (wait a week to respond? philosophy, why)	☐	☐	☐	☐
14. How would you respond to a parent who blames last year's teacher for a child's difficulty in school? (tact, steering a parent toward a solution)	☐	☐	☐	☐
15. Why do you want to be a teacher? What sets a good teacher apart from others? (commitment, enthusiasm)	☐	☐	☐	☐
16. What are your career goals? Classroom teacher, reading specialist, administrator? (professional strengths and interests)	☐	☐	☐	☐
17. Can you name two or three of your greatest strengths and weaknesses? (values, self-assessment)	☐	☐	☐	☐
18. Why should we hire you instead of the others? (persistence, self-assessment)	☐	☐	☐	☐

— — — — — — — — — — — — — — — **after the interview** — — — — — — — — — — — — — — — —

	4	3	2	1
19. Summary of professionalism, appearance, dress	☐	☐	☐	☐
20. Summary of oral communication skills: grammar, fluency, clarity	☐	☐	☐	☐

Note: It is important to assess a sample of the candidate's writing: perhaps a statement of educational philosophy, a description of a contemporary educational issues, etc.

Interpretation: The principal or interview committee may choose different approaches: the group may discuss each candidate independently of the others and reach consensus on the individual ratings *or* each interviewer may complete Form 9.1 for each candidate individually. Each column may be totaled with four points to checkmarks on the left, three points to the next column, two to the third column, and one point to checkmarks on the right column. Totals between 61–80 may be considered *highly qualified*, between 41–60 *typically qualified*, 21–40 *minimally qualified*, and 1–20 *not qualified*.

Candidate_____

Form 9.2				
READING-RELATED CRITERIA TO INTERVIEW SPECIAL READING TEACHERS				

Directions: In addition to information gleaned from Form 9.1, the principal and committee may want to address criteria to interview reading specialists. Again, questions and ordering are agreed upon. Space is provided to note important parts of candidate's responses following each question. After the interview, assess the quality of response by checking a column on the right.	Highly Qualified	Typically Qualified	Minimally Qualified	Not Qualified
Special Reading Teacher Interviews:	4	3	2	1

1. What are the key elements of a comprehensive reading program? (refer to Forms 4.19 and 4.20) .... ☐ ☐ ☐ ☐

2. What models of student assistance would you employ? Why? (pull-out, class-within-a-class, etc.) .... ☐ ☐ ☐ ☐

3. Who are your reading heroes, authors, speakers? Why? (awareness of trends, solid thinkers) .... ☐ ☐ ☐ ☐

4. Of what reading or language arts organizations are you a member? (professional development commitment) .... ☐ ☐ ☐ ☐

5. How do you view your role in the total building reading program? (manager, resource, model, remedial teacher) .... ☐ ☐ ☐ ☐

6. What is the scope of your experiences in teaching reading? (grade levels, strategies, approaches) .... ☐ ☐ ☐ ☐

7. What tasks would you set out to do prior to and at the opening of school? (materials for teachers and students, new students, new teachers, curriculum content, building philosophy) .... ☐ ☐ ☐ ☐

8. What assessment processes do you find most valuable? (knowledge of when to use and how to interpret standardized tests, basal tests, teacher-made tests, reading inventories, interest inventories, cloze tests, authentic assessment) .... ☐ ☐ ☐ ☐

9. How would you organize record-keeping to minimize work and maximize information (what data to keep, system, portfolios) .... ☐ ☐ ☐ ☐

10. How would you be a resource person to the faculty? (professional reading, organize study groups, alternative teaching processes and materials, incentives) .... ☐ ☐ ☐ ☐

11. Why do you want to be a reading specialist? (commitment, innovative, ideas, goals) .... ☐ ☐ ☐ ☐

Interpretation: Columns may be totaled, giving four points to checkmarks on the left, three to marks in the next column, two to the third, and one point to checkmarks in the right column. Totals between 34–44 may be considered *highly qualified*, between 23–33 *typically qualified*, between 12–22 *minimally qualified*, and between 1–11 *not qualified*.

ANNUAL GOAL-SETTING AND REVIEW   (see Form 9.3)

Administrators, Reading Advisory Boards, teachers, and community members review the reading curriculum, materials, instruction, assessment practices, and organizational trends for the school. Also, administrators assist teachers to examine their individual and collective knowledge base, experience, and teaching skills. This process is initiated by gaining from teachers their statements of goals they have for the school year.

Problem: School faculties become caught up in school-wide goals and buy into these goals superficially. They lack opportunity and know-how to assess and prioritize their personal, professional needs. Set goals may not be shared, evaluated, revised, and realized.

Rationale: Effective principals are cognizant of the varying skills, levels of experience, and background knowledge of the individual teachers of their faculties. They are able to build trust and to maintain a high level of morale and motivation among staff members. Consequently, they are able to assist teachers in setting professional goals, monitor their progress, and celebrate their successes. Those goal statements provide the focus for teachers' professional growth.

Procedures: The principal may wish to complete Form 9.3 to assess expertise and extent of practice assisting staff members to set goals that are realistic, achievable, relate to teacher effectiveness, and improve student learning. The Reading Advisory Board, as well as individual teachers, may also complete Form 9.3 to enable the administrator to compare judgments.

For Further Reading

Duke, D. (1990). "Setting Goals for Professional Development," *Educational Leadership*, 47, 8, 71–75.

Duke bases the article on the ingredients of time and collegial support. He advocates heightening awareness, with activities to break routine, change perspectives, examine assumptions, and read challenging materials.

Form 9.3
ANNUAL GOAL-SETTING AND REVIEW

Directions: While school-wide goals are important to a healthy school environment, teachers' individual goals must also relate to the total learning program. Below are criteria a principal may use to self-assess effectiveness of facilitating individual staff members in setting goals. Reading Advisory Boards and teachers may also assess the principal's effectiveness to provide comparative data.

Annual Goal-Setting and Review Criteria:	Highly Effective	Moderately Effective	Minimally Effective	Not Effective
	4	3	2	1
1. Establish rapport through informal conversations about teachers' families, interests, and concerns	☐	☐	☐	☐
2. Visit classrooms often on an informal, drop-in basis to maintain awareness of curriculum content, teaching strategies, and students' responsiveness ...	☐	☐	☐	☐
3. Frequently ask individual teachers what their needs are and follow through in meeting those needs	☐	☐	☐	☐
4. Make a point of speaking with each teacher each day that the principal is in the building	☐	☐	☐	☐
5. Encourage the sharing of ideas and humorous classroom happenings	☐	☐	☐	☐
6. Find opportunities to compliment teachers individually and collectively on a regular basis	☐	☐	☐	☐
7. Establish a procedure for school-wide goal setting	☐	☐	☐	☐
8. Set personal and professional goals and vision, and share those with the faculty and staff	☐	☐	☐	☐
9. Seek input from staff on prioritizing goals and developing a plan-of-action to meet them	☐	☐	☐	☐
10. Encourage the faculty to assess the principal's progress in goal attainment	☐	☐	☐	☐
11. Provide objective data and feedback at teachers' request which assists in goal-setting	☐	☐	☐	☐
12. Provide opportunities for faculty to examine their assumptions about reading by reading articles, listening to guest speakers, visiting other schools, etc.	☐	☐	☐	☐
13. Assist teachers in phrasing goals in observable terms	☐	☐	☐	☐

–continues–

Annual Goal-Setting and Review   -continued-

	4	3	2	1

14. Help teachers to brainstorm activities to reach goals .... ☐ ☐ ☐ ☐

15. Put teachers with similar goals in touch with each other to encourage networking .... ☐ ☐ ☐ ☐

16. Aid in developing a timeline for completing activities and meet with individual teachers on an agreed-upon schedule to monitor progress .... ☐ ☐ ☐ ☐

17. Encourage teachers to revise goals-in-progress based on periodic evaluation .... ☐ ☐ ☐ ☐

18. Discuss completion of goals in observable terms .... ☐ ☐ ☐ ☐

19. Celebrate successes with teachers .... ☐ ☐ ☐ ☐

20. Enable teachers to use successful completion of goals as a springboard to develop new goals .... ☐ ☐ ☐ ☐

Interpretation: Form 9.3 may be used in numerous ways. Principals' self-assessment of their role in helping teachers to set and attain goals is the obvious use. In a total program-planning process, the Reading Advisory Board may also study the principal's self-assessment to examine leadership compared to members' judgments. When a school needs teachers' feedback, faculty and staff might be asked to complete Form 9.3 and have the Board collate all perceptions. The principal or Board may tally items, giving four points to checkmarks in the left column, three to the next column, two to the third column, and one point to checkmarks in the right column. Totals between 61–80 may be considered highly effective, 41–60 moderately effective, 21–40 minimally effective, and 1–20 not effective.

TEACHERS' SELF-ASSESSMENT OF   (see Form 9.4)
READING LESSON FRAMEWORKS

Principals may wish to share concepts from Form 9.4 with teachers who need help in structuring their self-assessments. Teachers may strengthen professional competence and capacity for empowerment if they are able to identify reading lesson components, the primary vehicle for teaching children to read. To structure a framework for lessons lends confidence to teachers and helps them to monitor their efforts.

The Problem: Some teachers would not be able to develop comprehensive lessons without reference to teachers' manuals. Many do not learn to integrate curriculum concepts professionally. Some teachers may not be able to judge whether students have learned desired processes, strategies, or skills. Some principals may not know what makes good reading lessons.

Rationale: The quality of teachers' *pre-reading*, *during-reading*, and *post-reading* lesson decisions may, over time, profoundly influence students' abilities and feelings toward reading. Lessons that give students the support prior to, during, and after reading a story are the foundation.

Procedures: Teachers *and* principals may feel a need to know what makes a good reading lesson. The information may provide positive feedback, help teachers to know that they function effectively, or support them to focus their planning. Form 9.4 may be used for teachers' self-assessment of reading lessons. Principals may use Form 9.4 to work with new teachers, to help teachers who are not functioning well, or to structure planning conferences related to the pre-supervisory visit (Form 9.5).

For Further Reading

Cooper, J. D. (1993). *Literacy: Helping Children to Construct Meaning, Second Edition*. Boston: Houghton Mifflin Company, 64–91. (Wayside Road, Burlington, MA 01803. 1-800-733-1717.)

> The text is developed to aid preservice and inservice teachers to help children develop effective literacy. The book is founded on literacy concepts: thinking, reading, writing, speaking, and listening. Cooper advocates *real* literacy experiences, students' meaning construction and social interaction. Lesson frameworks are developed to support those contexts.

Duffy, G. G. & Roehler, L. R. (1989). *Improving Classroom Reading Instruction: A Decision-Making Approach*. New York: Random House, 205–209, 223–232. (McGraw-Hill, P. O. Box 545, Blacklick, OH 43004-0545. 212-512-3218.)

> The text is written to help teachers as professionals take control of their classroom instruction. The authors advocate uses of knowledge to make strong classroom decisions. Sections on classroom organization may be particularly helpful.

Form 9.4
TEACHERS' SELF-ASSESSMENT OF READING LESSON FRAMEWORKS

Directions: Teachers will find criteria to support self-assessment of reading lesson components. All criteria would not be used during any one lesson. Form 9.4 may be used in supervisory pre-visit conferences, Form 9.5. Teachers may opt to identify particular criteria to be addressed as they teach, or respond to the total worksheet, and self-respond to those items with checkmarks on the right.

Criteria for Reading Lesson Frameworks	Highly Effective	Moderately Effective	Minimally Effective	Not Effective
	4	3	2	1

Pre-reading activities:

1. Create with students an anticipatory set* to assure their focus for the lesson—to the point where students will be able to state what they will learn, and what they will be able to do that they could not do previously ..... ☐ ☐ ☐ ☐

2. Engage, or generate, background knowledge (prior knowledge) to expand students' text prediction effectiveness .... ☐ ☐ ☐ ☐

3. Use brainstorming and webbing to organize students' existing knowledge to *visualize* text before reading .... ☐ ☐ ☐ ☐

4. Develop unfamiliar concepts, not explicated in the text, through direct instruction or brainstorming.. ☐ ☐ ☐ ☐

5. Teach new vocabulary or terms, unexplained in the text, that students will need to know prior to reading the assignment .... ☐ ☐ ☐ ☐

6. Model the process, strategy, or skill that pupils will be able to perform as a result of the reading activity .... ☐ ☐ ☐ ☐

7. Offer guided practice for new processes, tools, or strategies to assure understanding .... ☐ ☐ ☐ ☐

8. Initiate a reading posture students will employ as they read the assignment: problem-solving question, predictions, survey-question, etc. .... ☐ ☐ ☐ ☐

During-reading activities:

9. Help pupils to become *active* readers who expect to understand texts as they read.. ☐ ☐ ☐ ☐

10. Support students' active stance with responses to problem-solving questions, confirmation of predictions, and pursuit of survey-question formats, etc., developed as a pre-reading focus .... ☐ ☐ ☐ ☐

11. Help readers to adapt their own think-along processes, those processes earlier modeled by teachers as group think-alouds* .... ☐ ☐ ☐ ☐

–continues–

Teachers' Self-Assessment of Reading Lesson Frameworks -continued-	4	3	2	1
12. Assist students to use story structures* to monitor text understanding	☐	☐	☐	☐
13. Show learners how to employ interactive text-reading processes, ReQuest* and reciprocal teaching* to read as engaged readers.................................	☐	☐	☐	☐
14. Teach pupils to apply metacognitive* structures to know what to do when they do not comprehend	☐	☐	☐	☐
15. Direct students to reread to confirm information that also requires use of particular strategies or skills	☐	☐	☐	☐

Post-reading activities:

	4	3	2	1
16. Initially, confirm that pupils have identified answers to prior problem-solving questions, confirmations of predictions, or applications of survey-question of the SQRRR* cycle	☐	☐	☐	☐
17. Use story structures to help students successfully participate in story retellings	☐	☐	☐	☐
18. Affirm or expand vocabulary or concepts taught in the pre-reading lesson segment	☐	☐	☐	☐
19. Use known words from the text to learn word analysis or decoding patterns, carrying those words back to context for confirmation	☐	☐	☐	☐
20. Provide independent practice for learning of any concepts, processes, strategies, skills, or tools taught during the pre-reading phase	☐	☐	☐	☐
21. Support process writing by asking students to write about their stories by using story grammars, maps, or frames	☐	☐	☐	☐
22. Teach students to use those story structures to organize their thinking, and as a result, monitor texts, comprehend, retell, or write stories	☐	☐	☐	☐
23. Take any new processes, strategies, etc., to the level of *transfer*, generalization, or automaticity, through application to multiple contexts	☐	☐	☐	☐
24. Use verbal interaction and brainstorming to enhance the love and excitement of reading and to build emotional and personal impact	☐	☐	☐	☐

Cover the page here and below if users are not to see the interpretation until later.

Interpretation: Teachers' responses to Form 9.4 may help them self-assess lesson delivery. Respondents may identify specific criteria, teach a focused process to address those criteria, and recheck perceptions using Form 9.4. Another way for participants to use the worksheet is to tally columns, giving four points to checkmarks in the left column, three to the next column, two to the third column, and one point to checkmarks in the right column. Totals between 70–92 may be considered *highly effective*, between 47–69 *moderately effective*, between 24–46 *minimally effective*, and between 1–23 *not effective*.

PROFESSIONAL DEVELOPMENT THROUGH SUPERVISION   (see Forms 9.5 to 9.7)

Administrators have a dual responsibility toward the delivery of reading instruction by their teachers: supervision and evaluation. In some instances, the roles overlap, causing confusion and a certain amount of distrust and hostility on the part of teachers. Treated independently of each other, evaluation is reserved for making decisions regarding salary increments, tenure, or termination. Teachers should be fully aware of the administrative role during observations and subsequent conferences.

Supervision, and more specifically, clinical supervision, is intended to help teachers analyze the instructional process based on data collected during observations, encouraging them to experiment with, modify or adapt curriculum, and broaden their teaching options. Acheson and Gall (2) further characterize clinical supervision as being *interactive versus directive, democratic versus authoritarian,* and *teacher-centered versus supervisor-centered.* The supervisory role is exercised in three phases: a planning conference with the teacher, the actual observation to collect specific data in a prescribed manner, and a feedback conference to complete the cycle.

Throughout the cycle, the principal acts as coach, rather than administrator or evaluator. The goal is to develop autonomy on the part of teachers to analyze and reflect upon teaching episodes to support continuous professional development. Administrators may use Forms 9.5 to 9.7 to track their own effectiveness through the three-part cycle of clinical supervision.

For Further Reading

Acheson, K. A. & Gall, M. D. (1992). *Techniques in the Clinical Supervision of Teachers: Preservice and Inservice Applications, Third Edition.* New York: Longman. (10 Bank Street, White Plains, NY 10606-1951. 914-993-5000.)

The authors offer a practical book on supervision and evaluation of teachers. The research-based volume helps teachers self-assess, interpret, and make decisions about their teaching using a clinical supervision model. The authors address empowerment,school reform, and accountability in the revision.

Stobbe, C. (1993). "Professional Partnerships," *Educational Leadership*, 51, 2, 40–41.

The author advocates teachers' establishing voluntary partnerships to act as researchers for each other. Teachers so often are isolated by assumptions and classroom walls. Traditional roles have not allowed teachers or principals to expand their opportunities for professional growth. The author's alternative evaluation process addresses prior limitations.

THE PLANNING CONFERENCE   (see Form 9.5)

The planning conference permits the teacher to set the stage for the actual observation. It is at the teacher's request that the supervisor visits the classroom setting to gather data to assist the teacher in assessing the lesson. Some teachers may need nudging to follow through. It is the supervisor's responsibility to have kept the lines of communication open so that the planning conference is fruitful.

The Problem: Teachers often feel suspicion and hostility regarding conferences and observations. Principals may lack the skills to question and probe in an effective way to build trust and to assist the teacher in streamlining the lesson plan.

Rationale: Developing a step-by-step process for planning conferences can help the teacher to attend to the details of a lesson and focus on specific activities to secure feedback. Skillful probes by the supervisor may clarify the teacher's thinking and increase responsibility for thorough planning.

Procedures: Both the supervisor and the teacher have clearly defined roles and obligations in the planning conference. It is only through careful monitoring and self-analysis that the planning conference can reach a level of automaticity. Administrators and teachers may find Form 9.5 helpful to define their respective roles in the planning conference. If the Reading Advisory Board assists the principal by providing feedback, it may look at all forms, collectively, to make inferences about needs.

For Further Reading

Acheson, K. A. & Gall, M. D. (1992). *Techniques in the Clinical Supervision of Teachers: Preservice and Inservice Applications, Third Edition*. New York: Longman. (10 Bank Street, White Plains, NY 10606-1951. 914-993-5000.)

> The authors offer a practical book on supervision and evaluation of teachers. The research-based volume helps teachers self-assess, interpret, and make decisions about their teaching using a clinical supervision model. The authors address empowerment, school reform, and accountability in the revision.

Costa, A. L. & Garmston, R. J. (1994). *Cognitive Coaching: A Foundation for Renaissance Schools*. Norwood, MA: Christopher-Gordon Publishers, Inc. (480 Washington Street, Norwood, MA 02062. 1-800-934-8322.)

> A practical text designed for staff developers, teacher leaders, supervisors, or principals. The purpose is to help instructional leaders to help classroom teachers become more effective. Step-by-step processes of coaching are explicated. A focus is developed for verbal strategies and cross-cultural communication.

Form 9.5 THE PLANNING CONFERENCE	Highly Effective	Moderately Effective	Minimally Effective	Not Effective

Directions: Administrators may want to check themselves routinely until they feel comfortable in the coaching role. Requesting teachers' periodicinput may verify the coaching effectiveness role. Below are criteria for effective conference planning. Checkmarks may be made on the right.

Planning Conference Criteria:	4	3	2	1
1. There is an atmosphere of trust between the administrator or supervisor and the teacher	☐	☐	☐	☐
2. Requests for conferencing and observation are made at the teacher's convenience	☐	☐	☐	☐
3. The teacher shares the lesson goals and objectives	☐	☐	☐	☐
4. Teaching strategies and possible decisions are rehearsed	☐	☐	☐	☐
5. The teacher determines the evidence of students' achievement	☐	☐	☐	☐
6. The teacher and supervisor, together, agree upon data the principal will record and collect, method of collection, and form of recording	☐	☐	☐	☐
7. The supervisor is told where to sit, stand, or move about the classroom to best facilitate the collection of data	☐	☐	☐	☐
8. The teacher, through mental rehearsal, may refine strategies, discover potential flaws in original thinking, and anticipate decisions that may need to be made on the spot	☐	☐	☐	☐
9. The teacher determines the time and place of the observation				
10. The supervisor helps the teacher to identify specific concerns about curriculum content, instructional process, and student behavior	☐	☐	☐	☐
11. The principal as supervisor collects the data without bias during the observation	☐	☐	☐	☐

Data collection options; the principal is able to

12. Script verbatim accounts recorded of specific behaviors: praise statements, verbal mannerisms, interchanges between teacher and students, etc.	☐	☐	☐	☐

–continues–

The Planning Conference   -continued-

	4	3	2	1

13. Collect data regarding the teacher's question-asking behavior so that the teacher may determine the cognitive level of questions, probing and stringing, multiple questions, rephrasing, redirecting, etc. .... ☐ ☐ ☐ ☐

14. Provide feedback regarding responses to student contributions: repetition, rephrasing, praise, criticism, length, variety, etc. .... ☐ ☐ ☐ ☐

15. Offer feedback on the teacher's directions and structuring statements: overview, summary, verbal cues to emphasize points, switching to new topics, etc. .... ☐ ☐ ☐ ☐

16. Use a seating chart to record movement of the teacher and students during the teaching episode, verbal flow between teacher and students, or between students and students, etc. .... ☐ ☐ ☐ ☐

17. Arrange for the option of audio or video recording of the lesson .... ☐ ☐ ☐ ☐

18. Log anecdotal notes during the lesson, describing the events as they happen, leaving the interpretation and evaluation to the teacher .... ☐ ☐ ☐ ☐

Cover the page here and below if users are not to see the interpretation until later.

Interpretation: The principal's role in coaching may have a strong impact on the professional growth of teachers. To gain feedback on planning conferences, participants may tally columns, giving four points to checkmarks in the left column, three to the next column, two to the third column, and one point to checkmarks in the right column. Totals between 55–72 may be judged *highly effective*, between 37–54 *moderately effective*, between 19–36 *minimally effective*, and between 1–18 *not effective*.

THE SUPERVISORY VISIT   (see Form 9.6)

Principals may view observations as necessary visits to complete fair evaluations of teachers with visits on a drop-in basis. Teachers often are grateful for principals' affirmation of positive instruction that is noted, motivating even further improvements.

The Problem: Frequently, managerial tasks fill the principal's day. The more important task of being an instructional leader and attending to classroom visits and observations may be pre-empted by drop-in visitors, phone calls, and paperwork. The teaching episode may be script-taped in its entirety and teachers given a copy of the script with few comments. Principals may not be proficient with information-gathering skills. In the classroom, observers may be distracted by unusual happenings, unscheduled exchanges among students, and the general ambiance of the setting.

Rationale: Effective observations are planned by the teacher and the supervisor, together. The principal's organization in preparation for the supervisory visit may be the most important part of the process. The principal's presence in the classroom remains neutral and non-participatory. Data gathering is focused and teachers are able to draw conclusions from the data and devise plans to change, enhance, or discard a lesson or reconsider a process.

Procedures: Classroom supervisory visits provide a structure to study the quality of classroom instruction. Both supervisors and teachers may find Form 9.6 helpful in monitoring their classroom visits.

For Further Reading

Goldhammer, R., et al. (1993). *Clinical Supervision: Special Methods for the Supervision of Teachers, Third Edition.* New York: Holt, Rinehart & Winston.

> The text supports principals and supervisors as instructional leaders, as they recommend spending half of their time engaged in curriculum planning, staff development, clinical supervision, and teacher evaluations. Each function is developed fully.

Wheeler, P. (1992). *Improving Classroom Observation Skills: Guidelines for Teacher Evaluation.* Livermore, CA: EREAPA Associates (ED 364 961).

> Wheeler suggests ways to improve objectivity, quality, and relevance of classroom observations. She explicates functions of the pre-, during-, and post-observation, and advises holding several observations, using multiple sources of information, and retaining documentation.

Form 9.6

THE SUPERVISORY VISIT OR OBSERVATION

Directions: The supervisory visit may provide some of the strongest support for professional development. Principals may check how well they perform during an observation by checking at the right. Occasional, corroborative checks may also be made by individual teachers.

Supervisory Visit or Observation Criteria:	Highly Effective 4	Moderately Effective 3	Minimally Effective 2	Not Effective 1
1. Arrives in ample time at the teacher's classroom	☐	☐	☐	☐
2. Positions himself/herself in the agreed-upon place to record the data, remaining as unobtrusive as possible	☐	☐	☐	☐
3. Has all of the materials (charts, data sheets, etc.) necessary to collect the data	☐	☐	☐	☐
4. Keeps eyes, ears, and mind on the task	☐	☐	☐	☐
5. Looks up regularly so as not to miss non-verbal exchanges	☐	☐	☐	☐
6. Keeps track of time in marginal notes	☐	☐	☐	☐
7. Uses abbreviations as much as possible to expedite note-taking	☐	☐	☐	☐
8. Uses tally marks to record repetitive patterns	☐	☐	☐	☐
9. Records information about the setting: information on the chalkboard, overhead transparencies	☐	☐	☐	☐
10. Records descriptively both positive and negative comments and happenings	☐	☐	☐	☐
11. Allows *at least* 30 minutes to observe, or better, stays for the entire lesson	☐	☐	☐	☐
12. Records the nature of any disruption, effects, and the time lost	☐	☐	☐	☐
13. Refrains from making any comments during the lesson	☐	☐	☐	☐
14. Does not permit interruptions during the data collection	☐	☐	☐	☐
15. Leaves as quietly as possible following the observation	☐	☐	☐	☐

–continues–

The Supervisory Visit of Observation -continued-

	4	3	2	1
16. Fills in the blanks immediately following the observation to preserve the chronological order	☐	☐	☐	☐
17. Reserves analysis until after the observation	☐	☐	☐	☐
18. Organizes data into a meaningful format for the teacher to analyze and interpret	☐	☐	☐	☐
19. Arranges the time for the reflecting conference	☐	☐	☐	☐

Cover the page here and below if users are not to see the interpretation until later.

Interpretation: Principals who wish to self-assess on their observation behaviors may give four points to checkmarks in the right column, three points to marks in the second column, two points to marks in the third column, and one point to checkmarks in the right column. Totals between 58–76 may be considered *highly effective*, 39–57 *moderately effective*, 20–38 *minimally effective*, and 1–19 *not effective*.

THE POST-OBSERVATION OR REFLECTING CONFERENCE   (see Form 9.7)

The third part of the clinical supervision cycle brings the two previous portions—planning conference and observation—together for comparison and contrast of the intended teaching episode with what actually transpired. The level of trust and degree of each person's experience will influence the effectiveness of the feedback conference.

The Problem: Oftentimes, the data collected during an observation are not studied, organized, or presented to a teacher in a usable format. Principals may feel compelled to dominate the conference in the guise of leadership. Teachers may lack confidence to interpret the data and use them to modify or set goals. The supervisor may find working with some teachers more difficult than with others.

Rationale: The supervisor who takes time to review and organize data, collected in accordance with the purpose of the observation, can lead a teacher to make connections between the teaching and responses of students. The connections can further lead to insightful conclusions regarding the viability of a strategy, effectiveness of the presentation, and possible avenues for growth. Timeliness (within 24 hours) is central to the effectiveness of this meeting.

Procedures: Supervisors may find it helpful to use Form 9.7 as a checklist to monitor their preparation for post-conferences, as well as to define their participatory roles. Teachers may also be asked to occasionally complete Form 9.7 at the conclusion of a post conference. The supervisory visit may then verify or refute the principal's self-perceptions.

For Further Reading

Aiex, N. K. (1993). *A Communicative Approach to Observation and Feedback*. (ED 364 926).

> The author views teacher observation and evaluation as a delicate process. As supervisors go through observation processes, supervisor-teacher rapport lends trust and mutual openness to grow. Mutually agreed upon observation criteria, too, lend trust.

Costa, A. L. & Garmston, R. J. (1994). *Cognitive Coaching: A Foundation for Renaissance Schools*. Norwood, MA: Christopher-Gordon Publishers, Inc. (480 Washington Street, Norwood, MA 02062. 1-800-934-8322.)

> A practical text designed for staff developers, teacher leaders, supervisors, or principals. The purpose is to help instructional leaders to help classroom teachers to become more effective. Step-by-step processes of coaching are explicated. The roles of verbal strategies and cross-cultural communication are interpreted.

Form 9.7

THE POST-OBSERVATION OR REFLECTING CONFERENCE

Directions: The post-conference requires advance preparation to assure an opportunity for reflection, analysis, and growth. Criteria are listed below. Supervisors may indicate on the right the degree to which criteria for a successful conference are being met.

Post-Observation Conference Criteria:	Highly Effective	Moderately Effective	Minimally Effective	Not Effective
	4	3	2	1
1. The supervisor allows time between the observation and post conference for the teacher to reflect	☐	☐	☐	☐
2. Objective data are presented in an organized manner to the teacher	☐	☐	☐	☐
3. The supervisor has prepared questions in advance to encourage the teacher's discussion	☐	☐	☐	☐
4. The teacher and supervisor analyze the data together to recreate the teaching episode	☐	☐	☐	☐
5. The supervisor elicits the teacher's reactions, i.e., feelings, opinions, inferences, regarding causes or consequences of student responses	☐	☐	☐	☐
6. The conference is *teacher-centered,* with the supervisor listening more and talking less	☐	☐	☐	☐
7. The principal acknowledges understanding with phrases such as "I know what you mean" and "I understand"	☐	☐	☐	☐
8. The supervisor refrains from criticizing, lecturing, or giving directions	☐	☐	☐	☐
9. If in doubt, the administrator paraphrases to check his/her comprehension	☐	☐	☐	☐
10. The principal asks clarifying questions to determine meaning of vague pronouns and action words or non-specific generalities: which students, when, how, tell me more	☐	☐	☐	☐
11. The supervisor uses the teacher's ideas to pursue a logical consequence or to investigate a similar situation	☐	☐	☐	☐
12. The principal supports the teacher's attempts to identify causal relationships	☐	☐	☐	☐

–continues–

The Post-Observation or Reflecting Conference -continued-	4	3	2	1
13. The teacher summarizes impressions and assessment of the lesson presentation and outcomes..	☐	☐	☐	☐
14. The teacher recalls factual data to support conclusions	☐	☐	☐	☐
15. The teacher makes inferences regarding the relationships teaching and students' achievement	☐	☐	☐	☐
16. The supervisor encourages the teacher to use the inferences to make decisions about altering, maintaining, or expanding instruction	☐	☐	☐	☐
17. The teacher and supervisor reach agreement on the goals for the next observation	☐	☐	☐	☐
18. The supervisor solicits input from the teacher regarding the value of the feedback conference and recommendations for refinements	☐	☐	☐	☐

Cover the page here and below if users are not to see the interpretation until later.

Interpretation: Principals may find it helpful to self-assess their conference skills across the teaching staff. A periodic check with a specific teacher could serve to maintain an objective perspective or indicate specific areas to work on with individual teachers. Participants may tally columns, giving four points to checkmarks in the left column, three to the next column, two the third column, and one point to checkmarks in the right column. Totals between 55–72 may be judged *highly effective*, 37–54 *moderately effective*, 19–36 *minimally effective*, and 1–18 *not effective*.

THE PRINCIPAL AS COACH

(see Form 9.8)

For a long time, principals viewed their instructional leaders' roles as authoritarian in nature and geared to the evaluative function of teachers. In recent years, the trend toward participatory decision-making, collegial assessment and planning, with a cognitive coaching emphasis, has evolved and grown. Cognitive coaching emerged from the work of Costa and Garmston (41). Successful coaching experiences arise out of trust between coach (i.e., principal) and teacher, a belief that the two are mutual leaders engaged in a drive toward achieving professional autonomy and interdependence.

The Problem: Principals may lack training and practice in the tenets of coaching. They may feel uncomfortable in being non-directive and non-judgmental. Teachers may also be unaccustomed to assuming responsibility and participating during pre- and post-conferences.

Rationale: Professional growth is stimulated when teachers take charge of their own needs. Principals who facilitate rather than direct conferences free teachers to critique themselves objectively, make inferences and deductions regarding their effectiveness, and monitor their growth.

Procedures: Principals may wish to self-assess the effectiveness of their coaching skills by completing Form 9.8. They may find that they routinely practice some of the skills. Other skills may require further reading, training, or supervised practice. At the same time, selected teachers may also complete Form 9.8 to assess their own roles as responsible conference participants and to affirm the principal's role as coach.

For Further Reading

Costa, A. L. & Garmston, R. J. (1994). *Cognitive Coaching: A Foundation for Renaissance Schools.* Norwood, MA: Christopher-Gordon Publishers, Inc. (480 Washington Street, Norwood, MA 02062. 1-800-934-8322.)

A practical text designed for staff developers, teacher leaders, supervisors, or principals. The purpose is to help instructional leaders to help classroom teachers to become more effective. Step-by-step processes of coaching are explicated. A focus is developed for verbal strategies and cross-cultural communication.

Garmston, R., et al. (1993). "Reflections on Cognitive Coaching," *Educational Leadership*, 51, 2, 57–61.

The purpose of cognitive coaching is to develop teachers' professional autonomy through self-monitoring. The concept's three-phase cycle—e.g., preconference, observation, and postconference—supports educators to become reflective about their teaching.

Form 9.8

THE PRINCIPAL AS COACH

Directions: Criteria may be found below regarding coaching relationships. Principals and teachers may check to the right the extent of effectiveness in supervisory conferences.

Criteria on Coaching Relationships:	Highly Effective	Moderately Effective	Minimally Effective	Not Effective
	4	3	2	1
1. The coach possesses the ability to enable and empower teachers to do their best	☐	☐	☐	☐
2. The principal is able to *stand in the teacher's shoes* and see things from that viewpoint	☐	☐	☐	☐
3. The principal acknowledges the teacher's goals, concerns, and experience level as a prerequisite for successful conferences	☐	☐	☐	☐
4. The administrator is aware of the ways the teacher processes information and capitalizes on that information	☐	☐	☐	☐
5. Both the principal and the teacher appear comfortable in their respective roles	☐	☐	☐	☐
6. During the conference, the principal is attuned to the teacher's posture, gestures, breathing, and other non-verbal indicators of comfort or stress and selectively matches them to verbal information	☐	☐	☐	☐
7. The coach exhibits non-judgmental verbal attributes such as				
a. providing data without interruption	☐	☐	☐	☐
b. asking open-ended questions	☐	☐	☐	☐
c. paraphrasing and summarizing to check understanding	☐	☐	☐	☐
d. empathizing to acknowledge feelings	☐	☐	☐	☐
8. The principal encourages and supports the teacher in making inferences and drawing conclusions about causal relationships	☐	☐	☐	☐
9. The coach engages the teacher in brainstorming activities	☐	☐	☐	☐

–continues–

The Principal as Coach	-continued-	4	3	2	1

10. The principal maintains flexibility to accommodate the various styles of individuals

    a. responds to teachers' preferred perceptual style: visual, auditory, kinesthetic—by listening to language cues and observing eye movements .... ☐ ☐ ☐ ☐

    b. is aware of teachers' innate cognitive style and maintains a professional distance with those who are task-oriented and analytical .... ☐ ☐ ☐ ☐

    c. develops collaborative, mentoring relationships with teachers who are people-oriented and intuitive .... ☐ ☐ ☐ ☐

11. The coach respects the teacher's educational belief system .... ☐ ☐ ☐ ☐

12. Fairness and consistency are apparent, regardless of gender or race, ethnicity, and culture .... ☐ ☐ ☐ ☐

13. Questions are asked in a way that teachers feel they have a variety of answers, any of which are suitable .... ☐ ☐ ☐ ☐

14. Rather than offering solutions, the principal taps the inner resources of the teacher .... ☐ ☐ ☐ ☐

15. There is an overarching belief that teachers can and will do their best .... ☐ ☐ ☐ ☐

16. There is a feeling of collaboration between principal and teacher, and among teachers .... ☐ ☐ ☐ ☐

Cover the page here and below if users are not to see the interpretation until later.

Interpretation: Respondents may tally columns, giving four points to checkmarks on the left, three to marks in the next column, two points to marks in the third column, and one point to checkmarks in the right column. Recognizing that some items have sub-categories, totals between 64–84 may be considered *highly effective*, between 43–63 *moderately effective*, between 22–42 *minimally effective*, and between 1–21 *not effective*.

PROFESSIONAL DEVELOPMENT THROUGH NETWORKING   (see Form 9.9)

Teachers who skillfully use cooperative learning in their classrooms are usually pleased that their students seem to learn a lot of information in a comfortable fashion and in a short time. Teachers could learn from the experiences of their students. Their efforts to share with colleagues are rewarded with new ideas, affirmation of their own teaching program, and a general sense of well-being about their profession.

The Problem: Principals and teachers often live in a small world of their own making. Many are reluctant to join professional organizations locally, state-wide, or nationally. Districts are not always able to allocate monies for teachers to attend professional conferences and institutes locally or out-of-town. Teachers may feel that it is easier to be at school than to retrench after having a substitute teacher in the class.

Rationale: Professional development goes beyond the local school or district setting. Innovations in the teaching of reading are usually introduced at the international or national meetings, and then at state conferences. The opportunities to share experiences with teachers from other locales is invigorating and refreshing. Hearing first-hand from a researcher or writer builds interest and understanding.

Procedures: Principals and Reading Advisory Board members are asked to assess how well they promote networking activities by using Form 9.9.

For Further Reading

Krovetz, M. & Cohick, D. (1993). "Professional Collegiality Can Lead to School Change," *Phi Delta Kappan*, 75, 74, 331–333.

> Professional development support teams replace traditional formal evaluation for certified staff in a district. The earlier system was judged meaningless and demoralizing. Although extra work is involved, teachers' responses are positive. Components include choice, support, stimulation, trust, and respect for peers.

Sanacore, J. (1993). "Using Study Groups to Create a Professional Community," *Journal of Reading*, 37, 1, 62–66.

> Traditional staff development is replaced with professional study groups. Strengths and weaknesses are described in the article. Components of effective study groups are provided and applications are suggested.

Form 9.9

PROFESSIONAL DEVELOPMENT THROUGH NETWORKING

Directions: Networking with teachers within a school, across the district, or at state, regional, and national meetings strengthens professionalism. Principals and Reading Advisory Board members are invited to check the efforts made at promoting networking activities.

Networking Criteria:	Highly Effective 4	Moderately Effective 3	Minimally Effective 2	Not Effective 1
1. Faculty and staff members are encouraged to meet as study groups on a regular basis to discuss specific issues of common interest.........................	☐	☐	☐	☐
2. Principals and teachers are treated equally; they collaboratively negotiate the agenda	☐	☐	☐	☐
3. All study group members share responsibility for discussions, research of professional literature, setting goals, trying and assessing new approaches and materials	☐	☐	☐	☐
4. Efforts are made to arrange meetings with teachers of the same grade level across the district to share specific reading topics..	☐	☐	☐	☐
5. Interest groups may meet regularly across the district or area, to study areas such as integrating reading and writing, using thematic units, multicultural literature, journals, portfolios, literature sets, etc.	☐	☐	☐	☐
6. Teachers present topics or review their professional reading at faculty meetings	☐	☐	☐	☐
7. The reading specialist or a Reading Advisory Board member may act as coordinator or liaison between the faculty and the local reading organization	☐	☐	☐	☐
8. Both teachers and principal join and attend meetings of the local reading organization	☐	☐	☐	☐
9. Subscriptions to journals such as *The Reading Teacher* and *Language Arts* are part of the periodical collection in the school library or media center......	☐	☐	☐	☐
10. A designated teacher reviews and highlights several articles from the above sources each month for the faculty and staff	☐	☐	☐	☐
11. Multiple copies of paperback editions of teaching strategy books are available for study group use	☐	☐	☐	☐

–continues–

Professional Development through Networking	-continued-	4	3	2	1

12. The principal budgets for a representative number of teachers (2 or 3) to attend the state reading conference and report back to the faculty and staff ☐ ☐ ☐ ☐

13. Memberships in the state and international organizations are encouraged .. ☐ ☐ ☐ ☐

14. The principal and reading specialist try to attend the national or international meetings on an alternating basis .... ☐ ☐ ☐ ☐

15. Teachers are encouraged to request district funds for partial or full payment to attend conventions, conferences, institutes, etc. .... ☐ ☐ ☐ ☐

16. District-funded conference attendees are expected to share their information with the local faculty and staff .... ☐ ☐ ☐ ☐

17. Principals scan flyers and brochures, especially of local presentations, and pass them on to teachers who have demonstrated interest .... ☐ ☐ ☐ ☐

18. Teachers, as groups and individually, are supported to prepare presentations for local, district, area, or state meetings .... ☐ ☐ ☐ ☐

Cover the page here and below if users are not to see the interpretation until later.

Interpretation: Respondents may tally columns, giving four points to checkmarks on the left, three points to marks in the next column, two to the third column, and one point to checkmarks in the right column. Networking totals between 55–72 may be judged *highly effective* between 37–54 *moderately effective*, between 19–36 *minimally effective*, and between 1–18 *not effective*.

STAFF DEVELOPMENT PLANNING   (see Forms 9.10 to 9.12)

Early administrator-directed inservice was based on brief workshops to implement curriculum changes. Gradually, workshops to introduce varieties of teaching skills and models emerged. Workshops tended to be fragmented, one-shot exposures with little follow-up. Teachers often were required to accumulate inservice hours to be eligible for salary advancement.

Today, staff development is more likely to emerge from comprehensive needs-assessment at the school or district level. Planners often take advantage of inservice provided by textbook publishers when they purchase new texts. Inservice may be scheduled over several after-school sessions spaced apart to permit opportunity for teachers to practice and then ask questions.

Some districts are large enough to send cadres of teachers and consultants to be trained by experts in strategies for specific areas. Groups may also attend local experts' sessions on general strategies. Well-known speakers and writers may be engaged to conduct content-specific general teaching strategies or even workshops dealing with school climate, effecting change, staff morale, parent involvement, and other current issues.

Regardless of the content, the realization of need, the timing, the commitment to see the workshop through, opportunities to practice under supervision, and local input, are all serious issues to resolve if staff development is to be worthwhile and become institutionalized. Respondents may study Form 9.10 to reflect upon what makes effective inservice workshops, Form 9.11 to consider a needs-base for staff development, and 9.12 to prioritize long-term plans.

For Further Reading

Wall, R. R. (1993). *Staff Development Programs in Public Schools: Successful Staff Development Programs Including the Role of the Classroom Teachers and Administrators* (ED 361 288).

> After reviewing the professional literature, Wall concluded that effective staff development incorporates a philosophy, cooperation, needs assessment to identify content, a strong delivery system with evaluations, in-school delivery, peer presentations, and quality time for inservice to take place.

EFFECTIVE STAFF DEVELOPMENT WORKSHOPS   (see Form 9.10)

The purpose of a staff development plan is to help teachers to improve instruction, resulting in more effective learning for each student. Workshops may answer questions about teachers' daily instructional problems. More often, perhaps, workshops may address contemporary educational development, keep faculties current, and enrich teaching repertoires.

The Problem: Teachers are all too familiar with the tiresome *dog and pony show* quality of staff development, planned by an administrator, with little relevance or interest, that occurs after a long teaching day. Experiencing those presentations leads many faculty members to be cautious about inservice sessions. Frequently, teachers are not able to contribute their ideas about needs, and may not be included in planning for staff development.

Rationale: Effective professional development is based on a long-term plan for instructional improvement in a school. Needs are carefully identified and working groups of teachers, principal, and central office administrator often plan inservice content to address both immediate and long-term needs. Needs-based, cooperative planning, may result in teachers' ownership of the process and active participation in its workshops.

Procedures: Reading Advisory Boards or principals may study Form 9.10 to consider criteria on good inservice delivery. Coupled with Form 9.10, the next worksheet, Form 9.11, may be used to develop a needs-base for planning.

For Further Reading

Wall, R. R. (1993). *Staff Development Programs in Public Schools: Successful Staff Development Programs Including the Role of the Classroom Teachers and Administrators* (ED 361 288).

> After reviewing the professional literature, Wall concluded that effective staff development incorporates a philosophy, cooperation, needs assessment to identify content, a strong delivery system with evaluations, in-school delivery, peer presentations, and quality time for inservice to take place.

Form 9.10

EFFECTIVE STAFF DEVELOPMENT WORKSHOPS

Directions: Administrators or Reading Advisory Boards will find below criteria to judge what makes a good inservice program. This information may help, somewhat, in planning. Respondents may check, on the right, their self-assessment of the degree of criteria's implementation.

Staff Development Workshop Criteria:	Highly Effective	Moderately Effective	Minimally Effective	Not Effective
	4	3	2	1
1. Staff development sessions each have a clear goal and framework of delivery	☐	☐	☐	☐
2. Inservice is based on needs-assessment, using instruments such as Form 9.11 or Forms 3.11 and 3.12 to define content	☐	☐	☐	☐
3. Needs (see Form 9.11) are defined, and prioritized by a voluntary committee or Board	☐	☐	☐	☐
4. Content of inservice should combine perceived instructional needs of teachers and the instructional thrust envisioned by leaders	☐	☐	☐	☐
5. The size of participating groups optimizes participation and intrinsic learning	☐	☐	☐	☐
6. Processes involve action, doing something, *hands on*, modeling, making materials, when possible, with theory and concepts imbedded	☐	☐	☐	☐
7. Workshops are focused and purposeful, but flexible to redirect for related needs	☐	☐	☐	☐
8. Each session is ended with a participants' evaluation of the program's effectiveness	☐	☐	☐	☐
9. School and central office administrators participate, both giving credibility to the importance, and to remain current	☐	☐	☐	☐

Interpretation: Form 9.10 may help administrators or Reading Advisory Boards to summarize the value of workshop sessions. Respondents may total each column, giving four points to checkmarks in the left column, three to the next column, two to the third column, and one point to checkmarks in the right column. Totals between 28–36 should be considered *highly effective* between 19–27 *moderately effective*, between 10–18 *minimally effective*, and between 1–9 *not effective*.

THE NEEDS-ASSESSMENT BASE   (see Form 9.11)

Effective staff development is responsive to teachers' needs. Content may be geared to implementing curricular changes, developing larger repertoires of strategies and skills, or improvement of internal health of the school as an organization.

The Problem: Data gathered from earlier chapters relate primarily to the reading program. Teachers' needs will be varied due to experience levels and prior participation in staff development opportunities. Principals find the task easier by prescribing the inservice themselves.

Rationale: Teachers develop ownership when their input is sought and used. Staff development that is directly related to day-to-day classroom activity is more likely to be institutionalized. In some schools and districts, a Professional Development Committee comprised largely of teachers, some local school administrators and central office administrators, analyze the data to develop district-wide goals. Teachers in the local setting develop a plan-of-action to tie into one or more of the district goals, as well as to their own particular needs.

Procedures: Principals will find it helpful to develop a needs-assessment instrument. Form 9.11 may serve as a baseline document, but may need to be adapted for local use. Information from Forms 3.11 and 3.12 may be adapted to faculty-based needs assessment.

For Further Reading

Boyd, B. (1993). *Transforming Teacher Staff Development* (ED 362 943).

> Boyd describes staff development that addresses affective and humanistic considerations. He supports proactive development, increased teacher empowerment, and strong collegiality. Needs of belonging and recognition of professionalism are developed as important components.

Wood, F., et al. (1993). *How to Organize a School-Based Staff Development Program.* Alexandria, VA: Association for Supervision and Curriculum Development. (1250 North Pitt Street, Alexandria, VA 22314-1453. 703-549-9110.)

> The authors develop a five-stage process for school improvement and strategies to learn how to: develop ownership and commitment of staff and the community, help faculty become aware of what is available and possible, create positive, productive inservice, and ensure that what is learned during training becomes part of daily school activities.

Form 9.11

NEEDS-ASSESSMENT FOR PROFESSIONAL DEVELOPMENT IN READING

Directions: Teachers and Reading Advisory Boards may benefit from needs statement feedback to plan staff development. Below are listed topics for professional development workshops. Teachers are asked to indicate their perceived needs on the right.

Perceived Staff Development Needs:	Top Priority	High Interest	Moderate Interest	Minimal Interest	No Interest
	5	4	3	2	1

1. Create interest, positive attitude, and appreciation in reading through

	5	4	3	2	1
a. reading incentive programs	☐	☐	☐	☐	☐
b. school-wide reading programs	☐	☐	☐	☐	☐
c. games and contests	☐	☐	☐	☐	☐
d. book talks by students or adults	☐	☐	☐	☐	☐

2. Capitalize on student affect

	5	4	3	2	1
a. extrinsic	☐	☐	☐	☐	☐
b. intrinsic	☐	☐	☐	☐	☐
c. reducing learner tension	☐	☐	☐	☐	☐
d. manipulating variables related to motivation, purpose, attitude, results, successes	☐	☐	☐	☐	☐

3. Select worthwhile practice activities

	5	4	3	2	1
a. matching activities to instructional input	☐	☐	☐	☐	☐
b. providing for mass and distributed practice	☐	☐	☐	☐	☐

4. Diagnosis of student needs

	5	4	3	2	1
a. determining reading levels	☐	☐	☐	☐	☐
b. using an Informal Reading Inventory* to assess primary areas of reading strength and difficulty	☐	☐	☐	☐	☐
c. completion and interpretation of a running record*	☐	☐	☐	☐	☐
d. administration and interpretation of a reading miscue inventory*	☐	☐	☐	☐	☐
e. use of the cloze* procedure	☐	☐	☐	☐	☐
f. interpretation of standardized test data	☐	☐	☐	☐	☐

–continues–

Needs-Assessment for Professional Development in Reading -continued-	5	4	3	2	1

5. Management of the classroom to economize time

   a. differentiated use of staff and faculty .... ☐ ☐ ☐ ☐ ☐

   b. intra- and inter-class grouping .... ☐ ☐ ☐ ☐ ☐

   c. utilizing parents, paraprofessionals .... ☐ ☐ ☐ ☐ ☐

   d. developing a peer tutoring program .... ☐ ☐ ☐ ☐ ☐

6. Overview of the reading curriculum

   a. comprehensive curriculum content .... ☐ ☐ ☐ ☐ ☐

   b. alignment of curriculum, assessment .... ☐ ☐ ☐ ☐ ☐

   c. prior grade level .... ☐ ☐ ☐ ☐ ☐

   d. following grade level .... ☐ ☐ ☐ ☐ ☐

7. Grouping in the classroom

   a. by grade level .... ☐ ☐ ☐ ☐ ☐

   b. for strategy and skill instruction .... ☐ ☐ ☐ ☐ ☐

   c. with sociograms .... ☐ ☐ ☐ ☐ ☐

   d. with interest inventories .... ☐ ☐ ☐ ☐ ☐

   e. with the use of learning centers .... ☐ ☐ ☐ ☐ ☐

   f. with cooperative grouping for literature sets .... ☐ ☐ ☐ ☐ ☐

8. Assessment of student progress

   a. selection of publishers' tools .... ☐ ☐ ☐ ☐ ☐

   b. role of performance assessment .... ☐ ☐ ☐ ☐ ☐

   c. development of teacher-made instruments .... ☐ ☐ ☐ ☐ ☐

   d. use of alternative assessment options .... ☐ ☐ ☐ ☐ ☐

   e. matching assessment options to perceptual styles .... ☐ ☐ ☐ ☐ ☐

9. Use of portfolios to

   a. collect student work to monitor progress .... ☐ ☐ ☐ ☐ ☐

   b. help students to organize their collection .... ☐ ☐ ☐ ☐ ☐

   c. teach students to self-assess .... ☐ ☐ ☐ ☐ ☐

   d. record growth in the reading process as well as products ..... ☐ ☐ ☐ ☐ ☐

–continues–

Needs-Assessment for Professional Development in Reading -continued-	5	4	3	2	1

10. Update teaching processes and strategies

a. emerging literacy/readiness .... ☐ ☐ ☐ ☐ ☐

b. narrative text comprehension .... ☐ ☐ ☐ ☐ ☐

c. expository text comprehension .... ☐ ☐ ☐ ☐ ☐

d. writing and reading .... ☐ ☐ ☐ ☐ ☐

e. meaning vocabulary .... ☐ ☐ ☐ ☐ ☐

f. literature-based instruction .... ☐ ☐ ☐ ☐ ☐

g. word analysis or decoding .... ☐ ☐ ☐ ☐ ☐

h. recreational reading .... ☐ ☐ ☐ ☐ ☐

i. rate and flexibility .... ☐ ☐ ☐ ☐ ☐

11. Sources of record-keeping

a. audio and video taping of oral reading over time intervals .... ☐ ☐ ☐ ☐ ☐

b. documentation of class participation .... ☐ ☐ ☐ ☐ ☐

c. development of anecdotal records .... ☐ ☐ ☐ ☐ ☐

d. development of observation checklists .... ☐ ☐ ☐ ☐ ☐

12. Use of prescriptive teaching procedures

a. selecting appropriate objectives .... ☐ ☐ ☐ ☐ ☐

b. matching materials to the objectives .... ☐ ☐ ☐ ☐ ☐

c. preparing a Directed Reading-Thinking Activity* .... ☐ ☐ ☐ ☐ ☐

13. Selection of reading materials

a. materials available in the local school .... ☐ ☐ ☐ ☐ ☐

b. preparing teacher-made materials .... ☐ ☐ ☐ ☐ ☐

c. selectively choosing commercial program materials .... ☐ ☐ ☐ ☐ ☐

d. development of a catalog or index for the grade level .... ☐ ☐ ☐ ☐ ☐

14. Identification of problem readers

a. characteristics .... ☐ ☐ ☐ ☐ ☐

b. causes of reading failure .... ☐ ☐ ☐ ☐ ☐

c. simplified classroom diagnostic processes .... ☐ ☐ ☐ ☐ ☐

d. referral and help for problem readers .... ☐ ☐ ☐ ☐ ☐

—continues—

Needs-Assessment for Professional Development in Reading -continued-	5	4	3	2	1

15. Integration of reading and writing

a. journal writing to respond to affect .... □ □ □ □ □

b. logging unfamiliar vocabulary .... □ □ □ □ □

c. imitating writers' style, craft, choice .... □ □ □ □ □

16. Choosing trade books to complement the reading program

a. story structure examples .... □ □ □ □ □

b. selection to study genre options .... □ □ □ □ □

c. choices for literature set study... □ □ □ □ □

d. titles to read to children .... □ □ □ □ □

e. non-fiction to enhance curriculum.. □ □ □ □ □

f. study formats to follow .... □ □ □ □ □

17. Beginning a whole language classroom

a. gaining a foundational belief system .... □ □ □ □ □

b. organizing a holistic environment .... □ □ □ □ □

c. learning to organize the time .... □ □ □ □ □

d. selection of trade books .... □ □ □ □ □

e. options for practice and enrichment .... □ □ □ □ □

f. assessment of pupils' learning .... □ □ □ □ □

18. Practice of cooperative learning options

a. basic tenets .... □ □ □ □ □

b. maximizing its use .... □ □ □ □ □

c. aligning cooperative learning to curriculum segments .... □ □ □ □ □

d. assessment of individual students, groups and group processes .... □ □ □ □ □

Cover the page here and below if users are not to see the interpretation until later.

Interpretation: The Reading Advisory Board may wish to record teachers' priority indicators for each item by using a blank Form 9.11 and tallying each column. Totals may be multiplied by the number of tallies in each category. The products may be added across, and ranked from high to low to determine areas of greatest perceived need or interest.

PREPARING FOR STAFF DEVELOPMENT SESSIONS   (see Forms 9.12 to 9.14)

Principals often may feel responsibile for presenting workshops for their faculties and staffs. Additionally, administrators may be aware that they work with teachers whose skills warrant their presenting workshops for the faculty. Careful planning may be expected to enhance administrators' or teachers' confidence and offer participants an organized session. The quality of sessions may improve current and eventual instruction in the school.

The Problem: Principals may not always understand how to prepare for organized and effective faculty workshops. Teachers who take ownership for their part in a school's reading program may have important ideas to present, but may be afraid to do things in front of their peers. They may teach well, but be unknowledgeable about how to organize workshops for adults.

Rationale: Planning for staff development presentations involves preparations *before*, *during*, and *after* presentations. Teachers or principals may develop the analogy that planning for staff development workshops is much like planning for good reading lessons. Workshops do contain variations on an anticipatory set, develop concepts about teaching children, check for peers' understanding, involve some organization into large groups, small groups, triads, dyads, etc., and present closure activities.

Procedures: Form 9.12 may be used for principals or faculty groups to self-assess their plans for workshop presentations. Forms 9.13 and 9.14 may be useful to gain feedback from participants about workshop effectiveness.

For Further Reading

Garmston, R., et al. (1993). "Reflections on Cognitive Coaching," *Educational Leadership*, 51, 2, 57–61.

> The purpose of cognitive coaching is to develop teachers' professional autonomy through self-monitoring. The concept's three-phase cycle—e.g., preconference, observation, and postconference—supports educators to become reflective about their teaching.

Sharp, P. A. (1993). *Sharing Your Good Ideas: A Workshop Facilitator's Handbook.* Portsmouth, NH: Heinemann Educational Books, Inc. (361 Hanover Street, Portsmouth, NH 03801-3912. 1-800-541-2086.)

> The book provides structures for teachers with little or no presentation experience to prepare workshops for colleagues. Content includes organizing for presentations, developing graphics and handouts, planning for participation, and evaluating the presentation and learning. Suggestions are given for beginning and ending workshops.

Form 9.12
PREPARING FOR STAFF DEVELOPMENT SESSIONS

Directions: Below, presenters will find criteria related to workshop preparations. Participants will find criteria below. On the right, presenters may self-assess their fulfillment of criteria.

Staff Development Presentation Criteria:	Thoroughly Prepared 4	Moderately Prepared 3	Minimally Prepared 2	Not Prepared 1

Prior to the presentation

1. Know the audience (their needs, awareness) .... ☐ ☐ ☐ ☐
2. Know the topic (do the warranted extensive reading, find more than one point of view) .... ☐ ☐ ☐ ☐
3. Plan the outline (giving attention to sequence), transparencies, charts, other visuals .... ☐ ☐ ☐ ☐
4. Plan participatory activities for the audience .... ☐ ☐ ☐ ☐
5. Prepare handouts (not verbatim of the speech) with space for note-taking .. ☐ ☐ ☐ ☐
6. Determine the time limits for each session part .... ☐ ☐ ☐ ☐
7. Rehearse, giving attention to the presentation as though you were in the audience .... ☐ ☐ ☐ ☐
8. Check that charts, transparencies, and other support materials are placed in the sequence you will use for the presentation .... ☐ ☐ ☐ ☐

During the presentation

9. Establish rapport with the audience, ask somebody to introduce you to provide prior credibility and stand still when introduced so people can assess what you are like .... ☐ ☐ ☐ ☐
10. Begin with a story that relates to yourself, the setting, the audience, or the topic .... ☐ ☐ ☐ ☐
11. Establish the comfort setting: tell people to get coffee during the presentation, to go to the bathroom without your permission .... ☐ ☐ ☐ ☐
12. Build in activities that allow people to move around, to work with other groups of people .... ☐ ☐ ☐ ☐
13. Remind yourself that you will be working with a diverse population; refrain from making judgmental statements .... ☐ ☐ ☐ ☐
14. Employ a sense of humor .... ☐ ☐ ☐ ☐

Preparing for Staff Development Sessions -continued-

		4	3	2	1
15.	Allow enough time for participants to take the notes they feel that they need	☐	☐	☐	☐
16.	As you are using transparencies during the presentation, check to see that their image is fully placed on the screen	☐	☐	☐	☐
17.	As a clincher, show students' work that exemplifies the concepts you are presenting in the workshop	☐	☐	☐	☐
18.	Check for understanding by asking application questions or have participants share with each other what they think the content was	☐	☐	☐	☐
19.	Be responsive to body language of the audience, perk up when members need to refocus; take appropriate coffee and rest breaks	☐	☐	☐	☐

At the end of the presentation

		4	3	2	1
20.	Develop closure for the workshop; you started by telling participants what you were going to do, you did it, now you will tell participants what you have done	☐	☐	☐	☐
21.	Ask workshop respondents to complete a workshop evaluation form (for examples of formats that might be used to develop an evaluation, see Forms 9.13 and 9.14)	☐	☐	☐	☐
22.	Analyze workshop feedback to identify strengths, weaknesses, and any areas that warrant follow-up action on your part	☐	☐	☐	☐

Interpretation: Presenters may self-assess by tallying responses, giving four points to marks in the left column, three to the next, two to the third column, and one point to checkmarks in the right column. Totals between 67–88 may be considered *thoroughly prepared*, between 45–66 *moderately prepared*, between 23–44 *minimally prepared*, and between 1–22 *not prepared*.

Form 9.13
SAMPLE OF A LICKERT SCALE WORKSHOP EVALUATION FORM

Directions: Below, presenters will find an example of possible workshop evaluation items for a session on expository text comprehension. A similar format might be developed for participants' workshop evaluations. Criteria are listed below and responses may be marked on the right. Checkmark options often provide four to seven choices.

Workshop Criteria:	Strongly Agree	Moderately Agree	Minimally Agree	Do Not Agree
	4	3	2	1
1. I acknowledge the importance of advance organizers* and structured overviews* to students' understanding of content texts (comments):	☐	☐	☐	☐
2. I realize how important predictions generated by students about text content before reading may be to their understanding when they read (comments):	☐	☐	☐	☐
3. I now appreciate the role of chapter-reading strategies such as the SQRRR* process we used during the workshop (comments):	☐	☐	☐	☐
4. The workshop was well organized and used my time well (comments):	☐	☐	☐	☐
5. Overall, this was an appropriately effective workshop (comments):	☐	☐	☐	☐

Interpretation: Respondents preparing workshops should find it obvious what the content was of the workshop example provided as Form 9.13. It may be noted that few items are used. Feedback tells the presenter how the session went, and lets participants know that their judgments are valued. This format allows those attending to make checkmarks, and presenters may tally responses to judge the session's effectiveness.

Form 9.14
SAMPLE OF AN OPEN-ENDED WORKSHOP EVALUATION FORM

Directions: Our hope is that the workshop has been beneficial to you. Below, you will find questions related to the workshop. Your responses will help us to evaluate the session, and revise future workshops. Your candid responses will be helpful to us.

1. What were your expectations for the workshop before it began?

2. What were, for you, the strengths of the workshop?

3. What ideas will you take away with you that you can use in your classroom?

4. What workshop content do you wish had been presented?

THE PRIORITIZED LONG-TERM PLAN   (see Form 9.15)

The central issue in staff development is whether student learning will be increased. Built into a long-term plan must be opportunities to assess both the efficacy of teachers' professional advancement, along with resulting improvements in students' literacy.

Efforts that are teacher-responsive, with schoolwide and district support, have the greatest chance for success (105). School districts often make one major change each year or two, local schools add one additional goal, and individual teachers, yet another. New teaching processes and curricula take more than one year to implement to the institutionalization stage.

The Problem: School districts do not always coordinate professional development with local school efforts. Staff development activities tend to be a year or less in implementation. Assessment and revision of goals are lacking. Teachers fail to see continuity in overall programming and view the activity as *another flash in the pan.*

Rationale: Professional development activities that are well thought out usually are related to the larger picture in an obvious fashion. Those activities are assessed, revised, and monitored on a continual basis to have a strong chance for success.

Procedures: Reading Advisory Boards, Professional Development Committees, and principals may want to use Form 9.15 as a guide for long-term planning of professional development activities.

For Further Reading

Joyce, B., *et al.* (1993). *The Self-Renewing School.* Alexandria, VA: Association for Supervision and Curriculum Development. (1250 North Pitt Street, Alexandria, VA 22314-1453. 703-549-9110.)

> The authors help readers to understand district restructuring by taking them through committee processes when looking at curriculum, staff development, and cultural change that have a research-base for improved student learning. Examples are provided of effective programs.

Wood, F., et al. (1993). *How to Organize a School-Based Staff Development Program.* Alexandria, VA: Association for Supervision and Curriculum Development. (address and telephone same as above.)

> The authors develop a five-stage process for school improvement and strategies to learn how to: develop ownership and commitment of staff and the community, help faculty become aware of what is available and possible, create positive, productive inservice, ensure that what is learned during training becomes part of daily school activities.

Form 9.15
PROCEDURES TO DEVELOP A PRIORITIZED LONG-TERM PLAN

Directions: A long-term plan helps a faculty to establish a reading and writing curriculum with a clear focus. Below are listed procedures to enhance the success of planning for professional development. Participants may check on the right the degree to which criteria have been implemented.

Long-Term Professional Development Plan:	Strongly Implemented 4	Moderately Implemented 3	Marginally Implemented 2	Not Implemented 1
1. Priorities have been established that reflect teacher needs and district support	☐	☐	☐	☐
2. Priorities are evaluated as to logical order for development	☐	☐	☐	☐
3. One priority is selected as the first to be developed	☐	☐	☐	☐
4. A flexible time line is developed allowing appropriate time for each of the stages of development	☐	☐	☐	☐
5. Faculty and staff members are randomly divided into study or work groups of 4–6 across grade levels and content areas	☐	☐	☐	☐
6. If this is a major change in reading curriculum, 10–15 days should be allotted for training over several months	☐	☐	☐	☐
7. Initial training in processes and strategies is spaced over several training episodes	☐	☐	☐	☐
8. Initial training includes both general theory and knowledge of expected effects	☐	☐	☐	☐
9. Study groups may meet to discuss supplemental reading	☐	☐	☐	☐
10. Trainers model the theory in practical settings with students	☐	☐	☐	☐
11. Trainers point out behaviors to note and tie behaviors to skill achievement	☐	☐	☐	☐
12. Videos are provided of trainers with students illustrating how to organize and instruct	☐	☐	☐	☐
13. As many as 20 demonstrations with varying ages and abilities of students can be made available for discussion and questions	☐	☐	☐	☐

–continues–

Procedures to Develop a Prioritized Long-Term Plan -continued-	4	3	2	1
14. Teachers are given opportunities to practice first with other teachers in the workshop setting	☐	☐	☐	☐
15. Trainers may provide follow-up demonstrations based on teachers' performances	☐	☐	☐	☐
16. At least six weeks (20–30 trials) should be allotted for teachers to practice in their individual classrooms	☐	☐	☐	☐
17. Teachers are assured that achieving control and comfort will be awkward at first	☐	☐	☐	☐
18. Study groups continue to meet, enabling teachers to share plans and to discuss experiences	☐	☐	☐	☐
19. Study groups keep a log or minutes of their meetings to share with the trainer and other study groups	☐	☐	☐	☐
20. Teachers are given opportunities to observe each other, but refrain from giving advice	☐	☐	☐	☐
21. Study groups begin to collect instructional materials to facilitate the new practice	☐	☐	☐	☐
22. Trainers meet with the entire staff to hear self-reports (logs, minutes), celebrate successes, and plan for follow-up training for problems encountered	☐	☐	☐	☐
23. Trainers decide when it is appropriate to move on with new information	☐	☐	☐	☐
24. As teachers demonstrate competence, the trainers set up a long-term schedule for coaching by peers and by the trainer	☐	☐	☐	☐
25. Effects specified earlier in the program are measured	☐	☐	☐	☐
26. Follow-up sessions with trainers are planned with wider time intervals	☐	☐	☐	☐
27. When teachers across all content areas and all grade levels feel competent and regularly use the new skill, process, or curriculum, the change has been institutionalized	☐	☐	☐	☐
28. The Reading Advisory Board begins the planning for another initiative	☐	☐	☐	☐
29. Teachers receive explicit information on how each new inservice activity supports the practices already in place..	☐	☐	☐	☐
30. Principals take caution not to begin more than one new project at a time	☐	☐	☐	☐

–continues–

Procedures to Develop a Prioritized Long-Term Plan -continued-	4	3	2	1
31. Care is given to allot release time or some incentive for after-school training	☐	☐	☐	☐
32. Principals work with teachers to facilitate time for teachers to observe each other	☐	☐	☐	☐
33. The time line indicates who is responsible for a particular meeting and what materials are needed	☐	☐	☐	☐
34. The training or workshop environment should be as comfortable as possible, considering the fatigue and stress of the school day	☐	☐	☐	☐
35. Progress is monitored continuously and the overall time line modified as needed	☐	☐	☐	☐
36. Reading Advisory Boards re-evaluate future workshops, make necessary revisions in priorities, and use practical information gained to schedule and plan a new timeline	☐	☐	☐	☐

Interpretation: To review long-term staff development, participants may tally columns, giving four points to checkmarks in the left column, three to marks in the second column, two to marks in the third column, and one point to checkmarks in the right column. Totals between 109–144 may be judged *strongly implemented*, 73–108 *moderately implemented*, 37–72 *marginally implemented*, and 1–36 *not implemented*.

SYNTHESIS OF PROFESSIONAL DEVELOPMENT   (see Form 9.16)

Faculty and staff may be helped to grow professionally in any number of ways. Setting a school *tone* of considering students and learning uppermost as school goals is a key role of principals. Supporting teachers to want to improve professionally, empowerment, is an important vehicle for growth.

The Problem: Helping teachers to take responsibility for their own professional advancement seems to call for intensified principals' efforts. Administrators may be unable to see the importance of positive skills to help teachers grow professionally. Some appear reluctant to *impose their will* upon teachers, and instead permit them to continue in existing ways.

Rationale: Any number of insights have emerged to help teachers to grow professionally. The importance of teachers' setting short-term and annual goals provides a strong focus. Teachers' seeking to increase the quality of their own reading lessons is a fundamental source of literacy improvement. The support of coaching, networking, and inservice workshops is designed to empower teachers to intrinsically increase teaching skills and to provide the knowledge for professional growth.

Procedures: Participants may reconsider Forms 9.1 to 9.15 to review concepts related to professional development. Summaries of those forms may be entered on Form 9.16. Judgments entered on Form 9.16 then may be applied to decisions about program strengths, needs, and priorities on Form 9.17. Finally, Forms 9.16 and 9.17 together may be used for the principal or Reading Advisory Board to develop Form 9.18, a staff development plan-of-action.

Comments and Cautions

Initial interviews to identify teachers with strong knowledge about teaching children to read and write represent the foundation of selecting teachers.

Teachers who, themselves, love reading and value its importance in children's lives are most likely to both teach children to read well and to develop their positive literacy affect.

Form 9.16
SYNTHESIS OF PROFESSIONAL DEVELOPMENT

Directions: For a Reading Advisory Board to gain synthesis of information on professional development, data from Forms 9.1–9.15 may be summarized below. Appropriate checkmarks may be made on the right. This information may support decisions related to program strengths, needs, and priorities of Form 9.17 and a plan-of-action of Form 9.18.

Criteria for Professional Development:	Thoroughly Implemented 4	Moderately Implemented 3	Minimally Implemented 2	Not Implemented 1
1. Selection of classroom and special reading teachers (see Forms 9.1 and 9.2)	☐	☐	☐	☐
2. Annual goal-setting and review (see Form 9.3)	☐	☐	☐	☐
3. Teachers' self-assessment of reading lessons (see Form 9.4)	☐	☐	☐	☐
4. Professional development through supervision (see Forms 9.5–9.7)	☐	☐	☐	☐
5. Cognitive coaching to support professional development (see Form 9.8)	☐	☐	☐	☐
6. Networking to enhance professional development (see Form 9.9)	☐	☐	☐	☐
7. Staff workshops that undergird professional development (see Form 9.10–9.15)	☐	☐	☐	☐

Interpretation: The principal or Reading Advisory Board may judge the scope of its professional development by examining responses in Form 9.16, using self-responses, and eliciting responses of faculty and staff in the school to gain comprehensive information about the program. Columns may be tallied, giving four points to checkmarks on the left, three points to marks in the next column, two points to marks in the third column, and one point to each checkmark in the right column. Totals between 22–28 may be considered *thoroughly implemented*, between 15–21 *moderately implemented*, between 8–14 *minimally implemented*, and between 1–7 *not implemented*.

<table>
<tr><td colspan="4" style="background:black;color:white;text-align:center">

Form 9.17

PROFESSIONAL DEVELOPMENT: STRENGTHS, NEEDS, AND PRIORITIES
</td></tr>
</table>

Directions: Administrators or Reading Advisory Board members will find, below, staff development options. On the right, space is provided to record program strengths, needs, and priorities, each to be developed after careful study of Form 9.16. To fully benefit from use of Form 9.16, review of Forms 9.1–9.15 may be beneficial

1. **Selection of Teachers**	*Strengths* 1. 2.	*Needs* 1. 2.	*Priorities* 1. 2.
2. **Goal-setting and Review**	*Strengths* 1. 2.	*Needs* 1. 2.	*Priorities* 1. 2.
3. **Self- assess-ment of Reading Lessons**	*Strengths* 1. 2.	*Needs* 1. 2.	*Priorities* 1. 2.
4. **Development through Supervision**	*Strengths* 1. 2.	*Needs* 1. 2.	*Priorities* 1. 2.
5. **Cognitive Coaching**	*Strengths* 1. 2.	*Needs* 1. 2.	*Priorities* 1. 2.
6. **Professional Networking**	*Strengths* 1. 2.	*Needs* 1. 2.	*Priorities* 1. 2.
7. **Staff Development Workshops**	*Strengths* 1. 2.	*Needs* 1. 2.	*Priorities* 1. 2.

Form 9.18
PROFESSIONAL DEVELOPMENT: PLAN-OF-ACTION

Directions: Administrators seeking to develop a comprehensive plan to improve teachers' professional development may benefit from being as specific as possible about what they seek to accomplish, how they will go about attaining improvement, and how they will know when they have reached their goals. A review of Forms 9.16 and 9.17 should lead the administrator to identify goals to pursue in the growth plan. Statements entered should be as simple, direct, and useful as possible.

1. Goal Statement: _____

2. Objectives:

    a) _____

    b) _____

    c) _____

3. Activities: Dates; time checkpoints:

    a) _____   * _____

    b) _____   * _____

    c) _____   * _____

    d) _____   * _____

    e) _____   * _____

4. Resources: (professional reading, consultation, visitations)

    a) _____   * _____

    b) _____   * _____

    c) _____   * _____

5. How I will know when my goal is accomplished:

_____

_____

_____

_____

CHAPTER 10

MANAGEMENT OF DIVERSITY IN READING PROGRAMS

Recent (1960's on) changes in American demographics have influenced educators' thinking. It is predicted that soon, one of three students enrolled in schools will be African-, Asian-, or Native-American. There is a decline in the percent of Euro-American students as cultural diversity increases. *Inclusion** also challenges contemporary educators.

Public schools will, increasingly, assume responsibility for alleviating the stresses on diverse students' differences. Further change may be expected as diverse school population enrollments increase. Those cultures do bring to schools non-conventional learning styles. Great variation among individuals means that educators must use suitable teaching strategies with all students.

Administrators, increasingly, work with their faculties and staffs to help them become more adaptable and flexible in meeting needs of populations of *at-risk* students. How teachers think about students and education makes a pronounced difference in student performance and achievement. When teachers understand, examine their beliefs, their culture and other cultures, they can be successful as they face teaching diverse learners.

Teaching diverse students to read should be a meaning-making process. This involves the use of literature-based texts, integrated reading and writing, and instruction that facilitates the learner's construction of meaning from print. Principals' challenges are to enhance faculty understanding and to monitor teachers as they attempt to meet students' special needs.

For Further Reading

"Celebrating Diversity in Teacher Education," (1994) *The Journal of the Association of Teacher Educators*, 16, 3, 1–86.

> A themed edition with eight articles on diversity in the classroom. Titles include: lessons from the multicultural teacher education literature, misconceptions about multicultural education, preparing teachers for diversity in classrooms, preparing student teachers for inclusion, and preparing future teachers to work with diverse families.

Kameenui, E. J. (1993). "Diverse Learners and the Tyranny of Time: Don't Fix Blame; Fix the Leaky Roof," *The Reading Teacher*, 46, 5, 376–83.

> The author's focus is on designing and implementing programs for special needs students. He decries the *right method* myth. Kameenui advocates opportunity to read, phonemic awareness, outside reading, and instruction in which pupils can succeed.

OVERVIEW OF READING DIVERSITY   (see Form 10.1)

Increasingly, school populations are made up of poor readers, disabled readers, language delayed, slow learners, crack babies, second language, culturally distinctive, and gifted, all of whom are considered diverse learners and may warrant special teaching assistance. Many come to school behind in literacy development and feel as though they are trying to *catch up*.

The Problem: Contemporary schools have more and more students with special needs. Administrators and teachers sense heightened needs to address diversity in classrooms. Principals and teachers may neither have awareness nor skills to adjust reading programs to provide successful experiences.

Rationale: Years ago, educators dealt with *individual differences* in preservice and inservice programs. Presently, the need is heightened, as teachers address whole classes, subgroups, or individuals. Teachers now gather new kinds of diagnostic data, and plan strategies to deal with populations of learners never before so extensively encountered by teachers.

Procedures: Administrators or Reading Advisory Board members may use Form 10.1 to help teachers self-assess their own awareness, or may use those data to gather program information or to monitor the program. That information may help planners determine whether the current program meets the needs, or warrants change.

For Further Reading

Finders, M. & Lewis, C. (1994). "Why Some Parents Don't Come to School," *Educational Leadership*, 51, 8, 50–54.

> The authors extol the value of examining barriers hindering some parents from involvement in school activities or their child's education. Typical reasons are described for non-participation.

Moll, L. (1992). "Bilingual Classroom Studies and Community Analysis: Some Recent Trends," *Educational Researcher*, 21, 2, 20–24.

> Moll argues that teachers' and researchers' roles should be redefined so that they collaborate better to bring about educational changes. Describes how research about children's communities can enhance bilingual understanding. Moll's sociocultural perspective identifies learning resources beyond the school.

Form 10.1
OVERVIEW OF READING DIVERSITY

Directions: Identifying diversity in classrooms can help teachers to be more effective. Below, respondents will find criteria related to diversity. On the right, administrators or Reading Advisory Boards may judge the extent of local implementation.

Diversity Criteria:	Thoroughly Implemented	Moderately Implemented	Marginally Implemented	Not Implemented
	4	3	2	1
1. The school recognizes that multiple perspectives and approaches will be necessary to meet the needs of diverse students	☐	☐	☐	☐
2. The school and its teachers have expectations that they will make a difference with all of the students in the school	☐	☐	☐	☐
3. Students are guided to learn through a strategic sequence of teacher-directed and student-centered activities	☐	☐	☐	☐
4. Diverse students are taught more thoroughly	☐	☐	☐	☐
5. Students are provided with highly frequent opportunities to read	☐	☐	☐	☐
6. Individual pupils are assessed regularly and remediated early	☐	☐	☐	☐
7. A variety of instructional arrangements (whole class, small group, etc.) is used to allow students to actively participate in literacy activities	☐	☐	☐	☐
8. Faculty members collaborate with one another in planning for diversity in classrooms	☐	☐	☐	☐
9. Principals expect teachers to adjust teaching strategies to meet the needs of all students	☐	☐	☐	☐
10. There is an ongoing assessment and refinement of the school's approach to diverse students	☐	☐	☐	☐
11. Teachers have opportunities to learn about characteristics of various culturally diverse student populations	☐	☐	☐	☐
12. Teachers have opportunities to learn characteristics and teaching approaches to use to be effective with academically diverse students at both ends of the learning spectrum	☐	☐	☐	☐

Cover the page at this point and below prior to photocopying if use is desired before referring to the interpretation.

Interpretation: Participants may tally columns, giving four points to marks in the left column, three points to the next, two points to the third column, and one point to marks in the right column. Totals between 37–48 may be judged *thoroughly implemented,* between 25–36 *moderately implemented,* 13–24 *minimally implemented,* and 1–12 *not implemented.*

AT-RISK STUDENTS AS DIVERSE LEARNERS   (see Form 10.2)

Teachers are faced with all kinds of social and learning problems that place pupils in what are called the *at-risk* groups. A review of the *Current Index to Journals in Education* shows at-risk problems based on poverty, abuse, violence, drugs, family dysfunction, suicide, and gangs. Those at-risk students' needs, manifested through total withdrawal, aggression, low interest, fear, poor concentration, and so on.

The Problem: Classroom teachers, without special training, are having more at-risk children placed in their classrooms than ever before. If support is provided, teachers' self-expectations are uncertain. If there is no support for the teacher, the problem is elevated.

Rationale: Contemporary schools are placed in a position where they are required to accommodate diverse students, which include those *at-risk* of learning to read. Schools and teachers are growing increasingly aware of the population of students who often require additional assistance in learning.

Procedures: Data taken from Form 10.2 may be used to gain background to support the current program, to monitor its functions, or make adjustments to it. That information may help planners to decide what should be done in the current program to meet the needs of those at-risk.

For Further Reading

Educational Leadership (1994), 51, 8, 12–15.

> A themed edition with particularly valuable articles on at-risk learners. The article by Erlich shows how stereotyping and negative concepts of diversity are unwholesome. The piece by Van Ausdall describes how multicultural books can broaden self-understanding and understanding of others.

Winfield, L. (1986). "Teacher Beliefs Toward At-Risk Students in Inner-Urban Schools," *The Urban Review,* 18, 4, 253–68.

> Urban teachers' beliefs are classified in several ways. Teachers may ignore low performance, judge that some type of assistance will improve learning, or shift the responsibility to others.

Form 10.2

AT-RISK STUDENTS AS DIVERSE LEARNERS

Directions: Among diverse students in classrooms are found at-risk students. Teachers must meet the needs of these individuals. Below, respondents will find criteria related to at-risk students. On the right, Reading Advisory Boards or principals may judge the extent of local implementation to meet those needs.

At-risk Program Criteria:	Thoroughly Implemented	Moderately Implemented	Marginally Implemented	Not Implemented
	4	3	2	1
1. The principal oversees the effort and keeps at the forefront goals and key concepts related to literacy of at-risk learners	☐	☐	☐	☐
2. The faculty makes strong attempts to gain participation of parents whose children are most at-risk of not learning to read	☐	☐	☐	☐
3. The administrator offers staff development workshops and professional conference attendance as needed	☐	☐	☐	☐
4. Teachers are able to identify at-risk students in the classroom and understand how to meet the needs of those students	☐	☐	☐	☐
5. The school has a way to assist teachers while they work with at-risk students to address discipline problems, school absences, parental neglect, social problems, etc.	☐	☐	☐	☐
6. Teachers provide stable, dependable reading class environments that engender trust	☐	☐	☐	☐
7. School personnel express authentic sincerity, empathy, and encouragement toward at-risk learners	☐	☐	☐	☐
8. Teachers are shown how to enable pupils to employ coping skills, perhaps sometimes using bibliotherapy*	☐	☐	☐	☐
9. Steps employed by teachers to help a child deal with rage are: acknowledge, cool down, verbalize (77)	☐	☐	☐	☐
10. Educators provide enlightened witness (77) models, others who have overcome similar adversity to build resilience * (14)	☐	☐	☐	☐
11. Educators acknowledge that children usually identify with parents, and that new behaviors, and new respect for literacy will occur as pupils identify strongly with teachers	☐	☐	☐	☐

–continues–

At-Risk Students as Diverse Learners   -continued-

	4	3	2	1

12. Proper reading materials are available to assist teachers in working with at-risk pupils .... ☐ ☐ ☐ ☐

13. Teachers explain reading and model strategies thoroughly in highly explicit ways .... ☐ ☐ ☐ ☐

14. Teachers build a standard English foundation, scaffolding across literacy gaps, while they accept and *expand* pupils' idioms and dialects .... ☐ ☐ ☐ ☐

15. Professionals teach a problem, concept, strategy, or skill in more than one way .... ☐ ☐ ☐ ☐

16. Teachers allow for frequent opportunities to read and participate in peer-response groups, often employing cooperative study groups .... ☐ ☐ ☐ ☐

17. Faculties attend to remediation early and frequently .... ☐ ☐ ☐ ☐

18. The school provides a time for parents to learn parenting skills to support their at-risk child's literacy advancement .... ☐ ☐ ☐ ☐

19. School personnel support and coordinate services between the school and social service intervention programs .... ☐ ☐ ☐ ☐

Cover the page at this point and below prior to photocopying if use is desired before referring to the interpretation.

Interpretation: Administrators or Reading Advisory Board members may tally columns, giving four points to marks in the left column, three points to the second column, two points to the third column, and one point to checkmarks in the right column. Totals between 58–76 may be viewed as criteria *thoroughly implemented*, between 39–57 *moderately implemented*, between 20–38 *minimally implemented*, and between 1–19 *not implemented*.

MULTICULTURAL STUDENTS AS DIVERSE LEARNERS   (see Form 10.3)

Increasing numbers of culturally diverse students are entering classrooms throughout the United States. Educators are experiencing the need to take steps to reflect the diversity of contemporary society in the materials they choose for teaching, along with the approaches and strategies they use to teach children, addressing racial, second-language, and ethnic diversity.

The Problem: Many teachers are middle-class whites who do not recognize that they are prejudiced, or appear to be prejudiced. They may not face the fact that they fail to equalize the school success of diverse learners.

Rationale: Teachers and administrators may function as key change agents in reforming curricula and teaching approaches for teaching *all* students. Racial, ethnic, and learning differences, and so on, often occur in schools without being recognized by teachers and administrators as warranting particular attention. The time has come for educators to change not only the curriculum but the teaching to equalize student achievement.

Procedures: Data from Form 10.3 may help the administrator or Reading Advisory Board to reflect upon their knowledge about multicultural students. The information may help planners assess how to become more aware of multicultural dimensions of classrooms, to monitor, and to implement new strategies toward developing equality in the classroom.

For Further Reading

Educational Leadership (1994), 51, 8, 28–31.

> A themed edition on multicultural education. Billings-Ladson writes about ways teachers use multicultural education to understanding self and others. Brandt reviews a conversation with James A. Banks (Director, U. of Washington Multicultural Education).

Strickland, D. S. (1994). "Educating African American Learners At Risk: Finding a Better Way," *Language Arts*, 72, 5, 328–35.

> The author describes effective language arts. She develops the case that literacy begins early and that its context is social. Strickland explicates the importance of language's being influenced by cultural contexts.

Tiedt, P. & Tiedt, I. M. (1990). *Multicultural Teaching: A Handbook of Activities, Information, and Resources*. Boston: Allyn & Bacon. (Dept 894, 160 Gould Street, Needham Heights, MA 02194-2310. 1-800-852-8024.)

> A volume with extensive information and activities for interpreting student diversity in classrooms. The underlying focus of the book is to help teachers present multicultural concepts and provide equity for diverse learners.

Form 10.3
MULTICULTURAL STUDENTS AS DIVERSE LEARNERS

Directions: Culturally diverse students are becoming more prevalent in classrooms. Below, Reading Advisory Boards or administrators will find criteria related to cultural diversity. On the right participants may check the extent of local implementation.

Multicultural Classroom Criteria:

	Thoroughly Implemented	Moderately Implemented	Marginally Implemented	Not Implemented
	4	3	2	1
1. The principal oversees school efforts to address cultural diversity, keeping goals and key concepts at the forefront	☐	☐	☐	☐
2. Faculty members value diversity and teach pupils to admire, accept, and appreciate racial, second-language, and ethnic diversity	☐	☐	☐	☐
3. Teachers provide successful language experiences for students in standard English	☐	☐	☐	☐
4. Educators and pupils accept language diversity, including dialects, giving respect to native speech while learning standard English	☐	☐	☐	☐
5. Appropriate intervention and support are available for language development of second-language students so that they can learn English	☐	☐	☐	☐
6. Teachers scaffold across the literacy gaps with students	☐	☐	☐	☐
7. Teachers carefully monitor their choice of words to reduce confusion of students who are not familiar with standard terms	☐	☐	☐	☐
8. Ethnic distinctiveness is honored and classmates study peers' cultures to develop understanding and acceptance while educating about the standard culture	☐	☐	☐	☐
9. Central and classroom library holdings include books about, and authors who represent cultures of students who attend the school	☐	☐	☐	☐
10. Classroom or textbook values that contradict justice and equality are not accepted	☐	☐	☐	☐
11. Teachers feel responsible for all students, and are held accountable for all students	☐	☐	☐	☐
12. Teachers' beliefs about diversity are analyzed, monitored, and self-examined since they influence teaching strategies and interactions with pupils	☐	☐	☐	☐

–continues–

Multicultural Students as Diverse Learners   -continued-

	4	3	2	1
13. Diversity issues are utilized all during the year, not just on celebration days	☐	☐	☐	☐
14. Instruction is modified to meet the learning needs among diverse groups, thus making academic achievement possible	☐	☐	☐	☐
15. Instructional materials are unbiased and non-stereotyped. They are genuine and contain authentic information. They are available to accommodate teaching to diverse groups	☐	☐	☐	☐
16. Literacy standards for diverse learners are appropriate, and all students gain the benefits that come from high expectations	☐	☐	☐	☐
17. Ongoing inservice programs on teaching diverse groups are available for administrators, teachers, and paraprofessionals	☐	☐	☐	☐
18. Collaboration exists among parents, teachers, and administrators concerning the role of diversity in the classroom and school	☐	☐	☐	☐
19. The school does value the ethnic and cultural diversity of its community, and uses diverse families as resource people to enhance the curriculum	☐	☐	☐	☐
20. Coordination exists and is ongoing between the school and social service intervention	☐	☐	☐	☐

Cover the page at this point and below prior to photocopying if use is desired before referring to the interpretation.

Interpretation: Columns may be tallied, giving four points to checkmarks in the left column, three points to marks in the second column, two points to the next column, and one point to marks in the right column. Totals between 61–80 may be judged *thoroughly implemented*, 41–60 *moderately implemented*, 21–40 *minimally implemented*, and 1–20 *not implemented*.

LEARNING DISABILITY STUDENTS AS DIVERSE LEARNERS   (see Form 10.4)

Learning disabilities (LD) are difficult to define, but tend to include students with differences between their present performance and their capabilities. LD students often are described as dysfunctional in processing information at the neurological level and require long-term treatment (113).

The Problem: Many teachers do not recognize that this population warrants specialized teaching, much of which may be provided by classroom teachers. Mildly disabled students may *fall through the cracks* in classrooms. LD students receive special services for an average of six years at a cost beyond regular education of about $9,906, in 1991 funds (54, 55). Those students often are unable to read adequately, even after expensive programs.

Rationale: Pupils may be taught using language, multisensory, data-based, or direct instruction models (89). An instructional focus is to show students how to compensate for faulty processing. Students may receive instruction in problem-solving, thinking skills, classifying, chunking,* and sequencing to organize for reading. Multiple modalities may be used to help students learn to process print accurately. LD pupils often benefit from work in cooperative group settings. Students may receive instruction as *inclusion* students, yet may require services outside of classroom settings.

Procedures: Reading Advisory Boards or administrators may use Form 10.4 to assess criteria related to services for learning disability students. A serious challenge for the principal is to support classroom teachers' roles in providing successful reading instruction for LD students.

For Further Reading

Lerner, J. (1993). *Learning Disabilities: Theories, Diagnosis, and Teaching Strategies, Sixth Edition.* Boston: Houghton Mifflin Company. (Wayside Road, Burlington, MA 01803. 1-800-733-1717.)

> Lerner's text, for undergraduate and graduate students, provides a broad view of the learning disabilities area for teachers, staff, and administrators. Its eclectic approach addresses theory, assessment, clinical teaching, and teaching techniques and materials.

Strichard, S. S. & Mangrum II, C. T. (1993). *Teaching Study Strategies to Students with Learning Disabilities.* Boston: Allyn and Bacon. (Dept. 894, 160 Gould Street, Needham Heights, MA 02194-2310. 1-800-852-8024.)

> A text for teaching learning disabled students beginning at the middle school level. Chapters contain a narrative, reproducible graphics, figures, and answers. Content includes study skills, reading mathematics problems, use of resources, use of the library, writing research papers, and test taking.

Form 10.4
LEARNING DISABILITY PUPILS AS DIVERSE LEARNERS

Directions: Learning disabled students ordinarily are more capable than their school performance indicates, and may have processing difficulties. Criteria are listed below. On the right, Reading Advisory Boards or principals may check the degree to which those criteria operate in the local school.

Criteria:

	Thoroughly Implemented 4	Moderately Implemented 3	Marginally Implemented 2	Not Implemented 1
1. The principal and program administrator jointly oversee the learning disabilities program and assist to advance goals and key elements of the program's effectiveness	☐	☐	☐	☐
2. The thrust of the parent interaction program is founded on getting as much home support as possible for the students' advancement	☐	☐	☐	☐
3. Decisions about whether classroom reading, partial inclusion, *class within a class*, or *pull-out* options are shared among the specialist, teacher, and principal	☐	☐	☐	☐
4. Close interaction is required between the classroom teacher and special education teacher	☐	☐	☐	☐
5. The focus is on teaching learning disability students strategies to learn how to learn	☐	☐	☐	☐
6. Students are taught compensating strategies, applying something different than their usual processes when text does not make sense	☐	☐	☐	☐
7. Teachers model a strategy over and over, and may state over and over its application to reading in various contexts	☐	☐	☐	☐
8. Teachers may ask pupils to practice new skills or strategies in multiple contexts to increase transfer beyond short-term memory	☐	☐	☐	☐
9. Students learn to use multiple modalities when identifying words, going beyond the usual visual and auditory by incorporating use of kinesthetic and tactile modalities (61, 139)	☐	☐	☐	☐
10. Mnemonic* processes are used whenever possible to develop structures for understanding and remembering	☐	☐	☐	☐
11. Instruction focuses on active involvement and task participation	☐	☐	☐	☐

–continues–

Learning Disablility Pupils as Diverse Learners	-continued-	4	3	2	1

12. Learners are shown how to monitor whether the text makes sense, and shown what to do when texts fail to make sense .... ☐ ☐ ☐ ☐

13. Pupils learn to listen to their tape-recorded prior oral reading to monitor when they have made mistakes, and to learn to avoid those mistakes in the future .... ☐ ☐ ☐ ☐

14. Teachers' directions are clear and simple for students to follow without confusion .... ☐ ☐ ☐ ☐

15. Teachers create environments to reduce distraction, whenever possible ..... ☐ ☐ ☐ ☐

16. Cooperative group activities are used to change learning to focus on social process and text meaning more than text accuracy or frustration with reading .... ☐ ☐ ☐ ☐

Cover the page at this point and below prior to photocopying if use is desired before referring to the interpretation.

Interpretation: Respondents may tally columns, giving four points to marks in the left column, three points to the next column, two points to the third, and one point to the right column. Totals between 49–64 are judged *thoroughly implemented*, between 33–48 *moderately implemented*, between 17–32 *minimally implemented*, and between 1–16 *not implemented*.

TITLE 1 STUDENTS AS DIVERSE LEARNERS　　(see Form 10.5)

Title 1 (formerly Chapter 1) provides federal funding to local education agencies for the education of economically disadvantaged children. For over 25 years, Title 1 funds have provided remedial services for disadvantaged students' basic skills with separate, compensatory instruction. Present legislation signals changes in instruction, assessment, and accountability.

The Problem: Title 1 is the largest federal elementary and secondary education program, yet key elements necessary to make Title 1 effective are evasive. Students do not tend to become good readers, even after extensive support. Students may be embarrassed to participate. Designed as a short-term compensatory program, students remain in Title 1 an average of five years at a cost beyond regular education, in 1991 dollars, of $4,715 (54, 55).

Rationale: Schools are provided specific funds to accommodate disadvantaged children. Local schools are enabled to purchase special reading materials to address distinctive needs. State education agencies are required to provide staff development to elevate teaching and learning. Parent participation is required, a concept that may improve home literacy efforts.

Procedures: Data taken from Form 10.5 may help the Reading Advisory Board or administrator to gain feedback, and to monitor, regarding the local Title 1 program. Decisions may then be made whether to maintain or revise present services.

For Further Reading

LeTendre, M. J. (1991). "Improving Chapter 1 Programs: We Can Do Better," *Phi Delta Kappan*, 72, 8, 576–80.

> LeTendre supports the idea that Chapter 1 students must succeed in regular classrooms with grade level capabilities. She advocates high learner expectations, elimination of stereotypes about learning abilites, and better coordinated classroom-specialist planning.

McCormick, K. (1990). *Chapter I: A Directors' Handbook for Parental Involvement.* (ED 333 967).

> The manual offers six goals: to inform parents, build school partnerships, train teachers, consult with parents, help parents to understand the school, and support second-language parents. Handouts, model letters, surveys, and agenda items are appended.

Slavin, R. E. (1991). "Chapter I: A Vision for the Next Quarter Century," *Phi Delta Kappan*, 72, 8, 586–89+.

> The author supports the prevention of reading failure, supports early intervention programs, enhanced regular classroom reading, improved assessment, and assured accountability.

Form 10.5
TITLE 1 STUDENTS AS DIVERSE LEARNERS

Directions: Among diverse students in classrooms are students identified for compensatory reading programs or Title 1 (formerly Chapter 1). Program characteristics are listed below. Administrators or Reading Advisory Boards may check on the right the extent of local implementation.

Criteria:	Thoroughly Implemented 4	Moderately Implemented 3	Marginally Implemented 2	Not Implemented 1
1. The principal and program director oversee jointly Title 1 services in the school, keeping goals and key elements at the forefront	☐	☐	☐	☐
2. The goal of Title 1 programs is to enable students to reach their achievable reading level and return functionally to regular instruction	☐	☐	☐	☐
3. The school applies *effective schools** practices, led by administrator's clearly stated goals and objectives that express *high expectations** for students	☐	☐	☐	☐
4. Children benefit from the trust that emerges from a positive classroom and school climate	☐	☐	☐	☐
5. The first instruction conducted by regular classroom teachers is unhurried and thorough for the most at-risk pupils	☐	☐	☐	☐
6. Classroom and special reading teachers participate in successful staff development, expressing an abiding concern to improve	☐	☐	☐	☐
7. Teachers in this school act on the belief that children can become successful readers	☐	☐	☐	☐
8. A powerful effort goes into prevention of reading failure	☐	☐	☐	☐
9. The teacher, specialist, and principal maintain coordination between classroom instruction and special services	☐	☐	☐	☐
10. The special reading teacher and classroom teacher determine for each child whether inclusion, *class within a class*, or pull-out is best	☐	☐	☐	☐
11. Case load decisions are based on children who can benefit from Title 1 services, considering other options for those whose needs warrant other services	☐	☐	☐	☐

--continues--

Title 1 Students as Diverse Learners	-continued-	4	3	2	1

12. Case load decisions focus on what is best for each student, considering supplementary, pull-out, classroom innovation, or inclusion options .... ☐ ☐ ☐ ☐

13. Instruction focuses on thinking/reading tasks more than paper and pencil work .... ☐ ☐ ☐ ☐

14. The instructional team of classroom teacher, special reading teacher, principal, and Title 1 coordinator monitor student progress, including NCE* gains, and provide feedback for each pupil .... ☐ ☐ ☐ ☐

15. Public recognition is awarded to children who excel, and to educators in the building who excel .... ☐ ☐ ☐ ☐

16. Support for the local program is consistent throughout the district, and is based on parents' feeling like partners with teachers .... ☐ ☐ ☐ ☐

17. Enrollment is monitored when 75 percent of students are low income and a school may be designated as a school-wide Title 1 school .... ☐ ☐ ☐ ☐

18. Program teachers and administrators are credentialed for their assignments .... ☐ ☐ ☐ ☐

19. Program evaluation data are used for the improvement of the program ...... ☐ ☐ ☐ ☐

Cover the page at this point and below prior to photocopying if use is desired before referring to the interpretation.

Interpretation: Respondents may tally columns, giving four points to marks in the left column, three points to the next column, two points to the third, and one point to the right column. Totals between 58–76 are judged *thoroughly implemented*, between 39–57 *moderately implemented*, between 20–38 *minimally implemented*, and between 1–19 *not implemented*.

SPECIAL EDUCATION STUDENTS AS DIVERSE LEARNERS   (see Form 10.6)

The diversity of pupils in special education may include those who are retarded, language delayed, physically handicapped, behavior disordered, and so on. Special education students may be placed in regular classrooms as *inclusion** pupils, in *resource rooms* full-time, or in some combination. Inclusion allows all special education pupils to become part of regular classroom activities.

The Problem: Parents first lobbied for separate, special programs and now lobby for regular classroom experiences for children. Teachers may not know how to address the challenges of *inclusion* in their classes. Classroom teachers often are left without extra help, and without the skills to succeed.

Rationale: Special education students placed in regular classes will participate in normal experiences, and classroom teachers are responsible for the IEPs* (individualized educational plan) of those students. Teachers may get special assistance to address the literacy needs of those pupils, yet schools may be ill prepared. A key concept is to help students to be attentive, and to monitor their attentiveness (86).

Procedures: Data from Form 10.6 may help the Reading Advisory Board or administrator to examine the role of the present reading program as it addresses special education students. Information may help planners to maintain the present course, to monitor, or to revise reading's place in special programs.

For Further Reading

Arnold, J. B. & Dodge, H. W. (1994). "Room for All," *American School Board Journal*, 181, 10, 22–26.

> The authors underscore first instruction in regular classrooms. They contend that, if support is needed, it should help students to function in classrooms. Descriptions and challenges of inclusion in classrooms are provided. Contemporary lawsuits are interpreted.

Sears, S., et al. (1994). "Meaningful Reading Instruction for Learners with Special Needs," *The Reading Teacher*, 47, 8, 632–38.

> The authors explain the planning and implementation of a meaning-based reading program for students with special learning needs. A program design is explained. Sample lessons are described.

Sears-King, M. (1994). *Curriculum-Based Assessment in Special Education*. San Diego: Singular Publishing Group. (4284 41st Street, San Diego, CA 92105. 619-521-8000.)

> The term curriculum-based assessment is presented in a structured, useful methodology for teachers to use with mild and moderate disabilites. The chapters would help any teacher to rethink teaching practices, instruction, and assessment.

Form 10.6

SPECIAL EDUCATION STUDENTS AS DIVERSE LEARNERS

Directions: Classroom teachers are becoming more responsible for the reading instruction of special education students. Respondents will find related criteria below. On the right, the Reading Advisory Board or administrator may signify the extent of implementation locally.

Criteria for Special Education:	Thoroughly Implemented 4	Moderately Implemented 3	Marginally Implemented 2	Not Implemented 1
1. The principal and program director, jointly, oversee special education, advancing program goals and key elements	☐	☐	☐	☐
2. Local data exist showing that special education students learn more in regular classes than in separate resource rooms	☐	☐	☐	☐
3. Special education students may be placed in regular classes if their IEPs* can be met	☐	☐	☐	☐
4. Linkages are established to connect the classroom teacher with adequate human resources and materials	☐	☐	☐	☐
5. Special education teachers may teach reading in resource rooms, or through inclusion in the classroom	☐	☐	☐	☐
6. Supplementary materials and technology are provided for special education students in regular classes	☐	☐	☐	☐
7. Classroom teachers require support to identify reading materials that special education students can read successfully	☐	☐	☐	☐
8. Classroom teachers require support and extra hands for organization, whether whole class, cooperative groups, pairs, class within a class, or individuals	☐	☐	☐	☐
9. Special education teachers meet with classroom teachers at least weekly to discuss individual students' needs	☐	☐	☐	☐
10. Ongoing special education inservice is provided for all teachers, particularly in support of any inclusion initiative	☐	☐	☐	☐
11. A key teaching function is to teach special education pupils how to *classify* information, which helps them learn how to learn, to read, to organize in their heads, and to better remember	☐	☐	☐	☐

–continues–

Special Education Students as Diverse Learners continued-	4	3	2	1
12. When classroom teachers learn how to use task analysis* they will be able to break complex processes into smaller, cumulative tasks for students	☐	☐	☐	☐
13. Direct instruction to increase chances of *memory* application will strengthen reading vocabulary and comprehension	☐	☐	☐	☐
14. Students are shown how to pay attention to key concepts and relevant information that support metacognitive strategies	☐	☐	☐	☐
15. Classes are organized into thematic, or unit, instruction to help special pupils tie together concepts from several academic areas into one lesson ..	☐	☐	☐	☐
16. Much of reading instruction may focus on functional reading—key words, signs, core sight words, survival words, and directions	☐	☐	☐	☐
17. Reading instruction may focus on generalization* (transfer of learning) related to comprehension and decoding for special students with use of multiple contexts and practice	☐	☐	☐	☐

Cover the page at this point and below prior to photocopying if use is desired before referring to the interpretation.

Interpretation: Columns may be tallied, giving four points to checkmarks in the left column, three points to those in the next column, two to the next column, and one point to marks in the right column. Totals between 52–68 may be viewed as *thoroughly implemented*, 35–51 *moderately implemented*, 18–34 *minimally implemented*, and between 1–17 as *not implemented*.

READING INTERVENTION PROGRAMS AND DIVERSE LEARNERS
(see Form 10.7)

Disenchantment with remedial education has led educators to consider new approaches, with a strong call for intervention to prevent difficulties in learning to read and write. The *up front* investment in prevention is proposed to reduce subsequent needs for retention, remediation, special education, transition rooms, and a range of programs to address learning difficulties.

The Problem: Remedial programs for children who have difficulty learning to read often have been ineffective. Remedial programs are expensive, students attend special classes for five-to-seven years, and students do not learn to read effectively, even with remediation (54, 55). Those students tend to lose hope and prefer not to be separated from classmates.

Rationale: Programs that enable intervention for young children before they encounter reading difficulties foster good mental health; those pupils do not grow up feeling failure (6). Intervention programs often result in children at-risk never realizing that they might have had difficulty. Several programs report documented, effective long-term results.

Procedures: Reading Advisory Boards or principals may complete Form 10.7 to study criteria common to intervention programs. Reference to Appendix C will provide titles, telephone numbers, and addresses of representative programs.

For Further Reading

Pinnell, G. S., et al. (1994). "Comparing Instructional Models for the Literacy Education of High-risk First Graders," *Reading Research Quarterly*, 29, 1, 9–39.

> Four treatment groups of first-grade children were each given distinctive reading intervention. Pinnell, Lyons, DeFord, Bryk, and Seltzer concluded that effective intervention variables were one-on-one instruction, lesson frameworks, and teachers' staff development.

Wasik, B. & Slavin, R. (1993). "Preventing Reading Failure with One-to-One Tutoring: A Review of Five Programs," *Reading Research Quarterly*, 28, 2, 178–99.

> The authors analyzed sixteen studies of five different one-on-one reading intervention tutoring methods and found mostly positive results. The five models vary in program components and results. The most complete programs have the greatest impact on reading advancement. Cost effectiveness is reviewed.

Form 10.7
READING INTERVENTION PROGRAMS AND DIVERSE LEARNERS

Directions: Intervention programs attempt to support students in achieving success prior to any possible experiences with failure. Criteria from one or more programs are listed below. On the right, Reading Advisory Board members or the principal may check the extent of local implementation of each criterion. To request program information, participants may refer to Appendix C.

Criteria:	Thoroughly Implemented 4	Moderately Implemented 3	Marginally Implemented 2	Not Implemented 1
1. The principal, special teacher, and program coordinator keep goals and key elements at the forefront for all school personnel	☐	☐	☐	☐
2. Intervention occurs very early in a child's schooling, and is designed to avoid the failure syndrome, preventing poor attitudes, negative motivation, and low self-esteem (6)	☐	☐	☐	☐
3. Children having reading difficulty require greater amounts of direct instruction, time-on-task, and engaged recreational reading time than do successful readers	☐	☐	☐	☐
4. The educational plan for each student is developed by a team, consisting of the special teacher, classroom teacher, parent(s), school counselor, trainer, and principal	☐	☐	☐	☐
5. Intervention program pupils' books are of a simple level to enable them to focus on the reading *process* and to get students doing a great deal of reading in a concentrated time...	☐	☐	☐	☐
6. Teachers conduct strategic teaching in which children are led to discover the reading process through teacher guidance and questions (34)	☐	☐	☐	☐
7. Instruction focuses on text meaning first, using visual and alphabetic information as a subsequent step to affirm meaning as children learn to read by reading (34, 72, 79,)	☐	☐	☐	☐
8. Repeated readings (204), even multiple readings of familiar texts, is an important component	☐	☐	☐	☐
9. The word analysis component may focus on the direct instruction of letters, sight words phonemic awareness (44, 72), phonics (194, 196), and spelling	☐	☐	☐	☐
10. Teachers conduct ongoing diagnosis as each child reads, creating the diagnostic loop that influences the next lesson	☐	☐	☐	☐

–continues–

Reading Intervention Programs and Diverse Learners -continued-	4	3	2	1
11. The reading intervention program contains a strong writing component	☐	☐	☐	☐
12. Any intervention program is based on the concept of high expectations with accelerated learning (124) as a foundation for learners	☐	☐	☐	☐
13. The intervention program has a strong parent involvement component (36) which increases students' achievement	☐	☐	☐	☐
14. The intervention program is based on intensive initial and long-term professional development of special teachers	☐	☐	☐	☐
15. Multiple assessments of each participating child occur, including assessments of the intervention program, standardized data, and classroom teacher-based evaluation	☐	☐	☐	☐
16. The intervention program has been shown to reduce subsequent need for Title 1, special education, transition room services, or retention	☐	☐	☐	☐
17. Assessment data are used to determine the intervention program's effectiveness, and to chart the course for improvement	☐	☐	☐	☐

Cover the page at this point and below prior to photocopying if use is desired before referring to the interpretation.

Interpretation: Columns may be tallied, giving four points to checkmarks in the left column, three points to those in the next column, two to the next column, and one point to marks in the right column. Totals between 52–68 may be viewed as *thoroughly implemented*, 35–51 *moderately implemented*, 18–34 *minimally implemented*, and between 1–17 as *not implemented.*

GIFTED STUDENTS AS DIVERSE LEARNERS   (see Form 10.8)

Gifted students are seen multidimensionally as possessing intelligence, aptitude, and ability beyond most students (188). While many gifted students are divergent thinkers, or creative, others do not share this attribute. External funding is available for most school districts.

The Problem: Many people in our society contend that gifted students do not need instructional attention or guidance. Gifted students often receive the same reading instruction as typical pupils, even though they can read several years above classmates. Those students may not be challenged intellectually or linguistically. Gifted students may be discouraged from developing their capabilities and made to feel uncomfortable.

Rationale: Gifted students may become society's future leaders; they have potential that is worth developing. The teachers' challenge is to offer a stimulating classroom environment and an enriched curriculum to help gifted students attain their capability. Regular classrooms may not adequately support gifted students to achieve to their capabilities, and enrichment may be warranted. Nevertheless, teachers should enrich their classrooms as much as possible, because environments have been shown to stimulate giftedness.

Procedures: Reading Advisory Boards or administrators may use Form 10.8 to evaluate present programmatic offerings for gifted students. The form may be used in deciding to maintain, monitor, or revise the present program.

For Further Reading

Calangelo, N. & Davis, G. (Eds.). (1991). *Handbook of Gifted Education*. Boston: Allyn and Bacon. (Dept. 894, 160 Gould Street, Needham Heights, MA 02194-2310. 1-800-852-8024.)

> This resource interprets issues, problems, and practical strategies for the education of gifted students. The text includes program models, teaching strategies, teaching for thinking and creativity, services, and other topics on the gifted.

Renzulli, J., et al. (1982). "Curriculum Compacting: An Essential Strategy for Working with Gifted Students," *Elementary School Journal*, 82, 3, 185–94.

> The authors endorse compacting and streamlining the curriculum to relieve gifted students of boredom. Instead, they advocate acceleration and enrichment activities, maintaining basics.

Shaughnessy, M. F. (1994). *Gifted and Reading* (ED 368 145).

> Shaughnessy advocates a variety of activities for gifted pupils, including use of guest speakers, books tied to the media, student creative writing, investigative activities, and higher order thinking activities. Reviews of literature and strategies are provided.

Form 10.8
GIFTED STUDENTS AS DIVERSE LEARNERS

Directions: Gifted students may warrant enriched curricula in schools. Administrators or Reading Advisory Boards may study Form 10.8 to examine criteria related to the education of gifted students. On the right, participants may check the extent of implementation of those criteria locally.

Criteria:

	Thoroughly Implemented 4	Moderately Implemented 3	Marginally Implemented 2	Not Implemented 1
1. The principal and program coordinator jointly oversee the program and articulate goals and key elements that create successful programs	☐	☐	☐	☐
2. The school has a written policy and plan on how the gifted program is developed, including class-within-a-class, inclusion, or pull-out model	☐	☐	☐	☐
3. Teachers in gifted programs hold appropriate professional certification	☐	☐	☐	☐
4. Teachers in gifted programs meet to explain the program to classroom teachers and parents	☐	☐	☐	☐
5. A definite plan exists to identify students for the gifted program	☐	☐	☐	☐
6. Teachers may show students how to develop problem-solving skills in reading and to understand research processes	☐	☐	☐	☐
7. Teachers use widely varied activities and curricular mediation to maintain motivation of gifted learners	☐	☐	☐	☐
8. Educators identify and use appropriate technology to advance gifted pupils' literacy advancement and learning	☐	☐	☐	☐
9. Pupils are shown ways to comprehend, analyze, and synthesize information from various sources such as reading, listening, conducting research, and experiencing directly	☐	☐	☐	☐
10. Learners are taught to solve problems in divergent ways, using reasoning and thinking skills other students may not be ready to use	☐	☐	☐	☐
11. Students are taught the searching skills of analysis and synthesis, to use reading to better learn how to learn independently	☐	☐	☐	☐
12. Students are helped to expand their use of creative language and expressive literary forms to better comprehend and to write more skillfully	☐	☐	☐	☐

–continues–

Gifted Students as Diverse Learners	-continued-	4	3	2	1

13. Learners are helped to develop social skills in cooperative group activities in which participative leadership and helping others may be nurtured .... ☐ ☐ ☐ ☐

14. Pupils' language may be enhanced with activities to extend fluency, imagery, humor, and multiple forms of expression .... ☐ ☐ ☐ ☐

15. Pupils are taught to read multiple sources to gather information, and to become analytical and critical in their synthesis of data .... ☐ ☐ ☐ ☐

16. Learning may be enriched through thematic curricular studies in which literature, the arts, and multiple disciplines are combined .... ☐ ☐ ☐ ☐

17. Students learn to function collaboratively rather than competitively to enhance confidence and leadership skills .... ☐ ☐ ☐ ☐

18. Teachers use widely varied activities and curricular mediation to maintain motivation of gifted learners .... ☐ ☐ ☐ ☐

19. Classroom teachers and teachers of gifted students are supported to attend conferences on gifted education .... ☐ ☐ ☐ ☐

20. There is a continuous, district-wide evaluation plan to monitor gifted education, and the local school's contribution is substantial .... ☐ ☐ ☐ ☐

Cover the page at this point and below prior to photocopying if use is desired before referring to the interpretation.

Interpretation: Columns may be tallied, giving four points to checkmarks in the left column, three points to those in the next column, two to the next column, and one point to marks in the right column. Totals between 61–80 may be viewed as *thoroughly implemented*, 41–60 *moderately implemented*, 21–40 *minimally implemented*, and between 1–20 as *not implemented*.

SYNTHESIS OF DIVERSE LEARNER LEADERSHIP (see Form 10.9)

The extent of student diversity in schools is increasing rapidly, and judging from demographic studies, can be predicted to increase into the next century. Implications for teaching children to read are staggering. Teachers may hope to meet the needs of all students, but may lack knowledge or skills.

The Problem: Reading Advisory Boards or administrators may not have a strong sense of what constitutes a balanced reading program for diverse students. Much may be the same as for mainstream students, but adapted to meet diversity needs. Staff development workshops and attitude shifts may be essential to change programs.

Rationale: A strong program to address the reading and language needs of diverse learners may increase students' school successes. The burden and responsibility seems to be shifting from school specialists to classroom teachers to meet the needs of diverse learners. Once strong programs are defined, the challenge is to develop resources and inservice.

Procedures: Administrators or Reading Advisory Boards may wish to summarize the way diversity in education is met using Forms 10.1 to 10.8. Checkmarks may be converted to Form 10.9 to evaluate overall strengths and weaknesses. From Form 10.9, priorities may be identified and entered on Form 10.10. The information may be used to develop an administrative plan-of-action, Form 10.11.

Comments and Cautions

Principals are often aware of the challenge to support classroom teachers as they teach children to read, and teachers do feel the pressure to address the reading needs of diverse pupils.

Many teachers do not want to acknowledge that student diversity is changing, and resist revisions in the way they teach.

Many teachers do not feel that it is *fair* to give extra help or assign less work to special needs students and still use the same grading system. Negative attitudes also may be found regarding a compacted curriculum for gifted students.

Form 10.9
SYNTHESIS OF DIVERSE LEARNER LEADERSHIP

Directions: Reading Advisory Board members may review Forms 10.1–10.8 to gather judgments related to completion of Form 10.9. Those data can then be applied to participants' checkmarks on the right signaling the extent of local implementation. Summary data may be applied to completion of Forms 10.10 and 10.11.

Criteria:	Thoroughly Implemented 4	Moderately Implemented 3	Marginally Implemented 2	Not Implemented 1
1. Review of the overview (see Form 10.1) shows reading needs of diverse students are met	☐	☐	☐	☐
2. The program for at-risk readers meets distinctive needs of that population (see Form 10.2)	☐	☐	☐	☐
3. Reading services to meet the needs of culturally diverse pupils lead those students to make strong gains (see Form 10.3)	☐	☐	☐	☐
4. Learning disability students in the program do advance in learning and affect of reading (see Form 10.4)	☐	☐	☐	☐
5. Students in Title 1 programs are moved back into regular instruction as fully functional readers (see Form 10.5)	☐	☐	☐	☐
6. Programs for special education pupils enhance their best opportunities for learning to read (see Form 10.6)	☐	☐	☐	☐
7. Early intervention programs are employed to reduce subsequent needs for special education, remedial programs, retention (see Form 10.7)	☐	☐	☐	☐
8. Gifted students have their intellectual, social, and academic needs met in reading programs at the local school (see Form 10.8)	☐	☐	☐	☐

Interpretation: Reading Advisory Boards or administrators may study checkmark patterns from various responses to Form 10.9. This information may help to decide whether attention to diversity, overall, is well directed in the school, or whether attention is appropriate. Another use may be for participants to check those components (items 2–8) which seem most in need of support and develop a plan to address those needs.

Form 10.10
DIVERSE LEARNERS: STRENGTHS, NEEDS, AND PRIORITIES

Directions: Administrators or Reading Advisory Board members will find, below, diversity education options. On the right, space is provided to record program strengths, needs, and priorities, each to be developed after careful study of Form 10.9. To fully benefit from use of Form 10.9, review of Forms 10.2–10.8 may be warranted.

1. At-risk Diverse Students	*Strengths* 1. 2.	*Needs* 1. 2.	*Priorities* 1. 2.
2. Multicultural Diverse Students	*Strengths* 1. 2.	*Needs* 1. 2.	*Priorities* 1. 2.
3. Learning Disability Diverse Students	*Strengths* 1. 2.	*Needs* 1. 2.	*Priorities* 1. 2.
4. Title 1 Diverse Students	*Strengths* 1. 2.	*Needs* 1. 2.	*Priorities* 1. 2.
5. Special Education Diverse Students	*Strengths* 1. 2.	*Needs* 1. 2.	*Priorities* 1. 2.
6. Reading Intervention Diverse Students	*Strengths* 1. 2.	*Needs* 1. 2.	*Priorities* 1. 2.
7. Gifted Students as Diverse Learners	*Strengths* 1. 2.	*Needs* 1. 2.	*Priorities* 1. 2.

Form 10.11
DIVERSE LEARNERS: ADMINISTRATIVE PLAN-OF-ACTION

Directions: Administrators seeking to develop a comprehensive plan to improve diversity education may benefit from being as specific as possible about what they seek to accomplish, how they will go about attaining improvement, and how they will know when they have reached their goals. A review of Forms 10.9 and 10.10 should lead the administrator to identify goals to pursue in the growth plan. Statements entered should be as simple, direct, and useful as possible.

1. Goal Statement: _____

2. Objectives:

    a) _____

    b) _____

    c) _____

3. Activities: Dates; time checkpoints:

    a) _____   * _____

    b) _____   * _____

    c) _____   * _____

    d) _____   * _____

    e) _____   * _____

4. Resources: (professional reading, consultation, visitations)

    a) _____   * _____

    b) _____   * _____

    c) _____   * _____

5. How I will know when my goal is accomplished:

_____

_____

_____

_____

CHAPTER 11

PARAPROFESSIONAL SUPPORT OF THE READING PROGRAM

The lives of children may be enriched, and the efforts of teachers may be expanded, with *extra sets of hands* in classrooms. Paraprofessionals, those employed as teacher aides, or volunteer parents may make valuable contributions to teaching and learning. Aides may nurture learning by such activities as reading to students, coaching their efforts, monitoring their shared reading and writing, or supervising. Adults who come into classrooms often function as public relations delegates, bringing community messages to the school and carrying word of positive school endeavors back to families.

School administrators often expend great effort to identify volunteers to help teachers. Invitations may be accompanied by questionnaires that ask parents about particular skills, talents, and interests they might share as they work with teachers and children. Careful planning is warranted as principals or Reading Advisory Boards (see Form 3.5) implement or manage paraprofessional programs. The support given to aides may increase their effectiveness, and often consists of workshops or other training activities. Public acknowledgment of the work of paraprofessionals may strengthen their enthusiasm, and it often compensates for the absence of volunteers' remuneration or employed aides' low pay.

Welcoming aides and volunteers into schools strengthens a principal's public relations plan, and leaves support people feeling that they may make a valuable contribution in the school. In addition, paraprofessionals who feel welcome and needed are enabled to operate in a warmer, more candid manner, which enriches interactions with children and teachers. Helping reluctant teachers to accept the contributions aides are able to make often increases their acceptance of additional adults operating in their classrooms.

OVERVIEW OF PARAPROFESSIONAL FUNCTIONS   (see Forms 11.1 and 11.2)

Two groups of people take the role of paraprofessionals; one is the parent volunteer and the other is the employed teacher aide. Identifying those people, creating viable roles for them, and making them feel welcome are important functions of administrators.

The Problem: Teachers have not always acknowledged that paraprofessionals would be helpful to them. Aides and volunteers might be left to feel unsuccessful and underappreciated. Paraprofessionals may never get the feedback that they are doing well.

Rationale: Extra hands at school usually benefit students, teachers, and administrators. Employed aides and volunteers can effectively undertake any number of roles to support reading programs. They may be able to supervise pupils' work, encourage their efforts, and function as effective role models. Keeping the community informed and involved about reading lends support to this important curriculum area, and those paraprofessionals are in positions to inform.

Procedures: Data taken from Form 11.1 may help the administrator or Reading Advisory Board to gain the background to support a paraprofessional program. That information may help planners to decide whether to initiate such a program, or may provide the basis for an existing program's improvements. To help a faculty consider acceptance of aides and volunteers, Form 11.2, or preferably a local story, might be shared by administrators.

For Further Reading

Jennings, J. M. (1992). "Parent Involvement Strategies for Inner-city Schools," *NASSP Bulletin*, 76, 548, 63–68.

> Jennings admonishes school principals to consider needs and interests of parents more than to push the school's agenda. He supports using community resources to involve parents in schools. The author advocates empowerment, school visits, volunteerism, and at-home activities.

Pickett, A. L., et al. (1993). *Promoting Effective Communications with Para-educators* (ED 357 586).

> Pickett's paper, presented at a professional conference, includes a variety of communication strategies, what paraprofessionals need to know about teachers, job descriptions, role assessments, a curriculum for paraprofessionals, effective tutorial use, and assessment.

Form 11.1
OVERVIEW OF PARAPROFESSIONAL FUNCTIONS

Directions: Use of paraprofessionals can improve teacher effectiveness, and both directly and indirectly benefit the lives of students. Below, respondents will find criteria related to volunteer and employed paraprofessional functions. On the right, principals or Reading Advisory Boards may judge the extent of local implementation.

Paraprofessional Criteria:	Thoroughly Implemented 4	Moderately Implemented 3	Marginally Implemented 2	Not Implemented 1
1. The school invites parents to volunteer their help in the reading program	☐	☐	☐	☐
2. Principals and teachers acknowledge the importance of having aides and volunteers	☐	☐	☐	☐
3. The school would be described as having a strong paraprofessional component...	☐	☐	☐	☐
4. Effort is made to match assignments to paraprofessionals' talents and schedules...	☐	☐	☐	☐
5. Informal needs-assessments are conducted to identify paraprofessionals' needs	☐	☐	☐	☐
6. Staff development exists to strengthen paraprofessionals' efforts to succeed...	☐	☐	☐	☐
7. Supervision of paraprofessionals is directed toward positive growth and contributions	☐	☐	☐	☐
8. Evaluation of paraprofessionals focuses on increased skills and public recognition	☐	☐	☐	☐
9. Administrators interpret school activities to paraprofessionals to enhance their roles and to support public relations	☐	☐	☐	☐

Cover the page at this point and below prior to photocopying if users are not to see the interpretation until later.

Interpretation: Respondents may tally columns, giving four points to the left column, three points to the second column, two the next column, and one to the column on the right. Totals between 28–36 may be considered *thoroughly implemented*, between 19–27 *moderately implemented*, between 10–18 *minimally implemented*, and between 1–9 *not implemented*.

Form 11.2

PARAPROFESSIONAL PROJECT SUCCESS STORY

Story of an actual school and how staff began using volunteers.

In a small (14 teachers) elementary school, 80 percent of parents returned a reading survey and indicated they wanted to: (1) know more about the school's reading program, and (2) be involved with the school on a volunteer basis. The school had a principal who was willing to investigate the use of volunteers in his school.

The principal, accompanied by three teachers, the reading specialist, and two parents, visited two nearby schools that had parent/community involvement. They were able to talk with the volunteers and meet with the principal. Discussion with the teachers helped with understanding strengths and problems. Being able to actually visualize the involvement that strengthened the reading program helped the school to get started. They were given handbooks prepared by the school for its volunteers.

After meeting with the Reading Advisory Board, the principal called a meeting of teachers, the librarian, and reading specialist to discuss the establishment of a volunteer program in their school. Several teachers were very apprehensive about parents coming into their rooms; however, the librarian stated that she could really use some assistance. The principal decided the project would begin with the librarian. He sent a letter to the parents and other community members inviting them to a meeting for prospective volunteers. In preparation, the librarian, principal, and reading teacher prepared a handbook of *Do's and Don'ts* for future volunteers.

Twenty people came to the meeting. After the principal explained that the school needed the volunteers at least twice a week for two to three hours in the library, only four people were actually willing or able to work. With those four, the days and time schedules were then established. The four were given the handbook and its contents were reviewed. On the first day, the principal and librarian met with the volunteers to review the handbook and explain what their duties would be. The principal made special name tags for them, and asked the librarian to direct the four people. The principal invited volunteers to talk with him if they had questions, comments, or concerns about their role.

The four persons were excellent volunteers. The volunteers shelved books, checked books in and out, and read to children, both in the library and in classrooms. They later started preparing the display materials for the bookcases in the hallway, and did some bulletin boards. By the end of the first year, some of the teachers were asking if *they* could possibly have some help in their classrooms. Then the principal knew it was time to take another step in bringing volunteers into the school. The project was a success story!

ELICITING PARAPROFESSIONAL SUPPORT   (see Forms 11.3 to 11.5)

Parents and school communities must understand school reading problems and needs if positive learning environments are to exist in the school and homes. The purpose, then, of assessing community and parent understandings of reading programs is to gain information to form positive climates, shared purposes, and mutual respect in support of literacy.

The Problem: Many schools and unconfident teachers seem to want parents and the general public to stay away from their classrooms and buildings. Yet apathy may be greatest in those families most in need of close school contact to support their children. Parents have not always felt welcome to visit or participate in school activities.

Rationale: Good reading programs that meet the needs of pupils exist only when educators collaborate closely with families and their community. Programs work best when all of the adults involved with students join together to plan and solve pupils' reading problems. Active involvement of parents and volunteers occurs when adults provide additional services as collaborators.

Procedures: Administrators or Reading Advisory Boards may use Forms 11.3 to 11.5 to initiate paraprofessional support for the reading program. Forms 11.3 to 11.4 may be used to invite participation. Responses to those forms will help to identify roles and talents of prospective paraprofessionals. Feedback from Form 11.5 will support decisions about the need for a coordinator, and help to define the role.

For Further Reading

Carter, D. A. (1993). "Community and Parent Involvement: A Road to School Improvement," *ERS Spectrum,* 11, 1, 39–46.

> Carter establishes criteria for effective parent involvement programs. She then describes several examples. She provides suggestions for managing school volunteer programs. The author recommends processes to establish partnership approaches to community involvement.

McDaniel, E. & Mack, V. H. (1992). *Involving Minority Parents of At-Risk Children: A Parent / School Partnership* (ED 358 533).

> A model program develops parent workshops, a learning resource center, incentives to reduce absenteeism, and a communications network. Pre- and post-surveys suggested that parents did benefit from participation. School achievement did increase. School attendance improved.

Form 11.3
INVITING COMMUNITY PARTICIPATION IN THE SCHOOL READING PROGRAM

Directions: We are inviting members of the community to become involved in the school's reading program. We will be able to use the help of people who are willing and interested. Would you fill in the following questionnaire, so we can plan for the educational future of students in this community? If you have questions, please feel free to call the school about your concerns. Below, please check on the right areas where you might be able to help.

Criteria for Participation in School Reading:	Yes	No
1. I am interested in the school's reading program, but I do not have the time to assist at school	☐	☐
2. I am interested in helping at school and have time to help	☐	☐
3. I would be able to read to students	☐	☐
4. I could listen to students read	☐	☐
5. I could help students with seatwork or practice activities	☐	☐
6. I would be willing to work in the library	☐	☐
7. I could prepare reading materials, photocopy, sort or organize student papers	☐	☐
8. I would help with preparing a reading newsletter	☐	☐
9. I could work on bulletin boards to encourage reading	☐	☐
10. I could accompany and/or offer transportation (where legal) for field trips	☐	☐

It would help us at school if you could volunteer on a regular schedule. An example would be a certain number of days a week (maybe two, three days) and a certain number of hours per day (perhaps one, three hours):

What time schedule could you give to the school? _____

_____

Other possible areas of service: _____

_____

Name _____ Address _____ Phone _____

Form 11.4
QUESTIONNAIRE TO DEVELOP A TALENT BANK

Full name
Mr.
Mrs. _____
Miss   Last   First   Initial

Home Address _____ Phone _____

Business Address _____ Phone _____

Children: Boys _____ Girls _____

1. Would you be willing to speak to a class or put on a demonstration? _____
   Please describe _____
   _____

2. Occupation _____
   Would you demonstrate and/or explain your occupation to groups of children? _____
   Would you permit individuals to visit you on the job? _____

3. Is your place of business available for field trips? _____
   What ages? _____

4. What kinds of educational materials could you make available through your employer, such as pamphlets on occupations, films, and other educational aids? _____
   _____

5. What interesting articles, hobbies, or collections do you have that you would be willing to share at school (perhaps stamps, paintings, ethnic items, items of cultural or racial diversity, science items, etc.): _____
   _____
   _____

6. Have you lived or traveled in other countries? ___ Where _____
   Have you traveled within the United States? ___ Where _____
   Do you have pictures, tapes, movies, or costumes of your travels? _____
   Would you be willing to share these with groups or individuals? _____

7. Do you know others who do not have children in school who might assist us?
   Name   **Contributions s/he could make**
   _____

Form 11.5
COORDINATOR OF PARAPROFESSIONAL PROGRAMS

Directions: Coordination of paraprofessionals may run from highly simple to extremely complex. Prospective tasks of coordination are listed below, and the opportunity exists on the right for a Reading Advisory Board or principal to judge the degree of present implementation.

Volunteers' Coordinator Criteria:	Thoroughly Implemented	Moderately Implemented	Not Implemented
	3	2	1
1. Plan, monitor, and assess the paraprofessional program in conjunction with the principal	☐	☐	☐
2. Tally and organize any information from Chapter 11 needed by the administrator, Reading Advisory Board, or teachers	☐	☐	☐
3. Attempt to find volunteers for total days	☐	☐	☐
4. Organize information for the principal on the kind of workshops needed by volunteers and teacher aides (see Forms 11.8 and 11.9)	☐	☐	☐
5. Keep a bulletin board for visitor and volunteer identification buttons	☐	☐	☐
6. Develop assignments for paraprofessionals (see Form 11.8)	☐	☐	☐
7. Organize a volunteer, parent, community, and teacher aide talent bank, catalog information (see Form 11.4), or create a card file	☐	☐	☐
8. Organize the volunteer and teacher aide work schedule (see Form 11.7)	☐	☐	☐
9. Plan, monitor, and arrange school recognitions of volunteer contributions (see Forms 11.10 and 11.12)	☐	☐	☐

Cover the page at this point and below prior to photocopying if users are not to see the interpretation until later.

Interpretation: Respondents may tally columns, giving three points to the left column, two points to the next, and one point to the column on the right. Totals between 19–27 may be considered *thoroughly implemented*, between 10–18 *moderately implemented,* and between 1–9 *not implemented.*

MANAGEMENT OF PARAPROFESSIONAL PERSONNEL   (see Forms 11.6 to 11.8)

Schools launching paraprofessional programs may find ways to invite participants, identify their skills and talents, provide workshop opportunities, and recognize their contributions. An organizational model appropriate for a school may enrich pupils' lives and teachers' effectiveness.

The Problem: Managing paraprofessional programs in large schools with numerous funded projects and several volunteers can be demanding and complex. Suiting paraprofessional assignments to appropriate staff involves thoughtful consideration. Supporting faculty with the help they need commands great effort.

Rationale: Work assignments that address the schedules and interests of volunteers increase chances that those paraprofessionals will continue to offer help. Employed aides, too, benefit schools most if assignments fit their talents and interests.

Procedures: The principal or Reading Advisory Board may use Forms 11.6 to 11.8 to formulate a management plan. The coordinator or administrator works with the Reading Advisory Board to develop a suitable model. Assignments are matched to the skills and interests of aides and volunteers The paraprofessional coordinator may use Form 11.7 to develop work schedules, and to gain paraprofessional feedback regarding scheduled assignments. Teacher responses to Form 11.8 may help the coordinator to prepare aides and volunteers for various assignments

For Further Reading

Pickett, A. L. (1988). *The Employment and Training of Paraprofessional Personnel: A Technical Assistance Manual for Administrators and Staff Developers*. NY: City University of New York (Ed 357 516).

> Pickett summarizes responsibilities of participants, increased use of paraprofessionals in ever more demanding roles, and suggestions for personnel practices and training. Six appendixes provide extensive practical guidelines.

Hermann, B. A. (Ed.). (1994). *The Volunteer Tutor's Toolbox*. Newark, DE: International Reading Association. (800 Barksdale Road, P.O. Box 8139, Newark, DE 19714-8139. 1-302-731-1600.)

> A practical resource for volunteers of any level. The text supports helping individual students to read better. Specific processes are presented on students' study skills, test-taking, and tutors' activities and strategies.

Form 11.6
ORGANIZATIONAL MODELS FOR VOLUNTEER PARTICIPATION

Directions: Several models exist for organizing volunteers. Some are suitable for small schools, others would be more effective in large schools. The Reading Advisory Board or principal may consider applicability of models to the local setting.

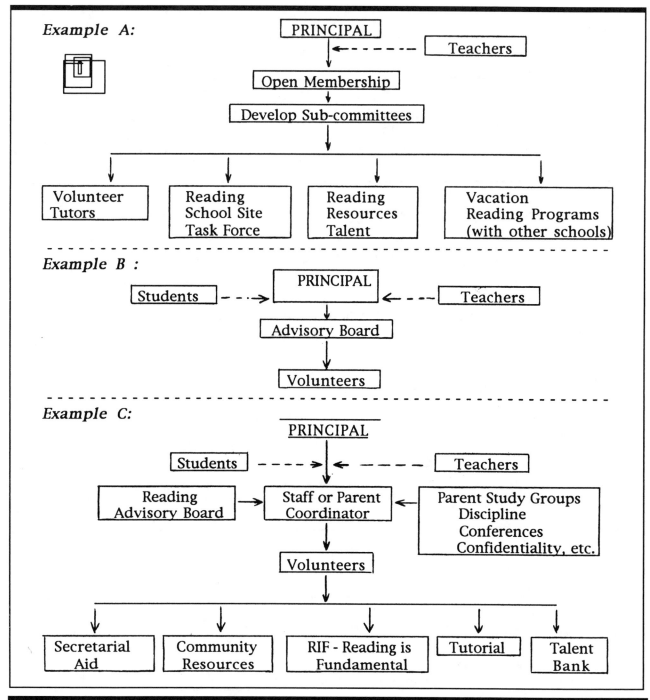

Form 11.7
VOLUNTEER AND PARAPROFESSIONAL WORK SCHEDULE

8:00–8:30   Meet with principal or coordinator.*

8:30–10:30   Tuesday–Thursday work assignment.

Volunteer's name _____

You are assigned to _____

Your duties are** _____

_____

_____

_____

Time:

- -

RESPONSES TO VOLUNTEER ASSIGNMENT***

Teacher(s) to whom assigned _____

The assignment was: Poor   Average   Excellent

Comments _____

_____

_____

_____

Signed _____   Dated _____

- -

*   If some volunteers come at different hours, the coordinator would need to be sure they are given a meeting time before the work.

**   Duties, written out as teachers' requests, may be attached.

***   The "Responses" format may be placed on the back of the "work schedule" form.

Form 11.8

ASSIGNMENTS FOR PARENT VOLUNTEERS AND EMPLOYED PARAPROFESSIONALS

Directions: Teachers usually wish to have aides conduct helpful projects. Additionally, support people would prefer to feel useful. Below are listed projects that teacher aides might pursue. On the right teachers may indicate whether the task is extremely important, fairly important, or unimportant in the classroom.

Possible Assignments for Aides	Extremely Important 3	Fairly Important 2	Not Important 1
1. Construct reading and learning games	☐	☐	☐
2. Listen to students practice reading	☐	☐	☐
3. Make learning center activities that enhance reading	☐	☐	☐
4. Assist students with practice work	☐	☐	☐
5. Check students' mastery of basic words	☐	☐	☐
6. Prepare student reading activities to be assigned by the teacher	☐	☐	☐
7. Do office work for teachers or administrators	☐	☐	☐
8. Take students on walking trips, or transport students on field trips, wherever legal	☐	☐	☐
9. Escort pupils to the library to select books	☐	☐	☐
10. Manage book club sales and distribution	☐	☐	☐
11. Read stories to pupils	☐	☐	☐
12. Listen to students as they read	☐	☐	☐
13. Listen to pairs of children read to each other	☐	☐	☐
14. Listen to the retellings of pupils after they have read silently	☐	☐	☐

–continues–

Assignments for Parent Volunteers and Employed Paraprofessionals -continued-	3	2	1
15. Develop a talent bank for the school or classroom (see Form 11.4)	☐	☐	☐
16. Prepare displays of student work	☐	☐	☐
17. Lend support to reading contests and activities	☐	☐	☐
18. Encourage others in the community who have the time to volunteer their help at school	☐	☐	☐
19. Administer reading attitude (Form 12.7) and reading interest (Form 12.8) inventories to small groups of students	☐	☐	☐
20. Exercise caution that paraprofessionals are not invading student privacy, but instead are effecting the fullest of student confidentiality	☐	☐	☐

Cover the page at this point and below prior to photocopying if users are not to see the interpretation until later.

Interpretation: Teachers who have filled out Form 11.8, responding to the use of teacher aides, provide valuable information for the Reading Advisory Board. After analysis, the Board may wish to show the faculty summaries of responses, seek feedback, and suggest ways of strengthening helpfulness of aides in classrooms, particularly in the context of creating changes in the reading program.

DEVELOPMENT OF PARAPROFESSIONALS   (see Forms 11.9 to 11.12)

Schools are fortunate when they can employ paraprofessionals to assist the faculty in educating children. Paraprofessionals are used in many ways, but predominately assist classroom teachers. Providing positive evaluative feedback on their work may increase their skills and extend their willingness to improve.

The Problem: Paraprofessionals usually are *everyday folks* without particular teaching skills. Their levels of interpersonal skills may not always nurture children in adequate ways. Some may feel insecure about organization, management, discipline, and so on.

Rationale: Aides and volunteers who participate in professional development are enabled to become more effective in the education of students. Paraprofessionals who respond to needs-questionnaires on workshops contribute to the training options available. Feedback from paraprofessionals may help school personnel to create better assignments.

Procedures: The coordinator of paraprofessional activities, or the principal, may administer Form 11.9 to get feedback on workshops that would benefit aides and volunteers. Responses to Form 11.10 will help coordinators or principals to support paraprofessionals, or to adjust conditions to increase effectiveness. Information gained from Form 11.11 will provide feedback on effectiveness. The principal may give summaries of the data from Forms 11.9 to 11.11 to paraprofessionals to interpret the status, and in separate audiences, to update faculty, in order to extend the quality of paraprofessional use.

For Further Reading

Anderson, N. A. (1989). "Increasing the Effectiveness of the Reading Aide: A Guide for Teachers," *Reading Horizons*, 29, 3, 153–61.

> The author suggests communication strategies and joint planning sessions to increase aides' effectiveness. Anderson builds the case that aides need helpful feedback and staff development to increase their strengths. Suggestions for content are included.

Pickett, A. L. (1989). *A Training Program to Prepare Teachers to Supervise and Work More Effectively with Paraprofessional Personnel.* New York: City University of New York (ED 357 515).

> A practical guide to support paraprofessional effectiveness. The author describes teacher and paraprofessional roles, support responsibilities of the administrator, and guidelines for use of training model materials. The module, with worksheet activities, case studies, and handouts, is described.

Form 11.9
WORKSHOP CONTENT FOR VOLUNTEERS AND PARAPROFESSIONALS

Directions: Below, criteria are listed as possible workshop topics. On the right, paraprofessionals may indicate whether they have great need, moderate need, or little need to learn about each topic. Of the possible topics, respondents might *place a circle around checkmarks for the three items* where participants feel the greatest need for workshops.

Criteria:	Great Need 3	Moderate Need 2	Little Need 1
1. Know what is expected of me as an aide or paraprofessional	☐	☐	☐
2. Know the policies and procedures that are stated in the school handbook ..	☐	☐	☐
3. Know the differences between the paraprofessional or aide's responsibilities in the classroom and those of the classroom teacher...................................	☐	☐	☐
4. Have adequate inservice reading training provided by the school district	☐	☐	☐
5. Communicate regularly with the classroom teacher and initiate conferences when appropriate	☐	☐	☐
6. Feel assured that the activities that I conduct are planned and discussed with the teacher in advance	☐	☐	☐
7. Feel confident that I have a systematic and organized way of reporting student progress to the teacher	☐	☐	☐
8. Understand the terms that are used in reading instruction	☐	☐	☐
9. Understand the various components of a reading and writing program	☐	☐	☐
10. Feel informed about the specific reading needs of children and how I should deal with those needs	☐	☐	☐
11. Be aware of pupils' instructional reading levels and what this means for a paraprofessional who supports children	☐	☐	☐
12. Have adequate materials to function effectively	☐	☐	☐
13. Conduct activities to help students' reading comprehension	☐	☐	☐
14. Ask students challenging questions concerning what they have read	☐	☐	☐
15. Direct the retellings that follow the silent reading activities	☐	☐	☐

–continues–

Workshop Contents for Volunteers and Paraprofessionals -continued-	3	2	1
16. Conduct activities to help pupils expand reading vocabulary	☐	☐	☐
17. Encourage pupils to learn to skip words and make reasonable guesses	☐	☐	☐
18. Test the meaning of unknown words against their context	☐	☐	☐
19. Apply phonic generalizations to decode words	☐	☐	☐
20. Be able to produce phonemes (sound) for graphemes (print) of the English language	☐	☐	☐
21. Apply syllabication patterns to unknown words	☐	☐	☐
22. Learn how to understand and enhance students' attitudes and interests in reading	☐	☐	☐
23. Manage the behavior of a group of students	☐	☐	☐
24. Understand the components of reading readiness or literacy emergence	☐	☐	☐
25. Keep students working "on task"	☐	☐	☐
26. Use the language experience approach with pupils to help them learn to read and write	☐	☐	☐
27. Ask individuals or small groups of children to read to you and support their reading	☐	☐	☐
28. Read stories to children with expression and fluency	☐	☐	☐
29. Become familiar with a variety of children's books in order to help students select good books to read	☐	☐	☐
30. Use creative drama, fingerplays, puppetry, and choral reading to develop oral language in children	☐	☐	☐
31. Make and use aids for teaching reading	☐	☐	☐
32. Help students improve their handwriting	☐	☐	☐
33. Write the alphabet and numerals properly in manuscript and in cursive	☐	☐	☐
34. Understand the general characteristics of students in reference to physical, emotional, social, and intellectual development	☐	☐	☐
35. Know the characteristics of children with learning problems	☐	☐	☐

–continues–

Workshop Contents for Volunteers and Paraprofessionals   -continued-

	3	2	1

36. Be aware of the legal privacy rights of students ....

37. Know what to do in the event of emergency situations, such as fire, tornado, injured or ill child, threatening intruder, or violent student behavior.....

Other topics that paraprofessionals need to have addressed:

Other topics that the Reading Advisory Board needs to address:

Cover the page at this point and below prior to photocopying if users are not to see the interpretation until later.

Interpretation: Information from Form 11.9 may be helpful to the coordinator, principal, or Reading Advisory Board as judgments are made regarding staff development of paraprofessionals. *Respondents have been asked to encircle three items where greatest need is felt.* Going back to tally encircled items will support the establishment of topical priorities. Planners may use individual responses to plan independent staff development and collate encircled items to identify areas in which group staff development workshops would be helpful.

Form 11.10

PARAPROFESSIONALS' RATING SCALE OF THE READING PROGRAM

Directions: Criteria listed below were developed to reflect on assignments of paraprofessionals. Respondents may read each criterion below and check themselves as aids. Comments should be written on the back of the form. Please *do not* sign your name.

Rating criteria for volunteer use:	Very Effective 4	Moderately Effective 3	Marginally Effective 2	Not Effective 1
1. Volunteers are sought actively to assist, and are made to feel wanted and needed	☐	☐	☐	☐
2. Enough are available to assist adequately in the reading program	☐	☐	☐	☐
3. Are well briefed as to their duties	☐	☐	☐	☐
4. Shown how to supervise practice reading	☐	☐	☐	☐
5. Are able to assist students with seatwork	☐	☐	☐	☐
6. Are capable of supervising paired or collaborative reading	☐	☐	☐	☐
7. Can monitor and encourage recreational reading	☐	☐	☐	☐
8. Are well qualified to perform their duties	☐	☐	☐	☐
9. Are readily accepted by classroom teachers	☐	☐	☐	☐
10. Are well aware of the parameters within which they are to operate	☐	☐	☐	☐
11. Are recognized by the principal, faculty, staff, and students for their contributions	☐	☐	☐	☐

Cover the page at this point and below prior to photocopying if users are not to see the interpretation until later.

Interpretation: Checkmarks may be totaled, giving four points to marks in the left column, three to marks in the second column, two to the next column, and one to the column on the right. Totals between 34–44 may be judged *very effective*, between 23–33 *moderately effective*, between 12–22 *marginally effective*, and between 1–11 *not effective*. Principals who ask aides for quarterly feedback to Form 11.10 could monitor their views of assignments.

FORM 11.11
PARAPROFESSIONAL EVALUATION

Directions: School personnel may sense the value of providing volunteers and employed paraprofessionals with feedback on their effectiveness. Forms such as those found below may be considered.

Example A: Teacher Aide Evaluation of Assignment

		Yes	No
1.	I have been made aware of the need to have me assist the reading program	_____	_____
2.	I feel that I was used effectively	_____	_____
3.	I knew what I was expected to do	_____	_____
4.	I had the background or training to do the task	_____	_____

Comments: _____

_____

Example B: Teacher Evaluation of Paraprofessional

		Yes	No
1.	I did wish to be assisted in my reading program	_____	_____
2.	I feel that the assistance I received was effective	_____	_____
3.	I helped the aide understand the assigned duties	_____	_____
4.	I provided the assignment for the coordinator at the beginning of the day	_____	_____
5.	I need to confer with my aide and coordinator	_____	_____

Comments: _____

_____

Example C: Pupil Evaluation of Volunteer

		Yes	No
1.	The volunteer helped me	_____	_____
2.	I liked the helper	_____	_____
3.	I felt successful when I worked with the aides	_____	_____

Comments: _____

_____

FORM 11.12

PARENT RECOGNITION CERTIFICATE

Directions: The certificate has value as a form that may be adapted to award to people who volunteer to support the reading program at schools. Adaptations, with use of local school logos, would personalize certificates.

CERTIFICATE OF APPRECIATION

PARENT VOLUNTEER
OUTSTANDING DEDICATION

The teachers, students, and staff of _____ School

extend their appreciation to

_____

for services during the year

19_____

_____   _____
(Principal)   (Superintendent)

SYNTHESIS OF PARAPROFESSIONAL   (see Forms 11.13 to 11.15)
SUPPORT OF THE READING PROGRAM

Translating extensive data on paraprofessional program needs (see Forms 11.1 to 11.12) into a functional plan-of-action is an important challenge to educators. Oftentimes, the full program improvement process (see Forms 2.3, 3.12) includes changes in the roles of paraprofessionals.

The Problem: Implementation or revisions of programs for aides or volunteers is a difficult task. Many prospective paraprofessionals feel unwelcome and poorly used. Supporting aides and volunteers to increase effectiveness warrants considerable time and leadership skills.

Rationale: The diversity of students in schools has increased remarkably in recent years. Use of paraprofessionals provides those *extra hands* so vitally needed to assist teachers, administrators, and staff. Use of paraprofessionals also supports family, school, and district collaboration, which helps students to read better.

Procedures: Educators may tie together data in Chapter 11. Those data may be summarized (Form 11.13), after referral to separate worksheets (Forms 11.3 to 11.12). Following extensive feedback from faculty and aides, administrators may establish strengths, needs, and priorities related to the paraprofessional program (see Form 11.14). A plan-of-action (see Form 11.15) may set the direction for program advances.

Comments and Cautions

Interviews of paraprofessionals may be almost as important as teacher interviews. These people may become very important to the reading program.

Paraprofessionals, as do teachers, warrant inservice training that occurs as they begin and throughout the time they participate in schools.

The quality of inservice provided for paraprofessionals will determine, in great part, the quality of service they are able to provide.

Teachers should participate in selected areas of the inservice offered for paraprofessionals, so that they will be aware of the developed skills.

Form 11.13
SYNTHESIS OF PARAPROFESSIONAL SUPPORT OF THE READING PROGRAM

Directions: Below, respondents will find statements addressing paraprofessional support of reading programs. On the right, members of the Reading Advisory Board, the principal, and faculty members may check the status of that criterion in the school.

Paraprofessional Support Criteria:	Thoroughly Implemented	Moderately Implemented	Not Implemented
	3	2	1
1. The school has sought participation from members of the community (see Form 11.3)	☐	☐	☐
2. The information gained from the community to form a talent bank of volunteer participants is satisfactory (see Form 11.4)	☐	☐	☐
3. The school has a successful format for the coordinator of volunteers (see Form 11.5)	☐	☐	☐
4. The organizational model used in the school is effective (see Form 11.6)	☐	☐	☐
5. The work schedule for volunteers and paraprofessionals operates functionally (see Form 11.7)	☐	☐	☐
6. The range of volunteer assignments is appropriate and successful (see Forms 11.8, 12.12)	☐	☐	☐
7. Adequate information is gathered to prepare workshop content for paraprofessionals (see Form 11.9)	☐	☐	☐
8. Feedback from volunteers on their feelings of effectiveness is sufficient (see Form 11.10)	☐	☐	☐
9. Evaluative feedback from paraprofessionals and regarding them is suitable (see Form 11.11)	☐	☐	☐
10. The school has designed a paraprofessional recognition certificate which works well (see Form 11.12)	☐	☐	☐

Interpretation: Principals or Reading Advisory Boards will want to retain strengths of the paraprofessional program and address needs. Respondents may examine self- and teacher-checkmarks above to judge whether implementation of any criteria is warranted to support the reading program.

Form 11.14

PARAPROFESSIONAL SUPPORT OF READING: STRENGTHS, NEEDS, AND PRIORITIES

Directions: Below, principals or Reading Advisory Board members will find categories of paraprofessional support for the reading program. On the right is provided space to enter summaries of reading program strengths, needs, and priorities.

	Strengths	Needs	Priorities
1. Overview of Para-professional Functions	1. 2.	1. 2.	1. 2.
2. Eliciting Para-professional Support	1. 2.	1. 2.	1. 2.
3. Management of Para-professional Personnel	1. 2.	1. 2.	1. 2.
4. Development of Para-professionals	1. 2.	1. 2.	1. 2.
5. Synthesis of Para-professional Support	1. 2.	1. 2.	1. 2.
6. Plan-of-Action for Para-professionals	1. 2.	1. 2.	1. 2.

Form 11.15

PLAN-OF-ACTION TO SUPPORT PARAPROFESSIONALS
IN THE SCHOOL READING PROGRAM

Directions: Administrators or Reading Advisory Boards seeking to improve the role of paraprofessionals as a part of program change may benefit from development of the plan-of-action. Participants should be as specific as possible regarding what they seek to accomplish, how they will pursue improvement, and how they will know when they have reached their goal. Application of Forms 11.13 and 11.14 conclusions may support writing the plan-of-action. Statements should be as simple, direct, and useful as possible.

1. Goal Statement: _____

2. Objectives:

   a) _____

   b) _____

   c) _____

3. Activities: Dates; time checkpoints:

   a) _____   * _____

   b) _____   * _____

   c) _____   * _____

   d) _____   * _____

   e) _____   * _____

4. Resources: (professional reading, consultation, visitations)

   a) _____   * _____

   b) _____   * _____

   c) _____   * _____

5. How I will know when my goal is accomplished:

   _____

   _____

   _____

   _____

CHAPTER 12

PUBLIC RELATIONS AND THE READING PROGRAM

A strong spirit of cooperation among schools, parents, and community members is highly desirable. That cooperation is enhanced by a free flow of communication in both directions—that is, from school to home and from home to school. The school that enjoys a positive reputation in the community, along with an abiding sense that parents believe their students are receiving a good education, often provides more favorable support than does the school that finds its community expressing suspicion, lack of confidence, and an undermining behavior toward the school. Questionnaires are provided to sample comments and parent sentiments.

One of the best ways to educate the public about an effective reading program and the resultant pupil literacy is to involve people. Administrators or Reading Advisory Boards (see Form 3.5) who develop public relations plans have the structure to inform the community, support community and school interaction, and create literacy exhibits to inform people. Gaining extensive information from families and community members about their views of the reading program builds a stronger literacy foundation.

There is considerable empirical evidence that parent involvement results in improved student reading scores. It also has been shown that when parents read with their children, the students are better prepared for learning to read at school. The very foundation of federally- and state-funded projects has been parent advisory committees and volunteers, recognizing that parent awareness is basic to educating children. Activities lend themselves to staff development workshops in which small groups brainstorm about implementation and use, sharing findings with the total faculty, to strengthen participant skills.

GAINING INPUT FROM HOME AND COMMUNITY   (see Form 12.1)

The purpose of assessing how well the community and parents understand the reading program is to gain information to develop a positive climate that results in improved student literacy. Parents who understand school reading goals may share common purposes, mutual respect, awareness, and positive learning environments.

The Problem: The administrator's problem often is that parents and community members do not provide strong support for literacy. Results may include parent apathy, distrust, and contempt, particularly in communities with sizable economically impoverished populations.

Rationale: It is much easier to inculcate a spirit of literacy in students when communities and parents support their children's reading development. People who work or volunteer in schools see needs and problems, express those needs back in the community, and often strengthen support for schools. A comprehensive plan for community involvement is presented.

Procedures: It is desirable for administrators to create a climate in which teachers want the help of outsiders. If teachers feel comfortable, and see the need for help, they will be better able to guide and welcome parents into their classes. Forms 12.1 and 12.2 provide support for administrators and Advisory Boards in securing community participation. Form 12.1 provides background information to develop a public relations structure. Form 12.2, the school logo, enables "identity," signals the importance of messages, and supports both informational and praiseworthy correspondence.

For Further Reading

Hennessey, A. (1992). "Getting the Word Out: Working with Your Local Reporter," *Phi Delta Kappan*, 74, 1, 82–84.

> Schools can increase their press coverage. Processes are suggested for working with members of the press. Local press agencies should be advised well in advance of scheduled events. Reporters appreciate administrators' sensitivity about newsworthiness. Rapid turnaround on prepublication copy is always appreciated.

Ordovensky, P. & Marx, G. (1993). *Working with the News Media*. Arlington, VA: American Association of School Administrators. (1801 North Moore Street, Alexandria, VA 22209. 1-703-528-0700.)

> Administrators can learn to develop positive working relationships with the press. Nineteen suggestions are offered, including news releases, fact sheets, media advisory access, news conferences, letters to editors, etc.

Form 12.1
PUBLIC RELATIONS FOR THE READING PROGRAM

Directions: Below are listed prospective activities for gaining community support of the reading program. On the right, school personnel may check whether the activity might be highly useful, somewhat useful, or not useful.

	Highly Useful	Somewhat Useful	Not Useful
Home/Volunteer Criteria:	3	2	1

1. *Invite community members to serve on a Reading Advisory Board or committee*

   a. Prepare agendas of substantial issues for discussion .... ☐ ☐ ☐

   b. Inform the Advisory Board about the reading program in an effort to gain support .... ☐ ☐ ☐

   c. Obtain recommendations from the Advisory Board .... ☐ ☐ ☐

   d. Encourage Board members to carry issues back to the community for discussion .... ☐ ☐ ☐

   e. Publicize recommendations from the Board .... ☐ ☐ ☐

2. *Prepare exhibits for the public to enjoy*

   a. Consider shopping malls, storefront windows, bank lobbies, etc., as locations for exhibits .... ☐ ☐ ☐

   b. Display the full range of reading program materials, going beyond basal texts and workbooks.. ☐ ☐ ☐

   c. Classes might depict favorite stories through dioramas, shadow boxes, mobiles, etc. .... ☐ ☐ ☐

   d. Exhibit a full set of reading program materials attractively and permanently in the school lobby .... ☐ ☐ ☐

   e. Conduct class, with desks, chairs, portable chalkboard, in a storefront or shopping center window all day .... ☐ ☐ ☐

   f. Invite parents to come to school to visit special reading program exhibits .... ☐ ☐ ☐

   g. Plan and participate in activities for Book Week and Library Week .... ☐ ☐ ☐

–continues–

Public Relations for the Reading Program	-continued-	3	2	1

3. Collect materials for a book fair

a. Invite the PTA Council or Advisory Board to publicize and manage the project .... ☐ ☐ ☐

b. Consider one of the commercial book fairs often advertised in teacher magazines .... ☐ ☐ ☐

c. Community members are asked to search their homes for surplus usable children's books .... ☐ ☐ ☐

d. Set up centers around the community where books may be deposited . ☐ ☐ ☐

e. Ask the PTA Council or Advisory Board to sort and organize the books ☐ ☐ ☐

f. With each book distribution, each child is given a book to keep as an effort to nurture reading .... ☐ ☐ ☐

g. Participate in Reading is Fundamental (RIF) to increase available book titles for students' personal ownership .... ☐ ☐ ☐

4. Extend television use with television scripts ☐ ☐ ☐

a. Secure scripts of special programs in advance .... ☐ ☐ ☐

b. Collect posters available from many sources: Public Broadcast System, Weekly Reader, Scholastic, Hallmark .... ☐ ☐ ☐

c. Request accompanying teachers' guides .... ☐ ☐ ☐

d. Use appropriate reading, writing, thinking activities for instruction .... ☐ ☐ ☐

e. Encourage students to read the script either in advance or while watching the program .... ☐ ☐ ☐

f. Create a press release demonstrating the benefits for promoting reading .... ☐ ☐ ☐

5. Prepare shopping lists for distribution

a. Solicit help of the Advisory Board or PTA .... ☐ ☐ ☐

b. Visit book stores, hobby shops, toy stores, etc. and make lists of items supporting reading .... ☐ ☐ ☐

c. Have lists include businesses where those items may be purchased .... ☐ ☐ ☐

d. Include comments about the learning benefits or reading benefits of items .... ☐ ☐ ☐

e. Distribute lists to families before holidays .... ☐ ☐ ☐

–continues–

Public Relations for the Reading Program -continued-	3	2	1

6. *Prepare summer reading lists*

a. Secure the help of the librarian	☐	☐	☐
b. Generate lists of books by grade levels	☐	☐	☐
c. Generate lists with mailing addresses for subscriptions to children's magazines	☐	☐	☐
d. Distribute to families shortly ahead of summer vacation or Christmas holidays (Children's Book Council, Reading Teacher)	☐	☐	☐

7. *Support reading contests*

a. Locate sources (Pizza Hut's Book-it, Six Flags' Day-at-the-Park, etc.) of contest incentives	☐	☐	☐
b. Distribute information to teachers and families	☐	☐	☐
c. Use internal school contests with coupons, prizes, or discounts contributed by local merchants	☐	☐	☐
d. Conduct assemblies to recognize individuals and classes that completed the most reading	☐	☐	☐
e. Secure a press release demonstrating the benefits of promoting reading	☐	☐	☐

8. *Send home reading progress letters*

a. Choose progress letters that convey more information than do report card grades	☐	☐	☐
b. Develop content that conveys just how well each child is moving through the curriculum	☐	☐	☐
c. Select progress letters that convey reading level, specific instructional emphasis, etc.	☐	☐	☐
d. Identify ways to indicate needs for special instruction	☐	☐	☐
e. Send home checklists of reading portfolio content	☐	☐	☐
f. Send home end-of-unit, end-of-volume letters available from textbook series publishers	☐	☐	☐
g. Consider whether the district should develop its own progress letters or use those provided by the publishers of textbooks used in the program	☐	☐	☐
h. Teachers may send home a letter-a-week with information about reading program activities and other school events	☐	☐	☐

–continues–

Public Relations for the Reading Program   -continued-

	3	2	1

9. *Develop a public relations plan*

a. Appoint a faculty member to be responsible for "selling the reading program" to the public .... ☐ ☐ ☐

b. Choose that faculty member with enthusiasm, potential, and capability to fulfill the project .... ☐ ☐ ☐

c. Meet regularly with the faculty member to plan and to provide assistance .... ☐ ☐ ☐

d. Invite other faculty in small groups to meet, plan, and brainstorm with the two of you ☐ ☐ ☐

e. Identify a prominent school location to promote reading with bulletin boards, showcases, displays .... ☐ ☐ ☐

f. Develop bulletin boards that convey themes studied around the school, such as Black history, literature-based study, etc. .... ☐ ☐ ☐

g. Create attractive activities with literature-based clues using well-known children's games such as Trivia, Bingo, Memory .... ☐ ☐ ☐

h. Develop riddles, guessing games and contests about books, authors, themes, or holidays, giving daily clues .... ☐ ☐ ☐

i. Develop short book reviews for local newspapers, reviews at both primary and intermediate levels .... ☐ ☐ ☐

j. Invite a photographer from the community newspaper to visit school and locate prospective photos for the paper .... ☐ ☐ ☐

k. Maintain contact with the local paper's editor to inquire what story content would be attractive .... ☐ ☐ ☐

l. Develop news releases of reading program events that are worthy of publication (local councils of the International Reading Association provide formats for successful news releases) .... ☐ ☐ ☐

m. Prepare tapes for radio broadcasts on community stations using children, parents, and teachers in various combinations as spot announcements or public service announcements .... ☐ ☐ ☐

–continues–

Public Relations for the Reading Program   -continued- | 3 | 2 | 1 |

10. *Develop a plan to increase volunteer involvement in the reading program*

   a.   Gain faculty support for community involvement (see Form 11.8) ....   ☐ ☐ ☐

   b.   Identify a faculty member or volunteer who will coordinate volunteer services (see Forms 11.5-11.6) ....   ☐ ☐ ☐

   c.   Secure willing volunteers (see Forms 11.3-11.4) ....   ☐ ☐ ☐

   d.   Develop a talent bank of contributors (see Form 11.4) ....   ☐ ☐ ☐

   e.   Plan ways in which present volunteers may recruit and solicit help from new volunteers ....   ☐ ☐ ☐

   f.   Identify volunteers who would prefer to work with children and, separately, people who prefer to work with materials and paperwork ....   ☐ ☐ ☐

   g.   Prepare a staff development plan for volunteers (see Form 11.9) ....   ☐ ☐ ☐

   h.   Develop a support system to train volunteers ....   ☐ ☐ ☐

   i.   Generate a way of recognizing the contributions made by volunteers (see Forms 11.10–11.12)..   ☐ ☐ ☐

Cover the page at this point and below prior to photocopying if use is desired before referring to the interpretation.

Interpretation: Participants have signaled responses to usefulness of prospective activities in Form 12.1. The Reading Advisory Board or principal may review strengths, recognize and celebrate their use. In areas where little use was found, and if those criteria may strengthen the literacy program, the Reading Advisory Board might create awareness and support for their use.

Form 12.2
USES OF THE SCHOOL LOGO

Directions: Correspondence using the school logo looks professional, attracts readers' attention, and tends to be taken seriously. Many notes may be written to highlight good things students have done, and the logo lets the reader know with a glance just who is sending the note. Brief notes, or memos may reduce the amount that actually needs to be written. Memos may come from teachers, the principal, or parent volunteer coordinators.

Example A: URGENT MEMOS IN REGULAR FORMAT

OUR SCHOOL LOGO

Memo to: _____

About:

_____

_____

_____

_____   _____
Principal   School

I M P O R T A N T

Example B: NEWSLETTERS WRITTEN BY STUDENTS AND STAFF

OUR SCHOOL LOGO

School   Principal

SECURING COMMUNITY FEEDBACK ON THE READING PROGRAM

(see Forms 12.3 and 12.4)

A close link between the community and its school is not easily attained. During the years their children are in school, parents tend to be more active, but after the school attendance years, families become less involved. An important way to help community members feel a sense of ownership is to ask them what they think about the reading program.

The Problem: School personnel, administrators, faculty, staff, and Reading Advisory Board members often have inaccurate beliefs about parent and community views of the school. Dysfunctional communication may be so extreme that families feel they are not wanted in schools. Some school personnel do hold contempt for some families— often the families most in need of school support.

Rationale: School employees who understand reading program views of families and the community are advantaged. Information is then available to fully interpret the program, enhancing community and family confidence in the school. That enhanced confidence may be converted indirectly to better pupil reading achievement.

Procedures: Questionnaires and informational forms are provided for the principal or Reading Advisory Board to obtain parent and community views of the reading program. Form 12.3 is designed to request feedback from parents, Form 12.4 views of community members.

For Further Reading

Carter, D. A. (1993). "Community and Parent Involvement: A Road to School Improvement," *ERS Spectrum,* 11, 1, 39–46.

> Carter defines elements of good parent involvement and describes effective examples. The author provides criteria to create and managing volunteer programs. Processes to develop partnerships are presented.

Fruchter, N., et al. (1992). *New Directions in Parent Involvement.* Washington, D. C.: Academy of Educational Development (ED 360 683).

> The authors review findings on effective parent involvement from 18 projects.

Ryan, T. E. (1992). "Parents as Partners Program," *School Community Journal*, 2, 2, 11–21.

> Conclusions were that parent involvement enhanced parent and student self-esteem, increased students' school success, and improved communication in a racially integrated school district.

Form 12.3
PARENT VIEWS OF READING PROGRAM EFFECTIVENESS

Directions: The questionnaire was developed to gain parent opinions about the reading program. After reading each statement below, parents are asked to indicate whether they agree or disagree. If there are comments, please write them on the back of the page. Please *do not* sign your name.

Parents' Views of Effectiveness Criteria:	Agree 2	Disagree 1

Beliefs and Practices

		Agree	Disagree
1.	The school supports and encourages a strong reading program	☐	☐
2.	Acquiring effective reading skills is essential to everyday living	☐	☐
3.	I encourage my child/children to read at home	☐	☐
4.	I purchase books and magazines for my children to read at home	☐	☐
5.	My children check out books from the public library	☐	☐
6.	I like to read	☐	☐
7.	I feel that the teachers have done a "good" job of teaching my child to read	☐	☐
8.	I feel that I have adequate knowledge about the school's reading program .	☐	☐
9.	I feel free to visit my child's reading class	☐	☐
10.	I believe that money spent on reading materials is money well spent	☐	☐

Information about the School

		Agree	Disagree
11.	I would like to know whether the teacher believes my child feels successful as a reader	☐	☐
12.	I would like to know whether my child seems to enjoy reading at school	☐	☐
13.	I would like to know more about how well my child actually is doing in reading class	☐	☐
14.	I would like to know more about how the school encourages recreational reading at school	☐	☐

–continues–

Parent Views of Reading Program Effectiveness -continued-	2	1
15. I would like to know more about reading workbooks and other seatwork	☐	☐
16. I feel that reading skills are being taught well in the subject areas as well as in reading class	☐	☐
17. I would like to know more about the writing my child does in school, how it ties in with the reading class	☐	☐
18. I am pleased with the school library, the choice of books, and reading-related study centers	☐	☐
19. The school provides books and materials that relate to my child's interests	☐	☐
20. I would like to know more about the reading program at the elementary school level	☐	☐
21. I would like to know more about the reading program at the middle school or junior high school level	☐	☐
22. I would like to know more about the reading program at the high school level	☐	☐

I am interested and willing to help with reading activities in my child's school (if so, please express this interest to the teacher or principal, or complete the tear-off below and send it to the principal)

— — — — — — — — — — — — — tear here — — — — — — — — — — — — — — — —

PARENT VIEWS OF READING

PROGRAM EFFECTIVENESS

Sign-up to Volunteer

Name _____

Address _____

Phone _____

Form 12.4
COMMUNITY VIEWS OF THE READING PROGRAM

Directions: The form was developed to gain feedback from community members on how well the school informs the public. Would you please read the criteria listed below and check on the right how well you feel the school is doing. Comments should be written on the back of this form. Please *do not* sign your name.

Community Views on Reading Criteria:

	Extreemely Well	Very Well	Fairly Well	Not Well
	4	3	2	1
1. Resource persons from the community are called upon to assist in special activities related to reading	☐	☐	☐	☐
2. Community facilities and institutions (such as museums, historical sites, zoos, etc.) are used when appropriate to create interest in reading about the community	☐	☐	☐	☐
3. Children are familiar with and use the community library and bookmobile services	☐	☐	☐	☐
4. When appropriate, business and industry personnel are asked to help the community become more concerned about reading	☐	☐	☐	☐
5. Changes in the reading program are adequately interpreted to the community	☐	☐	☐	☐
6. Pupils' progress in reading (as in state-mandated or local tests) is clearly interpreted to the community	☐	☐	☐	☐
7. Interesting and innovative practices in reading instruction are publicized in local news media	☐	☐	☐	☐
8. Parents and other interested citizens are invited to visit the school to observe the reading program and teaching	☐	☐	☐	☐
9. The reading program enjoys a good reputation in the community	☐	☐	☐	☐

Please place comments you desire to make on the back of the page.

ALLIANCES BETWEEN THE SCHOOL AND FAMILY   (see Forms 12.5 to 12.8)

Families that feel as though they are team members with school people are enabled to focus child-rearing toward children's literacy. In many cultures, teachers may be the only people who have the talents to help parents to nurture literacy at home. Periodic parent-teacher conferences provide the structure and great opportunity to be helpful when talking with parents.

The Problem: Many parents are not aware of things they can do at home that will increase chances of later high reading achievement. Bedtime and laptime reading, writing with invented spellings, and extensive nurturance of oral expression may be avoided, rather than nurtured.

Rationale: Parents who possess a strong sense of how to support children's literacy development may influence attitudes, confidence, and school skills. Outcomes that nurture attitudes of risk-taking, comfort with books, and oral skills of elaboration are the joys of teachers who extend growth at school.

Procedures: Administrators or Reading Advisory Boards may use Forms 12.5 to 12.8 to review important criteria, plan staff development activities, or gather needs-assessment data. Concepts to help parents at home, secure attitude and interest data, support school visits, and participate in parent-teacher conferences are provided.

For Further Reading

Comer, James P. (1980). *School Power: Implications of an Intervention Project.* New York: The Free Press (Macmillan). (Simon & Schuster, 200 Old Tappan Road, Old Tappan, NJ 07675. 1-800-223-2336.)

> Comer asserts that, in order to understand the problems schools face, we educators examine the use of power in our society. Alienation and distrust lead families to suspect the motives of educators and a sense of community often is lost, leaving schools powerless, but chaotic. The author shows the way to share power.

Hansen, B. J. & Mackey, P. E. (1993). *Your Public Schools: What You Can Do to Help Them.* North Haven, CT: Catbird Press. (16 Windsor Road, North Haven, CT 06473. 1-203-230-2391.)

> This text is written so that users may read any part that is useful at the moment. Section two is very helpful and includes strategies for educators: volunteering, clubs, mentoring, school councils and boards, school partnerships, and aides.

Spiegel, D. L. (1992). *A Portrait of Parents of Successful Readers.* Conference presentation at the National Reading Conference, San Antonio (ED 353 548).

> Spiegel analyzed numerous studies and concluded that parental roles are extremely important in creating children who can and will read. Those parents have high expectations for their children, read to them, and spend quality time with them.

Form 12.5

SUPPORT FOR MY PRE-K/SECOND-GRADE CHILD'S READING GROWTH AT HOME

Directions: Below, parents will find suggestions for helping their young child with reading growth. On the right, you might mark those activities that your family already enjoys, then mark those that they do not enjoy. You might use the latter to set goals for future family activities.

Young Children Reading at Home Criteria:	A Family Activity 2	Not A Family Activity 1
1. Praise and encourage your child. Confident children are more open and able to develop language, aiding reading	☐	☐
2. Encourage a great amount of conversation, recognizing that children who use oral language well have an advantage in later reading	☐	☐
3. Write stories as your child dictates them to you, then the two of you read the stories together	☐	☐
4. Model for your child the importance of reading by reading in his/her presence frequently	☐	☐
5. Read to your child frequently (of all suggestions in this worksheet, this may be the most important one)	☐	☐
6. When reading to your child, put great feeling and expression into stories	☐	☐
7. At times when you read to your child, leave out a word, or pause substantially, inviting her/him to provide the missing word	☐	☐
8. Invite others, such as siblings, relatives, and peers, to read to your child	☐	☐
9. Remember that fathers, grandfathers, and other significant male role models should read to your child	☐	☐
10. Provide bookshelf space for your child at eye level	☐	☐
11. Over time, develop an extensive collection of picture books, predictable books, and story books for your child	☐	☐
12. Develop bedtime stories as a favorite event of the day	☐	☐
13. Plan laptime as a time your child looks forward to sharing	☐	☐

–continues–

Support for my Pre-K/Second-Grade Child's Reading Growth at Home -continued-	2	1
14. Buy "read along" books and accompanying cassettes for your child to enjoy independently	☐	☐
15. Tape record your child's favorite stories so s/he can read along	☐	☐
16. Go with your child to the story hour at the local library	☐	☐
17. Develop a tradition of sharing nursery rhymes with your child	☐	☐
18. Provide appropriate pencils, crayons, markers, and a variety of paper for your child's writing	☐	☐
19. Encourage your child to write to you, accepting any markings or spellings without criticism, and read their stories to you and others	☐	☐

Form 12.6

ENRICHMENT OF MY ELEMENTARY SCHOOL-AGED CHILD'S READING AT HOME

Directions: Below, parents will find suggestions for helping elementary school-aged children with reading growth at home. You might mark on the right those activities your family uses in the first box, those they do not use on the last box. You might then consider which ideas from the far right box should be included in family activities.

Home Reading Criteria:	A Family Activity	Not A Family Activity
	2	1
1. Model your enjoyment of reading frequently when your child is present	☐	☐
2. Model your reading of the newspaper, showing parts of the paper as you read	☐	☐
3. Talk with your child about books you are reading, showing pictures when available. Read colorful parts to him/her	☐	☐
4. Talk with your child about favorite books that were read to you as a child	☐	☐
5. Work through the children's section of the newspaper with your child	☐	☐
6. When your child becomes an able reader, take turns; you read a page, the child reads a page, etc.	☐	☐
7. Listen to your child read aloud and listen to the "retellings" of the story without quizzing	☐	☐
8. Invite your child to practice reading into a cassette recorder and then listen to her/his own reading	☐	☐
9. Support, nurture and praise your child's writing, asking that he/she read it to you without your correcting	☐	☐
10. Encourage your child to write daily in a journal in which you might regularly write responses. Corrections should be avoided	☐	☐
11. Help your child set up his/her own personal library	☐	☐
12. Provide inexpensive, particularly popular children's books in your home	☐	☐
13. Encourage others to buy books for your child as birthday and holiday gifts .	☐	☐
14. Go with your child to local bookstores and browse through the children's section	☐	☐

–continues–

Enrichment of My Elementary School-Aged Child's Reading at Home   -continued-

	2	1
15. Take your child to the local library and obtain a library card for her/him	☐	☐
16. Take your child to the library frequently to select books	☐	☐
17. Arrange a time during the evening when your family members read together	☐	☐
18. During family reading time, try to minimize distractions that interrupt	☐	☐
19. Set family reading goals, with each person reading his or her own choices for a certain amount of time each day	☐	☐
20. Plan with your child the amount of time, and the quality of television s/he will watch	☐	☐
21. Watch children's television specials, based on good books, together as a family	☐	☐
22. Read seasonal and holiday stories together as a family	☐	☐

Form 12.7
INVENTORY OF READING ATTITUDES*

Name _____   Grade _____   Boy   Girl
             Last   First

School _____   Teacher _____

Date of Test _____
                    Month   Day   Year

To boys and girls:

This sheet has some questions about reading that can be answered YES or NO. Your answers will show what you usually think about reading. After each question is read to you, circle your answer.

INSTRUCTIONS TO PUPILS

Draw a circle around the word YES or NO, whichever shows your answer.

Sample A:

Yes   No   Do you like to read?

> If you like to read, you should have drawn a circle around the word YES in Sample A; if you do not like to read, you should have drawn a circle around the word NO.

Sample B:

Yes   No   Do you read as well as you would like to?

> If you read as well as you would like to, you should have drawn a circle around the word YES in Sample B; if not, you should have drawn a circle around the word NO.

Yes	No	1.	Do you like to read before you go to bed?
Yes	No	2.	Do you think that you are a poor reader?
Yes	No	3.	Are you interested in what other people read?
Yes	No	4.	Do you like to read when your mother and dad are reading?
Yes	No	5.	Is reading your favorite subject at school?
Yes	No	6.	If you could do anything you wanted to do, would reading be one of the things you would choose to do?
Yes	No	7.	Do you think that you are a good reader for your age?
Yes	No	8.	Do you like to read catalogs?
Yes	No	9.	Do you think that most things are more fun than reading?
Yes	No	10.	Do you like to read aloud for other children at school?

---

* Adapted from a questionnaire by the San Diego County School District.

–continues–

Inventory of Reading Atttitudes   -continued-

Yes	No	11.	Do you think reading recipes is fun?
Yes	No	12.	Do you like to tell stories?
Yes	No	13.	Do you like to read the newspapers?
Yes	No	14.	Do you like to read all kinds of books at school?
Yes	No	15.	Do you like to answer questions about things you have read?
Yes	No	16.	Do you think it is a waste of time to make rhymes with words?
Yes	No	17.	Do you like to talk about books you have read?
Yes	No	18.	Does reading make you feel good?
Yes	No	19.	Do you feel that reading time is the best part of the school day?
Yes	No	20	Do you find it hard to write about what you have read?
Yes	No	21.	Would you like to have more books to read?
Yes	No	22.	Do you like to read hard books?
Yes	No	23.	Do you think that there are many beautiful words in poems?
Yes	No	24.	Do you like to act out stories that you have read in books?
Yes	No	25.	Do you like to take reading tests?

Form 12.7a
KEY TO INVENTORY OF READING ATTITUDES

Key: Questions 2, 9, 16, and 20 should be answered no; the remaining questions usually should be answered yes.

Interpretation: (NORMS TABLE FOR GRADES 1–6):

Raw Scores	Interpretation
25	Superior
23–24	
21–22	Above Average
19–20	
16–18	Average
13–15	
10–13	Below Average
7–9	
0–6	Poor

Comment: The attitudes inventory may be used to gain individual pupil judgements about reading attitudes, or may be used to assess large groups of students' attitudes depending on whether the goal is to assess individuals or programs. In the context of the needs assessment chapter, the inventory's use is for program assessment.

Form 12.8

STUDENTS' READING INTEREST INVENTORY

Directions: Please write a very brief response to each question below:

1. What do you like to do in your spare time? _____
_____

2. What chores or jobs do you do at home? _____
_____

3. What are two of your favorite television programs? _____
_____

4. What are your hobbies? _____
_____

5. What are your favorite sports? _____
_____

6. What school subjects do you like the best? _____
_____

7. What kinds of books do you like to read? _____
_____

8. Do you belong to any clubs or groups? What are they? _____
_____

9. Do you take any special lessons? What are they? _____
_____

10. Do you ever go to the public library? _____
_____

11. If you had one wish, what would it be? _____
_____

12. What would you like to do when you are through with school? _____
_____

13. What kinds of music do you like? _____
_____

14. What are you interested in that you would like to tell me about? _____
_____

INTERPRETING PUPILS' READING PROGRESS   (see Forms 12.9 to 12.11)

Teachers who are able to interpret for parents the reading successes of pupils gain a strong sense of their trust. This communication also provides the chance for parents to ask questions that otherwise might not be raised. Parents tend not to understand technical reading terminology, and may ask for an explanation.

The Problem: Many parents feel uninformed about the literacy development of their children. Conference information may be vague and misleading. Some school people have difficulty telling parents about a reading problem when one arises. Visiting parents may not know what to look for in reading classes without an observational format—or even what they are seeing. Disorganized parent-teacher conferences display weak public relations.

Rationale: Parents who gain quality descriptions of their children's literacy status at school are enabled to complement the school role at home. Those parents may provide study time, homework supervision, family reading time, and any number of other activities that enrich school reading.

Procedures: Teachers have a great opportunity to interpret the program and a child's reading progress to parents when they visit, and when they participate in parent-teacher conferences. Form 12.9 may be offered to parents who observe a reading lesson. Forms 12.10 and 12.11 may be used by teachers to self-assess the way they conduct parent-teacher conferences.

For Further Reading

Granowsky, A. (1977). "Getting Together about your Children," *Partners in Learning*. Dallas TX: Dallas Independent School District. (Out of print.)

> Suggestions for teachers to work with parents. Strategies are suggested for planning teacher-parent conferences.

Klass, C. S., et al. (1993). "Home Visiting: Building a Bridge Between Home and School," *Equity and Choice*, 10, 1, 52–56.

> The purpose is to support collaboration between school and home. The authors describe goals for home visit programs and talk about the skills home visit participants would need to have.

Simic, M. R., et al. (1992). *The Curious Learner: Help Your Child Develop Academic and Creative Skills*. Bloomington, IN: Family Literacy Center (ED 362 930).

> The authors provide numerous suggestions for parents and educators to develop the academic skills of their children.

Form 12.9
WHEN I VISIT MY CHILD'S READING CLASS

Directions: Below are listed possible activities parents might look for when visiting their child's reading class. Visitors would not expect every activity to occur during any one visit, but this guide will provide a framework for observation. When the teacher states, "I will be . . .," you will have a good idea of what you will be able to observe, and may choose several items from the checklist that you will observe. A place is provided on the right to indicate whether or not you observed the activity. If you have questions, do not hesitate to talk with the teacher.

Classroom Visit Criteria:	Did Observe 2	Did Not Observe 1
1. Child interacted with the reading group or the class	☐	☐
2. Child seemed to be accepted in the group, his/her comments were acknowledged positively	☐	☐
3. Child is seated in such a way that s/he can participate easily	☐	☐
4. Child appeared interested throughout the reading lesson	☐	☐
5. Child followed the pre- and post-story reading activities carefully	☐	☐
6. Child seemed able to sit still and concentrate for adequate lengths of time	☐	☐
7. Child seemed able to recall parts or all of the story suitably	☐	☐
8. When reading aloud, child seemed to miss only words unimportant to understanding the story	☐	☐
9. When child missed words, s/he was not made to feel uncomfortable	☐	☐
10. During independent seatwork time, child pursued tasks in a serious manner	☐	☐
11. Preparing for seatwork, child listened to directions, then appeared to follow directions adequately	☐	☐
12. By the end of independent study time, child actually did complete the assigned work	☐	☐
13. Child participated in fun-reading, or recreational reading as a part of independent study time	☐	☐
14. Child appeared to be able to identify difficult words successfully	☐	☐
15. Child seemed to actually like reading class and felt successful	☐	☐

Form 12.10
PLANNING FOR PARENT-TEACHER CONFERENCES

Directions: Below are found planning activities to prepare for teacher conferences with parents, conducting conferences, and post-conference follow-up. As steps are completed, on the right the teacher might check whether the activity was satisfactory and whether follow-up is warranted.

Planning for Conferences Criteria	Well Conducted	Not Well Conducted
	2	1

Before the Conference

1. Develop a form to schedule times for parent-teacher conferences. Allow 20–30 minutes for each conference .... ☐ ☐

2. Send home parents' conference times on printed forms .... ☐ ☐

3. Call parents who send back their forms requesting different times and those parents who did not return forms .... ☐ ☐

4. Gather the following items for the conference: ☐ ☐

   a. Information describing the student's reading and mathematics status .. ☐ ☐

   b. Students' tests (achievement, mastery, end-of-level, end-of-unit, state-mandated) .... ☐ ☐

   c. Organized, comprehensive portfolios containing samples of reading and writing .... ☐ ☐

   d. Copies of district- or basal text-developed materials designed for parents .... ☐ ☐

   e. Other samples of each child's work .... ☐ ☐

   f. Students' reading book(s), favorite trade books, and mathematics books .... ☐ ☐

5. Be prepared to explain what is being done in school to teach the reading, writing, and mathematics programs .... ☐ ☐

6. Be prepared to discuss other subject areas, also .... ☐ ☐

7. Arrange a conference setting so that the parent will be comfortable. Sit beside the parent, not behind the desk .... ☐ ☐

8. Ask your students to encourage their parents to attend .... ☐ ☐

–continues–

Planning for Parent-Teacher Conferences -continued-	2	1

During the Conference

9. Extend a friendly and relaxed greeting .... ☐ ☐

10. Begin the conference on a positive note .... ☐ ☐

11. Focus on constructive suggestions and be specific, rather than vague .... ☐ ☐

12. Discuss the child's overall instructional level in reading, and functional levels in writing, and mathematics .... ☐ ☐

13. Explain the teaching materials and what you attempt to accomplish in your class .... ☐ ☐

14. Share results from any objective information available (test information, district curriculum, your program) .... ☐ ☐

15. Answer questions about other subject areas .... ☐ ☐

16. Encourage the parent to ask questions and share concerns. Listen, and then listen some more .... ☐ ☐

17. Ask the parent(s) to read to their child, listen to their child read, encourage their child to write, listen to any stories their child has written .... ☐ ☐

18. Assure the parent that you truly are interested in their child's school success. Discuss how the parent can keep in close contact with you .... ☐ ☐

19. Thank the parent for attending. Be sure parents realize how they can set up additional conferences .... ☐ ☐

20. As parents leave the conference, hand them an evaluation form to complete and leave at the office .... ☐ ☐

21. Make notes on the conference—record decisions, plans, problem areas, concerns, etc. .... ☐ ☐

22. Follow through by giving the parent(s) any materials or information you promised .... ☐ ☐

23. Complete the Self-assessment of Teacher-Parent Conference form (Form 12.11) .... ☐ ☐

Interpretation: Teachers may opt to examine Form 12.10 checkmarks, noting criteria that were well conducted, then noting items warranting improvement, seeking feedback from peer-coaching or the principal.

Form 12.11

SELF-ASSESSMENT OF TEACHER-PARENT CONFERENCE

Directions: The following criteria have been developed to provide for teachers' self-checking of the way each conference with parents was conducted. Teachers might ask themselves "Did I . . . "or "Was I . . . "

Conference Self-Assessment Criteria:	Well Conducted	Not Well Conducted
	2	1
1. Was I friendly	☐	☐
2. Did I allow the parent to express his/her concerns	☐	☐
3. Did I listen with understanding to the parent's viewpoints	☐	☐
4. Would I be able to restate clearly and accurately any strong concerns the parent had	☐	☐
5. Did I offer specific ideas and activities the parent could use at home to teach or support reading, writing, and mathematics	☐	☐
6. Did I explain clearly the child's instructional program	☐	☐
7. Did I explain carefully just how well the student is getting along in school, describing strengths and weaknesses, along with any specific needs	☐	☐
8. Was I able to describe the importance of parents' reading to their child at home	☐	☐
9. Was I able to encourage parents to listen to their child read to them at home	☐	☐
10. Was I able to adequately explain the importance of trips to the library and children's' books stores	☐	☐
11. Did I set up a way in which the parent and I can keep in close contact	☐	☐
12. Did I explain ways to communicate student progress	☐	☐
13. Did I support the parent to feel a true partnership	☐	☐

Interpretation: Teachers may wish to review checkmarks made on Form 12.11, identifying criteria on that they feel they are effective. They may then look at items which warrant attention, and through peer-coaching or consultation with a principal or consultant, work to improve on those criteria.

SYNTHESIS OF PUBLIC RELATIONS AND READING   (see Forms 12.12 to 12.14)

Good support for schools and reading programs will be enhanced as teachers and parents work together to benefit children. Even more, school performance may be increased. Teachers who work directly with community members are likely to find better support for tax and public relations efforts.

The Problem: Many schools and teachers who lack confidence seem to want parents to stay away from their buildings and classrooms. Teachers may not actually realize that teacher aides would be helpful to them. Parents may feel alienated and avoid school contact. In many cases, neither teachers nor parents may understand how much direct contact and communication will help the reading achievement of children.

Rationale: The benefits of using volunteers or employed paraprofessionals from local neighborhoods in schools are extensive. Extra "hands" in school may strengthen the work of teachers, staff, and administrators. Local people who can carry back to the community reports about the fine work that is being conducted in schools are good liaisons for school support. The most important benefit may be that children whose parents are involved in school do better in school than those whose parents have no contact.

Procedures: Form 12.12 affords the Reading Advisory Board, principal, or individual teachers an opportunity to self-assess and summarize the local public relations plan. Form 12.13 enables those same groups to identify the strengths and needs of public relations support, then set priorities for schools. Form 12.14 provides a structure for development of a plan-of-action to strengthen public relations related to the reading program.

Comments and Cautions

Children of parents who work at cross-purposes with schools miss advantages.

School personnel who do not work at gaining the trust of the community regarding their school's reading program compound their subsequent problems.

Form 12.12
SYNTHESIS OF PUBLIC RELATIONS AND READING

Directions: Below, principals or Reading Advisory Board members will find statements summarizing content of Forms found in Chapter 12. On the right, respondents will find a place to check whether the criterion's status is presently very strong, moderately strong, or in need of strengthening in the local school.

Criteria on Public Relations:	Very Strong	Moderately Strong	In Need of Strengthening
	3	2	1
1. Promoting the reading program positively (Forms 12.1 and 12.2)	☐	☐	☐
2. Securing community feedback on the Reading Program (Forms 12.3 and 12.4)	☐	☐	☐
3. Alliances between the school and the family (Forms 12.5–12.8)	☐	☐	☐
4. Interpreting pupil reading progress (Forms 12.9–12.11)	☐	☐	☐
5. Synthesis of public relations strengths, needs, and priorities (Form 12.12) ..	☐	☐	☐
6. Public Relations: Strengths, Needs, and Priorities (Form 12.13)	☐	☐	☐
7. Administrative plan-of-action for public relations (Form 12.14)	☐	☐	☐

Cover the page at this point and below prior to photocopying if use is desired before referring to the interpretation.

Interpretation: Reading Advisory Boards or principals seeking to assess the status of the school's public relations efforts may gain insight from self-assessment of Form 12.12. Columns may be totaled, giving three points to checkmarks in the left column, two points to marks in the center column, and one point to marks in the right column. Totals between 15–21 may be considered *very strong*, between 8–14 *moderately strong*, and those between 1–7 *in need of strengthening.*

Form 12.13

**PUBLIC RELATIONS SUPPORT FOR READING:
STRENGTHS, NEEDS, AND PRIORITIES**

Directions: Below, principals or Reading Advisory Board members will find categories of public relations support of the reading program just summarized in Form 12.12. On the right, space is provided to enter reading program support's strengths, needs, and priorities.

1. Promoting the Reading Program Positively	*Strengths* 1. 2.	*Needs* 1. 2.	*Priorities* 1. 2.
2. Securing Community Feedback on the Reading Program	*Strengths* 1. 2.	*Needs* 1. 2.	*Priorities* 1. 2.
3. Alliances between School and Family	*Strengths* 1. 2.	*Needs* 1. 2.	*Priorities* 1. 2.
4. Interpreting Pupils' Reading Progress	*Strengths* 1. 2.	*Needs* 1. 2.	*Priorities* 1. 2.
5. Administrative Plan-of-Action	*Strengths* 1. 2.	*Needs* 1. 2.	*Priorities* 1. 2.

Form 12.14
READING PROGRAM PUBLIC RELATIONS: PLAN-OF-ACTION

Directions: Principals seeking to develop a focus for professional growth may benefit from being as specific as possible about what they seek to accomplish, how they will go about attaining growth, and how they will know when they have reached their public relations goals. Reading Advisory Boards, during program-planning, might also find the plan-of-action useful. A review of the completed Form 12.12 should lead respondents to identify goals and pursue them purposefully. Statements entered should be as simple as warranted and as useful as possible.

1. Goal Statement: _____

2. Objectives:

   a) _____

   b) _____

   c) _____

3. Activities: Dates; time checkpoints:

   a) _____   * _____

   b) _____   * _____

   c) _____   * _____

   d) _____   * _____

   e) _____   * _____

4. Resources: (professional reading, consultation, visitations)

   a) _____   * _____

   b) _____   * _____

   c) _____   * _____

5. How I will know when my goal is accomplished:

   _____
   _____
   _____
   _____

GLOSSARY

Accelerated schools A concept of setting high expectations and offering at-risk students instruction following curriculum thinking employed in gifted education (125).

Advance organizers A concise overview (summary) of a larger text, such as a chapter, which is read to gain prior knowledge before reading the chapter. Schematic diagrams depict the vocabulary of a concept to be learned. Diagrams show relationships among new words in text material to be read, helping students to organize text concepts into categories (11, 134).

Anthologies Collections of children's literary works. Secondary schools have taught English literature from anthologies traditionally. A present movement leads book publishers to consider basal reading textbook series as anthologies.

Assessment Gaining information about students' learning; a term once referred to as testing, later measurement, subsequently evaluation, and now popularly labeled assessment.

At-risk Students whose culture or environment limits their learning to read, those who are bicultural or bilingual, and who often are from homes with economic poverty.

Authentic assessment See *Performance assessment.*

Automaticity The ability to process words, or decode, with fluency and accuracy, and without interrupting the reading process (168).

Bibliotherapy A counseling approach that nurtures troubled or divergent children's reading books related to their concern or problem to gain an external perspective on their troubles (126, 229).

Bond Reading Expectancy Formula A calculation to estimate students' potential or capability for reading, beyond present reading level:

$$\left(\frac{\text{I.Q.}}{100} \times \text{years of reading instruction} \right) + 1.0 = \text{Reading Expectancy}$$

Brainstorming A structured classroom discussion process in which teachers ask opening questions and multiple answers are encouraged, sometimes followed by analysis and synthesis.

Chapter 1 See *Title 1.*

Chunking Reading by perceiving and processing groups of words in meaningful units rather than a word at a time.

(Note: The Glossary contains items in text and forms marked with an asterik [*]).

Cloze test A reproduced passage with every nth word deleted and an underlined blank replacing that word. The reader's task is to write in missing words. Scoring and correlations with other assessments have been documented (19, 159).

Cognitive coaching Enabling teachers to be reflective and to critique their own teaching to bring improved teaching decisions to a level of automaticity (41).

Cognitive strategies Ties prior knowledge to information to be learned, activates structural connections between known and new, creates a setting for active learning, provides feedback, offers enough scaffolding, and takes advantage of the social context (135).

Collaborative learning See *Cooperative learning*.

Communication The sharing of messages to develop understanding between a sender and receiver, highly interrelated with decision-making and leadership qualities.

Constructivist classroom Classes in which teachers help children to construct meaning both as they read and write. The reading is based on use of authentic literature. Shared learning often evolves through cooperative activities that employ reading-across-the-curriculum and writing-across-the-curriculum. Some people believe this term will replace the term whole-language in reference to child-centered classes.

Cooperative learning Students work in study groups in which both individual and group contributions are important.

DEAR See *SSR*.

Direct instruction Focusing instruction on the desired strategy, process, or skill. Teaching is step-by-step, mastery of steps, corrections, teachers' diminished monitoring, practice, and review (73).

Drafting The process writing step in which students write a draft of their composition; first draft, revised draft.

DR-TA A text reading strategy that structures predictions, confirmations, and extensions of concepts. The process is initiated with questions about what will be in the text, generates multiple predictions, reads to confirm, predicts what will occur next in text, reads (197, 207).

Effective schools The study of schools, particularly urban schools, that are noted for achievement of unusual learning results (56).

Enlightened witness Shows how abuse can be overcome with sincerity toward clients, inspired confidence in them, encouragement, and support to develop successful coping skills. Teachers identify others with the same conflict for troubled pupils to study (77).

Feature matrix See *Semantic feature analysis*.

Fry Readability Formula A format used to calculate the difficulty level of reading materials (69).

Generalization The ability of students to transfer new learning to other contexts, skills, or situations (163, 201).

Graphophonic The cueing system that uses visual information—letters, sounds, spellings, etc. (75).

Herringbone A graphic structure to display who, what, where, when, how components of expository text reading.

IEP (individualized educational plan) A specifically tailored program designed to meet the distinctive individual needs of each special education student.

Inclusion Teaching of special education students in regular classrooms to allow instruction in the regular curriculum. As warranted, individual services are provided by special teachers and paraprofessionals to address their distinctive needs (188).

Informal Reading Inventory An individual assessment in which students read graded, short passages and answer questions. Teachers identify overall reading strengths and abilities, oral and silent reading comrehension patterns, rate analysis, and miscue analysis of decoding and comprehension of students (16, 160).

Information organizer A study or thinking map with graphics on which students may record study processes to understand and remember text.

Key word A variation on *Probable passages.*

K-W-L An expository text reading strategy in which students are asked to brainstorm what they know on a topic, what they wonder or want to know, prior to reading, and to confirm what they learned after reading. All brainstorming may be listed on the chalkboard to enable students to visualize the processes (140).

Language Experience Approach Classes prepare for a direct experience that is preplanned with children, completed, and used as the basis for discussion and creation of a story on chart paper or chalkboard restating the activity. Pupils discuss the activity, observe the teacher's recording of the experience, read the story, and reread (5, 88).

Learning strategies See *Cognitive strategies.*

Literature log. Periodic student responses to the reading they do. Teachers may provide feedback to students' comments.

Literature response journal See *Literature log.*

Literature sets A literature study group of students who read a text without direct instruction by the teacher. Students, semi-independently, read, discuss, and evaluate the text.

Mapping See *Semantic maps.*

Meaning making Reading comprehension or understanding text.

Metacognition Teaching students to become aware of the thinking they do as they are reading (228).

Mnemonics A device or rhyme that helps learners remember words, sequence, or concepts (113).

Modalities Going beyond the usual visual and auditory sensory information as learning disabled or reading disabled students learn to read, employing kinesthetic and tactile cues (61).

Multiple measures Use of several assessment instruments to gather reading data on pupils, perhaps including portfolios, standardized data, teacher observation, and criterion tests (215).

NCE (normal curve equivalent) A statistical calculation that allows performance on tests to be compared with other tests or with individual pupil performance over time.

Organizers See *Advance organizers*.

Overviews See *Structured overview*.

Peer editing The collaborative process in cooperative groups in which peers provide positive, helpful feedback on students' writing and make suggestions for revisions.

Performance assessment Represents procedures to evaluate literacy behavior of pupils' actual learning activities and performance in the classroom, frequently employing portfolios of students' work (214).

Phonemic awareness A metacognitive structure for decoding unknown words through development of phological awareness, employing an analogy or compare/contrast approach (72, 79).

Portfolios Collections of multiple samples of children's literacy work, accumulated by children in conjunction with the teacher, and accumulated over time, used to display and document children's literacy advancement (10, 81, 93).

Predictions Using previous information or prior knowledge to anticipate text content or identify words. Students may generate new predictions prior to reading by brainstorming shared information.

PreP A prereading plan (PreP), based on peer brainstorming, to develop interest in text and to diagnose students' background on a topic. The strategy fosters discussion and topical awareness (118).

Prior knowledge Information or knowledge students already know about, or which can be generated as they participate with peers in classroom brainstorming activities.

Probable passages Use of key words to make predictions about a text, then writing a possible story to compare with the actual text (231).

Publishing In process writing, the process of displaying written pieces, placing them in booklets, on bulletin boards, sharing with others (making pieces public).

QARs (Question-Answer-Relationship) Process of reading expository text when students analyze relationships between what a question asks for and what the text offers (158).

Readers' theater Class members read and/or narrate the characters' parts of stories, interpreting for classmates. Interpretation may bring life to characters through voice and gesture (185).

Reciprocal teaching A form of learning cognitive structures of texts when, before reading, teachers seek predictions and ask a question of students, who respond; then students elicit predictions of the teacher, before reading, and ask a question of the teacher who responds, etc. (128, 145).

ReQuest See *Reciprocal teaching*.

Resiliency Study of children who turn out well even when significant people in their lives are dysfunctional because of poverty or substance abuse, etc. The focus supports teachers who counsel pupils in turmoil because of family environment (14).

Retellings A structure that helps students understand whole text by reconstructing stories without teachers' interruption or questioning. Children use story grammar structures, implicitly, if they are able to retell accurately and comprehensively.

RIF (Reading is Fundamental) A federally funded program that provides revenue for local units to purchase books for children with matching funds.

Running Record Monitoring students oral reading by checking miscues for meaning, structure, and visual match (34).

Scaffolding Teachers' support to children to accomplish slightly more than they could do without support. Children are able to conduct the function independently, thereafter.

Semantic feature analysis Teachers prepare grids with new words or concepts listed across the side and features listed across the top to help students make decisions to classify and remember interrelationships.

Semantic maps A drawing that displays interrelationships within story parts, chapter sections, word meanings. Class's brainstorming results in teachers' webbing of comments as pupils watch, with the main topic as the central hub, branches indicating categories, and sub-branches displaying supporting details (89, 99, 100). Another concept is individuals' using prior knowledge to develop a diagram of what is to be read.

Semantics The cueing system that assists readers to gather meaning (75).

SQRRR (SQ3R) A chapter-reading structure for pupils' use of chapter heads and subheads while reading content textbooks, following processes of survey, question, read, recall, and review (164, 207).

SSR A school-wide process in which all school people—students, teachers, custodian, principal, cooks—set aside time for recreational reading without interruption. The process enables time for reading and models its importance (often entitled USSR, the "U" is labeled as uninterrupted).

Standard error of measurement The statistical calculation to predict the probabilities that a norm score on a standardized achievement test is accurate for individuals.

Standardized tests Published tests based on large field samples to measure students' reading ability and establish norms of performance for local group or individual comparison.

Story frames Adaptations of story grammars in which story components are provided, and students complete blanks by writing their responses to parts of stories or trade books they have read.

Story grammars Graphic or structural forms to help students visualize how stories are put together. Students learn to understand the role of setting, character, plot, problem, attempt, resolution, and ending. This understanding aids monitoring when students read, and supports structures of writing.

Story maps See *Story grammars*.

Story structures See *Story grammars*.

Strategy The mental structure or system students use as a plan to monitor their text reading, expanding generalizations of processes, thus heightening their awareness of how they read (156).

Structured overview A graphic display of chapter or unit headings of text materials to be studied, showing relationships among parts of that text. The overview is displayed, and concept arrangements are explained (12).

Syntax The cueing system to help students monitor grammatical functions as they read, using word order and sequence (77).

Task analysis Whenever a student cannot perform a task, the teacher breaks down complex tasks into simpler sub-tasks within the child's ability level. Activities are taught in sequence, and with each success, students move to the next level of the task.

Thematic study Units of study incorporate students' interdisciplinary study of content in themes or units. Cooperative groups of pupils use problem-solving processes to study and share content from multiple sources.

Think aloud A metacognitive strategy in which teachers or peers model thinking, describing their thoughts as they read through text, and as students follow along.

Title 1 Federally funded compensatory programs in reading, mathematics, and language arts for disadvantaged students (formerly called Chapter 1).

Trade books Library fiction and non-fiction books.

Transactivist Classroom see *Constructivist classroom*.

Transfer of learning See *Generalization*.

USSR (uninterrupted, sustained, silent reading) See *SSR*.

Webbing See *Semantic maps*.

Word maps Students effectively learn new words when they are tied to known words and concepts. New terms are classified into their superordinate and subordinate categories. Strategies involve tying new words to known words though graphic webs.

BIBLIOGRAPHY

1. Aaron, I. *et al.* (Eds.) (1979). *Principals' Reading Leadership Program.* Washington, D. C.: U. S. Office of Education.

2. Acheson, K. A. & Gall, M. D. (1992). *Techniques in the Clinical Supervision of Teachers: Preservice and Inservice Applications, Third Edition.* New York: Longman.

3. Adams, M. J. (1990). *Beginning to Read: Thinking and Learning About Print.* Cambridge, MA: The MIT Press.

4. Aiex, N. K. (1993). *A Communicative Approach to Observation and Feedback* (ED 364 926).

5. Allen, R. V. & Allen, C. (1982). *Language Experience Activities, Second Edition.* Boston: Houghton Mifflin Company.

6. Allington, R. L. (1992). "How to Get Information on Several Proven Programs for Accelerating the Progress of Low-achieving Children," *The Reading Teacher*, 46, 3, 246–48.

7. Anderson, N. A. & Graebell, L. C. (1988–89). "Prospective Topics for Paraprofessional Staff Develoment," *Journal of Reading Education*, 14, Winter, 26–28.

8. Anderson, R., *et al.* (Eds.). (1985). *Becoming a Nation of Readers.* Washington, D. C.: The National Institute of Education.

9. Arnold, J. B. & Dodge, H. W. (1994). "Room for All," *American School Board Journal*, 181, 10, 22–26.

10. *A to EZ Handbook: Staff Development Guide* (1993). New York: Macmillan/McGraw-Hill School Publishing Company.

11. Ausubel, D. P. (1978). *Educational Psychology, A Cognitive View.* New York: Holt, Rinehart and Winston.

12. Barron, R. (1969). "Research for the Classroom Teacher: Recent Developments on the Structured Overview as an Advanced Organizer," Edited by H. L. Herber & J. D. Riley. *Research in Reading in the Content Areas: The First Report.* Syracuse, NY: Reading and Language Arts Center, Syracuse University.

13. Barron, R. & Earle, R. A. (1973). "An Approach to Vocabulary Instruction," Edited by H. L. Herber & R. F. Barron. *Research in Reading in the Content Areas: Second Year Report.* Syracuse, NY: Reading and Language Arts Center, Syracuse University.

14. Benard, B. (1994). *Fostering Resiliency in Kids: Protective Factors in the Family, School, and Community*. San Francisco, CA: Western Regional Center for Drug-Free Schools and Communities.

15. Berman, W. C. & McLaughlin, M. (1975). "Federal Programs Supporting Change," *The Findings in Review*. Santa Monica, CA: Rand Corporation.

16. Betts, E. A. (1954). *Foundations of Reading Instruction, Third Edition, Revised*. New York: American Book Company.

17. Billings-Ladson, G. (1994). "What We Can Learn from Multicultural Education Research," *Educational Leadership*, 51, 8, 22–26.

18. Bond, G. L., *et al.* (1994). *Reading Difficulties: Their Diagnosis, and Correction, Seventh Edition*. Boston: Allyn and Bacon.

19. Bormuth, R. J. (1965). "Validities of Grammatical and Semantic Classifications of Cloze Test Scores." Edited by A. Figurel. *Reading and Inquiry,* 283–86. Newark, DE: International Reading Association.

20. Boyd, B. (1993). *Transforming Teacher Staff Development* (ED 362 943).

21. Brandt, R. (1994). "On Educating for Diversity: A Conversation with James A. Banks," *Educational Leadership,* 51, 8, 28–31.

22. Burnett, G. (1993). *Chapter I Statewide Project: Advantages and Limitations* (ED 363 668).

23. Calangelo, N. & Davis, G. (Eds.). (1991). *Handbook of Gifted Education*. Boston: Allyn and Bacon.

24. Calkins, L. M. (1994). *The Art of Teaching Writing, New Edition*. Portsmouth, NH: Heinemann Educational Books, Inc.

25. Canney, G. & Neuenfeldt, C. (1993). "Teachers' Preferences for Reading Materials," *Reading Improvement,* 30, 4, 238–45.

26. Carlson, R. V. & Awkerman, G. (Eds.). (1991). *Educational Planning: Concepts, Strategies, Practices*. New York: Longman.

27. Carr, J. F. & Harris, D. E. (1993). *Getting it Together: A Process Workbook for K-12 Curriculum Development, Implementation, and Assessment*. Needham Heights, MA: Allyn & Bacon, Inc.

28. Carrow-Moffett, P. A. (1993). "Change Agent Skills: Creating Leadership for School Renewal," *NASSP Bulletin,* 77, 552, 57–62.

29. Carter, D. A. (1993). "Community and Parent Involvement: A Road to School Improvement, *ERS Spectrum,* 11, 1, 39–46.

30. "Celebrating Diversity in Teacher Education" (1994). *The Journal of the Association of Teacher Educators,* 16, 3, 1–86.

31. Chall, J. S. (1983). *Stages of Reading Development*. New York: McGraw-Hill Book Company.

32. Chubb, J. E. & Moe, T. M. (1990). *Politics Markets America's Schools*. Washington, D. C.: The Brookings Institution.

33. Clay, M. M. (1991). *Becoming Literate: The Construction of Inner Control*. Auckland, NZ: Heinemann Education.

34. Clay, M. M. (1993). *Reading Recovery: A Guidebook for Teachers in Training.* Auckland, NZ: Heinemann Education.

35. Coleman, P., *et al.* (1993). "Seeking the Levers of Change: Participant Attitudes and School Improvement," *School Effectiveness and School Improvement,* 4, 1, 59–83.

36. Comer, J. P. (1980). *School Power: Implications of an Intervention Project.* New York: The Free Press (Macmillan).

37. Cook, D. M., *et al.* (1986). *A Guide to Curriculum Planning in Reading.* Madison, WI: The Wisconsin Department of Public Instruction.

38. Cooper, J. D. (1993). *Literacy: Helping Children Construct Meaning, Second Edition.* Boston: Houghton Mifflin Company.

39. Cooper, J. L. (1952). *The Effect of Adjustment of Basal Reading Materials on Reading Achievement.* Unpublished Doctoral Dissertation, Boston University.

40. Costa, A. L. (1989). "Re-assessing Assessment," *Educational Leadership,* 46, 7, 2–3.

41. Costa, A. L. & Garmston, R. J. (1994). *Cognitive Coaching: A Foundation for Renaissance Schools.* Norwood, MA: Christopher-Gordon Publishers, Inc.

42. Cullinan, B. E. & Galda, L. (1994). *Literature and the Child, Third Edition.* Ft. Worth, TX: Harcourt Brace College Publishers.

43. Cummings, C. (1990). *Managing a Cooperative Classroom.* Edmonds, WA: Teaching, Inc.

44. Cunningham, P. M. (1995). *Phonics They Use: Words for Reading and Writing.* New York: HarperCollins College Publishers.

45. Datta, L. E. (1980). "Changing Times: The Study of Federal Programs Supporting Educational Change and the Case for Local Problem Solving," *Teachers College Record,* 82, 1, 101–116.

46. Davey, B. (1983). "Think Aloud—Modeling the Cognitive Processes of Reading Comprehension," *Journal of Reading,* 27, 1, 44–47.

47. Dole, J. A., *et al.* (1990). *Guide to Selecting Basal Reading Programs.* Urbana, IL: Center for the Study of Reading.

48. Doll, R. S. (1992). *Curriculum Improvement: Decision Making and Process, Eighth Edition.* Boston: Allyn and Bacon.

49. Donohoe, T. (1993). "Finding the Way: Structure, Time, and Culture," *Phi Delta Kappan,* 75, 4, 298–305.

50. Duffy, G. G. & Roehler, L. R. (1989). *Improving Classroom Reading Instruction: A Decision-Making Approach.* New York: Random House, 205–209, 223–232.

51. Duke, D. L. (1990). "Setting Goals for Professional Development," *Educational Leadership,* 47, 8, 71–75.

52. Durkin, D. (1987). "Reading Comprehension Instruction in Five Basal Reader Series," *Reading Research Quarterly,* 16, 4, 515–44.

53. Durkin, D. (1993). *Teaching Them to Read, Sixth Edition.* Boston: Allyn and Bacon.

54. Dyer, P. C. (1992). "Reading Recovery: A Cost-Effectiveness and Educational-Outcomes Analysis," *ERS Spectrum: Journal of School Research and Information,* 10, 1, 10–19.

55. Dyer, P. C. (1995). "Estimating Cost-Effectiveness and Educational Outcomes: Retention, Remediation, Special Education, and Early Intervention." Edited by R. L. Allington & S. A. Walmsley. *No Quick Fix*. New York: Teachers College Press and Newark DE: International Reading Association.

56. Edmonds, R. (1985). "Characteristics of Effective Schools: Research and Implementation." Edited by J. Osborn, et al. *Reading Education: Foundations for a Literature America*. Lexington, MA: Lexington Books (D. C. Heath).

57. *Educational Leadership* (1994), 51, 8, (themed edition).

58. Elrich, M. (1994). "The Stereotype Within," *Educational Leadership*, 51, 8, 12–15.

59. English, F. W. (1992). *Deciding What to Teach and Test: Developing, Aligning, and Auditing the Curriculum*. Newbury Park, CA: Corwin Press, Inc.

60. Farr, R. & Carey, R. (1986). *Reading: What Can be Measured? Second Edition*. Newark, DE: International Reading Association.

61. Fernald, G. M. (1971). *Remedial Techniques in Basic School Subjects*. New York: McGraw-Hill Book Company.

62. Finders, M. & Lewis, C. (1994). "Why Some Parents Don't Come to School," *Educational Leadership*, 51, 8, 50–54.

63. Fitzgerald, J. (1980). "Research on Stories: Implications for Teachers." Edited by K. P. Muth. *Research into Practice*. Newark, DE: International Reading Association.

64. Flood, J., *et al.* (1992). "Am I Allowed to Group? Using Flexible Patterns for Effective Instruction," *The Reading Teacher*, 45, 8, 608–16.

65. Fowler, G. L. (1982). "Developing Comprehension Skills in Primary Students Through the Use of Story Frames," *The Reading Teacher*, 36, 2, 176–79.

66. Fox, C. A. F. (1992). "The Critical Ingredient of Making Change Happen," *NASSP Bulletin*, 76, 541, 71–77.

67. Frager, A. M. & Vanterpool, M. (1993). "Point-Counterpoint: Value of School Textbooks," *Reading Horizons*, 33, 3, 300–312.

68. Fruchter, N., *et al.* (1992). *New Directions in Parent Involvement*. Washington, D. C.: Academy of Educational Development (ED 360 683).

69. Fry, E. B. (1977). "Fry's Readability Graph: Clarifications, Validity, and Extension to Level 17," *Journal of Reading*, 21, 3, 242–252.

70. Galda, L., *et al.* (1993). *Language, Literacy, and the Child*. Ft. Worth, TX: Harcourt Brace Jovanovich College Publishers.

71. Garmston, R., et al. (1993). "Reflections on Cognitive Coaching," *Educational Leadership*, 51, 2, 57–61.

72. Gaskins, I. W., *et al.* (1988). "A Metacognitive Approach to Phonics: Using What You Know to Decode What you Don't Know," *Remedial and Special Education*, 9, 1, 36–41.

73. Gersten, R., *et al.* (1987). "Direct Instruction Research: The Third Decade," *Remedial and pecial Education*, 8, 6, 48–56.

74. Goldhammer, R., *et al.* (1993). *Clinical Supervision: Special Methods for the Supervision of Teachers, Third Edition*. New York: Holt, Rinehart & Winston.

75. Goodman, K. S. (1986). *What's Whole in Whole Language*. Portsmouth, NH: Heinemann Educational Books, Inc.

76. Goodman, Y. M. & Burke, C. (1972). *Reading Miscue Inventory: Procedures for Diagnosis and Evaluation*. New York: Macmillan.

77. Gootman, M. E. (1993). "Reaching and Teaching Abused Children," *Childhood Education*, 70, 1, 15–19.

78. Goswami, U. (1991). "Onset and Rime Awareness and Analogies in Reading," *Reading Research Quarterly*, 27, 2, 153–62.

79. Goswami, U. & Bryant P. (1990). *Phonological Skills and Learning to Read*. East Sussex, UK: Lawrence Erlbaum Associates, Ltd., Publishers.

80. Granowsky, A. (1977). "Getting Together about your Children," *Partners in Learning*. Dallas, TX: Dallas Independent School District.

81. Graves, D. H. (1992). *Portfolio Portraits*. Portsmouth, NH: Heinemann Educational Books, Inc.

82. Griffin, M. A. (1993). "Say It Like You Mean It," *School Businesss Affairs*, 59, 9, 15–19.

83. Gunning, T. G. (1992). *Creating Reading Instruction for all Children*. Boston: Allyn and Bacon.

84. Halpin, A. (1966). *Theory and Research in Administration*. Toronto: Collier Macmillan Canada, Ltd., 148–150.

85. Hansen, B. J. & Mackey, P. E. (1993). *Your Public Schools: What You Can Do to Help Them*. North Haven, CT: Catbird Press.

86. Haring, N. G., *et al.* (1994). *Exceptional Children and Youth, Sixth Edition*. New York: Macmillan College Publishing Company.

87. Harp, B. (Ed.). 1994. *Assessment and Evaluation for Student Centered Learning: Expanded Professional Version, Second Edition*. Norwood, MA: Christopher-Gordon Publishers, Inc.

88. Harp, B. & Brewer, J. (1991). *Reading and Writing: Teaching for the Connections*. San Diego, CA: Harcourt Brace Jovanovich, Publishers.

89. Heimlich, J. E. & Pittelman, S. D. (1986). *Semantic Mapping: Classroom Applications*. Newark, DE: International Reading Association.

90. Hennessey, A. (1992). "Getting the Word Out: Working with Your Local Reporter, *Phi Delta Kappan*, 74, 1, 82–84.

91. Herber, H. L. & Herber, J. N (1993). *Teaching Reading in Content Areas: with Reading, Writing, and Reasoning*. Boston: Allyn & Bacon.

92. Hermann, B. A. (Ed.). (1994). *The Volunteer Tutor's Toolbox*. Newark, DE: International Reading Association.

93. Hiebert, E. H. & Calfee, R. (1992). "Assessing Literacy: From Standardized Tests to Portfolios and Performances," Edited by S. J. Samuels and A. E. Farstrup. *What Research Has to Say about Reading Instruction, Second Edition*. Newark, DE: International Reading Association.

94. Hiebert, E. H. & Colt, J. M. (1989). "Patterns of Literature-based Reading Instruction," *The Reading Teacher*, 43, 1, 14–20.

95. Hill, B. C. & Ruptic, C. (1994). *Practical Aspects of Authentic Assessment: Putting the Pieces Together*. Norwood, MA: Christopher-Gordon Publishers, Inc.

96. Hughes, L. W. & Ubbens, G. C. (1994). *The Elementary Principal's Handbook: A Guide to Effective Action, Fourth Edition*. Des Moines, IA: Longwood Division.

97. Hunter, M. (1984). "Knowing, Teaching, and Supervising." Edited by P. L. Hosford. *Using What We Know About Teaching*. Yearbook of the Association for Supervision and Curriculum Development. Alexandria, VA: Association for Supervision and Curriculum Development.

98. Jennings, J. M. (1992). "Parent Involvement Strategies for Inner-City Schools," *NASSP Bulletin*, 76, 548, 63–68.

99. Johnson, D. D. & Pearson, P. D. (1984). *Teaching Reading Vocabulary, Second Edition*. New York: Holt, Rinehart & Winston.

100. Johnson, D. D., *et al.* (1986). "Semantic Mapping," *The Reading Teacher*, 39, 8, 778–83.

101. Johnson, D. W., *et al.* (1994). *The New Circles of Learning: Cooperation in the Classroom and School*. Alexandria, VA: Association for Supervision and Curriculum Development.

102. Jones, R. R. (1992). "Setting the Stage for Program Change," *Executive Educator*, 14, 3, 38–39.

103. Jongsma, K. S. (1991). "Grouping Children for Instruction: Some Guidelines," *The Reading Teacher*, 44, 8, 610–11.

104. Jongsma, K. S. (1992). "The Eyes of Textbooks are Upon You," *The Reading Teacher*, 46, 2, 158–60.

105. Joyce, B., *et al.* (1993). *The Self-Renewing School*. Alexandria, VA: Association for Supervision and Curriculum Development.

106. Kameenui, E. J. (1993). "Diverse Learners and the Tyrany of Time: Don't Fix Blame; Fix the Leaky Roof," *The Reading Teacher*, 46, 5, 376–83.

107. Kaufman, R. A. (1983). "Needs Assessment," Edited by F. W. English. *Fundamental Curriculum Decisions*. Alexandria, VA: Yearbook of the Association for Supervision and Curriculum Development, 53–67.

108. Kaufman, R. A. (1992). "Objectives and Needs Assessment: Basic Building Blocks," *Mapping Educational Success: Strategic Thinking and Planning for School Administrators*. Newbury Park, CA: Corwin Press, Inc.

109. Kaufman, R., *et al.* (1993). *Needs Assessment: A User's Guide, Second Edition*. Englewood Cliffs, NJ: Educational Technology Publications.

110. Keith, S. & Girling, R. H. (1991). *Education, Management, and Participation*. Boston, MA: Allyn & Bacon.

111. Kilian, L. J. (1992). "A School District Perspective on Appropriate Test-Preparation Practices . . .," *Educational Measurement: Issues and Practices*, 11, 4, 13–15+.

112. Kincade, K. M. & Stange, T. V. (1993). "Theory into Practice: Issues to Consider When Selecting Reading Software to Meet Different Readers' Needs," *Reading Horizons*, 34, 2, 151–69.

113. Kirk, S. A., *et al.* (1993). *Educating Exceptional Children, Seventh Edition*. Boston: Houghton Mifflin Company.

114. Klass, C. S., *et al.* (1993). "Home Visiting: Building a Bridge Between Home and School," *Equity and Choice*, 10, 1, 52–56.

115. Koblitz, D. (1993). "Starting the Year with Whole Language in Second Grade." Edited by O. Cochrane & E. Buchanan. *Teachers' Stories: Starting the Year with Whole Language*. Winnepeg, Canada: Whole Language Consultants Ltd.

116. Krovetz, M. & Cohick, D. (1993). "Professional Collegiality Can Lead to School Change," *Phi Delta Kappan*, 75, 74, 331–333.

117. Lamb, P. (1993). "Literature-Based Language Arts Programs: Promises and Problems," *Reading and Writing Quarterly: Overcoming Learning Difficulties*, 9, 2, 135–50.

118. Langer, J. A. (1981). "From Theory into Practice: A Prereading Plan." *Journal of Reading*, 25, 2, 152–56.

119. Lareau, A. (1987). "Social Class Differences in Family-School Relationships: The Importance of Cultural Capital," *Sociology of Education*, 60, 2, 73–85.

120. Lehr, F. & Osborn, J. (Eds.) (1994). *Reading, Language, and Literacy: Instruction for the Twenty-First Century*. Hillsdale, NJ: Lawrence Erlbaum Associates, Inc.

121. Lenz, B. K., *et al.* (1990). "Content Enhancement: A Model for Promoting the Acquisition of Content by Individuals with Learning Disabilities." Edited by T. E. Scruggs & B. Wong. *Intervention Research in Learning Disabilities*. New York: Springer.

122. Lerner, J. (1993). *Learning Disabilities: Theories, Diagnosis, and Teaching Strategies, Sixth Edition*. Boston: Allyn and Bacon.

123. LeTendre, M. J. (1991). "Improving Chapter 1 Programs: We Can Do Better," *Phi Delta Kappan*, 72, 8, 576–80.

124. Levin, H. M. (1991). "Accelerating the Progress of At-risk Students." Edited by A. C. Huston. *Children in Poverty*. London: Cambridge University Press.

125. Luce, W. M. (1994). "Principles for Principals," *Executive Educator*, 16, 8, 23–25.

126. Lumpkin, D. (1992). "Lifetime Reading by Teachers as Bibliotherapy." Edited by B. L. Hayes & K. Camperell. Twelfth Yearbook of the American Reading Forum, 51–57.

127. Lyman, H. (1991). *Test Scores and What they Mean, Fifth Edition*. Englewood Cliffs, NJ: Prentice-Hall.

128. Manzo, A. V. (1969). "The ReQuest Procedure," *Journal of Reading*, 13, 2, 123–26.

129. Mason, J. M. & Au, K. H. (1990). *Reading Instruction for Today, Second Edition*. New York: HarperCollins College Publishers.

130. McCormick, K. (1990). *Chapter I: A Directors' Handbook for Parental Involvement* (ED 333 967).

131. McDaniel, E. & Mack, V. H. (1992). *Involving Minority Parents of At-Risk Children: A Parent/School Partnership* (ED 358 533).

132. McGee, L. M. (1992). "Focus on Research: Exploring the Literature-based Reading Revolution," *Language Arts*, 69, 7, 529–37.

133. Melvin III, C. A. (1991). "Translating Deming's 14 Points for Education," *School Administrator*, 48, 9, 20–23.

134. Meng, K. & Patty, D. (1991). "Field Dependence and Contextual Organizers," *The Journal of Educational Research*, 84, 3, 183–89.

135. Mercer, C. D. (1994). "Learning Disabilities." Edited by N. G. Haring, *et al. Exceptional Children and Youth: Sixth Edition*. New York: Macmillan College Publishing Company.

136. Moll, L. (1992). "Bilingual Classroom Studies and Community Analysis: Some Recent Trends," *Educational Researcher*, 21, 2, 20–24.

137. Monahan, J., *et al.* (Eds). (1988). *New Directions in Reading Instruction*. Newark, DE: International Reading Association.

138. Moore, L., E. (1993). "Restructured Schools: How, Why Do they Work? *NASSP Bulletin*, 77, 553, 64–69.

139. Njiokiktjien, C. (1993). "Neurological Arguments for a Joint Developmental Dysphasia-Dyslexia Syndrome." Edited by A. M. Galaburda. *Dyslexia and Development: Neurobiological Aspects of Extra ordinary Brains*. Cambridge, MA: Harvard University Press, Pp. 205–236.

140. Ogle, D. M. (1986). "K-W-L: A Teaching Model that Develops Active Reading of Expository Text," *The Reading Teacher*, 39, 6, 564–70.

141. Oliva, P. F. (1992). *Developing the Curriculum, Third Edition*. New York: HarperCollins Publishers Inc.

142. Ordovensky, P. & Marx, G. (1993). *Working with the News Media*. Alexandria, VA: American Association of School Administrators.

143. Osborn, J. & Swengle, E. (1990). *A Guide to Selecting Basal Reading Programs: Overheads and Notes*. Urbana, IL: Center for the Study of Reading.

144. Pagels, C. F. & Adams, J. B. (1981). "Here's a Well-oiled Textbook Adoption Process," *Executive Educator*, 3, 12, 25–26.

145. Palinscar, A. S. & Brown, A. L. (1986). "Interactive Teaching to Promote Independent Learning from Text," *The Reading Teacher*, 39, 8, 171–77.

146. Parker, S. A. (1993). "So Now You're a School Leader: What Should You Do?" *Phi Delta Kappan*, 75, 3, 29–30.

147. Peck, G. (1989). "Facilitating Cooperative Grouping: A Forgotten Tool Gets it Started," *Academic Therapy*, 25, 2, 145–50.

148. Peterson, N. L. (1988). *Early Intervention for At-risk Children*. Denver: Love Publishing Company.

149. Pfeiffer, J. W. & Jones, J. E. (1972–1995+). *A Handbook of Structured Experiences for Human Relations Training, Annual Volumes*. San Diego, CA: University Associates.

150. Pickett, A. (1988). *The Employment and Training of Paraprofessional Personnel: A Technical Assistance Manual for Administrators and Staff Developers*. New York: City University of New York (ED 357 516).

151. Pickett, A. L. (1989). *A Training Program to Prepare Teachers to Supervise and Work More Effectively with Paraprofessional Personnel*. New York: City University of New York (Ed 357 515).

152. Pickett, A. L., et al. (1993). *Promoting Effective Communications with Para-educators* (ED 357 586).

153. Pikulski, J. J. (1994). "Preventing Reading Failure: A Review of Five Effective Programs," *The Reading Teacher*, 48, 1, 30–39.

154. Pinnell, G. S., *et al.* (1994). "Comparing Instructional Models for the Literacy Education of High-risk First Graders," *Reading Research Quarterly*, 29, 1, 9–39.

155. Powell, W. R. & Dunkeld, C. G. (1971). "Validity of the IRI Reading Levels," *Elementary English*, 48, 6, 637–42.

156. Pressley, M., *et al.* (1990). *Cognitive Strategy Instruction*. Cambridge, MA: Brookine Books.

157. Radencich, M. C. (1995). *Administration and Supervision of the Reading/Writing Program*. Boston: Allyn and Bacon.

158. Raffael, T. E. (1986). "Teaching Question Answer Relationships, Revisited," *The Reading Teacher*, 39, 6, 516–22.

159. Ransom, P. E. (1968). "Determining the Reading Levels of Elementary School Children by Cloze Testing." Edited by A. Figurel. *Forging Ahead in Reading*, 477–82. Newark, DE: International Reading Association.

160. Ransom, P. E. & Patty, D. (1984). "Informal Diagnosis of Reading Abilities." Edited by J. Baumann & D. D. Johnson. *Reading Instruction and the Beginning Teacher: A Practical Guide*, 122–141. Minneapolis, MN: Burgess Publishing Company (Macmillan).

161. Raywid, M. A. (1993). "Finding Time for Collaboration," *Educational Leadership*, 51, 1, 30–34.

162. Renzulli, J., *et al.* (1978). "Curriculum Compacting: An Essential Strategy for Working with Gifted Students," *Elementary School Journal*, 82, 3, 185–94.

163. Rivera, D. & Smith, D. D. (1988). "Using a Demonstration Strategy to Teach Midschool Students with Learning Disabilities How to Compute Long Division," *Journal of Learning Disabilities*, 21, 2, 77–81.

164. Robinson, F. (1961). *Effective Study*. New York: Harper and Row.

165. Ryan, T. E. (1992). "Parents as Partners Program," *School Community Journal*, 2, 2, 11–21.

166. Samuels, S. J. (1988). "Decoding and Automaticity: Helping Poor Readers become Automatic at Word Recognition," *The Reading Teacher*, 41, 8, 756–60.

167. Samuels, S. J. & Pearson, P. D. (Eds.). (1988). *Changing School Reading Programs: Principles, and Case Studies*. Newark, DE: International Reading Association.

168. Sanacore, J. (1992). "Intra Class Grouping with a Whole Language Thrust," *Reading and Writing Quarterly: Overcoming Learning Difficulties*, 8, 3, 295–303.

169. Sanacore, J. (1993). "Using Study Groups to Create a Professional Community," *Journal of Reading*, 37, 1, 62–66.

170. Sanacore, J. (1995). "Guidelines for Hiring Qualified Reading Professionals," *Journal of Reading*, 38, 5, 396–400.

171. Schlesinger, A. M. (1986). *The Cycles of American History*. Boston: Houghton Mifflin Company.

172. Schmuck, R. A. & Runkel, P. J. (1985, 1988). *The Handbook of Organizational Development in Schools, Third Edition*. Prospect Heights, IL: Waveland Press.

173. Searfoss, L. W. & Readence, J. E. (1994). *Helping Children Learn to Read, Third Edition*. Boston: Allyn and Bacon.

174. Sears-King, M. (1994). *Curriculum-Based Assessment in Special Education*. San Diego: Singular Publishing Group.

175. Shanahan, T. (Ed.). (1990). *Reading and Writing Together: New Perspectives for the Classroom*. Norwood, MA: Christopher-Gordon Publishers Inc.

176. Sharp, P. A. (1993). *Sharing Your Good Ideas: A Workshop Facilitator's Handbook*. Portsmouth, NH: Heinemann Educational Books, Inc.

177. Shaughnessy, M. F. (1994). *Gifted and Reading* (ED 368 145).

178. Shore, B., *et al.* (1991). *Recommended Practices in Gifted Education*. New York: Teachers College Press.

179. Short, K. E. *et al.* (1993). *Principal Study Groups and Teacher Study Groups: An Interactive and Innovative Approach to Curriculum Change* (ED 362 959).

180. Simic, M. R., *et al.* (1992). *The Curious Learner: Help Your Child Develop Academic and Creative Skills*, Bloomington, IN: Family Literacy Center.

181. Slavin, R. E. (1989). "PET and the Pendulum: Faddism in Education and How to Stop It," *Phi Delta Kappan*, 70, 10, 752–58.

182. Slavin, R. E. (1991). "Chapter I: A Vision for the Next Quarter Century," *Phi Delta Kappan*, 72, 8, 586–89+.

183. Slavin, R. E. (1993). "Ability Grouping in the Middle Grades: Achievement Effects and Alternatives," *Elementary School Journal*, 93, 5, 535–52.

184. Slotnik, W. J. (1993). "Core Concepts of Reform," *Executive Educator*, 15, 12, 32–34.

185. Sloyer, S. (1982). *Readers Theatre: Story Dramatization in the Classroom*. Urbana, IL: National Council of Teachers of English.

186. Slukarski, S. R. (1992). *Enhancing Professional Development through Reading Professional Literature* (ED 351 496).

187. Smith, C., (Ed). 1991. *Alternative Assessment of Performance in the Language Arts*. Bloomington, IN: Phi Delta Kappa & ERIC/RCS.

188. Smith, D. D. & Luckasson, R. (1995). *Special Education: Teaching in an Age of Challenge*. Boston: Allyn and Bacon.

189. Smith, F. (1985). *Reading Without Nonsense, Second Edition*. New York: Teachers College Press.

190. Smith, N. B. (1963). *Reading Instruction for Today's Children*. Englewood Cliffs, NJ: Prentice-Hall, Inc.

191. Smith, N. B. (1965). *American Reading Instruction: Its Development and Its Significance in Gaining a Perspective on Current Practices in Reading*. Newark DE: International Reading Association.

192. Smith, R. J. *et al.* (1978). *The School Reading Program: A Handbook for Teachers, Supervisors, and Specialists*. Boston: Houghton Mifflin Company.

193. Spencer, C. & Allen, M. G. (1989). *Grouping Students by Ability: A Review of the Literature* (ED 302 326).

194. Spiegel, D. L. (1992). *A Portrait of Parents of Successful Readers*. Conference presentation at the National Reading Conference, San Antonio (ED 353 548).

195. Stahl, S. A. (1992). "Saying the "p" Word: Nine Guidelines for Exemplary Phonics Instruction," *The Reading Teacher*, 45, 8, 618–625.

196. Stanovich, K. E. (1993–94). "Romance and Reality," *The Reading Teacher*, 47, 4, 180–91.

197. Stauffer, R. G. (1969). *Directing Reading Maturity as a Cognitive Process*. New York: Harper and Row.

198. Steinburg, C., *et al.* (1992). "Making Choices about Change," *Training and Development Journal*, 46, 3, 33–42.

199. Stewart, O. & Green, D. S. (1983). "Test-taking Skills for Standardized Tests of Reading, *The Reading Teacher*, 36, 7, 634–39.

200. Stobbe, C. (1993). "Professional Partners," *Educational Leadership*, 51, 2, 40–41.

201. Stokes, T. & Baer, D. (1977). "An Implicit Technology of Generalization," *Journal of Applied Behavior Analysis*, 10, 2, 349–67.

202. Strichard, S. S. & Mangrum II, C. T. (1993). *Teaching Study Strategies to Students with Learning Disabilities*. Boston: Allyn and Bacon.

203. Strickland, D. S. (1994). "Educating African American Learners At Risk: Finding a Better Way," *Language Arts*, 72, 5, 328–35.

204. Sulzby, E. (1985). "Children's Emergent Reading of Favorite Storybooks: A Developmental Approach," *Reading Research Quarterly*, 20, 4, 458–81.

205. Tiedt, P. & Tiedt, I. M. (1990). *Multicultural Teaching: A Handbook of Activities, Information, and Resources*. Boston: Allyn and Bacon.

206. Tierney, R. J., *et al.* (1990). *Reading Strategies and Practices, Third Edition*. Boston: Allyn and Bacon.

207. Tierney, R. J. & Pearson, P. D. (1992). "Learning to Learn from Text: A Framework for Improving Classroom Practice." Edited by E. K. Dishner, *et al. Reading in the Content Areas: Improving Classroom Instruction, Third Edition*. Dubuque, IA: Kendall/Hunt.

208. Tinker, M. A. & McCullough, C. M. (1968). *Teaching Elementary Reading, Third Edition*. New York: Appleton-Century-Crofts.

209. Ubbens, G. C. & Hughes, L. W. (1992). *The Principal: Creative Leadership for Effective Schools, Second Edition*. Boston: Allyn & Bacon.

210. Vacca, R. T. & Vacca, J. L. (1993). *Content Area Reading: Fourth Edition*. New York: HarperCollins College Publishers.

211. Vacca, J. L. *et al.* (1995). *Reading and Learning to Read, Third Edition*. New York: HarperCollins Publishers, Inc.

212. Valencia, S., *et al.* (1989). "Theory and Practice in Statewide Assessment: Closing the Gap," *Educational Leadership*. 46, 7, 57–63.

213. Valencia, S. W. (1992). "Commercially Available Language Arts Performance-based Assessments," *The Reading Teacher*, 45, 6, 468–70.

214. Valencia, S. W. & Greer, E. A. (1992). "Basal Assessment Systems: It's Not the Shoes," *The Reading Teacher*, 45, 8, 650–51.

215. Valencia, S. W., *et al.* (1994). *Authentic Assessment: Practices and Possibilities.* Newark, DE: International Reading Association.

216. Van Ausdall, B. W. (1994). "Books Offer Entry into Understanding Children," *Educational Leadership*, 51, 8, 32–35.

217. Vann, A. S. (1994). "The Pre-Employment Interview: Asking the Right Questions," *Principal*, 73, 3, 38–41.

218. Veatch, J. (1966). *Reading in the Elementary School.* New York: The Ronald Press.

219. Vroom, V. H. & Jago, A. G. (1988). *The New Leadership: Managing Participation in Organizations.* Englewood Cliffs, NJ: Prentice-Hall.

220. Wall, R. R. (1993). *Staff Development Programs in Public Schools: Successful Staff Development Programs Including the Role of the Classroom Teachers and Administrators* (ED 361 288).

221. Wasik, B. & Slavin, R. (1993). "Preventing Reading Failure with One-to-One Tutoring: A Review of Five Programs," *Reading Research Quarterly*, 28, 2, 178–99.

222. Wepner, S., *et al.* (Eds). (1995). *Administration and Supervision of Reading Programs, Second Edition.* New York: Teachers College Press.

223. Wepner, S. B. (1991). "Linking Technology to Genre-Based Reading," *The Reading Teacher*, 45, 1, 68–70.

224. Wheeler, P. (1992). *Improving Classroom Observation Skills: Guidelines for Teacher Evaluation.* Livermore, CA: EREAPA Associates (ED 364 961).

225. Wilson, M. C. (1947). "The Teacher's Problems in a Differentiated Reading Program," *Elementary English*, 24, 2, 77–85+.

226. Wilkinson, P. A. & Patty, D. (1993). "The Effects of Sentence Combining on the Reading Comprehension of Fourth Grade Students," *Research in the Teaching of English*, 27, 1, 104–123.

227. Winfield, L. (1986). "Teacher Beliefs Toward At-risk Students in Inner-Urban Schools," *The Urban Review*, 18, 4, 253–67.

228. Winograd, P. & Paris, S. G. (1988). "A Cognitive and Motivational Agenda for Reading Instruction," *Educational Leadership*, 46, 4, 30–36.

229. Wolf, J. & Penrod, D. (1980). "Bibliotherapy: A Classroom Approach to Sensitive Problems," *Gifted / Creative / Talented*, 15, 52–54.

230. Wood, F., et al. (1993). *How to Organize a School-Based Staff Development Program.* Alexandria, VA: Association for Supervision and Curriculum Development.

231. Wood, K. D. (1984). "Probable Passages: A Writing Strategy," *The Reading Teacher*, 37, 6, 496–99.

APPENDIX A

GRAPH FOR ESTIMATING READABILITY

GRAPH FOR ESTIMATING READABILITY—EXTENDED

by Edward Fry, Rutgers Univesity Reading Center, New Brunswick, NJ 08904

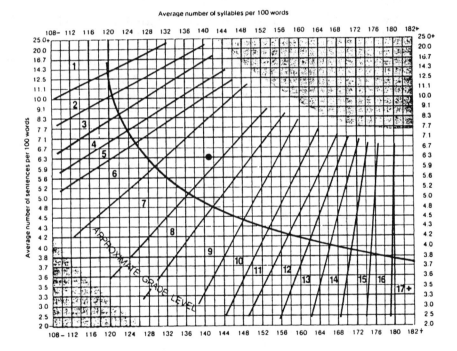

Average number of syllables per 100 words

Journal of Reading, 21, 3, 249

Note: This "extended graph" does not outmode or render the earlier (1968) version inoperative or inaccurate; it is an extension.
    (REPRODUCTION PERMITTED—NO COPYRIGHT)

Expanded Directions for Working Readability Graph

1. Randomly select three (3) sample passages and count out exactly 100 words each, beginning with the beginning of a sentence. Do count proper nouns, initializations, and numerals.

2. Count the number of sentences in the hundred words, estimating length of the fraction of the last sentence to the nearest one-tenth.

3. Count the total number of syllables in the 100-word passage. If you don't have a hand counter available, an easy way is to simply put a mark above every syllable over one in each word, then when you get to the end of the passage, count the number of marks and add 100. Small calculators can also be used as counters by pushing numeral 1, then push the + sign for each word or syllable when counting.

4. Enter graph with *average* sentence length and *average* number of syllables; plot dot where the two lines intersect. Area where dot is plotted will give you the approximate grade level.

5. If a great deal of variability is found in syllable count or sentence count, putting more samples into the average is desirable.

6. A word is defined as a group of symbols with a space on either side; thus, *Joe, IRA, 1945,* and *&* are each one word.

7. A syllable is defined as a phonetic syllable. Generally, there are as many syllables as vowel sounds. For example, *stopped* is one syllable and *wanted* is two syllables. When counting syllables for numerals and initializations, count one syllable for each symbol. For example, *1945* is four syllables, *IRA* is three syllables, and *&* is one syllable.

Journal of Reading, 21, 3, 249

408

APPENDIX B

Selected Professional Journals and Organizations

The School Administrator, American Association of School Administrators, 1801 North Moore Street, Arlington, VA 22209, 703-875-0748.

Educational Leadership, Association for Supervision and Curriculum Development, 1250 North Pitt Street, Alexandria, VA 22314-1403, 703-549-9110.

ERS Spectrum and *ERS Report*, 2000 Clarendon Road, Arlington, VA 22201, 703-243-2100.

Executive Educator, 1680 Duke Street, Alexandria, VA 22314, 703-838-6722.

Journal of Adolescent and Adult Literacy (formerly *The Journal of Reading*), International Reading Association, 800 Barksdale Road, P. O. Box 8139, Newark, DE 19714-8139, 1-800-336-READ or 1-302-731-1600.

Language Arts, National Council of Teachers of English, 1111 West Kenyon Road, Urbana, IL 61801-1096, 1-217-328-3870.

Principal, National Association of Elementary School Principals, 1615 Duke Street, Alexandria, VA 22314-1453, 703-524-1134.

Reading Horizons, Reading Center & Clinic, Western Michigan University, Kalamazoo, MI 49008, 616-387-3470.

Reading Research Quarterly, International Reading Association, 800 Barksdale Road, P. O. Box 8139, Newark, DE 19714-8139, 1-800-336-READ or 1-302-731-1600.

Research in the Teaching of English, National Council of Teachers of English, 1111 West Kenyon Road, Urbana, IL 61801-1096, 1-217-328-3870.

The Reading Teacher, International Reading Association, 800 Barksdale Road, P. O. Box 8139, Newark, DE 19714-8139, 1-800-336-READ or 1-302-731-1600.

APPENDIX C

INFORMATION SOURCES FOR SELECTED READING INTERVENTION PROGRAMS

Comment: The popularity of early intervention programs is due to the following factors: (1) children who otherwise might have failed tend to, instead, succeed, and (2) cost savings to districts multiply as fewer children require services. Programs described below offer initial and follow-up services and report documented results.

Accelerated Schools Dr. Henry Levin, Accelerated Schools Project, Center for Educational Research, 402 S CERAS, Stanford University, Stanford, CA 94305-3084. 415-723-0840 or 1676.

> High expectations and high academic achievement of pupils with active learning and collaboration strengthen results. Participating schools make commitments and are led to accelerate pupils rather than remediate, bringing at-risk pupils rapidly up to the mainstream.

EIR (Early Intervention in Reading) Dr. Barbara M. Taylor, Peik Hall, 129 Pillsbury Drive SE, University of Minnesota, Minneapolis, MN 612-625-1362.

> A supplemental program for first grade students working in about 20-minute sessions. Project-trained classroom teachers work with small groups of five to seven at-risk students who also receive regular instruction. About 80 percent are reading independently by May.

Reading Recovery Dr. Carol Lyons, Ohio Reading Recovery, The Ohio State University, 200 Ramseyer Hall, Columbus, OH 43210. 614-292-7807.

> A National Diffusion Network-documented program originating in New Zealand that takes the lowest first grade children, one-on-one, for half-hour daily lessons provided by teachers with special training. Nearly 90 percent read average or better in 12 to 20 weeks.

School Power Dr. James P. Comer, Yale Child Study Center, Yale University, P.O. Box 207900, New Haven, CT 06520. 203-785-2548.

> At local schools, governance, mental health, and staff-support groups undergird the program to create a positive school climate. A social skills curriculum for inner-city children is generated locally. Both children and parents are shown to experience bonding to the school.

Success for All Dr. Robert Slavin, Center for Research on Effective Schooling for Disadvantaged Students, Johns Hopkins University, 3505 North Charles Street, Baltimore, MD 21218. 401-516-8816.

> One-to-one trained tutors are a program foundation. Intervention is delivered through daily 90 minute reading/language arts sessions. Cooperative learning and structured writing processes support the advances in reading. Family support teams function in each school.

410

APPENDIX D

USE OF FORMS BY VARIOUS SCHOOL PERSONNEL

Directions: Forms from the *Resource Handbook* are listed below. On the right, participants will find the forms checked that may be useful to various educators. Columns are coded: Form number; Title, the name of the form; Page, the page the form will be found; Principal use; Advisory Board use; Central Office Administrative use; Supervisory use by supervisory or staff development personnel; Teachers, use by teachers.

Form	Title	Page	Principal	Advisory Board	Central Office	Supervisory	Teachers
1.1	Characteristics of Outstanding Reading Programs	3	X	X	X	X	X
1.5	Criteria Met By Outstanding Reading Programs	7	X	X	X	X	
1.6	Sources of Technical Assistance to Get Reading Program Help	10	X	X	X	X	X
2.1	The Reading Administrator As an Instructional Leader	14	X	X	X		
2.2	Reading Programs and School Effectiveness Research	20	X	X			
2.3	Change Processes and Improved Reading Programs	23	X	X			
2.4	School Climate in Reading Program Change	26	X	X			
2.5	Decision-Making Supports Program Goals	29	X	X			
2.6	Effective Communication Supports Program Change	32	X	X	X	X	X
2.7	Delegation of Tasks and Responsibilities	35	X	X	X	X	
2.8	Time Management Enhances Reading Leadership	38	X	X	X	X	X
2.9	Synthesis of Reading Program Leadership	44	X	X	X	X	
2.10	Prioritization of Reading Leadership Needs	45	X	X	X	X	
2.11	Personal Administrative Growth Plan	47	X	X	X	X	

Form	Title	Page	Principal	Advisory Board	Central Office	Supervisory	Teachers
3.1	Needs-Assessment and Reading Program-Planning	51	X	X			
3.2	Overview of Needs-Assessment and Program-Planning	53	X	X	X		X
3.3	Beliefs and Definitions Related to Reading Programs	56	X	X	X	X	X
3.4	Steps Taken During a Reading Needs-Assessment	59	X	X	X		X
3.5	Membership of the Reading Advisory Board	62	X	X	X		X
3.6	School Demographic Data for Program Study	64	X	X	X		
3.7	Assessment of Student Performance	66	X	X			
3.8	Needs-Assessment and Program-Planning Simulation	68	X	X			
3.9	Identification of Goals/Needs Discrepancies	72	X	X			
3.10	Needs-Based Establishment of Program Priorities	74	X	X			
3.11	Synthesis of Needs-Assessment and Program Planning	76	X	X	X		
3.12	Reading Program Strengths, Weaknesses, and Priorities	77	X	X	X		
3.13	Reading Program Strengths and Weaknesses: Plan-of-Action	79	X	X			
4.1	Assessment of Curricular Frameworks	83	X	X	X	X	
4.2	Preliminary Decisions about the Reading Curriculum	85	X	X	X	X	
4.3	The Emergence of Literacy	87	X	X	X	X	X
4.5	The Comprehension of Narrative Text	90	X	X	X	X	X
4.7	Expository Text Comprehension	93	X	X	X	X	X

Form	Title	Page	Principal	Advisory Board	Central Office	Supervisory	Teachers
4.9	Process Writing Supports Reading Comprehension	96	X	X	X	X	X
4.11	Development of Meaning Vocabulary	99	X	X	X	X	X
4.13	Literature-Based Reading and Writing	102	X	X	X	X	X
4.15	The Decoding/Word Analysis Instruction Cycle	105	X	X	X	X	X
4.17	The Recreational Reading Component	108	X	X	X	X	X
4.19	Curriculum Components of the Reading Program	111	X	X	X	X	X
4.20	The Reading Curriculum's Strengths, Weaknesses, and Priorities	112	X	X			
4.21	Reading Curriculum: Plan-of-Action	113	X	X			
5.1	Assessment of Reading Progress	118	X	X	X	X	X
5.2	Assessment Options for Local Consideration	119	X	X	X		
5.3	Standardized Achievement Tests in Reading Program Assessment	122	X	X	X	X	X
5.4	Performance/Portfolio Assessment	125	X	X	X	X	X
5.5	Basal-Reader/Literature-Based Assessments	132	X	X	X	X	X
5.6	Periodic Assessment: Literature Emergence	135	X	X	X	X	X
5.7	Periodic Assessment: Narrative Text Comprehension	136	X	X	X	X	X
5.8	Periodic Assessment: Expository Text Comprehension	137	X	X	X	X	X
5.9	Periodic Assessment: Writing about Reading	138	X	X	X	X	X

Form	Title	Page	Principal	Advisory Board	Central Office	Supervisory	Teachers
5.10	Periodic Assessment: Meaning Vocabulary	139	X	X	X	X	X
5.11	Periodic Assessment: Literature-Based Reading and Writing	140	X	X	X	X	X
5.12	Periodic Assessment: Word Analysis	141	X	X	X	X	X
5.13	Periodic Assessment: Recreational Reading	142	X	X	X	X	X
5.14	Coaching Students for Test-Taking	144	X	X	X	X	X
5.15	Summary of Assessment Components	151	X	X	X		
5.16	Reading Assessment: Strengths, Weaknesses, and Priorities	152	X	X	X	X	
5.17	Reading Assessment: Plan-of-Action	153	X	X			
6.1	Approaches to Reading Instruction	157	X	X	X	X	X
6.2	Overview of Reading Approaches	159	X	X	X	X	X
6.3	Basal Reading/Literature-Based Textbooks in the School Reading Curriculum	162	X	X	X	X	X
6.4	Whole Language in the School Reading Curriculum	166	X	X	X	X	X
6.5	The Language Experience Approach in the Reading Curriculum	170	X	X	X	X	X
6.6	Matrix to Judge Congruence of Reading Approach with Curriculum Content	173	X	X	X	X	X
6.7	Summary of Implementation of Approaches	177	X	X	X		
6.8	Reading Approach: Strengths, Needs, and Priorities	178	X	X	X		

Form	Title	Page	Principal	Advisory Board	Central Office	Supervisory	Teachers
6.9	Plan-of-Action for Reading Approaches	179	X	X			
7.1	Selection of Reading Materials	184	X	X	X	X	X
7.2	Basal or Literature-Based Series Selection	186	X	X	X	X	X
7.12	Evaluation of a Basal- or Literature-Based	200	X	X	X		
7.13	Synthesis of All Reading Programs Reviewed	201	X	X	X	X	
7.14	Criteria to Select Trade Books	203	X	X	X	X	
7.19	Matrix to Evaluate Trade Book Options	204	X	X	X	X	X
7.21	Selection of Reading Software Materials	212	X	X	X	X	X
7.22	Selection of Materials for Special Reading Programs	215	X	X	X		X
7.23	Selection of Professional Books for Teachers and Administrators	217	X	X	X	X	X
7.24	Synthesis to Select Instructional Reading Materials	219	X	X	X		
7.25	Selection of Instructional Reading Materials: Strengths, Needs, and Priorities	220	X	X	X		
7.26	Selection of Instructional Reading Materials: Administrative Plan-of-Action	221	X	X			
8.1	Reading Program Organization	226	X	X	X		
8.2	School-Level Reading Organizational Options	229	X	X	X		X
8.4	Classroom Reading Group Options	232	X	X	X	X	X
8.7	Management of Cooperative Groups	237	X	X	X	X	X

Form	Title	Page	Principal	Advisory Board	Central Office	Supervisory	Teachers
8.8	Use of Classroom Space for Reading	241	X	X	X	X	X
8.9	Assessment of Classroom Reading Groups	244	X	X	X	X	X
8.10	Synthesis of Reading Program Organization	247	X	X	X		
8.11	Reading Organization Strengths, Needs, and Priorities	248	X	X	X		
8.12	Reading Organization: Plan-of-Action	249	X	X			
9.1	Reading-Related Criteria to Interview Classroom Teachers	254	X	X	X	X	
9.2	Reading-Related Criteria to Interview Special Reading Teachers	256	X	X	X	X	
9.3	Annual Goal-Setting and Review	258	X	X			X
9.4	Teachers' Self-Assessment of Reading Lesson Frameworks	261	X	X			X
9.8	The Principal As Coach	274	X	X		X	X
9.9	Professional Development through Networking	277	X	X	X	X	X
9.10	Effective Staff Development Workshops	281	X	X	X	X	X
9.11	Needs-Assessment for Professional Development in Reading	283	X	X		X	X
9.12	Preparing for Staff Development Sessions	288	X	X		X	
9.15	Procedures to Develop a Prioritized Long-Term Plan	293	X	X	X	X	X
9.16	Synthesis of Professional Development	297	X	X			
9.17	Professional Development: Strengths, Needs, and Priorities	298	X	X			

Form	Title	Page	Principal	Advisory Board	Central Office	Supervisory	Teachers
9.18	Professional Development: Plan-of-Action	299	X	X			
10.1	Overview of Reading Diversity	304	X	X	X		
10.2	At-Risk Students as Diverse Learners	306	X	X	X	X	X
10.3	Multicultural Students as Diverse Learners	309	X	X	X	X	X
10.4	Learning Disability Students as Diverse Learners	312	X	X	X	X	X
10.5	Title 1 Students as Diverse Learners	315	X	X	X	X	X
10.6	Special Education Students as Diverse Learners	318	X	X	X	X	X
10.7	Reading Intervention Programs and Diverse Learners	321	X	X	X	X	X
10.8	Gifted Students as Diverse Learners	324	X	X	X	X	X
10.9	Synthesis of Diverse Learner Leadership	327	X	X			
10.10	Diverse Learners: Strengths, Needs, and Priorities	328	X	X			
10.11	Diverse Learners: Plan-of-Action	329	X	X			
11.1	Overview of Paraprofessional Functions	334	X	X			
11.3	Inviting Community Participation in the School Reading Program	337	X	X			X
11.5	Coordinator of Paraprofessional Programs	339	X				
11.6	Organizational Models for Volunteer Participation	341	X	X			
11.13	Synthesis of Paraprofessional Support of the Reading Program	353	X	X			

Form	Title	Page	Principal	Advisory Board	Central Office	Supervisory	Teachers
11.14	Paraprofessional Support of Reading: Strengths, Needs, and Priorities	354	X	X			
11.15	Plan-of-Action to Support Paraprofessionals in the School Reading Program	355	X	X			
12.1	Public Relations for the Reading Program	360	X	X	X		
12.3	Parent Views of Reading Program Effectiveness	367	X	X	X		X
12.4	Community Views of the Reading Program	369	X	X	X		
12.5	Support for My Pre-K/Second-Grade Child's Reading Growth at Home	371	X	X		X	X
12.6	Enrichment of My Elementary School Aged Child's Reading at Home	373	X	X		X	X
12.9	When I Visit My Child's Reading Class	380	X	X		X	X
12.10	Planning for Parent-Teacher Conferences	381	X	X		X	X
12.12	The Reading Program's Public Relations: Synthesis	385	X	X			
12.13	Public Relations Support for Reading: Strengths, Needs, and Priorities	386	X	X			
12.14	Reading Program Public Relations: Plan-of-Action	387	X	X	X		

AUTHOR INDEX

SUBJECT INDEX

ABOUT THE AUTHORS

Del Patty is a Reading Faculty Member and Reading Recovery Site Coordinator at Southern Illinois University. He received his Ed.D from Ball State University. His areas of special interest include reading recovery, performance assessment, and informal reading inventories.

Peggy E. Ransom is the Director of Professional Laboratory Experiences at Ball State University. She received the Ball State Teachers College Special Service Award for 1994 and earned her Ed.D in elementary education from Ball State University.

Janet D. Maschoff is an adjunct Assistant Professor at the University of Missouri. She is a former principal at Hazelwood School District in St. Louis, MO. She received her Ed.D from the University of Missouri and her special interests include mentoring new teachers and principals, and the supervision and evaluation of teachers.